JavaScript Goodies

by Joe Burns, Ph.D.

Second Edition

Pearson Technology Group
201 West 103rd Street Indianapolis, Indiana 46290

Praise for Joe's most recent book, *Web Site Design Goodies*

Those looking for design templates and HTML "how-to" will be disappointed. And a good thing, too. Instead, Joe Burns provides refreshing honesty and opinion, with intelligent advice on the key elements of Web site design, and advice which will still stand you in good stead long after HTML is a distant memory—a Web design guide for life.

Give a man a design template or code list, and you've fed him for one Web site. Give him this book, and you've set him on his way to building as many different Web sites as he needs. Instead of a paint-by-numbers approach, Joe uses his personable, conversational style to encourage self-development and design confidence.

At the same time, he provides in-depth comment on important Web site design issues, such as colors, technical wizardry, link placement, fonts, focus, and so on, and uses numerous examples, surveys, and site reviews to back up his points. Anyone who thinks they've done a good job with their Web site would do well to read this book and then reassess their work.

—*Mark Brownlow; VP Content, Internet Business Forum, Inc.;* `http://www.ibizhome.com/`

This is the kind of book an aspiring Web designer should read before learning HTML. For it is not just another HTML book, in fact it contains no HTML at all. The author presents pages followed by his opinion regarding the design. As Burns is the first to say, his opinions are not infallible; there can be circumstances where you may not want to follow his advice. However, he does know what he is talking about, so do not be hasty toward the contrary position.

I found the book easy to read, and the choices for sample sites were well made. Rather than making it easy for himself by picking sites that are awful, in general he chose pages that are quite good. If a site had been atrocious, the problems would have been obvious, even for a beginner. By choosing good ones, he could then point out the "flaws" that are easily overlooked.

This is a book that should be read either before or concurrently with a book that teaches the construction of pages. It is not necessary to know HTML to understand the material, and Web pages are like houses: You should first learn to read the blueprints before you start to build the walls.

—*Charles Ashbacher; author of Sams Teach Yourself XML in 24 Hours*

Another Superb Job by Joe Burns!

I have been working with Web pages for over four years, and I have taught Web design classes. I thought I had a good idea of what is involved with the design, setup, and marketing of a Web site. Now I find this book, and there are so many things I had never thought of before.

As with other Joe Burns books, this book is an excellent representation of what you can do if you have a little guidance to help you along. Burns is truly remarkable in the ways he is able to present ideas clearly yet make them understandable at the same time.

The book begins with an overview of what things to look for and what ideas to consider when planning and designing a Web site. Then Burns has you consider five questions before you begin the actual design layout—an approach that will help in making a better Web site.

There are other topics, like the 10 things you shouldn't put in the Web site, choosing a server and an ISP, text, and color; there is something for beginners and experts alike. Burns also spends time explaining links, images, and visual effects before moving on to counters and Web site promotion.

Overall, there is about everything you need to have to make sure you have a successful Web site right from the start and for years to come. A first-rate book from a first-rate author.

—Michael Woznicki

Praise for Author Joe Burns's HTML Goodies Web Site

From the Web Site Visitors

"I'd like to thank you for your HTML site. Instead of wasting time scouring the Internet, the code and examples on your site have made it so much easier to see my mistakes and to finally create a working Web site."

—Anthony Moore

"... your tutorial, page by page, word by word, told me every other thing I needed to know about Web design. It was like finding a gold mine. Your language was so impressive and so much direct to the heart that I always thought you [were] there talking to me, instead of me reading from your site. I saved all the pages of [HTMLGoodies.com] and [it] became the bible of my Web design."

—Barun Sen

"Thank you so much! Trying to learn how to use tables was causing my brain to pick up smoking. I understand now; thanks for explaining it in English."

—*Elizabeth Rotondi*

"Thanks thanks thanks for the wonderful (easy) primer! I am going day by day, and my page, boring though it is … is really coming along!"

—*Jean Van Minnen*

"… HTMLgoodies is an excellent Web site with plenty of GOLD content about HTML …. Well done on a superbly successful site!"

—*Carl Blythe*

"Thanks for the beautiful pieces of work. I salute you."

—*John J. Lacombe II;* `jlacombe@cpcug.org`; *Capital PC Users Group*

"This is not only a first-rate page but is also a huge help to me, and, my guess is, many, MANY people like me. These tutorials have helped me create my own page. Once again, thank you. You're terrific."

—*Rose Dewitt Bukater*

"You probably get dozens of thank-you notes each day, but I just wanted to add my own to the lot. Since I'm a just starting out in the HTML world, I've been visiting your tutorials a lot. Just wanted you to know I've learned more from your site than from any of the books I've bought!"

—*Dawn C. Lindley*

"Dear Mr. Really Smart Cool-Happening Dude, I would like to thank you because I have made the transition from FrontPage 98 to HTML all because of you. I spent months trying to learn HTML before I learned of your site, and at age 14 I fully understand the ins and outs of HTML 4. My page is in the works, and I owe it all to you."

—*Taylor Ackley*

"I just wanted to let you know that you are doing an amazing service to all of us weekend Webmasters. Thanks a million! P.S. My Web page looks and feels a thousand times better since I have been following your tutorials."

—*Aaron Joel Chettle; Seneca College Engineering*

"WOW!!!! ... I was always interested in setting up a Web page but was afraid that it would be too difficult for me to comprehend.... So my first introduction to HTML was actually YOUR primers ... and WOW!!!!!!! I went through ALL of them this very morning with my mouth hanging wide open .... I am still so surprised that I cannot gather any words to describe to you how I feel at this moment."

—*Ludwin L. Statie*

"I'm an old dog learning new tricks. I will be taking a Web publishing college course come August. I used your primer as a jump start. I really enjoyed your primer and thought it would ... help me. I now feel prepared for the college course and not so afraid to 'run with the big dogs.'"

—*Patricia Cuthbertson*

From the Media

"If you are just learning, or already know HTML, this site is the only place you'll need. Expert tutorials make learning Web design quick and easy. Definitely check this site out."

—*HTML Design Association*

"Dr. Joe Burns offers help at all levels—from novice to the expert."

—*Signal Magazine; January 26, 1998*

"Great stuff. Probably the best overall site reviewed here."

—*NetUser Magazine*

"If you're looking for information on HTML, you'll find it here."

—*USA Today Hot Site; March 23, 1998*

"His is a technical site that appeals to an exploding piece of the Internet pie—people building their own Web site."

—*PCNovice Guide to Building Web Sites; 1997*

"We would like permission to use your Web pages [HTML Goodies] to help teach [building] Web sites."

—*San Antonio Electronic Commerce Resource Center; February 10, 1998*

From Teachers

"If everyone wrote 'how-to' pages and books as well as you, boy life would be simpler."

—Deb Spearing Ph.D.; University Registrar, Ohio State University

"I am going to use your Goodies [to teach with] this summer! Awesome!"

—Cynthia Lanius; Rice University

"I hope your own students and colleagues appreciate the importance and magnitude of the service you provide to the discipline of communication technology via the Internet. In just a short time, Joe Burns has become a legend on the Internet among those who teach in this field."

—Raymond E. Schroeder; Professor of Communication, Springfield University

"The English classes at Union Alternative High School [are] using Dr. Joe Burns's Web site HTML Goodies as an online text book. Students now have Web pages they are proud of. They have learned to teach themselves unfamiliar subject matter. There is new excitement in the class; self-esteem is up. In a nutshell: We have succeeded. Thank you for helping, Dr. Burns."

—Aaron Wills; English teacher, Union School District, Union, MO

JavaScript Goodies, Second Edition

Copyright © 2002 by Que Publishing

International Standard Book Number: 0-7897-2612-2

Library of Congress Catalog Card Number: 2001094356

Printed in the United States of America

First Printing: November, 2001

04   03   02   01   4   3   2   1

Trademarks

Warning and Disclaimer

Associate Publisher
Dean Miller

Acquisitions Editor
Todd Green

Development Editor
Victoria Elzey

Technical Editor
Jim O'Donnell

Managing Editor
Thomas F. Hayes

Senior Editor
Susan Ross Moore

Production Editor
Megan Wade

Indexer
D&G Limited, LLC

Proofreader
Bob LaRoche

Team Coordinator
Cindy Teeters

Media Developer
Michael Hunter

Interior Design
Louisa Klucznik

Cover Design
Aren Howell

Page Layout
D&G Limited, LLC

Contents at a Glance

Contents

9 Putting It All Together   243

xvii

xxi

About the Authors

Joe Burns, Ph.D. is a professor at Southeastern Louisiana University where he teaches graduate and undergraduate classes in Web design and Internet-mediated communication. Joe is the Webmaster of HTML Goodies (`http://www.htmlgoodies.com`), a site devoted to teaching HTML and Web design that serves up close to seven million pages every month to almost a half-million individual readers. He is also an Internet consultant for Internet.com. Joe first became interested in the Internet while studying for his Ph.D. at Bowling Green State University. There he created HTML Goodies and first began teaching computer classes. Joe is currently working on the viability of delivering university-level classes over the Internet and the effect of teaching in a Web-based environment. Joe lives in Hammond, Louisiana, with his wife Tammy, and two cats, Chloe and Mardi.

Andree Growney is currently a software engineer at TERC, a nonprofit educational research and development company in Cambridge, Massachusetts, where she does Internet applications development. She has been working with computers for more than 20 years. A former programmer and systems analyst, she became infatuated with the Web early in its development. She was formerly the Webmaster at Susquehanna University in Selinsgrove, Pennsylvania, where she also taught client/server and other database-to-Web–related courses.

Dedication

Dedication by Joe Burns

This book is dedicated to my wife, Tammy, who never seems to think anything is outside of my grasp. Plus, she found that missing equal sign in Chapter 7 that kept me at bay for two hours.

Dedication by Andree Growney

To my husband, Wally, with all my love.

To Kristen, Todd, Eric, and Diann, for whom my love and admiration grow daily.

And in loving memory of my mother, Bess Schwedersky, who eyed computers suspiciously, but always supported me in whatever folly I chose to pursue.

Acknowledgments

Acknowledgments by Joe Burns

First and foremost, many, many thanks to Andree Growney who went into this project with me knowing full well that it might never become anything more than a series of Web pages. Hey, Andree! We got a book!

Thanks to Tiffany Taylor for content editing the first edition of this book. Compared to the *HTML Goodies* book, this was painless. Ditto the painless comments from Michelle Wyner at Netscape. Your tech editing was great. You pointed out concerns in a helpful manner, and I probably used your words more times than I should have.

As for this second edition of *JavaScript Goodies*: Big thanks to Todd Green for the go-ahead to get the project underway and not getting upset when I said I wanted to bulk the book up … way up. Thanks to Victoria Elzey for the DE work. Finally, thanks to Jim O'Donnell for tech editing this second edition. It's a much better, and more up-to-date, book now because of Jim's work.

Larry Augustine deserves thanks for allowing me to sit in my office at work and write when I should have been taking care of a radio station. I know you knew. Thanks for giving me the time.

Thanks to Ken Kopf for being there when I was at the end of my JavaScript rope. You helped more than you know.

Thanks to Mom and Dad for playing cheerleader after the last book and now for this one. Every person in Cleveland who came into contact with them was forced to listen to stories of their son, the author.

A big thank-you to Charles Spiro, a professor at Lord Fairfax Community College, who used this book for one of this Internet programming classes. He found, and helped repair, many of the concerns and problems in the first edition. Thanks Charles, you're a gentleman.

Dave … I'm a teacher because I wanted to be just like you.

Acknowledgments by Andree Growney

A special thank-you to our publisher, Dean Miller, and to everyone at Que who helped with the production of this book.

Thanks also to our wonderful technical and content editors, Michelle and Tiffany.

Special thanks to Mike Greene at EarthWeb for his encouragement.

Many, many thanks to my coauthor Joe Burns, for bringing me on board, and for the rare pleasure of laughing out loud while reading a computer book!

Tell Us What You Think!

As the reader of this book, *you* are our most important critic and commentator. We value your opinion and want to know what we're doing right, what we could do better, what areas you'd like to see us publish in, and any other words of wisdom you're willing to pass our way.

As an associate publisher for Que, I welcome your comments. You can fax, e-mail, or write me directly to let me know what you did or didn't like about this book—as well as what we can do to make our books stronger.

Please note that I cannot help you with technical problems related to the topic of this book, and that due to the high volume of mail I receive, I might not be able to reply to every message.

When you write, please be sure to include this book's title and author as well as your name and phone or fax number. I will carefully review your comments and share them with the author and editors who worked on the book.

Fax: 317-581-4666

E-mail: feedback@quepublishing.com

Mail: Publisher
            Que
            201 West 103rd Street
            Indianapolis, IN 46290 USA

An Introduction by Joe Burns

Welcome to *JavaScript Goodies, Second Edition*. I never thought I'd write a book, let alone a second edition. How about that?

The purpose of this book's lessons is to get you started writing your own JavaScript events.

If you've tried to learn JavaScript through a textbook or from the Internet, my guess is that you found it quite difficult. Me, too. After a while, the text melds into a large block of strange hieroglyphics equal to the Rosetta stone. I always feel like I'm deciphering the text rather than reading it.

Learning JavaScript is literally learning a new language. The text might look like English, but the construction of the sentences is quite different. This book teaches you JavaScript by coming at the language from an entirely new perspective. Instead of getting all the commands and then building a script, we'll start with the script and tear it down to its individual commands. In the process, you'll learn JavaScript programming.

Why Now?

In 1999, when HTML Goodies (http://www.htmlgoodies.com) was dedicated solely to HTML, I would get e-mail asking, "When are you going to put together a series of lessons for writing JavaScript?" Most readers of my sites know that I already have primers for HTML and for creating advertising banners, so why not JavaScript? Good question!

In an effort to put lessons together, I bought the books, read them, read them again, and gave up. JavaScript books, at least the four I've bulled through, are dry and hard to follow. They're textbooks, and we all know how fun those are to read. So, in an effort to not have to write JavaScript lessons at all, I created the Java Goodies Web site at http://www.java-goodies.com. There's no need to look for it—it has since been combined into JavaScripts.com. Ah, it's the way of the Web.

My purpose for starting JavaGoodies.com was to create the largest possible download source for JavaScript. I figured that instead of teaching you to make your own JavaScripts, I would supply you with as many ready-to-go scripts as I could. Well, it seemed like a smart idea at the time. JavaGoodies.com once had more than 1,000 scripts, and readers still wanted JavaScript lessons. I should have seen it coming.

My Coauthor

Andree Growney used to be the Director of Instructional Technology Support Services and Webmaster at the university where I worked and is a bit of a wizard at this JavaScript stuff. One day I asked if she would be interested in putting a book together on how to write JavaScript and posting it to the HTML Goodies Web site to test it out. To my great joy, Andree said yes. So, we got started.

We sat in her office and brainstormed until we came up with 30 JavaScript topics. Our thinking was, "If you've grasped these 30 lessons, you're well on your way to writing your own scripts." We then set to work creating scripts for each topic idea. I wrote the tutorials for my scripts; Andree wrote for hers. Then, we edited each other's work.

I finally set it all to hypertext, and it hit the Net in August 1998, as the HTML Goodies 30-Step JavaScript Primer series at http://www.htmlgoodies.com/primers/jsp/.

Wow! What a response. The bulk of the e-mail from the site didn't concern the content or the teaching method as much as the format for teaching JavaScript. E-mail after e-mail stated, "I understand this."

Mission accomplished.

How You Will Learn

My own method of learning the JavaScript language is the method these lessons—and hopefully you—will follow. I didn't set out to learn JavaScript following this book's method. It just happened that way. Let me explain.

Every script submitted to the Java Goodies site arrived via e-mail. Usually, the e-mail transmission did quite a number on it. Scripts always arrived bent, folded, and mutilated, and it was my job to put them back together so they would work again. After doing that a couple hundred times, I found I was using my reference books less and less. I could look at a script and see what the problem was. Error messages stopped sending me into a rage. Commands were becoming familiar. Formats and structure started to become friendly.

I was learning JavaScript. But I was learning it backward from the approach described in the books I had read. Everything I had seen to that point gave the commands and then built the script. So I thought, let's go the other way. Let's start with the script fully finished and then tear it apart. If we keep doing that over and over with new scripts, readers are bound to see patterns and common structures.

Forget trying to write from scratch right off. Let's get the readers altering finished scripts. There's a phenomenal sense of accomplishment if you can look at a script and alter where its output appears, or change the color of the text, or make numbers add up in different fashions.

With that sense of accomplishment comes the desire to learn more, to write a brand new script. The next thing you know, you're writing JavaScript.

More and more research shows that teaching by lecturing doesn't work. When you read a textbook, you are essentially being lectured. These primers are going to come at the subject from a different angle.

A professor of mine liked to say, "Tell me and I forget. Show me and I remember. Involve me and I learn." The purpose here is to involve you.

After the go-ahead was given to turn the JavaScript Primers into a book, I knew 30 lessons wouldn't be enough to satisfy the reader. The online users are right now screaming for the lessons to be expanded. So, I almost doubled the number of lessons. This book has 55 different scripts that we'll break down for your entertainment.

Furthermore, in this second edition, I've added 10 of the Script Tips from the HTML Goodies site. These are big, involved scripts broken down so you can understand how they work.

Each of the now 65 lessons display one JavaScript and tear it apart so you can see how it works. You see, you have to be taught *why* something works, not just be shown that it works. Case in point: David Copperfield doesn't close the door on his assistant, open it, and exclaim, "Son of a gun! She's gone again!" He knows why she disappeared. All you know is that he shut the door and she went away. You both know that the box works, but only he knows *why* it works. He will be in a better position to create another trick, whereas you'll just keep closing the door, hoping it'll work.

The Format of the Lessons

As I said before, this book contains 55 lessons in nine chapters. Each of those first 55 lessons follows the same format:

1. First, you get a brief concept statement regarding what the script is supposed to do and what the example is supposed to teach you.

2. Next, you see the script in text form.

3. Then, you see the script's effect. This book is fully supported online. I'll tell you how you can get all the scripts in the book into your own computer in a moment.

4. Next, we tear the script apart, looking closely at the building blocks used to create the whole. The purpose is for you to be able to read a JavaScript as you would a sentence.

5. Finally, each lesson has an assignment. You're asked to alter the script you've just worked on so that it will be a little different, or a lot different. Either way, you will be asked to create 55 new scripts from the 55 we give you.

Then, at the end of each chapter, you'll find a review lesson. We'll stop, quickly review the JavaScript commands you've learned up to that point, and then use them to create an entirely new script. This is where this book will hopefully start to come to life for you.

The Script Tips at the end of the book walk you through more scripts and further you along in your quest to understand this language.

I've been a college professor for a number of years now, and the hardest thing to teach students is that there comes a point where they have to look at the building blocks I've shown them and use those blocks to build something that is fully their own. Just mimicking what I show you here is not enough; you need to build something new.

Examples and Assignments

This is a book. You knew that. But we want this book to have an interactive feel to it. You should be able to see the JavaScripts in action. When you finish an assignment, you should be able to see a possible answer and be able to look at the source code to see how it could be done.

In an effort to help you do that, the wonderful staff at HTML Goodies and Java Goodies—me—has put together a packet that contains all this book's examples and assignment answers. How often do you get the answers up front? Just don't cheat and look before you try to do the assignment yourself, okay?

You can use the examples and assignments packet in one of two ways.

First, it's all available online at `http://www.htmlgoodies.com/JSBook/`. Please make a point of entering the address just as you see it. Note that the "J," "S," and "B" are capital letters. Log on to the Internet, and use your browser to look at the pages as you need to. You'll find an easy-to-follow chart of the examples and assignments by lesson. I also offer a direct URL to the required page right here in the book. Keep in mind that these pages were created for your use. Feel free to download one or all of them by clicking File and selecting Save As.

Second, you can download the entire packet of examples and assignments and install them right on to your own computer. It's very easy to grab and install. The packet contains all 55 scripts found in the book, along with all 55 assignments. It's available in Zip-file format. Follow these steps:

1. Log on to the Internet, and point your browser to `http://www.htmlgoodies.com/JSBook/JavaScriptGoodies.zip`. Again, make a point of following the capitalization pattern.

2. After you have the packet, unzip its contents into an empty folder on your hard drive.

3. Use a browser to open the file `index.html`, and you'll see links to all the examples and assignments.

Let's Get Started with JavaScript

Be careful going through these lessons. Often, a student will want to roll through the earlier lessons as quickly as possible. Most of the time that leads to commands being jumbled up in the mind. Your brain needs time to digest all of this. If I may make a suggestion: Don't do more than two or three lessons a day.

Students tell me they read the entire chapter, but they can't remember what they read. That's because getting to the end was the goal, not getting the most out of the reading. Speed kills. Give your brain time. Here's an example. You read all of this, right? Well, without looking back up the page, tell me the name of my coauthor. I've written it three times now.

You rolled before you crawled, before you walked, before you ran. Give your brain time to roll around the easy scripts.

Andree and I wish you the best of luck with your future JavaScripts.

Chapter 1

The Basics

This chapter contains the following lessons and scripts:

- What Is JavaScript?
- Lesson 1: Writing Text to a Web Page
- Lesson 2: Error Messages
- Lesson 3: Object Properties
- Lesson 4: Chapter Wrap-Up and Review

The purpose of this chapter is to get you started on the right JavaScript foot. In this chapter you'll learn how to work with JavaScript and how to create JavaScripts that print text to your HTML page, fix error messages, and tell the world what time it is.

What Is JavaScript?

First off, JavaScript is not Java. It's easy to get confused and think that Java and JavaScript are one and the same. Not so. Java is a programming language developed at Sun Microsystems. On the other hand, JavaScript is a programming language created by the good people at Netscape.

With Java, you create fully standalone programs that must go through a somewhat complex process of writing, compiling, and being referenced in your Web page. JavaScript, on the other hand, is simply text you type into your Web page much as you type in HTML tags and text. For JavaScript to work, the Web page it is in must be viewed with a browser that understands the JavaScript language, such as all Netscape browsers 2.0 and above. Some earlier versions of the Internet Explorer browsers have trouble with advanced JavaScript commands found in JavaScript version 1.1 and 1.2. The scripts in the book, however, stay mainly at the JavaScript 1.0 level and will run on both browsers. When writing JavaScript, remember that *JavaScript is not HTML!* I am often asked whether one is simply a different version of the other. Nope. The following sections outline the differences.

JavaScript Is Case Sensitive

In HTML, the tag <B> works the same as the tag <b>. That's because HTML doesn't differentiate between upper- and lowercase characters. Not so in JavaScript. You must pay very close attention to the capitalization of commands. Placing an uppercase character where a lowercase one should be causes an error.

Beware of Line Breaks and Spaces

HTML is very forgiving in terms of spaces and line breaks. It doesn't matter how many spaces you leave between words or paragraphs. In fact, there's no reason why you couldn't write an HTML document as one long line or skip 20 lines between every word. It doesn't matter.

The opposite is true in JavaScript. It makes a big difference where each line ends. Sometimes you can break (or *truncate*) a line of JavaScript, but not very often. Following is a single line of JavaScript:

```
document.write("<FONT COLOR='RED'>This Is Red Text</FONT>")
```

Those commands must all stay on one line. If you change this line to look something like this

```
document.write("<FONT COLOR='RED'>This Is Red Text</FONT>
")
```

the code will not work properly and will cause an error. (We'll get into errors and fixing them in Lesson 2.) Also, an extra space between two commands, or anywhere else a space doesn't belong, will cause an error.

Don't Set Margins

Whether you're writing or editing a script, you *cannot* allow margins to get in the way. Always edit your work in a text editor that has no margins. I don't mean margins set to their widest point. I mean *no margins*. You should be able to write off of the right side of the text screen for miles. Doing it any other way is going to cause you problems.

And now with some of the basics out of the way, let's get right to your first JavaScript!

Lesson 1: Writing Text to a Web Page

This first script is meant to introduce you to the very basics of creating and placing a JavaScript on your page. Simply type the following JavaScript into any existing HTML page of your Web site:

```
<SCRIPT LANGUAGE="javascript">
document.write("<FONT COLOR='RED'>This Is Red Text</FONT>")
</SCRIPT>
```

The concept of this script is to use JavaScript to place text on a Web page, as illustrated in Figure 1.1. In this case, the text will be red.

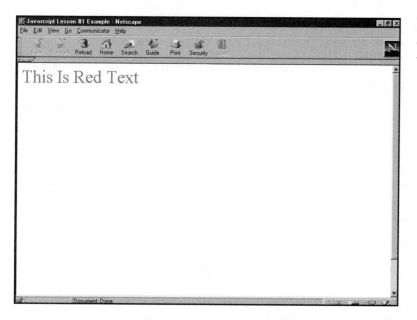

Figure 1.1
Putting red text on your HTML page.

To see the script working on your own computer, open Lesson One's Script Effect or point your browser to http://www.htmlgoodies.com/JSBook/lesson1effect.html.

Deconstructing the Script

Let's start at the top. The first line of the script looks like this:

```
<SCRIPT LANGUAGE="javascript">
```

That's HTML code to alert the browser that what immediately follows is going to be a JavaScript script. That seems simple enough. All JavaScripts start with this same command. We're writing this script in JavaScript version 1.0. Because no number follows the word javascript, the browser assumes by default that the following code is in JavaScript 1.0.

At the time of the writing of this second edition, the Internet Explorer browser 5.5 was out, as was Netscape Navigator 6.0. Both understand versions of JavaScript well above 1.0 and default to the latest version the browser understands. That means you can simply write LANGUAGE="javascript" and if the browser understands version 1.2, that will be the default. There's no real need to add the version number, but if you find yourself going beyond this book and getting into higher versions of JavaScript, adding the number at the end of the "javascript" is not a bad habit to get into.

That said ... what about that LANGUAGE="javascript" deal? Won't the browser simply default to the highest JavaScript version? Do you really need that anymore?

Yes, you need it. It's because there are other types of scripts: VBScript, for example. Using that LANGUAGE attribute keeps it straight in the browser's mind.

Because we're dealing with only three lines of text here, allow me to jump right to the end. The flag

```
</SCRIPT>
```

ends every JavaScript. No exceptions. Now, put that on a brain cell. That's the last time those two commands will be discussed. Remember, start with <SCRIPT LANGUAGE="javascript"> and end with </SCRIPT>.

Now we hit the meat of the script:

```
document.write("<FONT COLOR='RED'>This Is Red Text</FONT>")
```

This script is simple enough that you can just about guess what each little bit does, but let's go over it anyway so that we're all speaking with the same common terms.

The document holds the contents of the page within the browser window, including all the HTML code and JavaScript commands. If it helps you to simply think of document as the HTML document, that's fine.

That document will be altered by write-ing something to it. What will be written to the document is inside the parentheses.

Now we'll cover some terms. In JavaScript, the document is what's known as an *object*. The write that follows, separated by a period, is what is known as the object's *method*, an action to be performed on the object. So, the script is basically saying, take the object, something that already exists, and write something to it.

The open and close parentheses are called the *instance*. The text inside the parentheses is called the method's *parameters*. Are you with me so far?

Notice that what is inside the parentheses is encased in double quotation marks. In HTML, quotation marks are not always required. In JavaScript, they are. You must use them. And not only that, there's an exact way of using them.

The text inside the double quotation marks is simple text: It is written to the screen exactly as shown. Note the HTML flags within the double quotes. That's fine. The script is just going to write it all to the page.

But there are a couple of things to be concerned about when using a document.write() JavaScript command:

- You should recognize the text as a FONT flag that will turn text red. Notice that single quotation marks appear around the HTML attribute code <FONT COLOR='RED'>.

  If you use double quotes, the JavaScript thinks it's at the end of the line and you get only part of your text written to the object. You know you didn't intend that double quote to mean the end of the line, but the script doesn't. You'll most likely get an error message telling you something is wrong.

  Some people get around this concern by not using any quotes around HTML attributes. They write the previous command this way: <FONT COLOR=red>. Either way works, but if you decide to write using quotes around HTML attributes, remember this: Inside double quotes ... use single quotes.

- When writing text within double quotes, be careful not to use any words that are contractions. For example

  ```
  document.write("Don't go there!")
  ```

  That line of code produces a JavaScript error. You know that the single quote doesn't denote an attribute, but JavaScript doesn't know that. It thinks you've started an attribute, and when it doesn't find the ending single quote, an error results.

Note

If what you want is simply to have a single quote, such as in a contraction, place a backward slash in front of the quote mark. That slash is called an *escape character*. The format for the previous line of text would look like this:

```
document.write("Don\'t go there!")
```

What happens is the backslash escapes the script just long enough so the computer understands the single quote is meant to be text rather than part of the JavaScript code. Keep this concept in mind for later. I'll discuss it in much deeper detail in Chapter 2, "Popping Up Text with Mouse Events," when we begin popping up alert boxes.

If you simply must have more right now, I have an entire tutorial on escape characters at `http://www.htmlgoodies.com/beyond/escapecharacter.html`.

How Did the Text Become Red?

So, did the JavaScript actually turn the text red? No. The HTML did that for you. What the JavaScript did was write the code to the page. There it displayed and was shown as red thanks to the FONT FACE flag and attribute. The JavaScript was simply the delivery device. Neat, huh?

One More Thing

Look at this code and its result, shown in Figure 1.2:

```
<SCRIPT LANGUAGE="javascript">
document.write("This is the text that will be written to the page.");
document.write("But even though these lines of text are on different lines");
document.write("in this script, they will not reproduce the same way on the");
document.write("HTML document.");
</SCRIPT>
```

Notice how all the lines run together when written to the page even though the text is written in four lines. The reason is that the document.write statement just writes text to the page. It does not add any breaks when its lines stop.

How about that? The first lesson is over, and you've already got two very useful commands under your belt. Better yet, you know how to use them.

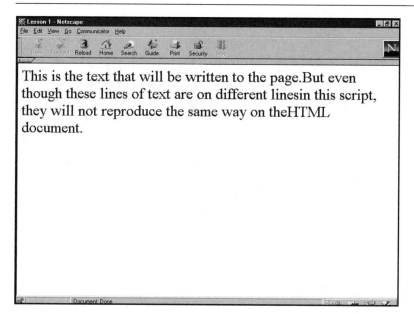

Figure 1.2
Multiple document.write *statements run together.*

Your Assignment

Each time you do an assignment, you'll need to copy the script described in the lesson so you can paste it into an HTML document and play with it. You probably already noticed this, but you can always copy and paste the script right from the sample Web page. If you're going online to see the examples, go to http://www.htmlgoodies.com/JSBook/ lesson1example.html.

Alter the previous script so that it will produce two lines of text, one red and one blue. *But* you must do this by writing more JavaScript commands, not by simply adding more HTML to the instance. Make the two bits of text write to two different lines rather than simply following each other on the same line.

You'll find one possible answer by clicking Lesson One Assignment or pointing your browser to http://www.htmlgoodies.com/JSBook/assignment1.html.

Lesson 2: Error Messages

You know what I've found missing from the myriad of JavaScript books I've read? They're missing a description of how to deal with error messages. I guess the assumption is that you'll get all your code right the first time and never see one. Welcome to reality.

If you've ever attempted to write or install a JavaScript on your Web pages, you know these little jewels are part of the fun. Just when you think you've got it right, boom, something like Figure 1.3 pops up.

Figure 1.3
A JavaScript error in version 3.x of Netscape Navigator.

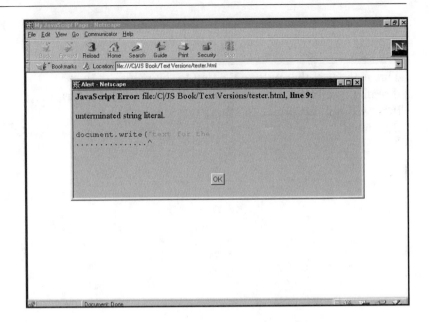

This lesson is intended to tell you what to do when you encounter error messages. I've worked through thousands of them. Now you're starting to write JavaScript, and you'll get your share of them, too. But first, let's look at the new face of error messages.

How Browsers Display the Error Messages

Figure 1.3 is a view of how error messages looked in Netscape Navigator before version 4.x browsers were released. After the version 4.x browsers came out, JavaScript version 1.3 was in vogue. Version 1.3 offered something new called the JavaScript Console. It looks similar to Figure 1.4.

The benefit of the JavaScript Console is that the errors are displayed in a single package. In contrast, the JavaScript errors in Navigator 3.x and below version browsers simply piled up one on top of another, resulting in a mess. The JavaScript Console displays all the errors on a scroll, showing the first error on top and following down the errors from there.

I actually enjoyed the way the errors displayed in Navigator version 3.x and below browsers because the errors were right there as soon as they occurred. You couldn't ignore them. The console is less intrusive, though. When you get an error in a 4.x browser, you're alerted to the error in the browser's status bar and asked to write "javascript:" in the Location (now Netsite) bar. That command brings up the JavaScript Console, where you see your errors.

14

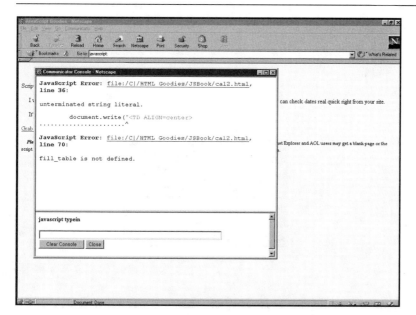

Figure 1.4
JavaScript errors in the Netscape Navigator JavaScript Console.

In some ways I like the old gray JavaScript error boxes popping up and in others I like the JavaScript Console. You can make your choice. If you do not find the JavaScript Console to your liking, try changing your browser to the older, gray-box method. It's an easy change; the instructions are on the Netscape Developer site at `http://developer.netscape.com/docs/technote/javascript/jsconsole.html`.

Note whom the author of that Netscape developer page is. It's Michelle Wyner. She tech edited the first edition of this book! Woo hoo!

You Internet Explorer fans get your errors as is shown in Figure 1.5.

JavaScript errors in Internet Explorer either pop up or they do not, depending on how you've set up your system. Again, I like my error messages to pop right up. You'll note in Figure 1.5 that the error box that pops up offers the ability to uncheck a box so that the gray dialog box won't pop up.

If you select that option, you'll still get a warning, but it won't be as blatant. A small, yellow triangle with an exclamation point will appear in the lower-left portion of the browser. Text will also proclaim that you have an error. You then click the yellow triangle and up will pop the error dialog box.

Gray box or no gray box? That is the question.

OK, now that you can actually understand your browsers and how they are trying to tell you that you have JavaScript errors, let's move along to how you can fix those errors.

Figure 1.5
An error being displayed in Internet Explorer.

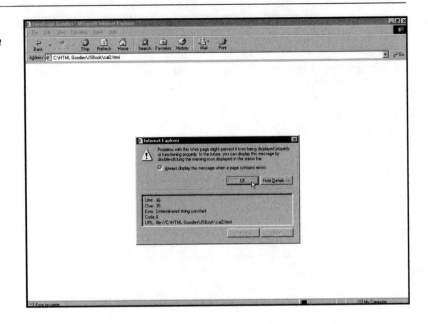

It is said that the best way to fix errors is to avoid creating them. That's a great deal easier said than done. However, you can up your chances of getting fewer error messages by writing in a text editor that does not have margins. Also, allow each line of JavaScript to remain on its own line. There's no need to break longer lines in two. In fact, doing that will probably throw errors. That said, I'll bet you get errors just about every time you start to play with this new language, so let's get into how to repair them.

The Two Types of Error Messages

There are basically two types of errors you can produce:

- **Syntax error**—This means that you've misspelled something, or the JavaScript is not configured correctly.
- **Runtime error**—This means that you have used an incorrect command and the JavaScript doesn't understand what you're trying to do.

Either way, they both mean the same thing: Somewhere, something's messed up.

Some programs do exist that will help you fix your errors—a process called *debugging*—but I still prefer to do it by hand. I wrote it, and I want to fix it, and it's actually easier than you think.

Fixing the Errors

The wonderful thing about a JavaScript error message box is that the little window that pops up tells you where and what the problem is. Look at the error message box previously shown in Figure 1.3. It's a syntax error, meaning I have not configured the script correctly, and the error is on line 9. What's more, the error message is pointing at the problem area. See the long line of dots and then the little caret pointing up? It's like the browser is saying, "Here's what I don't get."

When an error message denotes the line number in which the error occurred, you locate that line by counting down from the top of the HTML document, not the top of the JavaScript. You must also count blank lines. You might have a text editor program that offers to find a specific line for you, which is really helpful.

For instance, the following document has an error in line 9. It is a syntax error because the instance was not allowed to close on the same line on which it started. See how the last word and parenthesis were jumped to the next line?

```
<HTML>
<HEAD>
<TITLE>My JavaScript Page</TITLE>
</HEAD>

<BODY>

<SCRIPT LANGUAGE="javascript">
document.write("text for the
page" )

</SCRIPT>

</BODY>
</HTML>
```

After you've counted down and you're actually at the line that has an error, you need to decide what to do. More times than not, if it's a *syntax* error, one of the following is true:

- The line has been truncated. That means it has been chopped off early, such as in the previous example.
- Something is misspelled.
- You have used a double quotation mark where a single quotation mark should be. That's called using *unbalanced* quotes.
- You're missing a parenthesis.

17

If the error is *runtime*, the error message is pointing at a command that doesn't logically follow in the sequence. For instance, you might have used the code `document.wrote` instead of `document.write`.

Dealing with Multiple Errors

Nothing gives me heartburn faster than running a script and getting multiple errors. I used to think multiple boxes meant there were actually that many errors. But it's not always so.

JavaScript is an extremely logical language that likes to work in a linear fashion. Let's say you have 10 errors throughout a long script. When the error messages pile up, don't go after that last error first. It probably doesn't exist.

You see ... the first error in the script might very well be creating all the other errors. If you forgot to put a command in the third line of code, every subsequent line that needs that command to work will claim it has an error. So, fix the errors in sequence from bottom to top. I have found many times that a script threw 20 errors, but fixing only the first error solved all the subsequent errors.

The "Something's Not Defined" Error

You'll see this written on a few JavaScript error boxes before too long. This is a runtime error that means something in the script doesn't jibe quite right. The text that is throwing the error has come out of the clear blue sky—to the computer anyway. When I get a "not defined" error, I always make sure the text wasn't created by a longer line being truncated. If that's not the case, I try erasing the problem line. It can always be put back at another time. Typos do occur, so see whether this isn't one of those typos. It happens more times than you would believe.

There's not much more that can be said about error messages at this point. You now have enough knowledge to fix 99% of the problems that pop up. Just remember that getting error messages is actually a plus. If you didn't get them, all you would have is a blank page with no suggestion about what the problem might be.

Error messages are quite helpful if you think about them in the right light.

Your Assignment

 Go to your packet download and click the link that reads Lesson Two Assignment. You can also go right to it online at http://www.htmlgoodies.com/JSBook/assignment2.html.

When you click the link on that page, the script throws an error or two. You Netscape Navigator users might have to write `"javascript:"` into the Location bar to pop up the JavaScript Console and grab the error.

Your assignment is to fix the errors so that the script runs. Now, you probably won't recognize some of the commands in this script, but that doesn't matter. The error boxes that appear will give you enough information to make this script run.

HINT!!! You might get only one error when you first run it. The second error might come after you fix the first.

If the JavaScript runs correctly, the current date will display on the page.

 After you get the script to run, or give up trying, you can look at the corrected script by going to `http://www.htmlgoodies.com/JSBook/assignment2_answer.html`.

You'll find a short explanation of what had to be fixed right on the page.

Lesson 3: Object Properties

You should be starting to get an understanding of the hierarchy of JavaScript. In fact, hierarchy is quite important in this language, so much so that I devote an entire lesson, Lesson 13, to it.

You know there are objects, such as `document`, and methods, such as `write`. You know that methods act upon objects. And you know how to write the document and method format in JavaScript:

```
document.write("This writes to the page";)
```

In this lesson, you're introduced to a new part of the JavaScript hierarchy: object properties. A *property* is like a subsection of an object. It holds specific characteristics about the object. The object you're already familiar with—document—has a few properties, such as its background color, text color, and location. The four scripts in the next section each cover one of the following objects and a great many of their properties:

- `document`
- `navigator`—This object represents the browser.
- `history`—This object represents the list the browser keeps of all the pages the user visited during the current online session.
- `location`—This represents the current URL of the page that is being displayed.

Figure 1.6 shows the results of running the four scripts we'll examine.

Figure 1.6
The property scripts.

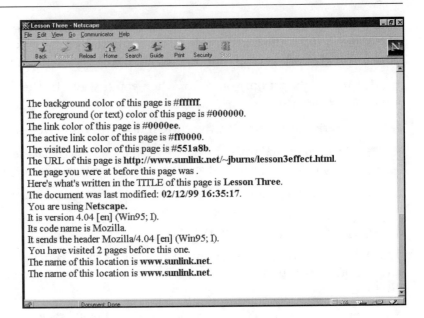

 You can see the effects of all the scripts by going to `http://www.htmlgoodies.com/JSBook/` `lesson3effect.html.`

The Property Scripts

There are actually four scripts in the following—but they all follow the same format: an
`object.property` statement placed into a `document.write()` statement to be written to the
page.

Writing document Object Properties

```
<SCRIPT LANGUAGE="javascript">
document.write("The background color of this page is <B>"
➥+document.bgColor+ "</B>.")
document.write("<BR>The foreground (or text) color
➥ of this page is <B>" +document.fgColor+ "</B>.")
document.write("<BR>The link color of this page is <B>"
➥ +document.linkColor+ "</B>.")
document.write("<BR>The active link color of this page is <B>"
➥ +document.alinkColor+ "</B>.")
document.write("<BR>The visited link color of this page is <B>"
➥ +document.vlinkColor+ "</B>.")
document.write("<BR>The URL of this page is <B>"
➥ +document.location+ "</B>.")
```

20

```
document.write("<BR>The page you were at before this page was <B>"
➥ +document.referrer+ "</B>.")
document.write("<BR>Here's what's written in the TITLE
➥ of this page is <B>" +document.title+ "</B>.")
document.write("<BR>The document was last modified: <B>"
➥ +document.lastModified+ "</B>.")
</SCRIPT>
```

Writing *navigator* Object Properties

```
<SCRIPT LANGUAGE="javascript">
document.write("You are using <B>" +navigator.appName+ ".</B><BR>")
document.write("It is version " +navigator.appVersion+ ".<BR>")
document.write("Its code name is " +navigator.appCodeName+ ".<BR>")
document.write("It sends the header " +navigator.userAgent+ "." );
</SCRIPT>
```

Writing *history* Object Properties

```
<SCRIPT LANGUAGE="javascript">
document.write("You have visited " +history.length+ "
➥ pages before this one.")
</SCRIPT>
```

Writing *location* Object Properties

```
<SCRIPT LANGUAGE="javascript">
document.write("The name of this location is <B>"
➥ + location.host + "</B>." )
</SCRIPT>
```

```
<SCRIPT LANGUAGE="javascript">
document.write("The name of this location is <B>"
➥ + location.hostname + "</B>." )
</SCRIPT>
```

Deconstructing the Scripts

Please notice that the format of calling a property is the same as attaching an object and a method. You write the object name, a dot, and then the property. The biggest difference in the appearance is there are no parentheses after the property. A method affects an object; a property already exists. You just want that property and nothing else, so there is no need for the parentheses instance. Plus, later in the book, you see that those parentheses are used to pass data around. The property already exists and thus has nothing that can be passed to it. Therefore, there's no need for the parentheses.

What Do Those Plus Signs Do?

Ah, you noticed that! You're very observant. Here's the first line of code from the first script:

```
document.write("The background color of this page is <B>"
➥ +document.bgColor+ "</B>.")
```

See the plus signs on either side of the code `document.bgColor`? Those plus signs are central to getting the results of the script.

You already know that whatever is within double quotation marks is written to the page. This is a `document.write` statement, after all.

Those plus signs are used in JavaScript to set aside the *object.property* code as something that should be returned. You don't want the text `document.bgColor` to appear on the page; you want the property that line of text represents. In this case, it's the document's background color.

By enclosing the `document.bgColor` statement in plus signs, connect what is returned as part of the entire line. It puts the three elements together on one line. The plus signs are used to concatenate the three elements.

Notice that `document.bgColor` is not surrounded by quotes, so it will not print as text. The value it represents, what is returned from the browser, will print. By using the plus signs, the first run of text, the return, and the last bit of text all run together on one line. The plus sign adds the three pieces together. Get it?

Hey! The Text Is Bold in Some Places!

Yes. That's another extra little trick thrown in for fun. Look at the code for any of the items that appear in bold. All I did was add the `<B>` and `</B>` statements on either side of the *object.property* code—inside the double quotation marks. Because this is a `document.write` statement, the bold commands are written to the page and then act upon the property that was returned. I wanted you to see that you could also affect what is returned from the script, rather than just the text you write within the `document.write` statement.

Just make sure the HTML commands are inside the double quotation marks so they are seen as text rather than part of the script commands. If you don't, you'll get an error.

Now let's find out what all these properties mean.

Properties of the document Object

The HTML document object properties are very popular in JavaScript. The script displays nine.

Pay close attention to the capitalization pattern of each property. Every time you write these properties, you must use that pattern. Why? Because that's the way JavaScript likes it:

- bgColor—Returns the background color in hexadecimal code.
- fgColor—Returns the foreground color in hexadecimal code.
- linkColor—Returns the link color in hexadecimal code.
- alinkColor—Returns the active link color in hexadecimal code.
- vlinkColor—Returns the visited link color in hexadecimal code.
- location—Returns the URL, or Web address, of the page. If you are not online, meaning no server is involved, this property returns the filename.
- referrer—Returns the page the user came from before the current page. If no page is available, this property returns a blank space. The one drawback to this command is that for a page to be recognized as a referring page, a click must have been made to get to the page containing the document.referrer code. If the page containing the document.referrer code was not arrived at by clicking, the property is returned as blank space. There are a few of these fun little bugs throughout JavaScript.
- title—Returns the text between the HTML document's TITLE commands.
- lastModified—Returns the date the page was last modified. The return is actually the date the page was uploaded to the server, or last saved on hard disk.

These document properties are not shown in the script:

- cookie—Returns the user's cookie text file
- anchors—Returns the number of HREF anchors on the page
- forms—Returns an array (listing) of the form items on a page
- links—Returns a number for each individual link

Properties of the navigator Object

People love these properties. The HTML Goodies e-mail box always gets questions about how to display browser characteristics. This is it. The object is navigator. After all, Netscape came up with JavaScript, so why not use its own browser's name to denote the browser object, right? Four properties are available. Once again, be careful of your capitalization:

- appName—Returns the name of the browser, such as Netscape or Microsoft Internet Explorer.
- appVersion—Returns the version number of the browser and the platform for which it is created.

- ● appCodeName—Returns the code name given to the browser. Netscape calls its browser Mozilla; Microsoft calls its browser Internet Explorer.

- ● userAgent—Returns the hypertext transfer protocol (HTTP) header used by the browser when working with servers so the server knows what it is dealing with. Web pages use HTTP protocol, so you write that at the beginning of each Web page address.

Knowing all this information about the browser is important. Later, we'll get into IF statements. Knowing the user's browser and version numbers allows you to say IF the browser is this, do this.

Properties of the history Object

This is a very popular object. Many readers want to be able to make links that take people back one or more pages, or forward one or more pages with one click. The purpose is to re-create the Back and Forward buttons at the top of the browser window.

Properties of the location Object

Location is JavaScript for URL, or the address of the page. The location object has eight properties, and you'll meet a few more later. However, these two properties are by far the most popular: host and hostname. The properties are equal in that they both do the same thing—return the URL in either IP number or text format depending on what format the server is using:

- ● location.host—Returns the URL plus the port the user is attached to
- ● location.hostname—Returns only the URL

If you are getting the same result with both commands, that means your server has not routed you to a specific port. In technical terms, the port property is "null".

By the way, these two commands will not work if you are running the page from your hard drive. You must be running this from a server for there to be an address for the script to return.

Your Assignment

Okay, smart person—do this: Using one of the previous object.property statements, write a JavaScript that creates a link to a page on your server on the HTML document. An example is if you're on www.you.com, the JavaScript would create a link to the page www.you.com/joe.html.

You can see a possible answer on your computer by opening Lesson Three Assignment in the download packet. But do yourself a favor. See it online at http:// www.htmlgoodies.com/ JSBook/assignment3.html. The answer requires that the page be on a server to get the effect—that should be a pretty good hint right there.

Lesson 4: Chapter Wrap-Up and Review

We've reached the end of Chapter 1. The concept of this lesson is to stop, review the JavaScript commands you've learned to this point, and build something new.

The chapters are progressively longer, and you'll be presented with this type of lesson at the end of each. Through years of teaching, Andree and I have learned that one of the hardest things for a student to do is to take what he or she has learned and apply it toward something outside the realm of the class. In short—make something new. We're going to try to force you to think past just what we're showing you in this book.

Table 1.1 shows the JavaScript commands you've seen up to now.

Table 1.1   JavaScript Commands Demonstrated in Chapter 1

Object	Methods	Properties
document	write()	alinkColor, bgColor, fgColor, linkColor, lastModified, location, referrer, title, vlinkColor
history		length
location		host, hostname
navigator		appCodeName, appName, appVersion, userAgent

You know what each of these commands does. Now let's use the commands to create something functional that's different from what you have seen so far. Enter the following JavaScript:

```
<SCRIPT LANGUAGE="javascript">
document.write("Go <A HREF=" +document.referrer+ ">
➥back</A> one page.")
</SCRIPT>
```

Figure 1.7 shows the script's effect.

Figure 1.7
The script creates a link to the previous Web page.

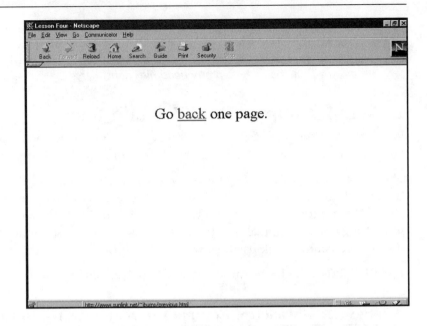

Go <u>back</u> one page.

To see the script's effect on your own computer, open Lesson Four's Script Effect in the download packet or see it online at http://www.htmlgoodies.com/JSBook/lesson4effect. html.

Notice that this script uses the document.referrer object property. It's best to see that online. The previous page address provides a link to click to get to the page with the document.referrer code, so you'll see the code's effect correctly.

Deconstructing the Script

The purpose of the script is to create a link back one page. Here's the line of code that does the trick:

```
document.write("Go <A HREF=" +document.referrer+ ">
➥back</A> one page.")
```

It's a basic document.write() formula that posts the code of a hypertext link to the page. Note there are no spaces before or next to the double quotation marks. That means the text returned from the document.referrer command will butt right up against the hypertext link text.

The movement back one page through the user's history list is created by returning the document's referrer property to the browser to act as a hypertext link. It's simple, and it's useful.

Your Assignment

Your final assignment in this chapter is to create something new and useful.

Take a moment and look back over the commands you've learned. What can you do with them? Remember that functionality does not always mean there has to be a flashy effect. You could use the commands to simply communicate with the user.

Here are a couple of suggestions:

- Create a page containing Internet Explorer–only commands and another containing Netscape Navigator–only commands. You could have the page read: You're using a ***** browser. Please click the ***** link below to go to a page made just for you. The ***** would be filled in using some of the commands we've discussed.

- Use the commands to talk to the viewer about the page. The text could read Thank you for coming in from **** to *****. I see you're using the ***** browser. Good choice.

 The code for both these examples is available for you to look at. Click Lesson Four Assignment on your download packet, or see it online at http://www.htmlgoodies.com/ JSBook/assignment4.html.

I got the second suggested effect by using multiple document.write codes. Think about how you would get the effect, and then go to the assignment page to see how I did it.

Chapter 2

Popping Up Text with Mouse Events

This chapter contains the following lessons and scripts:

Lesson 5: JavaScript's `onMouseOver` Event Handler

We've discussed objects, methods, and properties. Now let's start playing with events. Think of *events* as things that happen. They add life and interest to your Web site; they're things that make your viewers say, "Ooooooo," without your having to create large JavaScripts. *Event handlers* are the commands that detect the user's input and trigger an event.

Now allow me to throw a curve into the process. Events, created using event handlers, are JavaScript, but unlike what you've seen so far, they are "built in" to HTML code rather than standing alone. Event handlers are meant to be embedded, so they don't require the `<SCRIPT>` and `</SCRIPT>` flags. They themselves are not scripts but are small interfaces allowing for interaction between your page and your reader.

Several events exist, and we'll get to them, but let's start with one of the most popular ones: onMouseOver. Consider the following JavaScript:

```
<A HREF="http://www.htmlgoodies.com"
onMouseOver="window.status='Go to the Goodies Home Page';
    return true">Click Here</A>
```

The purpose of this script is to show text in the status bar, as shown in Figure 2.1, when your user rolls her mouse over the hypertext link.

Figure 2.1
The onMouseOver event in the script makes text appear in the status bar.

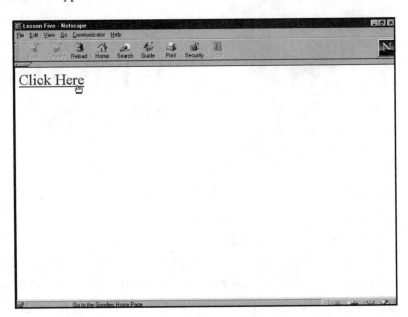

 To see the script working on your computer, click Lesson Five Script Effect One in your download packet or see it online at http://www.htmlgoodies.com/JSBook/lesson5effect1.html.

Deconstructing the Script

Knowing what you already know, this one just about explains itself. So let's look at it quickly and then start to play around with it.

First, onMouseOver (notice the capitalization pattern) is an event handler. In this case it is triggering when an event occurs in conjunction with the hypertext link. Does that make sense? We're using it *inside* the hypertext link.

The HTML format for the hypertext link remains the same. You use the same commands and the same double quotation marks. The event handler is stuck in right after the URL address, as you can see in the code. Now, just to be fair, the event handler doesn't have to be after the URL. It could go before, right after the A, but I like it sitting after the URL. It seems to be written in order when it's sitting after the URL. But, if you want it just after the A, go for it. To each their own.

The event is called for by writing onMouseOver= and then telling the browser to do something when the mouse actually does pass over. In this case, it's "window.status='Go to the Goodies Home Page'.

The pattern should look somewhat familiar now: two items separated by a period. The window is an object. It exists. status is a property of window and is the smaller section of the window where status messages go. You might be familiar with the traditional Document Done text that always appears in the status bar when an HTML page is finished loading. The window.status statement tells the browser where the following text should appear, which in this case is in the status bar.

> **Note**
>
> Is it getting confusing remembering which are properties and which are methods? I try to keep them straight by thinking that a method will usually be in the form of a verb, such as write or go. A property is a noun that exists as a smaller part of the item before the dot.

In the script, window.status is also followed by an equal sign (=) telling the browser that what follows is supposed to happen when the mouse actually does pass over. In this case, what follows is text *in single quotation marks*:

```
window.status='Go to the Goodies Home Page';
```

That text will show up in the status bar when the user rolls her mouse over the hypertext link.

Oh, Those Double and Single Quotation Marks

Match them up. When you use double quotation marks at the start of something, use double quotation marks at the end. If you use single quotation marks, use single quotation marks at the end.

The best method to keep the quotation marks straight in your own mind is to think that there is a hierarchy to them. I keep it straight by thinking that double quotation marks always go on the outside. Single quotation marks sit inside double quotation marks. If there's something inside single quotation marks, such as an HTML attribute, I don't give it quotation marks. Here's an example:

```
OnClick="location.href='page.html'"
```

See how the double quotation marks surround the single quotation marks? If you follow that hierarchy thinking, you're more likely to be sure the quotation marks line up single with single and double with double.

But that is simply a suggestion. As long as you make the quotation marks equal, you're good to go.

That said, make a point of keeping an eye on the quotation marks pattern in each of your scripts. They are, quote, important.

Get it? "Quote" important? Ha! I kill me.

The Semicolon

In JavaScript, the semicolon acts as a statement terminator—it basically says this code statement is done.

In this script, the semicolon is used because the effect we wanted to achieve through the event handler is finished:

```
onMouseOver="window.status='Go to the Goodies Home Page';
➥    return true">Click Here</A>
```

Now let's do something new.

So why not write the code to a new line? You did just fine without a semicolon in Chapter 1, "The Basics," when you wrote `document.write` statements. Well, that was a different story; each of those `document.write` statements sat on its own line and had only one function. This is different. Now there are two code statements: First there's `onMouseOver` and then that `return true` statement.

That's why this code is all on the same line separated by a semicolon. The JavaScript knows the two items are related, and now it also understands where one stops and the other begins, thanks to the semicolon.

It should be said here that even though that semicolon is not necessary, it is good practice to use one every time you end a line of code. It will help you quickly see where the lines end and help you be a better JavaScript author. Really. I wouldn't lie to you.

Now, what about that `return true` code?

return true

Those extra two words have quite a bearing on what happens when the mouse rolls over the link. If the words are present, the `return true` statement allows the script to overwrite whatever's there. Notice in the example that when the user rolls her mouse over the link, the text in the status bar is locked in. It doesn't change if she rolls over the link again and again. If you try this example yourself and refresh the page, you'll be able to see the effect a little better.

But what if you lose those two words? Well, let's think it out. If you do not have permission to overwrite what's in the status bar, then you can't overwrite what is in the status bar. When the mouse moves away from the link, the event will occur only once.

If you remember your HTML, the default is to display the URL to which the link is pointing. Then, after the mouse is off the link, the onMouseOver event takes place. The event occurs every time the mouse passes over the link. It's actually a better effect, in my opinion.

 To see what the effect would look like losing the return true code, click Lesson Five Script Effect Two in your download packet or see it online at http://www.htmlgoodies.com/ JSBook/lesson5effect2.html.

Other Properties, Other Uses

You know other objects must have properties, too. How about a page's background color? In HTML code, the attribute to change the background color is BGCOLOR. It's the same here, except now we're concerned again with capitalization. In JavaScript, it's written bgColor (capital C). So, let's think through creating a link that would change the window's background color using an onMouseOver event:

- First off, this will be a link, so it's a pretty good bet that the format is the same as the format in the earlier script. So, you should keep it.

- Are you changing the window, or are you changing your old standby, the document? Well, where does the BGCOLOR command go when you write a Web page? It'll be in the document, so that must be the object you're concerned with. Therefore, change window in the earlier code to document.

- You want to change the document object's background, so change status to bgColor.

- You no longer want text to appear, so change that text to a color. Let's use pink for this example.

- When the mouse moves over the link you probably want the color to stay whether the mouse runs over the links again or not, so you'll need to reenter the return true after the semicolon.

Here's the resulting JavaScript:

```
<A HREF="http://www.htmlgoodies.com"
➥onMouseOver="document.bgColor='pink'; return true">Click Here</A>
```

To see the background color effect, click Lesson Five Script Effect Three in your download packet or see it online at http://www.htmlgoodies.com/JSBook/lesson5effect3.html.

But what if you want both effects—the background color change and the text in the status bar? Okay, let's think it through: Common sense would suggest you write two onMouseOver commands. Let's try that.

The two commands are not separate from each other. You want them to occur at the same time, so you can't separate them using a semicolon because you know a semicolon is a statement terminator. Here's a new rule: Use a comma when setting multiple JavaScript events.

And what about all those pesky quotation marks? Remember that the double quotation marks go around the entire event handler statement, and single quotation marks go around the effects, such as text to be printed or in the color to be used:

- You want these two onMouseOver commands to happen as one, so you need double quotation marks only at the very beginning of the first event handler statement and at the very end of the second one. That way, the quotation marks surround it all, showing it to the browser as if it were one event.

- The single quotation marks surround the color and the text.

Here's the resulting JavaScript:

```
<A HREF="http://www.htmlgoodies.com"
onMouseOver="document.bgColor='pink',
➥onMouseOver=window.status='Go to the Goodies Home Page';
➥return true">Click Here</A>
```

 You can see this double effect by clicking Lesson Five Script Effect Four in your download packet, or see it online at http://www.htmlgoodies.com/JSBook/lesson5effect4.html.

These event handlers are great, and there are a slew of them. The next lesson discusses a whole handful.

Note

You might have noticed that the lessons are starting to "think things through" a bit. Remember that the JavaScript language is very logical. Later in this book is a lesson just on the hierarchy of items because the language is so logical. Just for now, though, try taking a few minutes before you write and thinking out what must happen for your idea to come to life in script.

Your Assignment

Let's see whether I can't trip you up on this one. I'm going to give you a new method for this assignment: alert(). What it does is pop up a small dialog box with text written above an OK button. See whether you can get the alert box to pop up when your mouse rolls across a hypertext link. Here's the format:

```
alert('text that appears on the alert box')
```

Think it through: What must happen first, second, and so on? It's actually quite simple (not that that's a hint or anything).

 See a possible answer by clicking Lesson Five Assignment in your packet download, or see it online at http://www.htmlgoodies.com/JSBook/assignment5.html.

Lesson 6: More Event Handlers

Well, now you've got the basic hang of event handlers. So let's look at another lesson and see a few more in action. Event handlers all work basically the same way. As long as you know the format of the event, and then think through the logic of getting it to run, you'll be able to place these all over your pages.

The onClick *Command*

Think about onMouseOver. You already know onMouseOver causes an event when the mouse is passed over a link. It can be used other places, too, but to this point you've only seen it used in a link. If passing over the link causes the event, clicking the link should be just as successful when you use the onClick event handler. That seems logical, yes?

I'll use the alert() method to show this one off. If you did the assignment from the last lesson, you know how it is used. But just for memory's sake, the alert() format goes like this:

```
alert('Text that appears on the alert box')
```

So, following the same pattern as the onMouseOver, you get this JavaScript:

```
<A HREF="http://www.htmlgoodies.com"
➥onClick="alert('You are off!');">Click Here</A>
```

The result appears in Figure 2.2.

Figure 2.2
Using onClick to display an alert box.

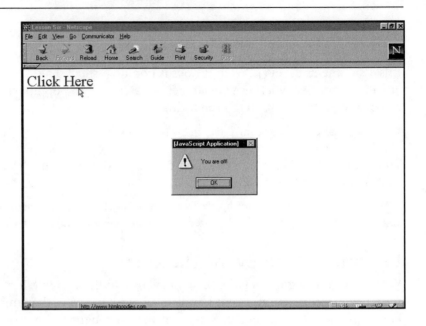

 See the effect on your computer by clicking Lesson Six Script's Effect in your download packet, or see it online at http://www.htmlgoodies.com/JSBook/lesson6effect.html.

The onFocus *Event Handler*

This is a great event handler that enables you to create action when your reader uses the mouse, tabs, or arrow keys to focus on one item on the page. This works for FORM object drop-down boxes, text boxes, and text area boxes.

Here's an example using a text box:

```
<FORM>
<INPUT TYPE="text" SIZE="30"
➥onFocus="window.status='Write your name in the box';">
</FORM>
```

Figure 2.3 shows the result of this JavaScript; as you can see, I followed the directions onscreen and entered my name.

Figure 2.3
When the text box has focus, the status bar text appears.

Tip

Never make an alert box the event of an onFocus event handler. Here's why: Let's say you had the onFocus set up on a text box, just the same way I do in the preceding code. You click the text box and the alert pops up. That causes focus to be lost from the text box. When you close the alert box, focus returns to the text box and the alert pops back up. It's a pretty nasty loop to get caught in.

 See the effect on your computer by clicking Lesson Six Script's Effect Two in your download packet, or see it online at http://www.htmlgoodies.com/JSBook/lesson6effect2.html.

The onBlur *Event Handler*

If you can focus on an item, you can *blur*, or lose focus, on an item. The onBlur event handler allows you to take focus off an item.

You can pretty much guess at the code, but here it is anyway:

```
<FORM>
<INPUT TYPE="text" SIZE="40" onBlur="alert(You changed your answer -
➥ Is it still correct?');">
</FORM>
```

The resulting effect appears in Figure 2.4.

37

Figure 2.4
This alert box appears after clicking off the text box.

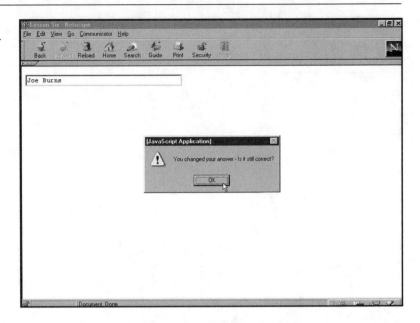

 See the effect on your computer by clicking Lesson Six Script's Effect Three in your download packet, or see it online at http://www.htmlgoodies.com/JSBook/lesson6effect3.html.

The onChange *Event Handler*

Its main function is to work as a check mechanism. If something changes, this event handler is enabled. Think of this as an event that ensures the user fills in what you are asking for:

```
<form>
<INPUT TYPE="text" SIZE="40"
➥onChange="alert('The text box has been changed')">
</form>
```

The result of this JavaScript appears in Figure 2.5.

 See the effect on your computer by clicking Lesson Six Script's Effect Four in your download packet, or see it online at http://www.htmlgoodies.com/JSBook/lesson6effect4.html.

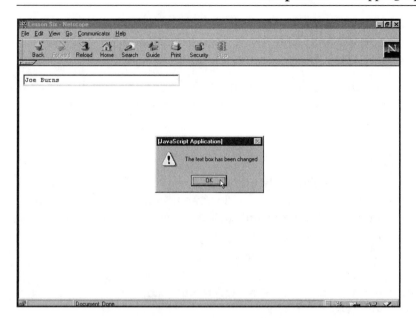

Figure 2.5
This alert box appears after the data in the text box is altered.

The onSubmit *Command*

This is the command everyone seems to want to lay his hands on. This command enables you to make the page change when the Submit button is clicked. People want this because they seem to require that wonderful effect when the user clicks a form's Submit button, and the page changes to another page that says Thanks for writing!

Here's the format:

```
<FORM>
<INPUT TYPE="submit"  onSubmit="alert('thanksalot.html')";>
</FORM>
```

 This event handler is difficult to show you as a figure, so see the effect on your computer by clicking Lesson Six Script's Effect Five in your download packet. Or see it online at http://www.htmlgoodies.com/JSBook/lesson6effect5.html.

location.href

You've probably noticed a few new commands in the previous script that respond to the Submit button, so let's look at one. location.href is the basic format for setting up a link to another page. The href property might be new to you, but if you've programmed in HTML at all, you can guess what it means. HREF stands for *H*ypertext *REF*erence, and it creates a link to another page. I use this format a great deal.

Just make a point of remembering the single and double quotation mark configuration. Double quotation marks surround location through the end of the command. The page the link sends the user to is surrounded in single quotation marks.

Remember, you have to surround the page location in quotation marks, but double quotation marks suggest to the browser that the command is over. So, use single quotation marks instead.

The onLoad *Event Handler*

The onLoad event handler is a great, and extremely useful, command. Unlike the other event handlers examined, onLoad sits within the HTML document's BODY flag. It's enacted when the page finishes loading into the browser window. The following example pops up a simple alert box to welcome the user to the page:

```
<BODY onLoad="alert('Thanks for coming to my page')">
```

Later in the book, you'll use the onLoad command to trigger larger scripts to start working. It will become a real tool in your JavaScript toolbox.

Figure 2.6 shows the result of the onLoad JavaScript.

Figure 2.6
An alert box pops up when the page loads.

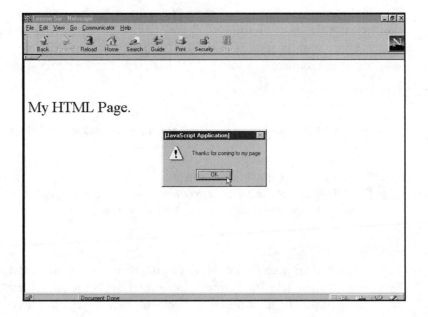

40

See the effect on your computer by clicking Lesson Six Script's Effect Six in your download packet, or see it online at http://www.htmlgoodies.com/JSBook/lesson6effect6.html.

Your Assignment

For this assignment, I want you to create a form that has some interaction with the user. I'm assuming you know how to create forms here. If forms are a bit foreign to you, see this HTML Goodies tutorial: http://www.htmlgoodies.com/tutors/forms.html.

The form should have four elements: a text box that asks for the person's name, two check boxes that ask whether the person prefers chocolate or vanilla, and a Submit button. Now, here's what I want to happen with each item:

- The text box should print `Put your name in here` in the status bar when the user fills it in.
- The two check boxes should write `You have chosen ---` in the status bar, indicating the user's choice.
- The Submit button should pop up an alert box thanking the user for filling out the form.

 See a possible answer on your own computer by clicking Lesson Six Assignment in your download packet, or see it online at http://www.htmlgoodies.com/JSBook/assignment6.html.

Lesson 7: `onUnload` **and** `onMouseOut`, **the After-Effect Commands**

Two after-effect event handler commands you should have in your arsenal are `onMouseOut` and `onUnload`. Again, watch the capitalization pattern.

You already know that the `onMouseOver` command makes things happen when the mouse passes over something on the HTML page. The `onMouseOut` command acts after the mouse leaves the link. You also know the `onLoad` command makes something happen when the HTML page fully loads. Well, the `onUnload` command makes something happen when the user unloads or leaves the page.

Both are quite useful, but try to keep the events that occur from your `onUnload` short. You don't want to slow the loading of the incoming page.

This script uses the `onUnload` event handler:

```
<BODY onUnload="alert('Leaving so soon?')">
```

41

This script uses the onMouseOut event handler:

```
<A HREF="thanksalot.html"
➦onMouseOver="window.status='Hey! Get off of me!'; return true
➦"onMouseOut="window.status='Much better - Thanks'; return true">
➦Place your mouse on and off of this</A>
```

The examples, shown in Figures 2.7a and 2.7b, actually use both scripts. In Figure 2.7a, a link on the HTML page produces text in the status bar both when the mouse passes over it and when the mouse leaves, thanks to the onMouseOver and onMouseOut event handlers. In Figure 2.7b, when you actually click the link, the onUnload event handler pops up the alert window with the text Leaving so soon?

Figure 2.7a
onMouseOut text appears in the status bar when the mouse leaves the link.

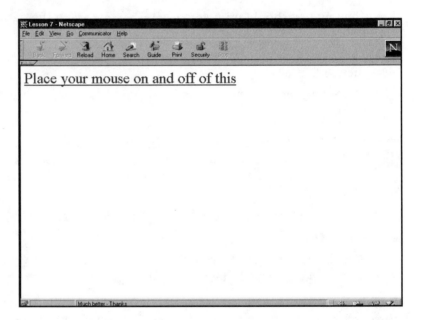

 See the effect on your computer by clicking Lesson Seven's Script Effect in your download packet, or see it online at http://www.htmlgoodies.com/JSBook/lesson7effect.html.

Deconstructing the Script

There's not a lot to tell that you probably haven't figured out for yourself at this point. The mouse-over effects are created by the onMouseOver and onMouseOut commands.

Please notice that unlike the simultaneous onMouseOver and bgColor effects from Lesson 5, the two commands here are quite separate from each other. You do not want these occurring at the same time.

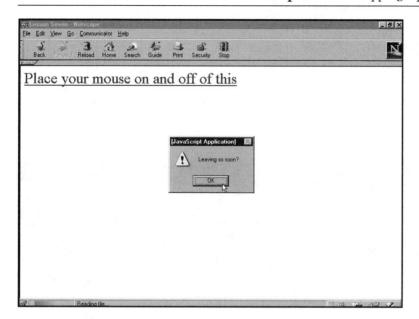

Figure 2.7b
An alert box is produced when the link is clicked.

You want one thing to happen when the mouse passes over the link and another to happen when the mouse moves off. So you write them as two totally separate commands, each containing its own `return true` statements, forcing the text to remain after the fact.

The effect when you're leaving the page is created by adding the `onUnload="alert('Leaving so soon?')"` command to the BODY flag of the HTML document.

Again, please notice the placements of the double and single quotation marks. You can't use the double quotation marks surrounding the text because that would mean double quotation marks inside of double quotation marks. The browser would see it as the end of a line, and not understand what follows—resulting in an error.

You'll get a lot of use out of these event handlers.

Your Assignment

You're going to use an `onUnload`, `onMouseOver`, and `onMouseOut` in this assignment. Here's what I want to happen:

- Create a page with a hypertext link. The link should place the text `Hello` *browser name* `user - Click here!` in the status bar when the mouse passes over.

- The text `You should leave` *page URL* `right away` should then appear when the mouse moves off the link.

● When the link is actually clicked, an alert should pop up that reads `Leaving so soon?` Do not use an `onClick` command to get the alert box; use the `onUnload` command.

Think about it for a minute. You've been able to get `document.property` returns to appear on the page. Now, how do you get them to appear in the status bar? You must combine the two formats you have learned so far in this chapter with what you learned in Chapter 1. You can do it.

Tip

The problem you'll run into involves the double and single quotation marks. Remember that in a `document.write` command, the double quotation marks mean text to be printed to the page. Well, now you have double quotation marks around the entire text for the `window.status` command, so those double quotation marks around the text are out the window. Use single quotation marks instead.

But in case you don't hit it on the first try, read the error messages. They'll tell you where the problem is.

See a possible answer to this assignment by clicking Lesson Seven Assignment in your download packet, or see it online at `http://www.htmlgoodies.com/JSBook/assignment7.html`.

Lesson 8: HTML 4.0, the `<SPAN>` Flag, and Some New Event Handlers

In late 1998, the World Wide Web Consortium (`http://www.w3c.org`) gave its thumbs-up to a new version of HTML, HTML 4.0. With the new version came new HTML flags, and with the new HTML flags came new JavaScript event handlers. As of the writing of this second edition, June 2001, a few of the new event handlers could be run using Internet Explorer 4.0, but Netscape Navigator couldn't run any of them. But time marches on, and soon these new event handlers will be in widespread use.

This lesson's example script shows three of those new event handlers in action. You'll also be introduced to a new HTML 4.0 delivery device flag, `<SPAN>`.

The `<SPAN>` *Flag*

First, let's look at the template for the sample script. It looks like this:

```
<SPAN JavaScript Event Handlers>Text on HTML Page</SPAN>
```

If you haven't seen the <SPAN> HTML flag before, be prepared to become very familiar with it. As HTML 4.0 comes more and more into the mainstream, this flag will become the darling of Web artists everywhere.

"What does it do," you ask? Nothing. Not a darn thing. The <SPAN> flag has no properties at all to affect or manipulate text or images in any way. In fact, if you take a piece of text and surround it with the <SPAN> and </SPAN> flags, you won't alter the text at all. The viewer wouldn't know it is there unless he looked at the source code.

But there has to be a reason this book is devoting page space to the <SPAN> flag. There is and with good reason.

<SPAN> is a delivery device. The flag itself has no effect. But that's the point. <SPAN>'s whole purpose is to act as a platform to carry other HTML attributes and JavaScript commands to text, images, tables, or whatever else you can think of to surround with <SPAN> and </SPAN>.

Look at the format again:

```
<SPAN JavaScript Event Handlers>Text on HTML Page</SPAN>
```

The text that is surrounded by the <SPAN> flags can include any event handler you've seen to this point. Once inside the <SPAN> flag, the event handler is enacted when the user interacts with the text in some way.

Here's an example before we get into the specifics of this lesson's script. Let's say you want to create a piece of text that acts as a hypertext link but doesn't carry the blue coloring or the underline. You want it to look like any other text. Believe it or not, this is actually a fairly popular request. HTML Goodies receives a fair amount of mail asking how it's done.

Think it out. The link will occur when the text is clicked. That would suggest you use the onClick event handler. Then you must set it so that when the user clicks, the page changes. You already know location.href as the code that creates a link. So let's build it.

The format would look like this:

```
<SPAN onClick="location.href='page.html'">Click to Go</SPAN>
```

 Now you have text that retains its color but carries with it the properties of a link, thanks to JavaScript. You can try the previous link by clicking Lesson Eight Script's Effect Two in your download packet, or see it online at http://www.htmlgoodies.com/JSBook/ lesson8effect2.html. Remember that this works only in Internet Explorer 4.0 or better.

The Sample Script

Now, let's look at this lesson's sample script:

```
<SPAN onMouseDown="window.status='Mouse Is Down'";
onMouseUp="window.status='Mouse Is Up'";
➡onDblClick="location.href='thanksalot.html'";>
Click on this text
</SPAN>
```

 The script's effect is shown in Figure 2.8. See the effect on your computer by clicking Lesson Eight's Script Effect in your download packet, or see it online at http://www.htmlgoodies. com/JSBook/lesson8effect.html.

Figure 2.8
Multiple event handlers are applied to this window.

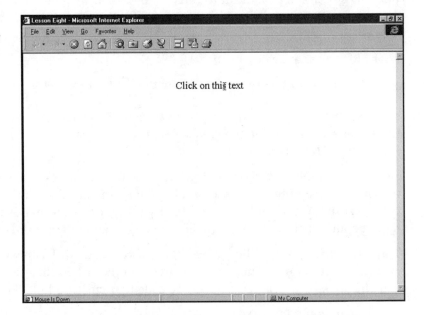

Make a point of looking at the example in an Internet Explorer browser, version 4.0 or higher. Those browsers support the HTML flags and JavaScript commands. By the time you're reading this, other browsers might support the code, too, but at the time of writing, Internet Explorer 4.0 (and above) was the only available browser to display this script properly.

Deconstructing the Script

The script starts with the <SPAN> flag. Three new JavaScript event handlers are inside the flag.

The first event handler, onMouseDown, is enacted when the user has her pointer on the text and clicks down. Notice the event handler is set up to place text in the status bar.

Although the semicolon is not necessary, I still use it to help me quickly see where each piece of code ends. It's my preference—you don't have to have it in your code.

The second event handler, onMouseUp, posts text to the status bar when the user lets the mouse click back up.

The third event handler, onDblClick, is put into use when the user double-clicks the link. In this script, the double-click sends the user to a new page named thanksalot.html.

The text that will appear on the HTML document page is then written after the <SPAN> flag.

Finally, the </SPAN> flag ends the entire format.

The New Event Handlers

You've seen three of them in this lesson's script, onMouseDown, onMouseUp, and onDblClick. Note the capitalization pattern of each.

Now that I've whet your appetite, here are a few other new event handlers and what they do:

- onKeyDown—Reacts when the user presses a key
- onKeyUp—Reacts when the user lets the key back up
- onKeyPress—Reacts when the user clicks a key up and down
- onMouseMove—Reacts when the user moves the mouse

Just remember that the event handlers in this lesson are not supported across the board yet, so use them sparingly, if at all. If you do use them, test them in a few different browsers on your own computer before posting the pages to the Web. If you can't run the command, your users probably can't either.

Your Assignment

Use the <SPAN> flag and a couple of event handlers on the text Green to Red so that when the mouse passes over it, the background turns green and when the mouse leaves the text, the background turns red. You'll get bonus points if you can get the page to change to purple when the user double-clicks.

HINT: Use Internet Explorer 4.0 or better to view your work.

 You can see a possible answer by clicking Lesson Eight Assignment in your download packet, or see it online at http://www.htmlgoodies.com/JSBook/assignment8.html.

Lesson 9: Let's Go!

So far, this chapter has dealt with user interaction through JavaScript event handlers. This particular lesson deals with a new method, go(). Although including a method with a group of event handlers seems a bit odd, it isn't. The go() method often acts along with event handlers to move your user through his history object.

This lesson's JavaScript is as follows:

```
<FORM>
<INPUT TYPE="button" VALUE="BACK" onClick="history.go(-1)">
<INPUT TYPE="button" VALUE="FORWARD" onCLick="history.go(1)">
</FORM>
```

This is a very popular use of the go() method. The code produces two buttons that act the same way as the Back and Forward buttons at the top of your browser window. Figure 2.9 shows these buttons in a browser.

Figure 2.9
Buttons that move users through their history objects.

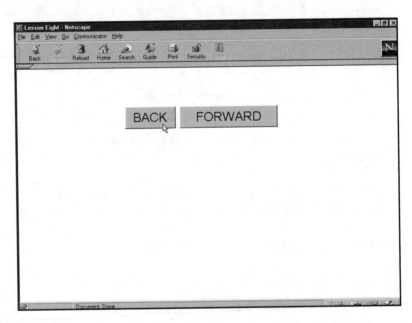

See the effect on your computer by clicking Lesson Nine's Script Effect in your download packet, or see it online at http://www.htmlgoodies.com/JSBook/lesson9effect.html.

Deconstructing the Script

The code for the two buttons is both HTML and JavaScript. The buttons are both FORM items created using this HTML code:

```
<FORM>
<INPUT TYPE="button" VALUE="BACK">
<INPUT TYPE="button" VALUE="FORWARD">
</FORM>
```

Using this format alone, the buttons will display, but they're little more than nice gray rectangles that don't actually do anything. It's the event handler and go() method that create the effect.

The Back Button

The code for the Back button looks like this:

```
<INPUT TYPE="button" VALUE="BACK" onClick="history.go(-1)">
```

Let's read it from left to right:

- INPUT—HTML code for an input item.
- TYPE="button"—Tells the browser that the input item will be a button.
- VALUE="BACK"—Puts the text on the button.
- onClick=—The event handler that will trigger what follows it when the user clicks the button.
- history.go—An object.method format JavaScript statement you should be pretty familiar with by now. history is the object; it represents the record the browser keeps of the user's current online session. Basically, it's a record of every page the user has been to, in order. The go method (parentheses left off on purpose) acts to move the user through that history object.
- (-1)—The instance of the method go. The -1 is telling the method to move one page back through the user's history object.

It would seem logical that if go(-1) is acceptable, go(-2) or go(-34) is also acceptable. They are. Just remember that the higher the number you put in that instance, the more pages the user will have had to have visited before coming to the current page. If the user is visiting the page containing this code first, the button is basically dead because there is no such thing as -1 in the history object.

However, there is one small exception to this rule. In Microsoft Internet Explorer 3.0, any negative value that is put into the go method parentheses sends the user back only one page. It's a known bug. You might want to keep that in mind when thinking about sending the user back multiple pages. Maybe one is enough.

The Forward Button

This code is similar to what you saw for the Back button:

```
<INPUT TYPE="button" VALUE="FORWARD" onCLick="history.go(1)">
```

The only two differences are as follows:

- VALUE= has been changed so that the button text now reads Forward, rather than Back.
- go() has been changed to now read a positive number, rather than a negative one. It moves the user forward through the history object list.

The method is the same, except that now when the user clicks the button, the next page up in the history object is loaded.

The Forward button is often dead because users might not have gone to another page and then returned to the page containing the code. However, I would still offer the button. Those who have gone to another page and returned can use it, and those who have not probably won't use it, knowing they didn't go anywhere. And if they do click the button, nothing will happen because there isn't a page to go to in the history object.

Your Assignment

The HTML Goodies site gets a great deal of mail asking how to set up guestbook, or form, pages so that when the user clicks to submit the page, either a thank-you page loads or the user is taken back to the page where he came from before clicking to fill out the guestbook.

The second scenario is your assignment. Create a small guestbook—one text box will do— so that when the user clicks to submit the form, he is taken back to the page he came from to fill out the guestbook form.

 You can see one possible answer by clicking Lesson Nine Assignment in your download packet, or see it online at http://www.htmlgoodies.com/JSBook/assignment9.html.

The page that loads following this link offers a link to the guestbook page. After the user fills in the text box and submits it, the original assignment page reloads.

Lesson 10: The Second End-of-Chapter Review

Once again, we're going to stop, look at the JavaScript commands you've learned up to this point, and build some new scripts. I'll offer one new script in this lesson and then make a suggestion or two for some new scripts. But keep in mind the purpose of these reviews is for you to take what you've learned so far and create a new and functional script to use on your pages.

Table 2.1 contains the object-related JavaScript commands you've learned up to now. In addition, you've seen these other JavaScript elements:

- The `alert()` method
- These event handlers: `onBlur`, `onChange`, `onClick`, `onDblClick`, `onFocus`, `onKeyDown`, `onKeyPress`, `onKeyUp`, `onLoad`, `onMouseDown`, `onMouseMove`, `onMouseOut`, `onMouseOver`, `onMouseUp`, and `onSubmit`
- The HTML 4.0 flag `<SPAN>`

Table 2.1   Object-Related JavaScript Commands Demonstrated in Chapters 1 and 2

Object	Methods	Properties
document	write()	alinkColor, bgColor, fgColor, linkColor, lastModified, location, referrer, title, vlinkColor
history	go()	length
location		host, hostname, href
navigator		appCodeName, appName, appVersion, userAgent
window		status

That's actually a pretty impressive list of commands. You can create some very nice JavaScripts out of just what I've listed, as you can see here:

```
<SPAN onClick="document.write('<FONT SIZE=+2>
➥To get to the other side.</FONT><FORM>
➥<INPUT TYPE=button VALUE=BACK onClick=history.go(-1)></FORM>')">
Why did the chicken cross the road?
</SPAN>
```

Allow me to explain a bit before you start copying the script. I am getting the before-and-after effect shown in Figures 2.10 and 2.11 by using only one `<SPAN>` flag. Remember that you can't break `document.write` commands into multiple lines because the script will throw an error. So, the entire preceding code should be kept on one long line. Also, because of the <SPAN> flag, you should look at this script's example in an Internet Explorer browser, version 4.0 or above.

Figure 2.10
The window before you click the text.

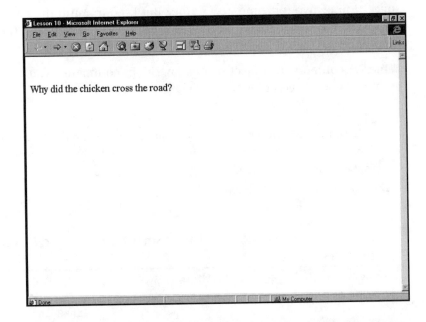

Figure 2.11
The window after you click the text.

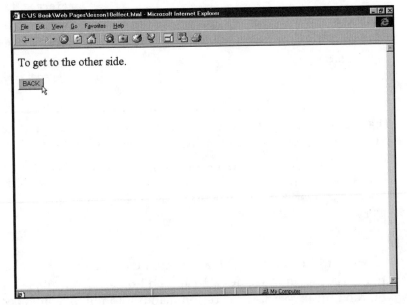

See the effect on your computer by clicking Lesson Ten's Script Effect in your download pack-et, or see it online at `http://www.htmlgoodies.com/JSBook/lesson10effect.html`.

Deconstructing the Script

When the script says `document.write`, it means `document.write`.

As you've been reading through this chapter, did you stop and wonder what would happen if you put a `document.write` statement after an event handler? Well, here's what happens: An entirely new document is written over the one currently in the browser window.

Look at the title bar in Figure 2.10: It says `Lesson Ten`. The title bar of Figure 2.11 says `JSBook\Web Pages\Lesson10effect.html`. The reason is that by putting the `document.write` command with an `onClick`, the browser did what you told it to. It wrote a brand-new page.

This is the code that did the trick:

```
<SPAN onClick="document.write('<FONT SIZE=+2>
➥To get to the other side.</FONT><FORM>
➥<INPUT TYPE=button VALUE=BACK onClick=history.go(-1)></FORM>')">
</SPAN>
```

I'll stress again that the code should all go on one line. The book page just isn't long enough to show it that way.

Let's take it piece by piece:

- `<SPAN>`—The HTML 4.0 code that acts as a delivery device so you can apply the `onClick` to an item, which in this case is text.

- `onClick=`—The event handler that triggers what follows it when the user clicks.

- `"document.write=`—The `object.method` statement used to write the text to the page. Please take note that double quotation marks appear before `document.write` and again at the very end of the `<SPAN>` flag, right before the `>`.

- Single quotation marks—These are around all the text within the `document.write` instance.

- `<FONT SIZE=+2>To get to the other side.</FONT>`—The basic HTML code that produces text at a font size of plus three.

- `<FORM><INPUT TYPE=button VALUE=BACK onClick=history.go(-1)></FORM>`—The HTML and JavaScript code that creates a Back button. You just saw that in Lesson 9. The code creates a button that moves the user back one page on his `history` object. Notice no quotation marks are around `button`, `BACK`, or `history.go(-1)`. You've already used double quotation marks around the `document.write` statement, and single quotation marks are used around the text in the instance. There's no quotation mark smaller than single quotation marks, so you don't use any.

● Finally, the text that will appear on the page is written in, and the `</SPAN>` flag ends the code.

As I said earlier in this chapter, JavaScript is very logical. When you're creating a new script, stop and think about what you want to happen, think about what must come before what, and then write the code in a linear fashion. You should be able to break it down like I broke down the preceding lines of code.

Now take some time to think about what you can do with the commands you already know.

Your Assignment

Make something of your own. May I suggest using the `document.location` statement to create a reload button?

Or how about a line of hypertext that takes the user to a new page without having to click? A simple mouse pass would create the change of the page.

 I have both of those suggested scripts available for you to view if you click Lesson Ten Assignment in your download packet. Or see it online at http://www.htmlgoodies. com/JSBook/assignment10.html.

But first, go make your own!

Using Escape Characters

In this chapter's lessons, I have you popping up alert boxes and writing text to HTML pages. I mentioned in Chapter 1 that you have to be careful of writing contractions such as "isn't" or "you're" because they contain a single quotation mark. You know that that single quotation mark doesn't end the JavaScript line, but the JavaScript doesn't. It sees a quote and acts on it, which usually causes a pretty big error.

But you can't very well write only to alert boxes and `document.write` text and never use a single quotation mark. Furthermore, what if you want a line break or a tab setting in your statements?

The answer is the use of escape characters. Let's talk a little about aesthetics.

The Alert Example

Figure 2.12 is a quick example of using escape characters in an alert box.

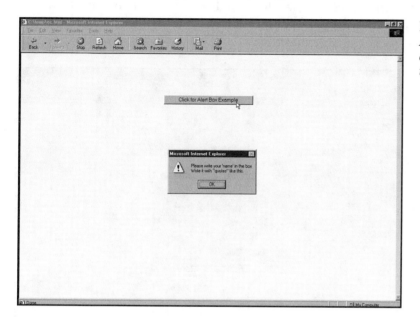

Figure 2.12
An alert box using escape characters to format the text.

Here's the code for the alert button:

```
alert("Please write your \'name\' in the box\rWrite it with \"quotes\" like
➥this.")
```

The JavaScript code should be all on one line.

Look closely at Figure 2.12 and then at the code. You'll notice the single quotes were created with this: \'.

The return, or line break, was created with this: \r.

The double quote was created with this: \".

The backslash is the key. If you use that backslash in front of the quotation marks or the letter "r", you escape the coding long enough for the script to understand you want the character to represent text rather than a command to be used in the coding. That's why it's called an *escape* character. Get it?

A Bigger Alert Box Example

I used four different escape characters in this example—the three shown previously and \t to create a tab effect. Note I sometimes used two to get a double tab or a double return. Again, look at Figure 2.13 and then at the code and pick out what escape character did what.

Figure 2.13
An alert box using many escape characters to format the text.

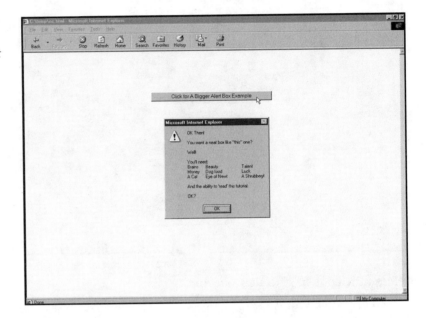

Now here's the code. This should all be written on one long line. Just make a point of going through it piece by piece, and you'll see each of the escape characters at work:

```
alert("OK Then!\r\rYou want a neat box like \"this\" one?\r\rWell!\r\rYou\'ll
need:\rBrains\tBeauty\t\tTalent\rMoney\tDog food\t\tLuck\rA Cat\tEye of Newt\tA
➥Shrubbery!\r\rAnd the ability to \'read\' this tutorial.\r\rOK?")
```

Get it?

The document.write Example

You wouldn't want to use the return character in a document.write because it's better to literally write a BR or P flag to the page. Hopefully, you remembered that from all the way back in Chapter 1. Where these escape characters come in handy is situations in which you need to use a double or single quotation mark, yet you do not want to end the line. For example, let's say the following line has to be written with a document.write command:

We're going to "need" to know where you're going tonight, young man!

Anybody else have parents that sounded like that? Mine did. It was the only sentence I could think of that had a single and double quote in it. Huh. I guess I have issues to work out. Here's the code:

```
<SCRIPT LANGUAGE="javascript">
document.write('We\'re going to \"need\" to know where you\'re going tonight,
➥young man!')
</SCRIPT>
```

Read slowly and pick out the escape characters.

I'll bet those little blips of information just made someone's life a little easier. At least now you'll have fewer alert boxes that do not talk in contractions.

Okay, that's the end of aesthetics. Let's get back to JavaScript coding.

Chapter 3

Manipulating Data and the Hierarchy of JavaScript

This chapter contains the following lessons and scripts:

- Lesson 11: Prompts and Variables
- Lesson 12: Dates and Times
- Lesson 13: Hierarchy of Objects
- Lesson 14: Creating a Function
- Lesson 15: An Introduction to Arrays
- Lesson 16: The Third End-of-Chapter Review—A <BODY> Flag Script

The JavaScript commands in this chapter are grouped together because they all deal with data in some way, shape, or form. That data can consist of dates, times, or input from the user. In addition, each of these lessons introduces you to one of the most important topics in JavaScript—the hierarchy of objects.

You have already been introduced to JavaScript hierarchy in the object.method and object.property statements in Lesson Nine (see Chapter 2, "Popping Up Text with Mouse Events"). But now you'll learn about creating hierarchy with variables and other types of JavaScript data.

As Lesson 13 in this chapter states, "… after you understand the hierarchy of objects, you've conquered JavaScript."

Lesson 11: Prompts and Variables

This lesson has two concepts. First is the prompt box, which you use when you want to prompt the user for information. The second, creating variables, is one you'll use throughout the remainder of your JavaScript life. Let's begin by examining these concepts.

Creating a Variable

The concept of variables is paramount in JavaScript, so you must know how to create them. When you create a variable, you are denoting a one-word (or one-letter) representation for the output of a JavaScript command line. Remember when you were posting the name of the browser to the page using the method appName? When you placed the name in the document.write statement, you wrote out the entire navigator.appName. Because you did it only once, it wasn't so hard. But what if you wanted to write it ten times across the same page? Writing those characters again and again would get boring.

So you assign a variable to represent the output of the method. Let's say you choose the variable NA. That way, you would have to write navigator.appName only once and assign NA to it. The rest of the way through, you would write only NA when you wanted the navigator.appName.

Please keep in mind that the variable is "NA" with two capital letters. You'll need to follow whatever capitalization pattern you choose every time you call for the variable you created because JavaScript is case sensitive. You could also have a variable "na" in the same script, and it would be seen as completely different from "NA". Please understand I'm just making a point by showing "NA" and "na" together. You would never want to do that in a script simply because it would be confusing. The point I want to make is to be aware of your capitalization when creating variable names.

Are you still with me? Let's get back to this example.

This lesson's script uses the following line to denote a variable:

```
var username = prompt ("Write your name in the box below", "Write it here")
```

We created the variable following this format:

- var proclaims that the word immediately following will be the variable name.
- username is the name of the variable. I made this up. It didn't have to be this long; in fact, I could have made it N if I wanted. It's always best to create the variable names in such a way that you can easily remember what the variables represent.
- The equal sign (=) denotes that the variable name will equal the output of the commands that follow. In this case, the variable will represent the output of the prompt box.

One more thing: Variable names can be just about any word or combination of letters and numbers you want; however, some variable names are off limits.

For instance, you should not create a variable name that is the same word as a JavaScript command. You'll know you didn't mean for the word to be used as a command, but the computer won't.

In addition to not using JavaScript commands as variable names, Appendix C, "JavaScript Reserved Variable Words," has a list of other words you should avoid. Some of the words are already in use as JavaScript commands, and some are reserved words that will be used in upcoming JavaScript versions. You might want to take a quick look at the list before going further.

I've found that as long as you create a variable name that is representative of the data, you shouldn't run into any trouble, but just to be sure, take a look at Appendix C.

Please notice that no quotation marks surround either var or the variable name. Just follow one word with the next as shown in the code. The JavaScript will understand what you're saying.

The Prompt *Command*

I used a new command for this example: prompt. This method pops up a box prompting the user for a response.

Here's the basic format of the prompt:

```
var variable_name = prompt("Message on the gray box","Default Reply")
```

The default reply is the text that will appear in the user-entry field on the prompt box. You should include text in case the user doesn't fill anything in. That way, you'll have some-thing for the JavaScript to work with.

But if you like the look of an empty user-entry field on the prompt box, that's fine. If the user doesn't enter any text, the text null will be returned for you.

In case you're wondering ... to get a blank white box in the user-entry field, do not write any text between the second set of quotation marks. And yes, you need the quotation marks even if they're empty. If you do not put the second set of quotation marks in, the white box will read undefined.

The var and the variable name you assigned are included in the format. They have to be; otherwise, you'll get the prompt, but nothing will be done with the data the user enters.

The Sample Script

Now you're back to creating full JavaScripts rather than just adding events to HTML, so you'll need to again start using the full `<SCRIPT LANGUAGE="javascript">` to `</SCRIPT>` format.

Here's what you're going to do. You'll ask the user for his name and assign a variable to that name. After the variable is assigned, you can enter it in a `document.write` line that posts the user's name to the page. The script is as follows:

```
<SCRIPT LANGUAGE="javascript">
/*This script is intended to take information from the user
and place it upon the page*/
var username = prompt ("Write your name in the box below",
➥"Write it here");
document.write("Hello " + username + ". Welcome to my page!");
</SCRIPT>
```

This script brings up a prompt box asking for the user's name, as shown in Figure 3.1. Figure 3.2 shows the result after the user enters his name and clicks OK.

Figure 3.1
The prompt box asks for the user's name.

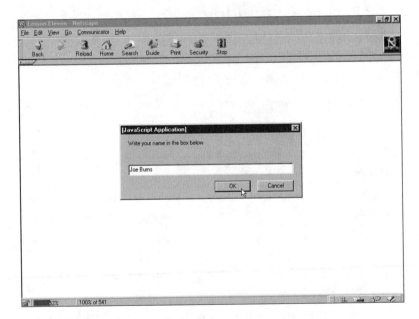

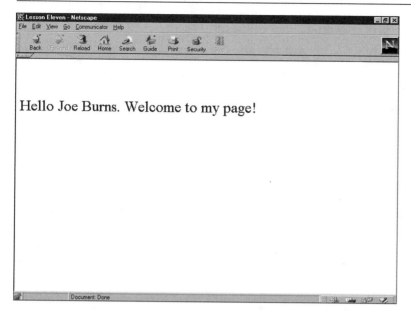

Figure 3.2
The script responds appropriately to the user's input.

To see this script's effect on your computer, click Lesson Eleven Effect in your download packet, or see it online at `http://www.htmlgoodies.com/JSBook/lesson11effect.html`.

Wait! What Are Those /* and */ Things?

Yeah, I stuck in two extra commands that comment out text in the script. When you *comment out* something, the text sits in the source code for you and anyone else who's interested to read it, but it won't affect the script nor show up on the resulting page. It's a great way to add copyrights, tell what the script does, and generally help yourself along by adding instruction text that's not part of the script.

These comment commands allow for multiple lines. Just have /* at the beginning and */ at the end, and everything in between will comment out. You can write a whole paragraph of commented text as long as it is between the two comment commands—it won't affect the script in any way.

Deconstructing the Script

Now that you know all the parts of the prompt, let's examine the meat of the script:

```
var user_name = prompt ("Write your name in the box below",
➥"Write it here");
document.write("Hello " + username + ". Welcome to my page!");
```

63

- The variable name `username` is assigned to the output of the prompt.
- The prompt asks the user to write his name in the box. The white box reads `"Write it here"`.
- A semicolon ends the line because I wanted it there. It is not necessary.
- The `document.write` statement calls for the text `"Hello "` (space for continuity).
- The plus sign (+) denotes that what follows will write right after the line of text.
- `username` is representative of the output of the prompt. No quotation marks are used—we don't want it printed.
- Another plus sign is used.
- `". Welcome to my page!"`, with a period and a space for continuity, completes the text.
- The semicolon is placed on purpose to show me that the line has ended.

That's all.

Please make a point of truly understanding the concept of variables before you proceed. Variables are used extensively in this language. If you're lost at this point, reread the lesson.

Your Assignment

... is a review.

Let's combine a couple of the commands you've learned so far with the new variable and prompt commands you just learned.

Here's what I want you to do:

- Create two prompts. One will ask for the user's first name, and one will ask for the user's last name. Don't let this throw you—just create two fully formed prompt lines in the preceding script and assign each one a different variable name. One will simply follow the other in the script.
- Using the prompts, create this line of text: `Hello first-name last-name. I see you are using browser-name. Thanks for coming to document-title.`

  BUT! Write the code so that the `browser-name` and `document title` items are called by the variables `BN` and `PT`, respectively.
- Think it through, and then write the script. There are bonus points if you comment out a couple of lines.

You can see a possible answer to this assignment on your own computer by clicking Lesson Eleven Assignment in your download packet, or see it online at `http://www.htmlgoodies.com/JSBook/assignment11.html`.

Lesson 12: Dates and Times

What's nice about writing JavaScript right to a Web page is all the stuff that already exists that you can grab and display.

This lesson talks about how you can display existing information using a new object, `Date`, and seven new methods: `getDay()`, `getDate()`, `getMonth()`, `getYear()`, `getHours()`, `getMinutes()`, and `getSeconds()`.

`Date` is an object that contains the current day of the week, month, day of the month, current hour, current minute, current second, and current year. All that and looks, too, huh?

So, if `Date` has all that, why use any of the methods? Because you might not want all that stuff every time. What if you want only the day of the week? Then you use `getDay()` to extract just that day of the week from the `Date` object.

The Date and Time Methods

Even before beginning to delve into the sample script, let's discuss each of the `Date` object methods. They are quirky to say the least.

First, all seven methods return numbers rather than text. It would be nice if `getDay()` would give you Monday, or Wednesday, or Saturday, but it doesn't. It gives you a number between 0 and 6.

Between 0 and 6?

Yes. Allow me to introduce you to one of the more frustrating aspects of JavaScript.

JavaScript counts start at 0. The number 0 is equal to the first element of a list in JavaScript's mind.

The common week starts on Sunday and ends on Saturday. You might see it differently, but JavaScript sees the seven-day week as Sunday through Saturday. Those seven days are in JavaScript's mind as being numbered from 0 (Sunday) through 6 (Saturday).

So, if you call for `getDay()` and it's Wednesday, you will actually get only the number 3 returned. Goofy, yes, but that's what happens.

But so what? The previous script doesn't call for the day of the week. True, but it does call for the month. JavaScript counts that up from 0, too. Thus, the number returned for the month is always one less than you would expect.

The Methods and What They Return

Here's a quick rundown of each method and what it returns. It'll help you to understand what pops up on your page when using the variable, as I'll show:

- getDate()—Believe it or not, this one acts normally. It returns the day of the month as the correctly numbered day of the month.
- getDay()—Returns the numbers 0 (Sunday) through 6 (Saturday), depending on the day of the week.
- getHours()—Returns the hour of the day in a 24-hour format counting the hours up from 0 through 23.
- getMinutes()—Returns the minute of the hours counting up from 0 up through 59, but this one isn't bad. There actually is a 0 at the top of the hour, so we're good to go with getMinutes.
- getMonth()—Returns the month of the year counting up from 0. The month of February therefore returns the number 1.
- getSeconds()—Returns the second of the minute counting up from 0 to 59. This method, like getMinutes, is okay in that there is actually a 0 at the top of the hour.
- getFullYear()—Returns the 4-digit year. JavaScript ran into a little trouble when the Y2K bug hit. The original year command, getYear(), returned only a two-digit year. When it was 1999, that was okay. But when 2000 began, instead of returning 00, the command returned 100. Oops. Do yourself a favor and start using getFullYear() exclusively. It's a quick fix that works pretty well.

The Sample Script

Take a look at this lesson's script:

```
<SCRIPT LANGUAGE="JavaScript">
//This script posts the exact day and time you arrived
RightNow = new Date();
document.write("Today's date is " + RightNow.getMonth()+ "-")
document.write("+ RightNow.getDate() + "-" + RightNow.getFullYear() + ".")
document.write("You entered this Web Page at exactly: "
➥ + RightNow.getHours() + "hours")
document.write("+ RightNow.getMinutes() + " minutes and "
➥ + RightNow.getSeconds() + " seconds")
</SCRIPT>
```

The script displays the date and time the page was loaded with this script, as shown in Figure 3.3.

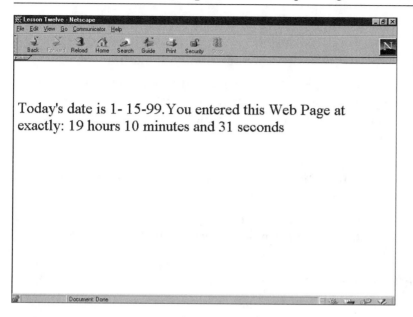

Figure 3.3
The date and time methods display a variety of useful information.

 To see this script's effect on your computer, click Lesson Eleven Effect in your download packet, or see it online at `http://www.htmlgoodies.com/JSBook/lesson12effect.html.`

Wait! What's That // Thing?

You are an observant one, aren't you? That double slash denotes a single comment line inside the script. It means that the text that follows will not be used in the process, but rather will just be reprinted as is. It works just like the multiline comment you saw in Lesson 11, earlier in this chapter. You can add as many of them as you want, as long as each line starts with the double slash.

You also can use the double slashes at the end of a line of JavaScript to remind yourself, or tell your users, what the line of JavaScript will do. Here's an example:

```
document.write("text")   //This writes text to the page
```

Deconstructing the Script

If you look at the sample script, you'll see that the effect is created by asking the script to write the month, date, year, hour, minute, and second to the page. The extra verbiage stuck in there just makes it obvious what you're looking at.

Let's start with the first one called for in the preceding script—the month—and then we can start to break down how this works. As stated before, getMonth() is a method. That said, we now must concern ourselves with what object getMonth() is a method of.

It might appear from the script that get*Something*() is a method of document. Not so—the method of document is write. getMonth() is actually a method of the object Date. Look up at the script and you'll see that Date is set aside in the command:

```
RightNow = new Date();
```

What is happening here is we are setting aside the object for the method getMonth() to work on. Actually, we're creating a new Date object to work with in the script.

Date, remember, contains all the date and time information you'll need. In fact, when you use one of the get*Something*() methods, you're simply extracting one section of what Date possesses.

I'll prove that to you. Here's code that uses only the Date object without any method:

```
<SCRIPT LANGUAGE="javascript">
document.write("Here's some information: " +Date()+ ".")
</SCRIPT>
```

With just that, look at Figure 3.4 to see all the good stuff you get.

Figure 3.4
Using the Date object yields a lot of information.

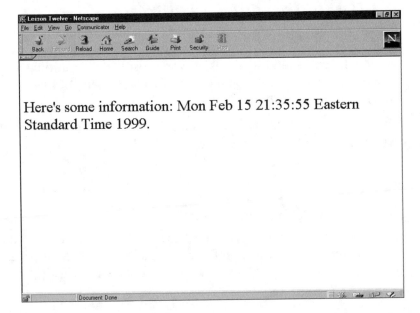

68

Defining a Variable for the Date *Object*

The variable name given to the Date object in the sample script is RightNow. Now, I could have called it Zork or Fred, for all the browser cares. It doesn't matter as long as the object is given an original name that isn't found in JavaScript. See Appendix C for a list of unusable words.

If that seems backwards to you, it does to me, too. It seems like it should be new Date = RightNow, but it isn't. You're learning a new language, and you have to play by its rules.

The earlier command is saying this: RightNow is the variable that represents a new Date();.

But why "new" Date? The date has to be new so that you get a new date every time the page is entered or reloaded. Without the new command, the date would remain static. You reinforce the fact that the date has to be new by giving it a variable name, too.

Hooray! You have your object variable name set so that your getMonth() method can act on it. You want this month to be printed on the page, so you need to have a document.write() statement in there somewhere. You also know that what appears in the parentheses is printed on the page, so put together a smaller version of the big script in this lesson by following a logical process:

1. You need to place the <SCRIPT LANGUAGE="javascript"> first.
2. Then, insert a comment line that tells what this thing does.
3. You'll need to create a new Date object before you can call on the getMonth() portion, so insert that. Make sure the call ends with a semicolon.
4. Now you can place the document.write() statement.
5. Inside the document.write's incidence, follow the same format as in Lesson 1 in Chapter 1, "The Basics."
6. Text that is to be printed must be inside double quotation marks.
7. Finish up with </SCRIPT>.

Here's what you get:

```
<SCRIPT LANGUAGE="javascript">
//This script will post the name of the month
RightNow = new Date();
document.write("This is the month " + RightNow.getMonth ".")
</SCRIPT>
```

Look at the full script again. That long line of text doesn't look so tough now. It's simply the RightNow object variable name followed by the next getSomething() method. I separated each with a hyphen; remember the hyphen is to be printed so it must be in quotation marks.

Building the Lines of `document.write` *Code*

I won't go through it all because you probably have the swing of it by now, so I'll discuss just the date portion of the script. It looks like this:

```
document.write("Today's date is " + RightNow.getMonth()+ "-")
document.write(+ RightNow.getDate() + "-" + RightNow.getYear() + ".")
```

- It starts with `"Today's date is "`, with a space at the end for continuity.
- The plus sign is next.
- `RightNow.getMonth()` is added without quotation marks because we do not want that printed—we want the number returned.
- Another plus sign follows.
- Now, a hyphen appears in quotation marks to separate it from the next number. No space is used because we want the next number to butt right up against it.
- Next comes a plus sign.
- Then comes the next `document.write` statement.
- It starts with a plus sign because the first item in this statement is a return.
- Now `RightNow.getDate` is added because we want the number of the day (no quotation marks).
- A plus sign is next.
- Another hyphen appears in quotation marks so it is printed right to the page.
- Another plus sign is next.
- Last is another new method, `RightNow.getYear`, which returns the number of the year.

Just continue to follow this same format, and the script will print out what you tell it to. So now you can tell everyone what time it is. But as Chicago sang, "Does anybody really know what time it is? Does anybody really care?"

Wait! What About Some of the Numbers Being One Off?

It's actually pretty easy to fix. So far, you've seen the plus sign used to surround text so that it acts as a return rather than printing to the page.

That plus sign can also act as a, well, as a plus sign intended to add things together. We'll get more into the mathematics of JavaScript in Chapter 5, "Forms: A Great Way to Interact with Your Users," but for now, let's just do some simple addition.

To get the returns from `getDay()`, `getMonth()`, and `getSeconds()` to display correctly, you must add a couple of steps to the process.

To return the correct number, you need to return each of the `method.objects` (listed earlier) and assign each a variable name.

Also, when you assign a variable name, you must add 1. Here's an example of a script that returns the date in ##/##/#### format:

```
<SCRIPT LANGUAGE="javascript">
RightNow = new Date();
var dy = RightNow.getDate() + 1
var mth = RightNow.getMonth() + 1
var yr = RightNow.getFullYear()
document.write(+ dy + "/" + mth + "/" + yr + ".")
</SCRIPT>
```

See the format? I assigned the variable name `dy` to the code that would return the number representing the day of the week and added 1. Then, in the `document.write` statement, I called only for the variable name `dy`. That returns the number returned by `RightNow.getDay()` plus 1.

Now it's correct.

I did the same for `RightNow.getMonth()`. The command `getFullYear()` returns the entire four-digit year.

Your Assignment

This one isn't so tough:

- Write a script that asks for the user's name through a prompt.
- Use that name to write a piece of text that reads `Welcome` *user-name*. `It is` *minutes* `past` *hour*. `Thanks for coming.`
- Now, here's the kicker: Make that text appear in an alert that pops up when the page loads.
- Bonus points are available if you call for the minutes and hours by using variable names.

 You can see a possible answer on your own computer by clicking Lesson Twelve Assignment in your download packet, or see it online at `http://www.htmlgoodies.com/JSBook/assignment12.html`.

Lesson 13: Hierarchy of Objects

Whoa! Let's pause and get familiar with the concept of hierarchy. What better time to stop than lucky Lesson 13?

You know that JavaScript has objects, which are similar to nouns. You also know that objects have properties that describe how objects look, just as adjectives describe nouns.

You also know that objects have methods, or actions, that can be performed to the object. Different objects have access to different properties and methods. But what follows what, and which of these is most important? How do you write the code to the page so that the JavaScript understands that this is a property of this, and this method is to act upon this object? You do it by writing objects, methods, and properties in a hierarchical fashion.

Now you'll learn THE secret to understanding JavaScript—the hierarchy of objects, illustrated in Figure 3.5. Don't tell a soul, but after you understand the hierarchy of objects, you've conquered JavaScript!

Figure 3.5
The concept of an object hierarchy.

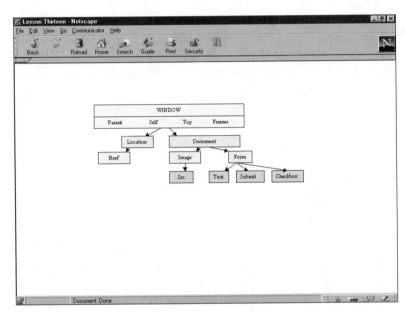

Click Here *You can either see this diagram up close by clicking Lesson Thirteen Script's Effect or see it online at* http://www.htmlgoodies.com/JSBook/lesson13effect.html.

Please understand that the image is not a complete representation of the hierarchy of JavaScript; it represents only what you've learned up to this point.

Terms, Terms, Terms: DOM

The purpose of this book is to teach you JavaScript in the friendliest and most easy-to-understand method possible.

Figure 3.5 shows the hierarchy of JavaScript. That hierarchy actually has a term—it's called a *Document Object Model*, or DOM for short.

I don't use the term because it really doesn't tell you, the reader, anything. In fact, at the level you're at, it might actually be confusing.

I use the term *hierarchy statement* because it is a better representation of the code.

Just keep in mind at your next party full of technical people that the true term is DOM, or Document Object Model.

The Hierarchy of Objects' Effects

All references begin with the top object, the window (the browser screen), and go down. window is the highest-level object in JavaScript. So much so that JavaScript doesn't even require that you use it in your code. JavaScript just understands that, unless told otherwise, everything happens within the browser window.

That means that everything you've seen so far actually should be written with the object window at the beginning, like so:

```
window.document.write
window.RightNow.getDay()
window.default.status
```

If you want to write your code this way, great, but it's not required, obviously, because the top-level object, window, is understood to be the overriding object.

Here are some examples. Notice they follow the hierarchy pattern from Figure 3.5, from top to bottom:

```
document.mypic.src = "pic1.gif"
```

Again, window is not needed at the very beginning because it is assumed that all this is inside the window. This references an image named mypic, changing its contents to pic1.gif. Did you follow that? document is the page the item is on, mypic is the item's name, and SRC is the item's source.

It is getting smaller going left to right, one inside the other. It's similar to how a page contains a sentence, a sentence contains a word, and a word contains a letter. Look at this example:

```
document.write(location.href)
```

write() is a method of the document object, and location.href returns the full URL of the window. Notice that location and document are at the same level. They are written to the left of the only dot. However, one has a method following it (write), and the other has a property following it (href).

That means you get the location of that same-level document denoted by `document.write`, even though one hierarchy statement is sitting in the instance—the parentheses—of the other. Both `document.write` and `location.href` act within the same document window because they are at the same level. Still with me?

Deconstructing the Hierarchy of Objects

What's most confusing about this is that some objects are also properties. I'm referencing Figure 3.5 again here:

- `window` is just an object.
- `document` is an object inside the window.
- `form` is a property of `document`, but it is also an object with its own properties.
- `value` and `src` are just properties.

Not all objects and properties are displayed here. However, this should be enough to help you understand this format. All references start at the top with `window` and go down, writing them left to right, separated by dots.

You therefore can't write `document.mytext.myform` or `mypic.src.document` because they are not in correct order. The order must go biggest to smallest from left to right.

A Very Important Concept

Order is paramount in hierarchy. It will come into play when we start to talk about forms in Chapter 6, "Mathematics, Random Things, and Loops."

Let's say you have an HTML text box on your page, and the user writes something in the text box. To return the contents of that text box using JavaScript, you must use the property value; for example, `document.myform.mytext.value`. Just writing `document.myform.mytext` gives information about the form field but not its contents. The `value` command returns what is written inside the text box.

Just know that an HTML form field, like a text box or a radio button, is given a name. In the preceding example, it's `myform`. If you call for that alone, you'll get information about the form item itself, just like `getDay()` returns the day number. But if you want what is written in the form element itself, you must add `value` to the end of the hierarchy statement. Now you're one level below the form field itself. You're at the level of what the user wrote—what is contained within the form.

Think of `value` as a reading of what something is or is not at a specific time. A check box can have a value of on or off depending on whether it has been clicked. A text box field can have a value of "hidden" if you don't want the user to see it. And, as noted previously, a TEXT field can have input written to it, which is that field's value. Get it?

Maybe not yet, but you will. Hierarchy is at the very heart of JavaScript. We will talk about hierarchy a great deal throughout the rest of the book.

Your Assignment

Here's a little bit of code for you to look at:

```
<FORM>
<INPUT TYPE="button" Value="Click Here"
onClick="parent.frames[1].location='zippy5.html';
parent.frames[2].location='zippy6.html';
parent.frames[3].location='zippy7.html';"
</FORM>
```

You can see the basic format as a FORM button, but what does all that stuff after the onClick stand for?

Follow the thought process from the preceding lesson and without looking at the answer, make a point of writing down what you think this script does.

Also—think about how it does it.

 You can see a full tutorial on what that link does by clicking Lesson Thirteen Assignment in your download packet, or see it online at http://www.htmlgoodies.com/JSBook/ assignment13.html.

Lesson 14: Creating a Function

In the creation of a variable, you assign a one-word title to the output of a JavaScript command or event. Creating a function is doing the same thing, except you are assigning a title to an entire series of commands. You are combining many JavaScript commands into one.

Here's an example. Let's say you have some JavaScript code that grabs the hour, minute, and second. Then you have some code that writes that code to the page. You want the return from that code to appear on the page four times. There's no reason why you couldn't write the code again and again. It will work just fine, but wouldn't assigning a one-word title to both pieces of code be easier? Then you could call for the two pieces of code by just calling on that one word.

It's good programming, too, because you must call on only one name to get an effect. Your page isn't full of extra, and probably confusing, code.

To illustrate, let's use a script that's actually in two parts: the script itself, which contains the function; and the onLoad event handler, which triggers the function to work.

Here are both parts:

```
<SCRIPT LANGUAGE="javascript">
<!-- Hide from browsers that do not understand JavaScript
function dateinbar()
{
var d = new Date();
var y = d.getFullYear();
var m = d.getMonth() + 1;
var d = d.getDate();
var t = m + '/' + d + '/' + y + ' ';
defaultStatus = "You arrived at the page on " + t + ".";
}
// end hiding -->
</SCRIPT>
```

And here's the onLoad command in the <BODY>:

```
<BODY BGCOLOR="FFFFcc" onLoad="dateinbar()">
```

The script's effect displays in the status bar, as shown in Figure 3.6.

We kept basically the same type of date script we've been using in past lessons so it would all look somewhat familiar to you. See how we assigned the get*Something*() method's variable names and added 1?

Figure 3.6
The function displays the date in the status bar.

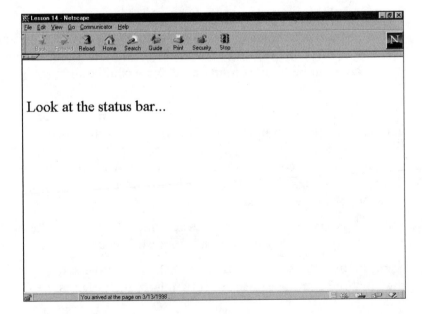

You can see this effect on your computer by clicking Lesson Fourteen Script's Effect, or see it online at `http://www.htmlgoodies.com/JSBook/lesson14effect.html`.

Hey! What Are Those <!-- *and* --> *Things?*

They're yet another couple of extra commands stuck in for good measure. Those probably look familiar to you because they're the two comment flags you use to comment out text in an HTML document. It looks like this:

```
<!-- The text in here would comment out -->
```

I am using them here because, believe it or not, there are still browsers out there that do not read JavaScript. I wrote this section on June 28, 2001, and yes, even today there are browsers that will not read JavaScript. By using these comment commands, the text of the JavaScript is commented out so that it isn't printed on the page. You see, if the browser doesn't understand JavaScript, it sees that text as something to be printed on the page, and it looks bad. But if you use the comment flags, the browser that can't read JavaScript happily ignores the text and displays the page.

If you use these comment flags, there are a few very important rules to follow.

The commands go inside the <SCRIPT> and </SCRIPT> flags. If you put them outside those commands, you would comment out the entire JavaScript on all browsers and nothing would run. The <!-- flag can be followed by a line of text as long as the text is all on the same line. The --> flag must be commented out using the double slashes; otherwise, the JavaScript thinks the command is part of the script, causing an error.

Notice you can also put some text before it because it is commented out. No, you do not have to use text along with these commands. I put the text in because it made explaining the purpose of the flags easier. Follow the format and placement style discussed earlier, and you'll have no trouble.

Deconstructing the Script

Two things are happening here. The first is the script section that creates the function. The second is the command found in the HTML <BODY> flag that triggers the function to work. Let's look at the concept of the function first:

```
function dateinbar()
{
var d = new Date();
var y = d.getFullYear() + 1900;
var m = d.getMonth() + 1;
var d = d.getDate();
```

```
var t = m + '/' + d + '/' + y + ' ';
defaultStatus = "You arrived at the page on " + t + ".";
}
```

The format is straightforward:

- The function is given a name by writing `function` and then the name you want to assign to the function. It's very similar to the way you create a variable name.

  But please note that the function name has the parentheses following it the same way that method commands do. I always keep it straight by thinking that in creating a function, I am actually creating a new method for performing a task.

- A variable is made for the year. Another variable is assigned to the month, and another for the day.

- A fourth variable, `t`, is created to represent the entire date format. It should look familiar. It was created to enable you to call for the full date anywhere in the HTML document by just calling for `t`.

- The last command is new to you:

  ```
  defaultStatus = "You arrived at the page on " + t + ".";
  ```

  `defaultStatus` is a property of the object `window`. Its purpose is to place text into the status bar at the bottom of the browser window.

There's only one status bar, so that has to be the default.

The `onLoad=` Command

The command `onLoad` tells the browser that upon loading the page, do what follows. In this case, what follows is the function `dateinbar()`.

This `onLoad=`*functionname*`()` command format is almost always found in the `BODY` portion of the HTML document.

Placement of These Items

Where you put the two sections—the function and the `onLoad` command—is important. You know the `onLoad` command goes in the `BODY` portion. The script that contains the function should be placed between the `<HEAD>` and `</HEAD>` commands in the HTML document. You can actually stick it anywhere on the page and it'll run, but placing it after the `onLoad` command causes it to start after the entire page has been loaded. Putting it before the `onLoad` command places it in the computer's memory first, so it's there ready to go when the `onLoad` calls for it.

A Word About Global and Local Variables

Okay, now you understand how to assign a variable name and how to create a function. What you might not know is that variables are seen differently by JavaScript, depending on whether they are inside the function or outside the function.

JavaScript allows for two levels of variables, local and global.

Local variables are variables that are viable only within a function. JavaScript understands that whenever a variable is encased within a function, that variable name is viable only inside that function. That way, if you copy and paste a script onto a page that already has a script on it, any existing variables that are equally named will not clash as long as that variable name is found within a function.

Global variables are variables that are not found within functions, and thus *can* clash with the existing variables on the same page.

Here's an example:

```
<SCRIPT LANGUAGE="javascript">
var joe = 12
function writeit()
{
var joe = "Joe Burns"
document.write(joe)
}
</SCRIPT>
```

The variable joe is used twice, but because one is found outside the function (the global variable) and one is found inside the function (the local variable), the two will not clash.

Now, with all that said it is *not* a good idea to follow the preceding format and use like variable names within your scripts. The purpose of the local variables being hidden is far more for protection against clashes with other scripts on the same page than clashes with variable names within the same script.

Name all your variables descriptively and differently, and you'll run into very few, if any, problems.

Your Assignment

Just about any group of JavaScript commands that produce an effect can be set into a function format. In fact, your assignment today is to try to prove that theory.

This one's a little involved:

1. Create a function that calls for two prompts. The first asks for the person's first name, whereas the second prompt asks for the person's last name.

2. Then, in the same function, have an alert box pop up with the text Hello *first name last name*. Welcome to *page address*, My Great Page!

3. Make sure you make a variable for the page address.

4. If you want to make this assignment a little more fun, present My Great Page to the viewer some other way than simply writing it in text in the alert command. Make a variable for that, too.

You can see a possible answer by clicking Lesson Fourteen Assignment in your download packet, or see it online at http://www.htmlgoodies.com/JSBook/assignment14.html.

Lesson 15: An Introduction to Arrays

Let's return to Lesson 12. When you used any one of the getSomething() date or time methods, a number representing the Date object property was returned. In some cases, such as the hour and day of the month, that's fine, but for other Date returns it isn't so good. Take getDay(), for example. As you probably thought, it's not very helpful to have the days of the week returned as 0, 1, 2, 3, 4, 5, or 6.

The best approach is to take the number that's returned and change it into text. That makes more sense and is easier to read.

Here's how:

```
<SCRIPT LANGUAGE="JavaScript">
var dayName=new Array("Sunday","Monday","Tuesday",
➥"Wednesday","Thursday","Friday","Saturday")
var y=new Date();
document.write("Today is "+dayName[y.getDay()] + ".");
</SCRIPT>
```

Figure 3.7 shows the result of this script. You can also see this effect on your computer by clicking Lesson Fifteen Script's Effect, or see it online at http://www.htmlgoodies. com/JSBook/lesson15effect.html.

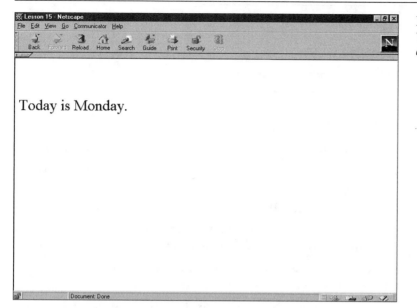

Figure 3.7
The function displays the day of the week.

Deconstructing the Script

Let's start with the same rule that started Lesson 12:

JavaScript starts counting at 0.

That's why the month number is always returned one less than what the month actually is. JavaScript starts counting January at 0.

For this lesson, we'll add to the preceding rule:

JavaScript counts everything you give it and always starts counting at 0.

If you offer JavaScript a list of simple text items, such as a number of names or words (known in JavaScript as *literals*), the script will assign numbers to the items in that list. Guess what number it assigns to the first item? That's right: 0.

So let's give JavaScript a long list of things—the days of the week. But like everything else, you can't just throw a bunch of words in a script and hope the browser picks up what you mean. There is a method to offering a long list of items, such as the days of the week.

It's called creating an *array*.

Setting Up the Array

Here's the array line from the sample script:

```
var dayName=new Array("Sunday","Monday","Tuesday",
➡"Wednesday","Thursday","Friday","Saturday")
```

The format for creating an array is pretty simple:

1. You assign the array of literals a variable name. In this case, I called the array `dayName`.
2. You tell the browser that this is a new array by writing `new Array`. That makes sense. Note the capitalization pattern.
3. The array of literals is placed within parentheses.
4. Each new array item is surrounded with double quotation marks. Remember that each array item is text, and that requires double quotation marks.
5. Each array item is separated from the next by a comma, no spaces. You can have spaces if you want, but I feel this format looks a little cleaner.
6. The big question is in what order to put the array items. Here the answer is easy: You know that the days of the week are represented Sunday through to Saturday, 0–6. So, you list Sunday first because you know it will receive the 0 both from the `getDay()` method and from the JavaScript assigning numbers to the array. That makes it a pretty sure bet that a 0 will return Sunday to the page.

Later in the book, we'll discuss arrays that do not come with a 0 through whatever pattern is already set. That gets a little more complicated. For now, we'll stay with the rather easy-to-create arrays because JavaScript has set the order for us already.

Grabbing a Piece of the Array

Now that you've set up the seven-day text array, you need to create a method to return the numeric day of the week through the `getDay()` method, and then turn that number into the correct day from the array.

Here's the code that does it:

```
var y=new Date();
document.write("Today is "+dayName[y.getDay()] + ".");
```

The first line should be familiar by now. A variable, y, is set up that represents the `new Date()`.

The `document.write` statement should also look familiar. The text within the double quotation marks writes to the page, whereas the text within the plus signs returns something to the page in its place.

Here's the magic in the script:

```
dayName[y.getDay()]
```

The code turns the attention of the return to the array, `dayName`.

The code in the brackets is the same format used to return the numeric day of the week number: *variablename*`.getDay()`.

The `y.getDay()` is replaced by a number representing the day of the week, like it always is.

So what the command is actually saying is *Go to this array[find this number]*.

If you were running this script on a Monday, the `y.getDay()` would return the number 1. The browser would see the command `dayName[y.getDay()]` as `dayName[1]` and would return the text in the array associated with the number 1. The number 1 is Monday because JavaScript counts up from 0.

Get it? Good.

Your Assignment

Use the previous instructions and array to create a script that prints this line to the page:
`Today is `*`Day-Of-The-Week`*` in the month of `*`Month-Name`*`.`

You already know the format for the day of the week. Now create an array that returns the name of the month. Just follow the pattern shown earlier to create the array, and remember to give the new array a new variable name. You can't have two variables in the same script with the same name.

Remember, even in months, JavaScript starts counting at 0.

 You can see a possible answer by clicking Lesson Fifteen Assignment in your download packet, or see it online at `http://www.htmlgoodies.com/JSBook/assignment15.html`.

Lesson 16: The Third End-of-Chapter Review—A `<BODY>` Flag Script

If you stopped at this point, you would do just fine. What you have is sufficient to create some wonderful scripts.

But why stop now? Let's review!

Table 3.1 contains the object-related JavaScript commands you've learned up to now. In addition, you've been introduced to these JavaScript concepts:

- The alert() method and the prompt() method
- These event handlers: onBlur, onChange, onClick, onDblClick, onFocus, onKeyDown, onKeyPress, onKeyUp, onLoad, onMouseDown, onMouseMove, onMouseOut, onMouseOver, onMouseUp, onSubmit
- The HTML 4.0 flag <SPAN>
- Creating variable names
- Creating a function

Table 3.1   Object-Related JavaScript Commands Demonstrated in Chapters 1–3

Object	Methods	Properties
date	getDate(), getDay(), getHours(), getMinutes(), getMonth(), getSeconds(), getYear()	
document	write()	alinkColor, bgColor, fgColor, linkColor, lastModified, location, referrer, title, vlinkColor
history	go()	length
location		host, hostname, href
navigator		appCodeName, appName, appVersion, userAgent
window		defaultstatus, status

Next, let's use some of these commands to create a script that helps the viewer create the page. The script will ask the viewer what background and text colors she would like. Then, the page will display with those colors. Finally, the viewer will be told, in the status bar, Here's your *color* background and *color* text.

The script is as follows:

```
<SCRIPT LANGUAGE="javascript">
var color = prompt("What color would you like the page's background to be","")
var txtcolor = prompt("What color would you like the text to be?","")
document.write("<BODY BGCOLOR=" +color+ " TEXT=" +txtcolor+ ">")
defaultStatus="Here's your " +color+ " background and " +txtcolor+ " text"
</SCRIPT>
```

Figure 3.8 shows the script's effect.

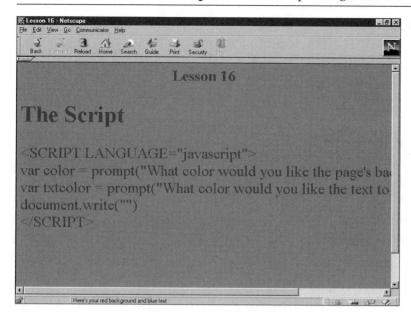

Figure 3.8
The script creates a page with the user's desired background color and text color.

 You can see this effect on your computer by clicking Lesson Sixteen Script's Effect, or see it online at `http://www.htmlgoodies.com/JSBook/lesson16effect.html`.

Deconstructing the Script

The script starts by setting a couple of variables using prompts. You need to get the user's input on what background and text color she wants, so this seems as good a way as any.

The variables are `color` and `txtcolor`, respectively. The code looks like this:

```
var color = prompt("What color would you like the page's background to be","")
var txtcolor = prompt("What color would you like the text to be?","")
```

Now that you have the input from the user, you'll need to use that data to alter the page. The real beauty of this script is its placement on the page.

Up until now, each of the scripts in this book had no real placement concerns. The script could pretty much sit anywhere in an HTML document, and the results would display. Now, though, you are concerned with where this script will place its output.

The script must write its line of text so that that line of text becomes the HTML document's <BODY> flag.

The quickest way to implement the user's background and text color requests is to write them to the <BODY> flag. So that's what you did. This script's main purpose is to write the HTML document's <BODY> flag to the page, so you must ensure that the entire script sits right where the body command needs to sit on the HTML page. And, of course, you need to ensure that you don't write a <BODY> into the HTML document yourself. You need to let the script do that for you.

Here's the code that writes the <BODY> flag:

```
document.write("<BODY BGCOLOR=" +color+ " TEXT=" +txtcolor+ ">")
```

The colors are entered as return variables inside the two plus signs. That way, what the user writes in the prompt is what is returned.

Status Bar, Too?

But the script goes a little further than just writing a <BODY> flag. It also places the viewer's data to the status bar, almost as if the page were served to her.

Here's the line of code that does it:

```
defaultStatus="Here's your " +color+ " background and " +txtcolor+ " text"
```

It follows the same format as the document.write statement, with text surrounded by double quotation marks and return variables surrounded by plus signs, except in this case the text is sent to the status bar.

Your Assignment

Okay, your turn. Make a new script—something that adds to your page. I stuck with prompts and variables for my example.

If you want to, may I suggest creating a Mad-Lib party game? It's that game where you're asked for a noun, a verb, a state, and things like that. Then, you read the sentence you created using those words. And you know from playing it that the sentence never makes any sense.

It would be your first JavaScript game.

For my brand-new script, I created a button that, when clicked, displays the current date and time. It's rather simple. (You should try the Mad-Lib game or something even more helpful.)

 You can see a possible answer to making the button that shows the date and time by clicking Lesson Sixteen Assignment in your download packet, or see it online at http://www. htmlgoodies.com/JSBook/assignment16.html.

Chapter 4

Flipping Images and Opening Windows with Mouse Events

This chapter contains the following lessons and scripts:

- Lesson 17: An Image Flip Using `onMouseOver` and Preloading Images
- Lesson 18: An Image Flip with a Function
- Lesson 19: Opening New Windows
- Lesson 20: Opening a Window with a Function
- Lesson 21: The `confirm` Method, with an Introduction to `if` and `else`
- Lesson 22: The Fourth End-of-Chapter Review—Some Jumping Jacks

Up to this point, each of the JavaScripts you've built has dealt with altering, changing, or writing text to the page. Sure, there's been some color, but there has to be more than text manipulation in JavaScript. In this chapter, you'll start to look at manipulating images, opening new windows, and offering users a choice, rather than simply taking information from them.

Lesson 17: An Image Flip Using `onMouseOver` and Preloading Images

An image flip is a great effect. Some people call it a *mouse rollover* or an *image rollover*. The user rolls her mouse pointer over an image, and it changes to a new image. When the mouse leaves the image, the image changes back. It's a very popular event on the Web.

This example goes back to the use of the onMouseOver and onMouseOut event handlers. You use the event handler to affect not only text, but also the space the image is sitting in. Here's the script:

```
<A HREF="http://www.cnn.com"
onMouseOver="document.pic1.src='menu1on.gif'"
onMouseOut="document.pic1.src='menu1off.gif'">
<IMG SRC="menu1off.gif" BORDER=0 NAME="pic1"></a>
```

It'll take two figures to show you this one. Take a look at Figures 4.1 and 4.2.

Figure 4.1
The page looks like this when the mouse is off the image.

 You can see the effect on your own computer by clicking Lesson Seventeen Example in your download packet, or see it online at http://www.htmlgoodies.com/JSBook/ lesson17example.html.

In this example—and the ones that follow, for that matter—the images are all the same size. You don't need to use same-size images for your image flips, but it's a good idea. It really heightens the look.

Notice again that there is no need for the <SCRIPT> and </SCRIPT> tags. You're using event handlers again. The JavaScript onMouseOver and onMouseOut events are built into an <A HREF> HTML flag, so not only is this an image flip, it's also a hypertext link.

Also notice that by including BORDER="0" in the <IMG SRC> tag, no link box appears around the image.

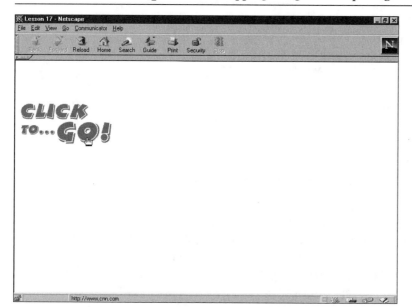

Figure 4.2
*When the mouse is on
the image, the message
changes.*

Deconstructing the Script

From what you already know about event handlers, you should be able to go a long way toward picking this one apart by yourself. When the mouse is off the image space, the image `menu1off.gif` is displayed. That's the image displayed when the page first loads; it's also the image called for in the `<IMG SRC>` flag. When the mouse is on the image, the `menu1on.gif` image is shown.

The NAME Attribute

Notice the `<IMG SRC>` flag has been given a `NAME=` attribute. In this example, the name given to the image—or more correctly, the space the image is occupying—is `pic1`.

That `NAME=` attribute becomes quite important if you want to put multiple image flips on the same page. For every new image flip you put on the page, you must choose a different name for the new image space. Here's an example of three image flips in a row:

```
<A HREF="http://www.htmlgoodies.com"
onMouseOver="document.pic1.src='menu1on.gif'"
onMouseOut="document.pic1.src='menu1off.gif'">
<IMG SRC="menu1off.gif" BORDER=0 NAME="pic1"> </A>

<A HREF="http://www.developer.com"
onMouseOver="document.pic2.src='menu1on.gif'"
onMouseOut="document.pic2.src='menu1off.gif'">
<IMG SRC="menu1off.gif" BORDER=0 NAME="pic2"> </A>
```

```
<A HREF="http://www.javagoodies.com"
onMouseOver="document.pic3.src='menu1on.gif'"
onMouseOut="document.pic3.src='menu1off.gif'">
<IMG SRC="menu1off.gif" BORDER=0 NAME="pic3"> </A>
```

Not only were the links changed to new locations, but notice also that all the names were changed, both in the <IMG SRC> and in the hierarchy statements.

The Hierarchy Statement

The name of the space the image is sitting in, pic1 in this case, is referenced in the hierarchy statement referenced by the onMouseOver and onMouseOut statements. The hierarchy statement, document.pic1.src, reads this way:

- window is implied. You could have written this with the object window at the beginning, but as you read in Lesson 13 in Chapter 3, "Manipulating Data and the Hierarchy of JavaScript," it is not necessary. JavaScript simply assumes all that is going on is going on inside a browser window.

- document refers to the current HTML document object.

- pic1 is the name of the space the image will occupy. You swap out images within a space occupied by an image, and you make up that NAME and stick it in the <IMG SRC> flag.

- src is a property of the image object that enables you to load a new image into the current image's space.

When the mouse passes over the space occupied by the image, the onMouseOver event handler springs into action, replacing the menu1off.gif image with the menu1on.gif image.

The process might take a second or two to allow the image that will display to be loaded into the browser. But you can cut down on that time by preloading the image.

Preloading Images

Through JavaScript, you can set up code that downloads images into the user's browser cache for later use. Using the previous image flip code, the menu1off.gif image loads to the cache because it is being called for by the HTML document in the <IMG SRC>.

If the term *cache* is new to you, here's what's so great about it: The cache is a section of your hard drive, set aside by your browser, so it can store files after it has displayed them for you. Have you noticed how much faster a page loads after you've first seen it? That's because the browser is not reading the images and text from the server anymore. It is reading them from your hard drive.

By pre-caching, or preloading, images for your user, when she starts to use the image flip, the browser works quickly the first time without having to contact the server again for the image it wants to display. It's a very clever way of doing things.

Here, you need to call for the menu1on.gif to load into the cache with the rest of the page. Then, when the image flip is called for, the menu1on.gif is there ready and waiting to be posted. The flips will go much faster the first time around because the browser isn't waiting for the server to be contacted and the new image to be loaded.

Here's the code that performs the preload:

```
<SCRIPT LANGUAGE="javascript">


Image1= new Image(200,200)

Image1.src = "menu1on.gif"

</SCRIPT>
```

The preload occurs thanks to a completely different script from the image flip. The format follows this pattern:

- ● `Image1 = new Image(200,200)` assigns a variable name to a new image that is 200 pixels wide by 200 tall. The script doesn't know what the image is yet; it just knows that now the image will be brought into the cache under that variable name.
- ● `Image1.src = "menu1on.gif"` tells the JavaScript the source, or path, to find the image.

The preceding JavaScript loads the image into the browser cache under the variable name `Image1`. But the name used to pull the image into the cache becomes immaterial because you never call for the image by that variable name. You call for it only by its true, or *literal*, name: menu1on.gif.

The purpose of the preceding JavaScript is to load the image to the browser cache, period. The variable names assigned mean nothing past a format you must use to get that behind-the-scenes download to occur.

Let's say you had multiple images to download. Again, the variable names don't matter, so you might as well just keeping adding one to the variable name Image1. Preloading three images might look like this:

```
<SCRIPT LANGUAGE="javascript">

Image1= new Image(200,200)
Image1.src = "menu1on.gif"
```

```
Image2= new Image(125,15)
Image2.src = "line.gif"

Image3= new Image(20,10)
Image3.src = "button.gif"
</SCRIPT>
```

Notice each new two-line command group is given a new variable name and a new image to preload. The height and width parameters have also changed to fit the image.

Put this script between the <HEAD> flags in your script, and the preloaded images should be waiting in the cache when your user tries the image flips for the first time.

Your Assignment

Take this sample code and add a few comments so that when the mouse is on the image, the status bar reads, Oh, Click it! Then, when the mouse is off the image, the status bar should read, Click to go!

Here's a hint: return true.

 To see a possible answer on your own computer, click Lesson Seventeen Assignment in your download packet, or see it online at http://www.htmlgoodies.com/JSBook/ assignment17.html.

Lesson 18: An Image Flip with a Function

Here is another example of onMouseOver and onMouseOut event handlers being used to create an image flip effect. But this time, instead of including the JavaScript statements to swap pictures in the <A HREF> tag, the event is called for in a function.

To show you where each of the parts should be placed on your page, this display includes the entire HTML document format:

```
<HTML>
<HEAD>
<TITLE>Javascript Example 18</TITLE>
<SCRIPT LANGUAGE="JavaScript">
function up()
{
document.mypic.src="up.gif"
}
function down()
{
document.mypic.src="down.gif"
```

```
}
</SCRIPT>
</HEAD>
<BODY>
<CENTER>
<h2>Sample Animation</h2>
<A HREF=http://www.htmlgoodies.com onMouseOver="up()"
➥ onMouseOut="down()"; return true>
<IMG SRC="down.gif" NAME="mypic" BORDER=0></A>
</BODY>
</HTML>
```

It's a simple image flip animation with onMouseOver and onMouseOut event handlers in a function. In the example, if you mouse over and out quickly, this looks like an animation of a stick figure doing jumping jacks.

Andree did the artwork shown in Figures 4.3 and 4.4. I take no responsibility for that.

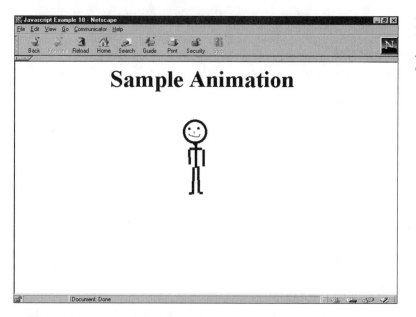

Figure 4.3
The stick figure stands up straight when the mouse is off the image.

 You can see the man (I think it's a man) doing jumping jacks on your own computer by clicking Lesson Eighteen Example in your download packet, or see it online at http://www.htmlgoodies.com/JSBook/lesson18example.html.

There aren't a whole lot of external words on the page. I just took the preceding code and pasted it into an HTML document.

Figure 4.4
The figure does a jumping jack when the mouse is on the image.

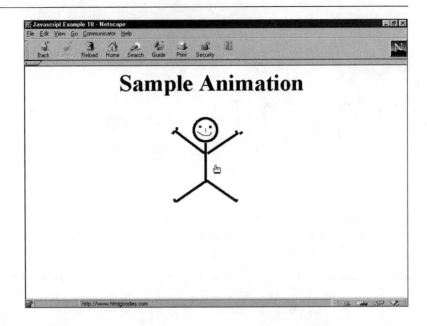

Deconstructing the Script

In this example you are calling for two different images, so you need two separate functions. Here's what they look like:

```
<SCRIPT LANGUAGE="JavaScript">
function up()
{
document.mypic.src="up.gif"
}
function down()
{
document.mypic.src="down.gif"
}
</SCRIPT>
```

Look again at the format for creating a function.

The command `function` is followed immediately by the name of the function followed by the two parentheses. In this case, the parentheses are empty because you are passing nothing to the function. Later in the book, we'll discuss putting parameters into the parentheses so that information can be passed to the function. The commands that make up the function are housed within left and right braces ({}).

The functions are equal to the statements used in the previous JavaScript lesson on image flips. Remember the hierarchy statements? Here the function contains the statements, rather than adding them into the <A HREF> flag.

The format for the hierarchy statement is document, and then comes the NAME assigned to the image space, and finally the SRC path to the image.

The two functions were named up() and down(). The names could have been just about anything, but we used these two because of the actual position of the man doing jumping jacks.

Calling for the Function

Now let's look at the call for the function:

```
<A HREF="http://www.htmlgoodies.com" onMouseOver="up()"
➥ onMouseOut="down()"; return true>
<IMG SRC="down.gif" NAME="mypic"  BORDER=0></A>
```

The format is close to that used in Lesson 15 (see Chapter 3), but a function is called on here, rather than the hierarchy statement being included in the HREF command itself.

By calling for the function name following onMouseOver and onMouseOff, in effect, what is included in the function statements is replaced with the function name.

The code onMouseOver="up()" basically means this:

```
onMouseOver="document.mypic.src='up.gif'"
```

More Than One Image Flip

Remember from Lesson 17, earlier in this chapter, that if you want to create multiple image flips on a page, you must continue using new NAME= attributes to separate each image space in the browser's mind? It's the same thing here, except now you must create whole new function names in addition to new NAME= attributes.

For example, suppose you want to place on the page another JavaScript image flip, similar to the first example. You would create two new functions by copying and pasting the same functions shown earlier and altering the function name. The easiest and quickest method is to add the number 2.

Then, you also have to change the NAME=. So, you change the name to mypic2. But be sure you change the name of the image space every time it appears.

Now you get code that looks like this in the HEAD commands:

```
<SCRIPT LANGUAGE="JavaScript">
function up()
{
document.mypic.src="up.gif"
}
function down()
{
document.mypic.src="down.gif"
}
function up2()
{
document.mypic2.src="upagain.gif"
}
function down2()
{
document.mypic2.src="downagain.gif"
}
</SCRIPT>
```

You also get code like the following to call for the two different images:

```
<A HREF="http://www.htmlgoodies.com" onMouseOver="up()"
➥ onMouseOut="down()"; return true>
<IMG SRC="down.gif" NAME="mypic"  BORDER=0></A>

<a href="http://www.htmlgoodies.com" onMouseOver="up2()"
➥ onMouseOut="down2()"; return true>
<IMG SRC="downagain.gif" NAME="mypic2"  BORDER=0></A>
```

See how the new functions are linked to a specific image space through the NAME=, and all the image space names were changed? Follow that process every time you add a new image flip, and you can put hundreds on the same page. Well, maybe not hundreds—just about 100 will probably do the trick.

Preloading Those Images

Keep in mind that you can help your viewer along by preloading the images that will be called for in the flip.

Here again is the format:

```
<SCRIPT LANGUAGE="javascript">

Image1= new Image(200,200)
```

```
Image1.src = "menu1on.gif"
```

```
</SCRIPT>
```

It'll help your user greatly because she won't be sitting around waiting.

Your Assignment

First, you need to get four images. If you can supply them, that's great. If not, I have four for you at

- http://www.htmlgoodies.com/JSBook/img1.gif
- http://www.htmlgoodies.com/JSBook/img2.gif
- http://www.htmlgoodies.com/JSBook/img3.gif
- http://www.htmlgoodies.com/JSBook/img4.gif

Download them into your computer. Use the function and code shown earlier to make `img1.gif` and `img2.gif` to create an image flip, and then get `img3.gif` and `img4.gif` to do an image flip. You will create two image flips from the preceding code.

TIP

Watch the order in which you put the images in the function. You'll know you have it right when you roll your pointer over the image and it flips correctly. If it stays flipped, you're out of order.

 To see a possible answer on your own computer, click Lesson Eighteen Assignment in your download packet, or see it online at http://www.htmlgoodies.com/JSBook/assignment18.html.

Lesson 19: Opening New Windows

This is the first of two lessons about opening a new window through JavaScript. This first new-window lesson deals with the JavaScript commands you would use to open a new window that displays a second HTML document.

Let's get started with a basic script:

```
<SCRIPT LANGUAGE="javascript">
window.open('opened.html','joe',config='height=300,width=300')
</SCRIPT>
```

The script's effect appears in Figure 4.5.

Figure 4.5
The script opens a new window.

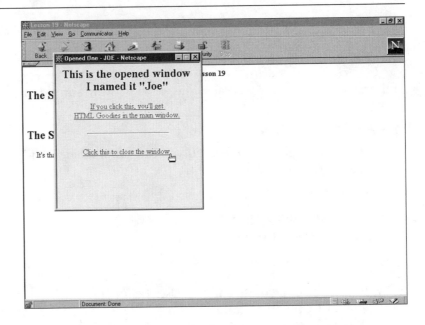

 You can try the script yourself by clicking Lesson Nineteen Script's Effect in your download packet, or see it online at http://www.htmlgoodies.com/JSBook/lesson19example.html.

NOTE

This script only opens the window. The links that appear in the new window were written on the HTML page that filled the new window, but what about those links in the new window? They're functional, too.

If you look at this example in your download packet or online, you'll see that a link in the little window loads a new page in the big window, and then you'll see a link closes the little window. It's like fireworks at a fairground. You can even say "Oooo" and "Ahhh," if the mood strikes you.

I'll get to those links in the little window and how they are written to control the main window, as well as how to close the window itself, later in this chapter.

Deconstructing the Script

Let's start by talking about the placement of this script in your HTML document. Until now, I have always said it's good to place scripts up high in the document so they can run early in the page load. When you're dealing with a function, the script goes up in the head commands. Here, I would like to make a different suggestion.

If you're going to open a second window, put the commands that do it down pretty low in the HTML document. In fact, make them last. The reasoning is simple: The page loads—then the new window pops up. If you have the commands first, the new window pops up before the viewer gets to see what's there in the big window. There's also a greater chance that the user will close the little window before it can be used.

That's just my opinion, of course. You can actually place this script anywhere in the document you want. It'll run from wherever it sits. I just think the order of the window popping last is more beneficial to your viewers.

Let's look at the basic window-opening code again:

```
<SCRIPT LANGUAGE="javascript">
window.open('opened.html','joe',config='height=300,width=300')
</SCRIPT>
```

The code `window.open` couldn't be more blatant. `window` is the object, and `open` is the method that acts on it. That's the easy part. Now you get to configure the window.

Configuring the Window

This is all that good stuff in the instance of the command (that's the parentheses, remember?). Here's the format you need to follow:

```
('URL of document in window', 'New Window Name', config='New Window Parameters')
```

Here's the command from the script with the current elements:

```
('opened.html', 'joe', config='height=300,width=300')
```

- ⚪ `opened.html` is the URL of the page that will appear in the new window. If the page is from your server, or in a different directory, you'll need to add the `http://` stuff or a directory path so the browser can find it.
- ⚪ `joe` is the name of the new window. This will be important in a moment.
- ⚪ `config=` means that what follows will configure the window. Currently, there are only a couple of configuration settings—the height and the width of the window—but there are many more window parameters you can set.

The `Config` Commands

The `config` commands in this script open a new window that is 300 pixels wide by 300 pixels tall.

Numerous features work under the `config=` command. `height` and `width` are two you already know. They work by adding the number wide by number tall in pixels. The remainder of these commands all work using yes or no, depending on whether or not you want to include the element in your page. Remember that even if you use every one of these attributes, you should be sure to run them all together just as you did the height and width in the sample script. A space equals an error. Here are the Config commands and what they do:

- toolbar=—The toolbar is the line of buttons at the top of the browser window that contains Back, Forward, Stop, Reload, and other buttons.
- menubar=—The menu bar is the line of items labeled File, Edit, View, Go, and so on, which gives the user access to menus of options.
- scrollbars=—I wouldn't make a new window that would need scrollbars. I think it kills the effect.
- resizable=—Denotes whether the user can change the size of the window by dragging the window's resize area.
- location=—The location bar is the space at the top of the browser window where the page URL is displayed.
- directories=—This is the bar at the top of the Netscape browser window that has the bookmarks and such.
- status=—Denotes whether the window will contain a status bar.

Here's an example of what code would look like using some of these commands:

```
('opened.html', 'joe', config='height=300,width=300,
➥toolbar=no,menubar=0,status=1')
```

You should notice that for the toolbar, no is used because we didn't want one. For the menu bar and status bars, we used 0 and 1. Which is right?

Well, you can use either. Remember that JavaScript counts everything … and … it starts counting from 0. To JavaScript, 0 means *no*, and 1 means *yes*.

Of course, you can always use the words *yes* and *no*. I just wanted to make you aware that, once again, JavaScript was counting and it was counting up from 0.

What About the Title Bar?

In case you're wondering whether you can lose the title bar, and apparently you are, the answer is no. That's a given. You get it, like it or not.

Tags in the New Window

The new window that pops up can be more than a frame for the HTML document that is posted inside. As you can see from the new window in this lesson's example, I made the background a nice greenish-blue. Also, there were two links.

The first link opens the HTML Goodies site in the main window. This is the code that makes it happen:

```
<A HREF="http://www.htmlgoodies.com" TARGET="main"></A>
```

Whether you know it or not, the big window has a name, main. There's no need for you to name it main—that's already done from the start for you. It's the default name of the big window. In fact, it has two names: parent and opener. If you use either one of them as the target, the output of the hypertext link in the new window will display in the big window. It's another little extra from the friendly folks at JavaScript, Inc. (Netscape, actually. It invented JavaScript.)

All I did was add the command TARGET="--" to the <A HREF> flag and enter parent to indicate where the page should load.

But what if you wanted the page to load in the small window? In that case, you would add nothing. You should know from basic HTML that any hypertext link, by default, loads into its own window. Just make a link to appear in the little window and when your user clicks, the page will display in the little window.

Multiple Windows

You can actually have multiple windows by adding multiple window.open commands. Just be sure to give each window a different name. Then, you can have links from window to window, as long as you continue to target the links correctly.

Suppose you have this code on your main window page:

```
<SCRIPT LANGUAGE="javascript">
window.open('opened.html','joe',config='height=300,width=300')
</SCRIPT>
<SCRIPT LANGUAGE="javascript">
window.open('nextopened.html','andree', config='height=300,width=300')
</SCRIPT>
```

Two windows will pop up. Then, as long as you set the links correctly, you could target links from one window to the next. This HTML code, which shows up in the small window named joe, would target a link to open in the second small window named andree:

```
<A HREF="page.html" TARGET="andree">Click</A>
```

As long as you keep the names straight, you can target your links to the main window or any one of the smaller windows that have opened.

Closing the Window

In the original example for this lesson, the second link on the new window closed it. Here's the format to do that:

```
<A HREF="" onClick="self.close()">Click To Close</A>
```

It's a basic `<A HREF>` link that points to nothing. See the empty quotation marks following the `HREF=`? Setting the link to point to nothing disallows another page to load. The command that actually closes the window is `onClick="self.close()"`.

`self` is a property of window, whereas the command `close` is a method that does the dirty work.

Some people would rather their windows not be closed by a simple link. They believe a button looks much more official, and there's some merit in that. If you would rather use a button to close your window, here's the code:

```
<FORM>
<INPUT TYPE="button" VALUE="Click to Close the Window" onClick="self.close()">
</FORM>
```

One More Thing—Opening the Window on Call

Let's say you wanted to open a window on command rather than just having it simply happen when the person logs in. Try this:

```
<SCRIPT LANGUAGE="javascript">

function openIt()
{
window.open('000.html', 'joe', config='height=300,width=300');
}
</SCRIPT>

<A HREF="javascript:onClick=openIt()">Click to open New window</A>
```

It's a small function that contains the commands to open a new window. I only have the height and width in there, but any of the `config` commands will fit.

Then, a basic hypertext link is set to enact `"javascript"`. That JavaScript command is an `onClick` that triggers the function. I know I say that usually functions sit up in the HEAD for the document, whereas the HTML that calls for them sits in the BODY. If you want to set this code up that way, fine; the browser won't care. I, however, simply drop the whole block of code—function and all—right where I want the link to go.

You just need to be sure that the function sits above the link in the code. If you keep the format shown previously, you'll have no troubles.

Your Assignment

I didn't get a chance to show you all the extra little functions that are available in action. So, your assignment is to write a script that opens a new window incorporating every one of these features:

- Make the window 300 pixels tall by 500 pixels wide.
- Include a location bar and a status bar.
- Don't include a toolbar, menu bar, scrollbar, or directories.
- Make the new window resizable.

There should be two links:

- One opens a new page in the main window.
- The second page opens a new page in the same window.
- The second page that opens in the small window should have the links to close the window.

Oh, and make the background yellow (ffff00).

 To see a possible answer on your own computer, click Lesson Nineteen Assignment in your download packet, or see it online at http://www.htmlgoodies.com/JSBook/ assignment19.html.

Lesson 20: Opening a Window with a Function

In Lesson 19, earlier in this chapter, you opened a new window using the window.open command. That window was then filled with a different HTML document you named in the instance.

Here, you'll create a new window function where the new window, and all its contents, will be carried along in the same HTML document. It is literally the equivalent of two pages in one.

Lessons 17 and 18 discussed preloading images for your image flips. Think of this as preloading a second page. Here's the sample script:

```
<SCRIPT LANGUAGE="javascript">
function openindex()
{
```

```
var OpenWindow=window.open("", "newwin", "height=300,width=300");
OpenWindow.document.write("<HTML>")
OpenWindow.document.write("<TITLE>New Window</TITLE>")
OpenWindow.document.write("<BODY BGCOLOR='00ffff'>")
OpenWindow.document.write("<CENTER>")
OpenWindow.document.write("<font size=+1> New Window</font><P>")
OpenWindow.document.write("<a href= 'http://www.htmlgoodies.com' target='main'>")
OpenWindow.document.write("This will open<BR> in the main window</a><p>")
OpenWindow.document.write("<P><HR WIDTH='60%'><P>")
OpenWindow.document.write("<a href='' onClick='self.close()'>
➥ This closes the window</a><p>")
OpenWindow.document.write("</CENTER>")
OpenWindow.document.write("</HTML>")
}
</SCRIPT>
```

And in the BODY command is this code:

```
onLoad="openindex()"
```

The script's effect is exactly the same as in Lesson 19, as you can see in Figure 4.6. The same size window opens and contains the same two links. The difference is that it was all done with one page.

Figure 4.6
This script opens a new window.

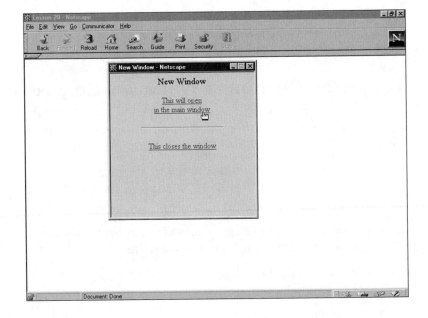

104

You can try the script yourself by clicking Lesson Twenty Script's Effect in your download packet, or see it online at http://www.htmlgoodies.com/JSBook/lesson20example.html.

Deconstructing the Script

The main script, the code between the <SCRIPT> and </SCRIPT> that contains the function, is placed between the <HEAD> and </HEAD>, as are most functions.

The function is named openindex(), in the normal fashion.

Then, the braces surround what the function will do when called on.

Now we get to the meat of the script. The variable OpenWindow is created to represent the window.open("instance") command. It looks like this:

```
var OpenWindow=window.open("", "newwin", "height=300,width=300');
```

The format is familiar. The only real difference is that there is no URL writing the first set of quotation marks. See the empty double quotation marks? They tell the browser to look to the script to find the new window information, rather than looking for another page somewhere on the server.

It's very similar to not placing a URL in the command that closed the window. It wouldn't close if it had something to load. Same here—it wouldn't look to the script if it had something else to load.

Now you start to build the HTML page that will go inside the new window. Here's the first line of text:

```
OpenWindow.document.write("<HTML>")
```

This format should also look somewhat familiar. The command is saying that this line of text should be written on the variable OpenWindow (the new window).

Look back at the full script. That format is followed again and again, writing line after line of text. There's no reason there can't be hundreds of lines of text creating a fully functioning HTML document.

I would suggest again that you pay close attention to the double and single quotation mark patterns.

Finally, the function is triggered in the BODY command through an onLoad event handler.

Getting the Window on Call

Maybe you don't want this window to open when the page loads. The effect might be better if the page opened when the user clicked a link or a button.

You would follow the same patterns outlined in Lesson 19, except here the user's click would activate the function rather than call for a new window.

Here's the format for a hypertext link that opens the window:

```
<A HREF="currentpage.html" onClick="openindex()">Click To Open 'joe'</A>
```

And here's the code for the button:

```
<FORM>
<INPUT TYPE="button" VALUE="Click to Open a New Window" onClick="openindex()">
</FORM>
```

Your Assignment

For this assignment, you'll create a window that opens using a function. Please make the document that appears in the window have a green background.

In addition, make the TITLE command read Hello *user name* - Here is your window! You can gather the user's name through a prompt. Of course, make a link that closes the window.

The big concern now is where to put the prompt. Think about when you want it to appear. If you want the prompt to appear when the user first enters the page, put it in the document outside the function. If you want the prompt to appear when the new window is called for, put it in the function. Put it first in the function.

 To see a possible answer on your own computer, click Lesson Twenty Assignment in your download packet, or see it online at http://www.htmlgoodies.com/JSBook/ assignment20. html.

Lesson 21: The confirm() Method, with an Introduction to if and else

The confirm() method acts very much like the alert() method, except confirm() adds a Cancel button to the dialog box. You should use alert() to simply pass along information to the user. confirm() is best for when you want some feedback.

If you use the confirm() method by itself, it doesn't do much except post the OK and Cancel buttons. No matter which button you choose, you go in.

Add the if and else commands, and you start to get some neat effects.

First, let's look at the basic format. This script doesn't do much:

```
<SCRIPT LANGUAGE="javascript">
confirm("Are you sure you want to enter?")
</SCRIPT>
```

Look familiar? It should. It's the same format as an alert(), except the word *confirm* is used instead of *alert*. Figure 4.7 shows an example of what this little script does.

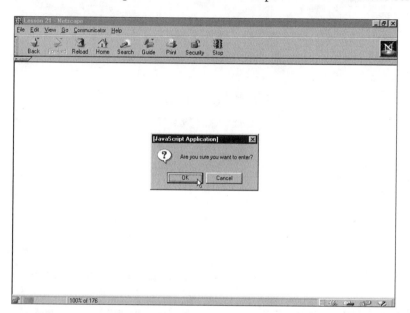

Figure 4.7
The script displays a confirm box.

 You can try the confirm box yourself by clicking Lesson Twenty-One Script's Effect One in your download packet, or see it online at http://www.htmlgoodies.com/JSBook/ lesson21example.html.

As you saw, if you looked, no matter which button you click, you got to see the page load.

Now here's the same script with some new additions:

```
<SCRIPT LANGUAGE="javascript">
if (confirm("Are you sure you want to enter Effect Two?") )
{
location.href='lesson21effect2c.html'
alert("Good choice")
}
else
{
```

```
    alert("Then you'll stay right here")
    }
</SCRIPT>
```

You can see what you get in Figure 4.8. The effect works best if you are coming from another page to see it. When you open the page listed previously, you'll get a link. Click the link, and then you'll see the effect.

Figure 4.8
The confirm box after clicking OK.

 You can try the second confirm box yourself by clicking Lesson Twenty-One Script's Effect Two in your download packet, or see it online at `http://www.htmlgoodies.com/JSBook/lesson21effect2.html`.

Now we're getting somewhere. Here's a link that asks you whether you want to enter. Except this time, if you click OK, you'll enter the site. If you click Cancel, you won't.

Three pages are actually involved in the effect:

- The page with the `Click To Go!` link.
- The page that contains the `confirm` script. This page displays if the user clicks Cancel. In the preceding example, if this page loads, the text `"Chicken!"` shows up.
- The page that displays if the user clicks OK. This is the page URL in the `confirm` script.

Try the script again. See whether you can pick out the three pages.

Deconstructing the Script

The process of the script is quite logical, as is all JavaScript. First, the script makes the statement:

```
if (confirm("Are you sure you want to enter HTML Goodies?") )
```

The if means, "Here is your chance to make a choice."

Before going on, look at the multiple uses of parentheses. The if statement always has an instance, and that means parentheses. But you also know that confirm(), too, has parentheses. That's fine. Just use the parentheses like you normally would, and you'll get the previous look. Notice how the parentheses from the if command simply surround the entire confirm() method, including its parentheses. Let's get back to the script.

Because this is a choice, options are available. In this case, a confirm() method is used to offer two choices—OK and Cancel. I think of them as yes and no.

Immediately following the if statement are the commands to be carried out for each choice. Please notice the commands are encased inside those lovely little braces ({}). Because curly brackets are involved, you might think that what is encased is a function. I guess if you want to think of it that way, that's fine, but technically it isn't. That's just the format of an if statement. The commands in the first set of braces are what should happen if the user clicks OK:

```
{
location.href='lesson21effect2c.html'
alert("Good choice")
}
```

The line location.href creates a link. If that's the choice the user makes, you have a basic alert proclaiming Good Choice.

But what if the user clicks Cancel? You already know that the commands that immediately follow the if statement are what occur if the user clicks OK.

Notice that right after the first set of braces ends, the word else pops up.

Think of the command else as meaning *if not*. So, the code

```
else
{
alert("Then you'll stay right here")
}
```

means *if not, post the alert message and do not change the page.*

Put it all together, and you get the effect of giving the user a choice—enter or don't enter. And you've also set up an event to occur either way.

Your Assignment

Don't get nervous! You can do this. Your assignment is to turn the commands discussed here into a function. Oh, and make it so that when the user chooses not to go in, not only does the alert pop up, but the status bar of the window reads Chicken!

If you really want to be fancy, when the person clicks OK, make the page open up on a new window.

 To see a possible answer on your own computer, click Lesson Twenty-One Assignment in your download packet, or see it online at http://www.htmlgoodies.com/JSBook/ assignment21.html.

By the way, to see the answer, you actually have to click the Cancel button. Sorry about the "Chicken!" in the status bar. I mean it in the nicest way.

Lesson 22: The Fourth End-of-Chapter Review—Some Jumping Jacks

The scripts and commands in this chapter are real crowd pleasers, so this should be a pretty good end-of-chapter wrap-up.

The following lists the commands you've learned so far. Read them over and start thinking about how you could use them to create something new and functional to use on your pages.

Table 4.1 contains the object-related JavaScript commands we've discussed. In addition, you've been introduced to these other JavaScript concepts:

- The alert(), confirm(), and prompt() methods
- The if/else conditional statement
- These event handlers: onBlur, onChange, onClick, onDblClick, onFocus, onKeyDown, onKeyPress, onKeyUp, onLoad, onMouseDown, onMouseMove, onMouseOut, onMouseOver, onMouseUp, and onSubmit
- The HTML 4.0 flag <SPAN>
- Creating variable names
- Creating a function

Table 4.1   Object-Related JavaScript Commands Demonstrated in Chapters 1–4

Object	Methods	Properties
date	getDate(), getDay(), getHours(), getMinutes(), getMonth(), getSeconds(), getYear()	
document	write()	alinkColor, bgColor, fgColor, linkColor, lastModified, location, referrer, title, vlinkColor
history	go()	length
location		host, hostname, href
navigator		appCodeName, appName, appVersion, userAgent
window	close()	defaultstatus, directories, location, menubar, resizable, self, scrollbars, status, toolbar

Here's a script that puts some of the JavaScript commands to work:

```
<FORM>
<INPUT TYPE="button" VALUE="Jump!"
onClick="document.jj.src='up.gif', window.status='Put me down!'; return true">
<INPUT TYPE="button" VALUE="Stop"
➥ onClick="document.jj.src='down.gif', window.status='Thank you!'">?
</FORM>
<IMG SRC="up.gif" NAME="jj">
```

We're using Andree's wonderful artwork again for this one. You already know how to make the jumping jack images work as an image flip. This script enables your user to decide when the person jumps by clicking form buttons, as you can see in Figure 4.9. Better yet, the little image yells at the person clicking the buttons in the status bar.

 You can try the manual jumping jacks yourself by clicking Lesson Twenty-Two Script's Effect One in your download packet, or see it online at http://www.htmlgoodies.com/JSBook/ lesson22effect.html.

Figure 4.9
Manual jumping jacks.

Deconstructing the Script

What you've got here is basically something that's fun. Stop and think about the uses of changing an image when a click occurs. You could make one of the images a solid color—for example, the same color as the background so that when the user clicks, it appears as if the image comes up out of nowhere.

You could use one of the buttons as a link and have the image change when the user clicks. It would be great for clicks where the user stays at the same page. A link to a file to be downloaded is a good example.

The concept I want to get across here is that images and the items that control them do not have to be in the same HTML flag like the image flips.

As long as you keep the names equal in the hierarchy statements, you can separate the buttons and the images completely, as has been done here.

Let's break it down.

The Form Buttons

The code for the form buttons looks like this:

```
<FORM>
<INPUT TYPE="button" VALUE="Jump!"
onClick="document.jj.src='up.gif', window.status='Put me down!'; return true">
```

```
<INPUT TYPE="button" VALUE="Stop"
➥onClick="document.jj.src='down.gif'; window.status='Thank you!'">?
</FORM>
```

The only reason one `<FORM>` and one `</FORM>` flag are used to make the two buttons is because that allows the buttons to sit on the same line. If separate `<FORM>` and `</FORM>` flags were used for each button, they would have stacked on top of each other.

Changing the Image

Here's the code that creates the image flip:

```
onClick="document.jj.src='up.gif'
```

You should recognize the `onClick` event handler by now, but the hierarchy statement might still be a little new. Let's take it piece by piece, biggest to smallest, left to right:

- `document` is the HTML document the buttons and images sit on.
- `jj` is the name you have assigned to the image command.
- `src` stands for the source of the image.
- After an equal sign, the image name—or URL if necessary—is written in.

The Text in the Status Bar

The text in the status bar is produced at the same time as the click, so you get that `window.status` command right next to the `onClick` event handler, separated by a comma. It looks like this:

```
, window.status='Put me down!'; return true"
```

The `return true` statement ensures the text will act only when the click occurs.

The second button is put together the same way, but is calling for the original image. Thus, it appears you are putting the jumping jacks man down.

The Image

The image code should look pretty familiar:

```
<IMG SRC="up.gif" NAME="jj">
```

The `NAME` attribute is used to connect this image with the buttons that sit just above it. In the hierarchy statement in the buttons, the name `jj` was used. Here you can see how `jj` was connected to the image.

Now, see whether you can think of a few more interesting ways to use the button to image link. There have to be a hundred good things that can come out of my giggling at the little stick figure screaming for me to stop.

Your Assignment

As always, your assignment is to look over the commands you've learned and create something new, interesting, and functional to put on your Web page. But as always, I make a suggestion.

Can you alter the confirm() script in Lesson 21 so that when the user clicks Cancel, he is taken back one page?

That way, the user would go back to where he came from, rather than to the page that contains the script loading. Try it.

 To see a possible answer on your own computer, click Lesson Twenty-Two Assignment in your download packet, or see it online at http://www.htmlgoodies.com/JSBook/ assignment22.html.

Chapter 5

Forms: A Great Way to Interact with Your Users

This chapter contains the following lessons and scripts:

Until this point, you have gathered information from the user mostly through a prompt. This chapter looks at using JavaScript commands along with HTML form flags. Users will be able to enter their data into form fields and send the results along to you or use the form elements as new methods of choosing links.

I should state here that the following forms are all simply mailto: format scripts. We have not gone as far as attaching the output of the script to a CGI, as is commonplace today.

I mention that because Internet Explorer and Netscape Navigator handle mailto: forms differently. Netscape browsers enable you to submit a mailto: form and have the information sent to an e-mail address as a packet. Internet Explorer, on the other hand, most likely opens a new mail message in whatever mail program you're using.

Supposedly, IE 4.0 and better act on forms as Netscape does, but the user must have filled out all the mail preferences for it to work. You can't always be sure of that.

The possibilities of what you can do with JavaScript and HTML forms are endless. Just remember that when using a form to submit information, IE users might have some trouble.

Lesson 23: What Is Written in the Text Box?

When you are dealing with form elements, there are three basic JavaScript events you want to be able to perform:

- Extract the information from the fields so you can use it for other purposes.
- Display information in a form element.
- Send the information to yourself via e-mail.

This lesson deals with the first event. Someone has written something into a form field on your HTML document, and now you want to extract and display back to that person what she wrote in the field.

In this lesson, pay close attention to how the form elements are named and the format of the JavaScript hierarchy statement. Those two elements are, by far, the most important concepts in this lesson—and possibly this chapter.

The sample script is being displayed in full HTML format to show the placement of the elements:

```
<HTML>
<HEAD>
<TITLE>Lesson 23</TITLE>
<SCRIPT LANGUAGE="JavaScript">
function readit()
{
alert("You wrote " + document.myform.thebox.value + " in the box.")
}
</SCRIPT>
</HEAD>
<BODY>
<FORM NAME="myform">
Write something in the box. <INPUT TYPE="text" NAME="thebox"><p>
<INPUT TYPE="button" VALUE="Then Click Here" onClick="readit()">
</FORM>
```

```
</BODY>
</HTML>
```

In Figure 5.1, I've entered my name into the box and clicked the button.

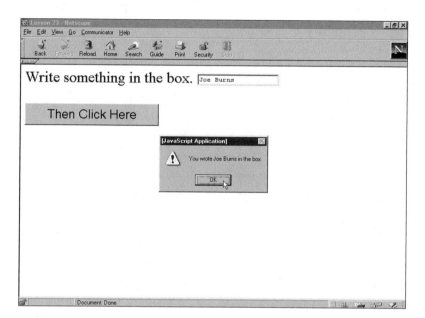

Figure 5.1
Displaying text box data.

 To see the effect on your own computer click Lesson Twenty-Three Script's Effect in your download packet, or see it online at http://www.htmlgoodies.com/JSBook/lesson23effect.html.

Deconstructing the Script

When you start working with forms, the uses of the hierarchy statement and NAME attributes become very important. We will move through this script from top to bottom, often referencing from the function to the form elements.

The Function

The function's purpose in this script is to take the information written to the text box and display it as part of an alert() box. It looks like this:

```
<SCRIPT LANGUAGE="JavaScript">
function readit()
{
alert("You wrote " + document.myform.thebox.value + " in the box.")
```

117

```
    }
  </SCRIPT>
```

The `alert()` format should be familiar. The new coding is the longer, more specific hierarchy statement representing what is written in the box. The hierarchy statement reads like this:

```
document.myform.thebox.value
```

Without a more in-depth explanation, now let's stop and look at the HTML form elements. You need to become familiar with them to understand the hierarchy statement when we discuss it again. The FORM code is as follows:

```
<FORM NAME="myform">
Write something in the box. <INPUT TYPE="text" NAME="thebox"><p>
<INPUT TYPE="button" VALUE="Then Click Here" onClick="readit()">
</FORM>
```

Here is each line of the form and what it means:

- `<FORM NAME="myform">` is the overriding form command that starts the entire form process. The NAME= attribute gives the entire form a name. You must do this even if only one form is on the page—every form must have an overriding name.
- `<INPUT TYPE="text" NAME="thebox">` is the name of the form element you are most concerned with. This is the element where I typed in my name. The NAME= attribute in this case gives a name to the form element.

  Now the form itself has a name, and the form element has a name. It is important that you make that separation in your mind. The form is now named myform, and the specific form element is named thebox.

- `<INPUT TYPE="button" VALUE="Then Click Here" onClick="readit()">` is the button the user clicked to get the alert. The JavaScript in this button is an event handler that calls on the previous function, onClick="readit()".
- `</FORM>` ends the HTML form section of the script.

Back to the Hierarchy Statement

Here is the hierarchy statement from the function, one more time:

```
document.myform.thebox.value
```

Remember that in hierarchy statements, things go from biggest to smallest, left to right. In this case, the hierarchy statement is narrowing down the items on the page until we get to the specific text I typed in the box:

118

- document refers to the HTML document sitting inside the browser window.
- myform is the name of the form on the page. Again, because only one form is on the page, this seems unnecessary, but this is JavaScript. You have to follow the syntax.
- thebox is the name of the text box form element where I typed in my name.
- value is the JavaScript representation of what I typed in the box.

Now here's the entire alert() command from the previous function:

```
alert("You wrote " + document.myform.thebox.value + " in the box.")
```

The format is very similar to what you did in earlier lessons. You gathered information from the user—usually in the form of a prompt—and then returned that value to the page through an alert() or a document.write.

This is exactly the same method, except you are gathering the text written into a text box through a hierarchy statement pointed right at the value.

The more things change, the more they stay the same.

The Entire Process

So, what is happening in this JavaScript?

The function is loaded into the browser's memory, but nothing is actually done with it. It isn't needed until the form button is clicked.

After something is typed into the form box, the user then clicks the button.

The button click triggers the function, which starts to post an alert box. However, if the button isn't clicked, nothing happens. But let's assume the user clicks the button. The text of the alert box calls for the value of a form element, thebox, inside a form, myform, on the current document.

After that data is retrieved, the alert box is posted—end of JavaScript.

Your Assignment

Your assignment should take a little bit of brainpower. Take the preceding script, and add a second text box to it. You'll have to assign it a NAME, of course.

Then, get the alert button to pop up and read Hello *firstname lastname*!

You'll get extra points if you can turn the long hierarchy statements into variable names.

 You can see a possible answer to this assignment on your own computer by clicking Lesson Twenty-Three Assignment in your download packet, or see it online at http://www. htmlgoodies.com/JSBook/assignment23.html.

Lesson 24: Passing Information to the Function

Now that you understand the concept of how to extract the value from a form item, let's play with it a bit. This lesson's script posts a series of alert boxes that tell you the values in the boxes, change the text to all uppercase, and then change it to all lowercase.

After all the alert boxes have finished, text will show up in a third text box thanking the user for watching the show.

The concept is this: If you can take information out of a form element, you can certainly put it back. Here's the code:

```
<SCRIPT LANGUAGE="JavaScript">
function readitagain()
{
var greeting="Hello "

alert(greeting + document.myform.fname.value + " " + document.myform.lname.value)

alert("length of first name " + document.myform.fname.value.length)

alert("First name in ALL CAPS: " + document.myform.fname.value.toUpperCase())

alert("Full name in all lowercase letters: "
➥ + document.myform.fname.value.toLowerCase() + " "
➥ + document.myform.lname.value.toLowerCase())

document.myform.receiver.value= ("Thanks " + document.myform.fname.value + ".")

}
</SCRIPT>
<FORM NAME="myform">
What is your First Name? <INPUT TYPE="text" NAME="fname"><p>
What is your Last Name? <INPUT TYPE="text" NAME="lname"><p>
<INPUT TYPE="button" VALUE="Submit" onClick="readitagain()"><P>
Look Here after Alert Boxes: <INPUT TYPE="text" NAME="receiver"><P>
</FORM>
```

Figure 5.2 shows the script's effect.

 You can try the script for yourself by clicking Lesson Twenty-Four Script's Effect in your download packet, or see it online at `http://www.htmlgoodies.com/JSBook/lesson24effect.html`*.*

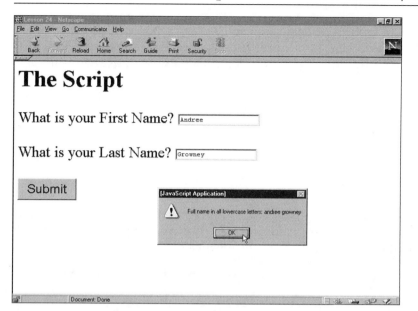

Figure 5.2
This alert box changes a name to lowercase letters.

Deconstructing the Script

Let's start at the bottom and work our way back up the scale of the script. Here are the four form elements first:

```
<FORM NAME="myform">
What is your First Name? <INPUT TYPE="text" NAME="fname"><p>
What is your Last Name? <INPUT TYPE="text" NAME="lname"><p>
<INPUT TYPE="button" VALUE="Submit" onClick="readitagain()"><P>
Look Here after Alert Boxes: <INPUT TYPE="text" NAME="receiver"><P>
</FORM>
```

- The entire form has been named `myform`. That goes first, immediately following `document` in the hierarchy statement.

- The first text box is named `fname`. It contains the first name, which makes sense.

- The second text box is named `lname`. It contains the last name. Again, that's logical.

- The input button is the familiar format. It is used to trigger the earlier function you called `readitagain()`.

- The third text box is named `receiver` because it receives something from the function.

Okay, now you know the players, so let's get to the plays found in the function.

The Alert Boxes

Probably the easiest way to break down this script is to look at each element in the function. You might have already noticed that the function is a long list of alerts that run one right after the other.

Finally, there's a hierarchy statement pointing at something. We'll look at that last. But first, here are the alerts:

```
var greeting="Hello "

alert(greeting + document.myform.fname.value + " " + document.myform.lname.value)
```

The first alert shown in the preceding code uses a variable greeting to place the word *Hello*. Do you find it funny that the variable name is longer than the actual word and space it's representing? Me, too, but all this is to teach, so that's how we did it.

Then, the first and last name are called for from the text boxes using the full hierarchy statements.

No surprises here:

```
alert("length of first name " + document.myform.fname.value.length)
```

Here's something new. The alert posts the length, in letters, or whatever is entered in the first text box.

You might have taken it from the earlier lesson that value was at the end of the hierarchy food chain when it came to forms. That was true for that lesson, but not for all of JavaScript. value has a couple of properties, actually; its length is just one of them. The JavaScript counts the letters, spaces, and any symbols in the value and posts the number it comes up with.

Luckily, in this case, JavaScript does not start counting at 0.

Once again, you see a familiar hierarchy statement with something stuck on the end of it:

```
alert("First name in ALL CAPS: " + document.myform.fname.value.toUpperCase())
```

This statement takes the information from the first name box and changes all the letters to uppercase.

It's done by attaching the toUpperCase() method on the very end. Please note that toUpperCase() is a method, and you need those parentheses at the end.

If you can change letters to uppercase, it follows logically that you can change them to lowercase:

```
alert("Full name in all lowercase letters: "
➡ + document.myform.fname.value.toLowerCase() + " "
➡ + document.myform.lname.value.toLowerCase())
```

It's done by following the same formula shown earlier, but you change the method at the end to toLowerCase(). Again, note the parentheses because toLowerCase() is a method.

Writing to the Text Box

Now you get to the most interesting part of this script. How did we get that text to show up in the text box? Here's the line of code that did it:

```
document.myform.receiver.value= ("Thanks " + document.myform.fname.value + ".")
```

The concept is fairly straightforward. When you use the hierarchy statement document.myform.receiver.value as a return, you get the value of the text box returned.

But if you turn the process around and use the hierarchy statement as a target, as is being done in the previous code, the statement places the value rather than returning it.

That's why the text in the instance pops into the box.

Your Assignment

Okay, smart person! Try to do this one:

- Create a script that has two prompts. The first prompt asks for a name, whereas the second one asks for a home state.
- After the two prompts have been filled in, two text boxes and a button should appear.
- When the user clicks the button, the first text box should read Your name is *name*.
- The second box should read You are from *state*.
- Both effects should occur with one click of the button.

 You can see a possible answer to this assignment on your own computer by clicking Lesson Twenty-Four Assignment in your download packet, or see it online at http://www. htmlgoodies.com/JSBook/assignment24.html.

Lesson 25: Calling Functions with Forms

At face value, this lesson's script might seem rather simple, but its workings are quite new and rather important. Up until now, the functions you created have been stable—they couldn't be altered by the user.

This script allows your users to pass information from form elements to the function itself before the function runs.

The following script again shows the full HTML document. (Forms always begin with <FORM> and end with </FORM>. No surprises here yet, just good old HTML!) Here's the code:

```
<HTML>
<HEAD>
<SCRIPT LANGUAGE="JavaScript">
function newcolor(color)
{
alert("You Chose " + color)
document.bgColor=color
}
</SCRIPT>
</HEAD>
<BODY>
<h3>Select a Background Color</h3>
<FORM>
<INPUT TYPE="button" VALUE="Blue" onClick="newcolor('lightblue')">
<INPUT TYPE="button" VALUE="Pink" onClick="newcolor('pink')">
</FORM>
</BODY>
</HTML>
```

As you can see in Figure 5.3, this script uses form buttons to enable users to choose a background color, either blue or pink.

Figure 5.3
Describing the change in color in a message box.

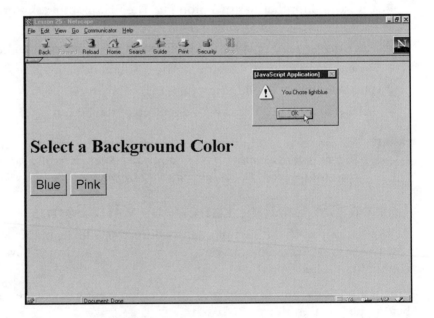

You can try the script for yourself by clicking Lesson Twenty-Five Script's Effect in your download packet, or see it online at http://www.htmlgoodies.com/JSBook/lesson25effect. html.

Literals

We mentioned this term in passing before, but now you can add it to your JavaScript vocabulary. A *literal* is a data value that appears directly in a program and can be a string in double or single quotation marks, a value, or numbers. Even NULL is considered to be a literal. Just remember that a literal is solid; it can't be altered.

String

A *string* is any run of letters or numbers within single or double quotation marks. Therefore, the following section from the sample script defines the literal string lightblue:

```
onClick="newcolor('lightblue')
```

You might now ask, so what? Well, the *so what* is this: When you place text into a format like this, it becomes a literal, and you can't then use the text for something else.

Let's say you set up this script with literals such as document.title and Date(). You know that you want the page title and the full date returned, but JavaScript doesn't see it like that. It sees those commands only as text, just as they're written and not what they would normally represent. Therefore, it displays them as such, and you get Date() written to the page rather than what Date() would normally return.

Go ahead—try it. Drive yourself nuts.

Deconstructing the Script

Here are the script's input items again:

```
function newcolor(color)
{
alert("You chose " + color)
document.bgColor=color
}
<form>
<INPUT TYPE="button" VALUE="blue" onClick="newcolor('lightblue')">
<INPUT TYPE="button" VALUE="Pink" onClick="newcolor('pink')">
</form>
```

Here's the basic concept: You are passing a literal string, `'lightblue'` or `'pink'`, to the function `newcolor(color)`.

Basically, the function is waiting until it is called on and given the information it needs to perform.

Remember that in all functions up until this point, the parentheses were empty. The function had all the parts it needed. Here, however, it does not have the required parts, and it won't until someone clicks a button.

Look again at the form button code. The buttons contain the function format in their `onClick=`, but this time the function has the data it needs: a color command.

Think of it this way: The function line at the top of the script is sitting there with a variable name inside the function instance. Here, it's `color`. When a user triggers the `onClick` in the button, the same function name is used. But this time, there is a real color name in the instance, and it is assigned the variable name it replaced—`color`.

So, how does the JavaScript know that the word *color* in the original function is only a variable name? It doesn't. In fact, the JavaScript never even looked at it. The function text was loaded into memory, but until it's triggered by the button, the function never runs.

That's good to know because we've set up a basic template, `function()`. Every time the user clicks, the function is given a new `function()` header, but the `function()` is run with the new value in the parentheses, `lightblue` or `pink`.

If you set up your `onClicks` to include the same text as the function, when the click is made, the `onClick function()` statement replaces the old function line and assigns the variable name to the new string brought up from the button.

Until now, functions were static. They did what they were written to do. Now you can write functions with a `function()` header and let the user pass along what she wants to happen.

This is a fairly difficult concept to grasp, but look over the script again, and follow its path from the button back up to the top of the function.

Your Assignment

Alter the script in this lesson so that you now have three buttons: blue, yellow, and green. Make the same background effect occur, but lose the alert button and post a text box.

When you click one of the color buttons, the background color should change right away and the text box should read `You Chose color`.

You'll get bonus points if you change all the variable names to new words.

You can see a possible answer to this assignment on your own computer by clicking Lesson Twenty-Five Assignment in your download packet, or see it online at http://www. htmlgoodies.com/JSBook/assignment25.html.

Lesson 26: Form Fields and the `Value` Property

This lesson takes the last one a little further. You'll transfer information into the function again, but this time you'll transfer a string the user enters into a field. The string will then be used to create a hypertext link and send a search to Yahoo!:

```
<SCRIPT LANGUAGE="JavaScript">
function Gofindit()
{
var searchfor = document.formsearch.findthis.value;
var FullSearchUrl =  "http://av.yahoo.com/bin/query?p=" + searchfor ;
location.href = FullSearchUrl;
}
</SCRIPT>
<FORM NAME="formsearch">
Search Yahoo for: <INPUT NAME="findthis" SIZE="40" TYPE="text">
<INPUT TYPE="button" VALUE="Go Find It" onClick="Gofindit()">
</FORM>
```

Figure 5.4 shows the script in action.

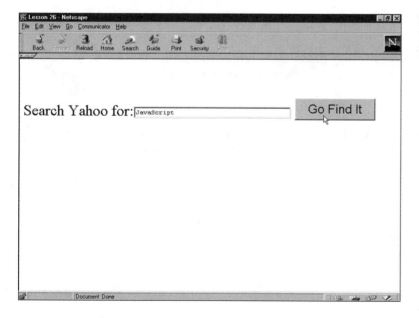

Figure 5.4
The form is ready to search Yahoo!

You can try the script for yourself by clicking Lesson Twenty-Six Script's Effect in your download packet, or see it online at http://www.htmlgoodies.com/JSBook/lesson26effect. html.

Deconstructing the Script

Do you remember that at the very beginning of this chapter I said there were two main reasons for using forms?

The first reason is to accept and manipulate input from your users. The second is to allow information to be sent back to you or around the Internet.

We have arrived at reason number two.

The Function

The function Gofindit() is created in the normal fashion:

```
function Gofindit()
{
var searchfor = document.formsearch.findthis.value;
var FullSearchUrl =  "http://av.yahoo.com/bin/query?p=" + searchfor ;
location.href = FullSearchUrl;
}
```

That's a good title for this one, don't you think?

Three variables are set up. This is a wonderful example of one variable building from the one before it.

The first assigns searchfor to a hierarchy statement representing the text box where the user will enter his keyword. At this point, assuming everything is correct, you should be able to pick out that the name of the form must be formsearch and the name of the text box must be findthis.

Another variable is created: FullSearchUrl. FullSearchUrl is the address to Yahoo's search engine, plus the variable you just created representing the value of the text box.

Finally, location.href is assigned FullSearchUrl, which represents the entire URL and input, a string literal, from the user.

By going to all this trouble, you get the entire URL, plus the text input, down to one word that you could easily put with location.href. It's a very clean form of coding.

The HTML Form Code

Let's move on to the FORM flags. There are two flags this time around. One is a text box that receives a string from the user, and the other is a button that enacts the function.

It looks like this:

```
<FORM NAME="formsearch">
Search Yahoo for: <INPUT NAME="findthis" SIZE="40" TYPE="text">
<INPUT TYPE="button" VALUE="Go Find It" onClick="Gofindit()">
</FORM>
```

The entire form is named `formsearch`. The TEXT box has been named `findthis`. But you knew that without looking.

The form button has the `onClick="Gofindit()"` command that triggers the function. Finally, be sure you have a `</FORM>` command to kill the form. Mission accomplished.

What Happens

The user enters a literal string to the box and clicks the button to begin the search. The function is triggered, and the value is taken from the text box. The value is attached to the Yahoo! URL, which connects and performs a search. The full URL is assigned a variable name and given to a `location.href` command. The information is then sent on its way.

Your Assignment

Alter the script so that it uses a search engine other than Yahoo! Also, change the script so that when the user clicks, an alert pops up that reads `Going to Search....`

You might have to go to a different search engine and look at its code to be able to do this assignment.

 You can see a possible answer to this assignment on your own computer by clicking Lesson Twenty-Six Assignment in your download packet, or see it online at `http://www. htmlgoodies.com/JSBook/assignment26.html`.

Lesson 27: Pull-Down Menu of Links

Ever since the HTML Goodies Web site first started putting up JavaScript examples, this has been one of the most requested scripts. People just seem to love the look of it. It is nice.

This is a simple drop-down box made with form commands. You select the link you want and click the button to complete the link, as you can see in Figure 5.5:

```
<SCRIPT LANGUAGE="javascript">
function LinkUp()
{
var number = document.DropDown.DDlinks.selectedIndex;
location.href = document.DropDown.DDlinks.options[number].value;
}
```

```
</SCRIPT>

<FORM NAME="DropDown">
<SELECT NAME="DDlinks">
<OPTION SELECTED>Choose a Link
<OPTION VALUE="page.html"> Page One
<OPTION VALUE="page2.html"> Page Two
<OPTION VALUE="page3.html"> Page Three
</SELECT>

<INPUT TYPE="BUTTON" VALUE="Click to Go!" onClick="LinkUp()">
</FORM>
```

Figure 5.5
Selecting a link from a drop-down list.

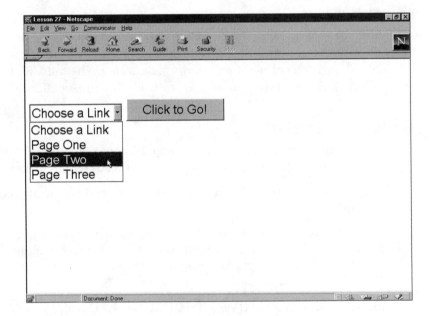

 You can try the script for yourself by clicking Lesson Twenty-Seven Script's Effect in your download packet, or see it online at http://www.htmlgoodies.com/JSBook/ lesson27effect.html.

Deconstructing the Script

Keep two concepts in mind as we go through this deconstruction:

- JavaScript counts everything starting at 0.
- If the HTML form element can't accept a value, you assign it one.

The HTML Form Code

We'll start this from the ground up. Here is the HTML form code:

```
<FORM NAME="DropDown">
<SELECT NAME="DDlinks">
<OPTION SELECTED>Choose a Link
<OPTION VALUE="page.html"> Page One
<OPTION VALUE="page2.html"> Page Two
<OPTION VALUE="page3.html"> Page Three
</SELECT>

<INPUT TYPE="BUTTON" VALUE="Click to Go!" onClick="LinkUp()">
</FORM>
```

Let's get the vitals out of the way first:

- The name of the entire form is DropDown. It is a name I assigned it.

- The name of this SELECT form element is DDlinks. It stands for *drop-down links* and is a name I assigned.

- The first OPTION flag is not part of the Links menu simply because I chose to not make it part of the Links menu. The code <OPTION SELECTED>Choose a Link displays the text Choose a Link on the drop-down box before it has been clicked.

- The next three OPTION statements are links. They have been given VALUEs of page.html, page2.html, and page3.html, respectively. Those are the three links the user can choose from.

  It is important that you see the VALUE is the actual link, and not the text that follows. Because the drop-down link format is not something that accepts data from a viewer, it can't accept a literal string. But it can have one assigned to it, so that's what we did.

- </SELECT> ends the SELECT drop-down menu box.

- The button code should be familiar by now. It is set with an onClick trigger to activate the function, which we'll get to next.

- </FORM> ends the code.

The Function

This is where the magic happens. It might look complicated at first, but if you've read up to this point, you should have no trouble understanding what's here. Except for two commands, you've actually seen it all before. The function is enacted after a choice is made and the user clicks the button triggering it to start. Here's the function:

```
function LinkUp()
{
```

```
var number = document.DropDown.DDlinks.selectedIndex;
location.href = document.DropDown.DDlinks.options[number].value;
}
```

The function is called `LinkUp()`—a name we made up.

First, a variable, `number`, is created that represents the number of a link in the drop-down menu.

If you follow along in the hierarchy statement from left to right, `document` is first. Then comes the name of the form itself, `DropDown`, followed by the name of the form element, `DDlinks`. Last in the statement is that new thing, `selectedIndex`.

selectedIndex

This is the command that makes it possible to turn this drop-down menu into a series of links.

Remember that JavaScript counts everything and starts at 0. That means the four items in this list have all been assigned a number, 0–3, starting with the first `OPTION SELECTED` item, even though it will never come into play.

The `selectedIndex` command enables you to choose one of the items on the list and grab its number. We make it a *selected Index*. Get it?

Setting Up Link Properties

Now that you have a variable set up that represents the number of the item in the drop-down box, you can start setting up the link properties of the JavaScript.

Here's the code that does that:

```
location.href = document.DropDown.DDlinks.options[number].value;
```

You know that `location.href` means a link, but a link to what? It's a link to a specific value from the drop-down menu. You know the values are all URLs, so the purpose of this line is to grab a specific value chosen by the user.

It's done with another hierarchy statement. `document` leads it off, and it is followed by the name of the form itself, the name of the form element, and then the option.

In this case, think of the user's option as a property of an array of strings. This drop-down box is as good an array as any other, so you want an option. But which one? The one the user chooses. You know which one he selects because the option is given the number of the choice through the `number` variable in brackets.

So, if the user selects the last option in the drop-down menu, the user gets the number 3 returned to the `options` property. JavaScript counts everything, starting at 0.

Then the hierarchy gets going and asks for the `value` of the number returned.

The value is a URL, and the process is complete. The hierarchy link returns a specific value, and the link is performed.

It's a very clever method of drawing a link out of the drop-down menu and using it to make a connection.

Wait! I'm Getting an Error

We missed something, didn't we? One of the biggest problems you'll run into when writing a JavaScript that interacts with a user is setting up a contingent for every choice the user makes.

We would love it if all our users would simply select one of the three links and then click. Well, some won't. Some will simply click without selecting a link. They will click while the text `Choose a Link` is still showing. If a user clicks while that text is showing, he'll get an error. Try it yourself.

So, what do you do about it? You set up a plan that will so something if the user clicks that link. The easiest fix is to set a `VALUE` for the first line and make that value the same page. That way, if the person clicks, the page simply reloads.

The code will look like this:

```
<FORM NAME="DropDown">
<SELECT NAME="DDlinks">
<OPTION SELECTED VALUE="lesson27effect.html">Choose a Link
<OPTION VALUE="page.html"> Page One
<OPTION VALUE="page2.html"> Page Two
<OPTION VALUE="page3.html"> Page Three
</SELECT>
```

Later in this book, you'll write code that's a little fancier and does more than simply reload the page.

Your Assignment

This is mostly an assignment to see whether you have the ability to keep everything straight.

Using the previous script, copy and paste it a second time on the page. When your page displays, there should be two drop-down boxes: one of them going to links on your site, and one of them going to links off your site.

You know you're obviously going to need to change the values to change the links, but be careful. You'll need to change a few other things as well.

Remember to put in a VALUE for each of the elements so that no matter what the user selects, he will not get an error.

 You can see a possible answer to this assignment on your own computer by clicking Lesson Twenty-Seven Assignment in your download packet, or see it online at http://www. htmlgoodies.com/JSBook/assignment27.html.

Lesson 28: A Guestbook with All the Bells and Whistles

Whenever you hear someone talking about forms, it's a good bet he wants to use the forms to act as a Guestbook for his site.

Most people can get the mail just fine through basic HTML form code, but then they want more, and the Guestbook in this lesson carries every one of the bells and whistles. After you understand it, you can apply only the parts you like to your own site's Guestbook, or use the whole thing.

This Guestbook is a JavaScript-driven event that opens with two prompts. One asks for the person's name, and the second asks for the person's e-mail address.

The Guestbook page then displays. After the user types in the text box and clicks Submit, a second window pops up thanking him for his e-mail, which is written there for him to see.

When the e-mail arrives in your mailbox, the subject line will read Mail from user's name at user's e-mail address.

You'll be the envy of Web designers everywhere.

It actually takes three different scripts and then some HTML form code to make this technique work:

```
<SCRIPT LANGUAGE="javascript">
var name = prompt("What is your name?","Write It Here")
var email = prompt("What is your email address", "Write It Here")
</SCRIPT>

<SCRIPT LANGUAGE="javascript">
function verify()
{
var OpenWindow=window.open("", "newwin", "height=300,width=300");
OpenWindow.document.write("<HTML>")
OpenWindow.document.write("<TITLE>Thanks for Writing</TITLE>")
```

```
OpenWindow.document.write("<BODY BGCOLOR='ffffcc'>")
OpenWindow.document.write("<CENTER>")
OpenWindow.document.write("Thank you <B>" + name +
➡ "</B> from <B>" +email+ "</B><P>")
OpenWindow.document.write("Your message <P><I>"
➡ + document.gbookForm.maintext.value + "</I><P>")
OpenWindow.document.write("from " + name + " / " +email+ "<P>")
OpenWindow.document.write("will be sent along when you close this window.<p>")
OpenWindow.document.write("<CENTER>")
OpenWindow.document.write("<FORM><INPUT TYPE='button'
➡ VALUE='Close Window'  onClick='self.close()'></FORM>")
OpenWindow.document.write("</CENTER>")
OpenWindow.document.write("</HTML>")
}
</SCRIPT>


<SCRIPT LANGUAGE='javascript'>
document.write("<FORM METHOD='post'
➡ ACTION='mailto:jburns@sunlink.net?Subject=Mail from "
➡ +name+ " at " +email+ "' ENCTYPE='text/plain' NAME='gbookForm'>")
</SCRIPT>

<b>What would you like to tell me?<BR></b>
<TEXTAREA COLS="40"  ROWS="20" NAME="maintext"></TEXTAREA><P>
<INPUT TYPE="submit" VALUE="Send It"  onClick="verify()">
</FORM>
```

As you can see in Figure 5.6, the Guestbook is set up to send the output to Joe Burns. So, if you want to write me, this is the place to do it. It's coming to a mailbox set up just for this Guestbook.

 You can try the script for yourself by clicking Lesson Twenty-Eight Script's Effect in your download packet, or see it online at http://www.htmlgoodies.com/JSBook/ lesson28effect.html.

Deconstructing the Script

There is a lot to this script, so let's talk about it script by script; then at the end, we'll put it all together into one working Guestbook package.

135

JavaScript Goodies

Figure 5.6
Results of clicking the Send It button.

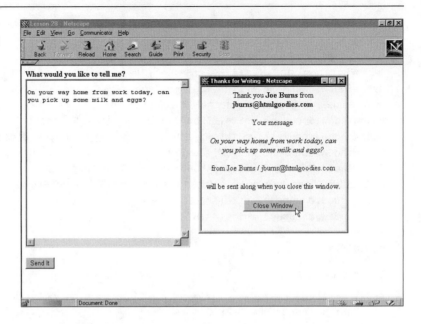

The Prompt Script

We'll start where the Guestbook event starts. The first thing that occurs when the page loads is that a couple of prompts pop up asking for your name and e-mail address:

```
<SCRIPT LANGUAGE="javascript">
var name = prompt("What is your name?","Write It Here")
var email = prompt("What is your email address", "Write It Here")
</SCRIPT>
```

There shouldn't be any surprises here. The prompts are in the traditional format. Just remember that the prompt that asks for the name is assigned the variable name, and the prompt that asks for the e-mail is given the variable email.

Those variable names will become quite important later.

The Verification Window Script

This is the script that creates the smaller window that pops up when the user clicks to submit the Guestbook data:

```
<SCRIPT LANGUAGE="javascript">
function verify()
{
var OpenWindow=window.open("", "newwin", "height=300,width=300");
OpenWindow.document.write("<HTML>")
```

136

```
OpenWindow.document.write("<TITLE>Thanks for Writing</TITLE>")
OpenWindow.document.write("<BODY BGCOLOR='ffffcc'>")
OpenWindow.document.write("<CENTER>")
OpenWindow.document.write("Thank you <B>" + name + "</B> from <B>"
➥ +email+ "</B><P>")
OpenWindow.document.write("Your message <P><I>"
➥ + document.gbookForm.maintext.value + "</I><P>")
OpenWindow.document.write("from " + name + " / " +email+ "<P>")
OpenWindow.document.write("will be sent along when you close this window.<p>")
OpenWindow.document.write("<CENTER>")
OpenWindow.document.write("<FORM><INPUT TYPE='button'
➥ VALUE='Close Window' onClick='self.close()'></FORM>")
OpenWindow.document.write("</CENTER>")
OpenWindow.document.write("</HTML>")
}
</SCRIPT>
```

We used the format from Lesson 20, opening a new window with a function and named the function verify().

The window opens 300 pixels wide and 300 pixels tall. The background is an off-yellow represented by the hex code ffffcc, and the text in the new window is centered.

Now, we get into how all the relevant text was entered into the window. Remember that you assigned the variables name and email to the information from the two prompts in the first script. Here those returned literal strings come into play. The line

```
OpenWindow.document.write("Thank you <B>" + name + "</B> from <B>"
➥ +email+ "</B><P>")
```

writes the text Thank you name from e-mail@address.com to the news window. It's a nice personal touch. Pay close attention to where the double quotation marks fall as well as where the <B> and </B> flags come into play.

In the next line, you make the connection with the HTML form items that are yet to come in this deconstruction:

```
OpenWindow.document.write("Your message <P><I>"
➥ + document.gbookForm.maintext.value + "</I><P>")
```

Notice first the hierarchy statement that takes the information from the <TEXTAREA> box.

It starts with a document; then, it calls for a form named gbookForm, a form element named maintext, and finally that form element's value.

137

When the HTML in the instance is written to the page, you get the text Your Message followed by what the user typed in the <TEXTAREA> box. It's a very clean effect.

The next lines of code again list the user's name and e-mail address using the name and email returns from the prompts. That might look like overkill because those two pieces of information were already posted; we put them in, though, because it gave the appearance that the information was posted as a signature.

The next code creates a traditional button that closes the window, and the last two document.write lines close the HTML document being written to the new window's page.

The <FORM> *Flag Script*

In Chapter 3, "Manipulating Data and the Hierarchy of JavaScript," Lesson 16 talked about using the input from a user to build a line of HTML. The big concern was that the script must be sitting right where the line of HTML code itself will sit.

That's what the following code does. A simple document.write line is used to create the main HTML <FORM> flag:

```
<SCRIPT LANGUAGE='javascript'>
document.write("<FORM METHOD='post'
➥ ACTION='mailto:jburns@sunlink.net?Subject=Mail from "
➥ +name+ " at " +email+ "' ENCTYPE='text/plain' NAME='gbookForm'>")
</SCRIPT>
```

By doing this, you can use the literal returns from prompts to make the ACTION text actually write the user's name and e-mail address.

NOTE

Please note that the previous line is truncated into a couple of lines. That's bad, but the book page just isn't long enough. When you get this to your page, make sure it all goes on one line.

This was the line in the code that took the longest time to build. Look at all the double and single quotation marks. It gets rather hairy, but we stuck to it, error after error, and got the effect.

As you might have guessed from the previous hierarchy statement, the name of this entire form is gbookForm.

The Rest of the FORM *Items*

It's not written here because the main <FORM> flag is in a script by itself, but this is the remainder of the FORM gbookForm:

```
<b>What would you like to tell me?<BR></b>
<TEXTAREA COLS="40"  ROWS="20" NAME="maintext"></TEXTAREA><P>
<INPUT TYPE="submit" VALUE="Send It"  onClick="verify()">
</FORM>
```

The <TEXTAREA> element is named maintext. This is an HTML tip, but remember that when you use a <TEXTAREA> box, it requires an end flag.

Look at the button code. This is quite important. Notice the TYPE is set to submit. You are submitting this form; therefore, if you just wrote in that the type was equal to button, the format would not work. This button not only activates the function verify()—note the onClick=—but it also sends the form.

Wait!

The little window says the button on it sends the mail. I know, but it's part of the illusion of the Guestbook. It was done on purpose. The actual mail-sending dirty work was accomplished by the TYPE="submit" button.

It's done so that the user stops for a moment to read the window. That way the browser is given a spot of downtime during which to send the mail.

Clever, no?

What Is Happening?

The process of the Guestbook is pretty straightforward:

- ◉ The user enters the page and is asked for her name and e-mail address.
- ◉ Those two literal strings are assigned the variables name and email, respectively.
- ◉ The rest of the page loads. The new <FORM> flag, with the user's name and e-mail address, is written to the page.
- ◉ The user types in the <TEXTAREA> box and clicks the Submit button.
- ◉ The function is triggered, and a new page is displayed showing the user what she wrote.

- In the background, the mail is being sent while the user reads the mail and thinks what a fantastic Guestbook you have.

- The mail arrives in your box with a subject line which tells you that you have mail from a specific person with a specific e-mail address.

Your Assignment

This was quite a large, multiscript event, but can you add one more touch to it?

When the user clicks the Send It button, can you make a page that reads Thanks A Lot load into the mail window and still get that new little window?

 You can see a possible answer to this assignment on your own computer by clicking Lesson Twenty-Eight Assignment in your download packet, or see it online at http://www. htmlgoodies.com/JSBook/assignment28.html.

Lesson 29: The Fifth End-of-Chapter Review—Posting Link Descriptions While Users Pass Over

I'm going to list the commands you've learned so far again. Read them over, and start thinking how you could use them to create something new and functional to use on your pages.

Table 5.1 contains the object-related JavaScript commands we've discussed. In addition, you've been introduced to these other JavaScript concepts:

- The alert(), confirm(), and prompt() methods
- The if/else conditional statement
- These event handlers: onBlur, onChange, onClick, onDblClick, onFocus, onKeyDown, onKeyPress, onKeyUp, onLoad, onMouseDown, onMouseMove, onMouseOut, onMouseOver, onMouseUp, and onSubmit
- The HTML 4.0 flag <SPAN>
- Creating variable names
- Creating a function
- HTML form items
- The form item attribute NAME=
- These form item properties: length, value, and selectedIndex
- These form item methods: toLowerCase and toUpperCase()

Table 5.1   Object-Related JavaScript Commands Demonstrated in Chapters 1–5

Object	Methods	Properties
date	getDate(), getDay(), getHours(), getMinutes(), getMonth(), getSeconds(), getYear()	
document	write()	alinkColor, bgColor, fgColor, linkColor, lastModified, location, referrer, title, vlinkColor
history	go()	length
location		host, hostname, href
navigator		appCodeName, appName, appVersion, userAgent
window	close()	defaultstatus, directories, location, menubar, resizable, self, scrollbars, status, toolbar

Here's a script that puts some of the JavaScript commands to work:

```
<TABLE BORDER="0"><TD>

<A HREF="http://www.htmlgoodes.com"
onMouseOver="document.pic1.src='flip1b.gif',
document.PostText.Receive.value='This link points toward the
➥ HTML Goodies Home Page'"
onMouseOut="document.pic1.src='flip1.gif'"><img src="flip1.gif"
➥ NAME="pic1" border="0"></a>

<A HREF="http://www.JavaGoodies.com"
onMouseOver="document.pic2.src='flip1b.gif',
document.PostText.Receive.value='Click here to go to JavaGoodies'"
onMouseOut="document.pic2.src='flip1.gif'"><img src="flip1.gif"
➥ NAME="pic2" border="0"></a>

<A HREF="http://www.internet.com"
onMouseOver="document.pic3.src='flip1b.gif',
document.PostText.Receive.value='This is HTML Goodies parent company.
➥    Go see what they are all about.'"
➥ onMouseOut="document.pic3.src='flip1.gif'">
```

```
<img src="flip1.gif" NAME="pic3" border="0"></a>

</TD>
<TD>

<FORM NAME="PostText">
<TEXTAREA COLS="20" ROWS="20" they go."
➡   NAME="Receive" wrap="virtual"></TEXTAREA>
</FORM>

</TD>
</TABLE>
```

We're going to combine some image flips with form items in this example. There will be three image flip mystery links sitting to the left of a <TEXTAREA> box. When you pass your mouse over the top of each link, a description of where that link points will pop up in the <TEXTAREA> box, as shown in Figure 5.7.

Think about how you would do it, and then read how we did it.

Figure 5.7
Image flips posting text to a form item.

 You can try the script for yourself by clicking Lesson Twenty-Nine Script's Effect in your download packet, or see it online at http://www.htmlgoodies.com/JSBook/ lesson29effect.html.

Deconstructing the Script

Let's take this script apart piece by piece. We'll start with its layout and design. Until now, the layout of the scripts didn't much matter. The output was posted somewhere, and the look didn't come into play.

Well, now the layout does matter. The layout is set so that the buttons are all on the left of the <TEXTAREA> box. We got that look through a simple two-celled TABLE layout:

```
<TABLE BORDER="0">
<TD>
The image flips went in here
</TD><TD>
The <TEXTAREA> box went in here
</TD>
</TABLE>
```

However, let me offer a word of caution. When you use tables and JavaScript, you can run into trouble. It's not enough trouble for me to say never use tables and JavaScript together. But be aware that placing HTML elements and JavaScript into table formats, especially if you put different code sections into different table cells, can cause trouble and throw errors.

If you are trying to combine tables and JavaScript and are getting errors, try eliminating the tables. If the script runs, that was your problem. Find a different layout and design format.

The Form

Let's go a little backwards. We're going to start with the form and the <TEXTAREA> box first. It looks like this:

```
<FORM NAME="PostText">
<TEXTAREA COLS="20" ROWS="20" NAME="Receive" wrap="virtual"></TEXTAREA>
</FORM>
```

The form itself is named PostText, and the <TEXTAREA> box is named Receive.

What I wanted to show was a new HTML attribute that will help with script: WRAP="virtual". The code makes the text that will fall into this box wrap at the end, rather than just running off the right. It's really necessary to get the effect we're shooting for.

Now that you know the elements required to create a hierarchy statement, let's get to the image flips.

The Image Flips

This is where all the magic occurs. Here's the first image flip:

```
<A HREF="http://www.htmlgoodes.com"
onMouseOver="document.pic1.src='flip1b.gif',
document.PostText.Receive.value='This link points toward the
➥ HTML Goodies Home Page'"
onMouseOut="document.pic1.src='flip1.gif'"><img src="flip1.gif"
➥ NAME="pic1" border="0"></a>
```

If you learn this one, the others will fall right into place. They follow the same pattern.

This is a lot of text, but the script will work best if everything shown in the previous code snippet is allowed to stay on one line, one very long line.

The format for the image flips is pretty basic. The onMouseOver points to the document, and then the name of the image space (pic1), and finally the src (flip1b.gif).

But notice that immediately following that, we've placed a comma and then a hierarchy statement pointing at the <TEXTAREA> box. It reads as follows:

```
,document.PostText.Receive.value='This link points toward the
➥ HTML Goodies Home Page'"
```

That is what places the text into the box. The hierarchy statement refers to the document, the form we named PostText, and the form element we named Receive; then it sets its value to 'This link points toward the HTML Goodies Home Page'.

Because the two hierarchy statements were separated by a comma, the onMouseOver triggers them both. The image flips, and the text pops up in the box.

A neat effect indeed.

Image Flips

Just remember that when you are doing multiple image flips on the same page, you must always give each image space a new name and change that name out in each image flip's hierarchy statements.

Your Assignment

At the end of the chapters, your assignment is always to create a new and functional script from what you know to this point, but I always make a suggestion.

Can you create a drop-down box that will answer people's questions? For example, create a drop-down box that people can use to find out what HTML code they should use to get an effect. Make the box read, What is the code for? When the user opens the box, she can choose from bold, italic, and underline.

After the user has made her choice, she will click a button and a text box will show her the code.

Remember that the user could very well click the button even though she has not selected anything. Make the text Pick One Please pop into the text box if that happens.

 You can see a possible answer to this assignment on your own computer by clicking Lesson Twenty-Nine Assignment in your download packet, or see it online at http://www. htmlgoodies.com/JSBook/assignment29.html.

Chapter 6

Mathematics, Random Things, and Loops

This chapter contains the following lessons and scripts:

- Lesson 30: Math Operators
- Lesson 31: Mathematics and Forms
- Lesson 32: Creating Random Numbers with a Date
- Lesson 33: Creating Random Numbers Through Mathematics
- Lesson 34: Producing Random Statements and Images
- Lesson 35: Introduction to `for` Loops
- Lesson 36: Introduction to `while` Loops
- Lesson 37: End-of-Chapter Review—A Browser-Detect Script

From Joe Burns: One of the first things I ever saw done with JavaScript involved entering numbers on a page and having that page perform a mathematical computation using those numbers. The actual example was to figure a 15% tip. I thought that was the greatest thing I had ever seen. In fact, I wrote a script that does the same thing in Lesson 31, later in this chapter.

The purpose of this chapter is to take you back to math class, teach you how to make random events occur, and teach you how to use math to create JavaScript loops. All these events are seldom standalone items. Math typically is used to create a greater event. Case in point: Generating random numbers is nice, but what good is it unless the numbers help you to win the lottery?

Hey! That's a great idea for a script.

But you have to walk before you can run, so let's start with the basics of JavaScript mathematics.

Lesson 30: Math Operators

This page will not only show you how to use numeric values to perform computation with JavaScript, but it will also test your basic math skills. There might be a test later. Its purpose is to introduce you to mathematical operators, something you'll use often. If you have done any type of computer programming before, you should be experiencing déjà vu! If not, don't panic. Using this script, I'll give you an easy introduction:

```
<SCRIPT LANGUAGE="javascript">

var result = 10 * 2 + 1 / 3 - 7
alert ("the answer to 10 * 2 + 1 / 3 - 7   is " +result + ".")

var numsums = 10 + 2
alert("10 + 2 is " + numsums)

var x = 10
alert("ten is " + x)

var y = x * 2
alert("10 * 2 = " + y)

var z = "Hello " + "Good Bye"
alert(z)

</SCRIPT>
```

The script's effect appears in Figure 6.1.

 To see the effect on your own computer, click Lesson Thirty Script's Effect in your download packet, or see it online at http://www.htmlgoodies.com/JSBook/ lesson30effect.html.

The Arithmetic Operators

I think it would be hard to get to this point in the book and not be able to figure this one out pretty quickly. But it's not the makeup of the script that's important. The purpose here is to show you the JavaScript binary operators.

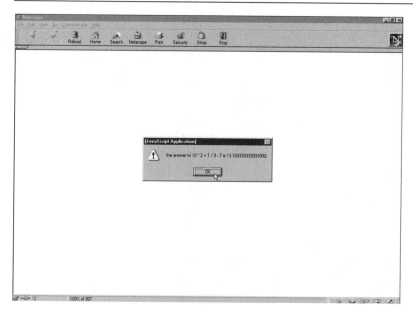

Figure 6.1
Alert box displaying math answers.

That's a fancy way to refer to the addition (+), subtraction (-), multiplication (*), and division (/) symbols.

Percent (%) is also a binary operator. Its technical name is a *modulus operator*. However, it doesn't create percentages. You actually have to create the percentages by hand, dividing one number into the other. The percent sign only returns any number left over, a *remainder*, in a division equation.

For example, the code `10 % 2` would return `0` because 2 divides into 10 evenly. But `10 % 3` would return the number `1`. That's what's left over.

Deconstructing the Super Math Script

Well, maybe it's not super, but it makes its point.

Each two-line piece of code sets up a mathematical equation or number usage and then uses an `alert` method to display the answers. Here's the quick rundown:

```
var result = 10 * 2 + 1 / 3 - 7
alert ("the answer to 10 * 2 + 1 / 3 - 7  is " +result + ".")
```

We tried to create an equation that would use all the traditional binary operators. This is what came out. The answer is 13.333333333.

When you look at the equation, it might seem that the JavaScript is doing the wrong calculation. If you pull out a calculator and follow the format, you might come up with this:

10*2+1 (that equals 21) / 3-7 (that equals -4)

Right? Well, JavaScript doesn't see it that way. Remember, we're dealing with a computer here. That computer just bulls through, left to right, without stopping to see this as a division problem. If you simply read the equation straight through, you'll get the answer the computer did.

10*2 (equals 20) + 1/0 (1 divided) / = 13.333333

So how do you get around the computer bulling through? Parentheses, my friend. Remember that from high school algebra? In math, the stuff in the parentheses is calculated first. Same here. If I wanted to turn this into a division problem with an equation on either side of the slash, it would look like this:

```
var result = (10 * 2 + 1) / (3 - 7)
```

Be careful when you put together mathematical equations in your JavaScript. Make sure the computer is figuring out what you want it to figure out. Always check the math against a calculator before offering your work to the public.

```
var numsums = 10 + 2
alert("10 + 2 is " + numsums)
```

The script sets a numsums variable. Can you see that it's equal to 12 (10+2)? The script transfers that variable to an alert box and displays that 10 + 2 = the variable, or 12:

```
var x = 10
alert("ten is " + x)
```

Another variable, x, is set to equal 10. The alert box then displays that value:

```
var y = x * 2
alert("10 X 2 = " + y)
```

Another variable, y, is set to equal the x variable multiplied by 2. That should be 20, right? It is. The answer is displayed in the alert method:

```
var z = "Hello " + "Good Bye"
alert(z)
```

Finally, the variable z is created, showing you can connect text using the computation symbols. That variable is then displayed using the alert boxes. (That will become very important later.)

The nice thing about the binary operator (+) is that it fulfils two duties. If it is placed between two numbers, it adds them. On the other hand, if it is placed between two strings, it puts them together into a single string, a process known as *concatenation*.

In Terms of Numbers and Binary Operators

Never put quotation marks around numbers. If you do put quotation marks around a number, it becomes a string. That's bad. For example, if you run the equation "3"+4, you will get 34 because the quotation marks made the "3" a string and set the 4 to a string, "4"; the plus sign simply put the two items together rather than adding them. If you want 7 to be the result, don't use any quotation marks so the plus sign sees both the 3 and the 4 as numbers.

Your Assignment

Write a script in which a prompt is used to ask the user for a number between 2 and 10. Then, have that number's square display on the page.

You do know what a square is, right? The number times itself.

 You can see a possible answer to this assignment on your own computer by clicking Lesson Thirty Assignment in your download packet, or see it online at http://www. htmlgoodies.com/JSBook/assignment30.html.

Lesson 31: Mathematics and Forms

After Chapter 5, "Forms: A Great Way to Interact with Your Users," you should be pretty familiar with entering data into form fields and then getting values to show up.

Let's take a look at that tip script that impressed Joe so much. It's basic, but it does the trick:

```
<SCRIPT LANGUAGE="javascript">
function figureItOut()
{
var dinCost = document.meal.dinner.value
var tipCost = dinCost * .15
var bigtipCost = dinCost * .25
document.meal.tip.value = tipCost
document.meal.bigtip.value = bigtipCost
```

```
   }
   </SCRIPT>

   <FORM NAME="meal">

   How much was dinner? $<INPUT TYPE="text" NAME="dinner"><BR>

   <INPUT TYPE="button" VALUE = "OK, Hit Me!" onClick="figureItOut()"><P>

   You should tip: $<INPUT TYPE="text" NAME="tip"><BR>

   A big tipper would leave 25% $<INPUT TYPE="text" NAME="bigtip"><BR>

   </FORM>
```

This script accepts input from the user, manipulates the data, and then posts an answer. Very clever. You can see the script's effect in Figure 6.2.

Figure 6.2
How much should you tip?

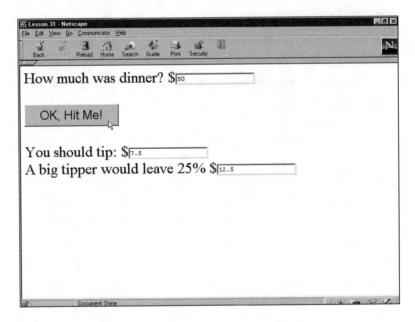

 To see the effect on your own computer, click Lesson Thirty-One Script's Effect in your download packet, or see it online at http://www.htmlgoodies.com/JSBook/lesson31effect.html.

Deconstructing the Script

We'll start with the form elements this time around because they are probably still somewhat fresh in your mind:

```
<FORM NAME="meal">
How much was dinner? $<INPUT TYPE="text" NAME="dinner"><BR>
<INPUT TYPE="button" VALUE = "OK, Hit Me!" onClick="figureItOut()"><P>
You should tip: $<INPUT TYPE="text" NAME="tip"><BR>
A big tipper would leave 25% $<INPUT TYPE="text" NAME="bigtip"><BR>
</FORM>
```

First, note the formal names. The entire form is called `meal`, and the first input text box is called `dinner`. The button is set up to trigger a function called, smartly enough, `figureItOut()`.

The results of the normal 15% tip shows up in a text box called `tip`, and the larger 25% tip result displays in a text box called `bigtip`.

Okay, now you know the players, so let's get to the plays of the script:

```
function figureItOut()
{
var dinCost = document.meal.dinner.value
var tipCost = dinCost * .15
var bigtipCost = dinCost * .25
document.meal.tip.value = tipCost
document.meal.bigtip.value = bigtipCost
}
</SCRIPT>
```

We could have written out the hierarchy statement for the text box that accepted the user's data, but because it was going to be used at least twice, we decided to assign a variable to it. `document.meal.dinner.value` was assigned the variable `dinCost`.

Now that we have that variable, we can start to create some mathematical equations with it.

The variable `tipCost` was assigned to the cost of dinner multiplied by the traditional 15%, or .15, tip. Remember that the `%` sign does not mean percentage—it means the remainder of a multiplication. That's why we use the .15 and .25 rather than 15% and 25%.

The variable `bigtipCost` was assigned to the cost of dinner and multiplied by the better tip amount 25%, or .25.

Now you need to get those values into the correct form items when you click the button. This is done by these lines of code:

```
document.meal.tip.value = tipCost
document.meal.bigtip.value = bigtipCost
```

Notice the hierarchy statement points at the two form elements set up to receive the data. The values assigned to each box are the variable names that represent the equations set up a moment ago.

When you put the whole process together, the function figures the tip amounts, assigns variable names to them, and writes them to the form element.

Nothing to it.

Your Assignment

Until now, you have had it easy with the math. Now let's try something a little harder. Can you create a two–text box form with a button in the middle that changes Celsius degrees to Fahrenheit degrees?

Here's the equation:

```
Fahrenheit = (Celsius X 9/5)+32
```

In case you want to get clever, Fahrenheit to Celsius is done using this formula:

```
(Fahrenheit - 32) X 5/9
```

TIP

You'll do best by taking each section of the equation and making it its own variable. You can then do the equation with text, and you'll be sure the numbers within the parentheses are being figured by themselves.

 You can see a possible answer to this assignment on your own computer by clicking Lesson Thirty-One Assignment in your download packet, or see it online at `http://www.htmlgoodies.com/JSBook/assignment31.html`.

Lesson 32: Creating Random Numbers with a Date

This example introduces you to random numbers. People love random numbers for some reason. Here's our example:

```
<SCRIPT LANGUAGE="JavaScript">
function rand()
{
```

```
var now=new Date()
var num=(now.getSeconds())%9
var numEnd=num+1
alert(numEnd)
}
</SCRIPT>
<FORM>
<INPUT TYPE="button" VALUE="Random Number from 1 to 10" onClick="rand()">
</FORM>
```

You can see the script's effect in Figure 6.3.

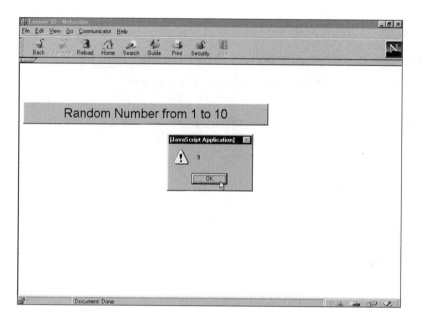

Figure 6.3
Generating a random number.

 To see the effect on your own computer, click Lesson Thirty-Two Script's Effect in your download packet, or see it online at http://www.htmlgoodies.com/JSBook/ lesson32effect.html.

Notice this in the script: The number after the % is the ending number. The following example picks a random number between 1 and 10.

But wait! The number after the % is 9! And there's that % sign we keep mentioning for some reason. Keep reading to find out why.

Deconstructing the Script

We'll start with the function this time:

```
function rand()
{
var now=new Date()
var num=(now.getSeconds())%9
var numEnd=num+1
alert(numEnd)
}
```

It takes a few steps to get the random number.

First, you must set aside a function. We called ours rand().

Next, we set aside a variable that will act as a method called new Date().

Another variable, called num, is set aside. It contains the method getSeconds() to grab a number between 0 and 59.

JavaScript counts everything and starts counting from 0. The number returned from getSeconds() is divided by 9, and a remainder is returned. Remember that the % sign returns only the remainder of a division.

The remainder has one number added to it. That number is assigned the variable name numEnd.

The alert() method then displays the number.

How Does That Give a Random Number?

Here's the concept. 9 divides into 0 through 60 approximately 6.7 times. So, every six and a half seconds or so, a new number can be returned.

Let's say the second returned is 54. 9 divides into 54 with a result of 6. That's a perfect number. There is no remainder. Therefore, the remainder is 0. Remember that the % sign returns only the remainder of a division. 1 is added, and the random number is 1.

Here's another example. The second return is 22. 9 divides into it 2.4 times. 4 is the remainder. 1 is added to it, and you get a random number of 5.

You'll never get a 0 returned as the random number because 1 is always added to the mix.

It's hard to believe it works, but it does.

The Form Items

```
<FORM>
<INPUT TYPE="button" VALUE="Random Number from 1 to 10" onClick="rand()">
</FORM>
```

There's no real need to name the form or the form items in this case. None of the elements comes into play. The button is simply there to act as a trigger to produce the number through the rand() function.

It's a neat trick.

Your Assignment

Do you play the lottery? Let's create a JavaScript that picks the three-digit daily lotto drawing numbers. You have to return three random numbers, 0–9.

Make the numbers appear on an alert box. For good measure, put the text Good Luck! in the status bar.

TIP

If you use getSeconds() for all three number generators, you'll always get all three numbers the same.

 You can see a possible answer to this assignment on your own computer by clicking Lesson Thirty-Two Assignment in your download packet, or see it online at http://www. htmlgoodies.com/JSBook/assignment32.html.

Lesson 33: Creating Random Numbers Through Mathematics

This script enables you to create a random number using JavaScript mathematics statements rather than relying on a date return:

```
<SCRIPT LANGUAGE="javscript">
var num = Math.round(35 * Math.random());
document.write("Random number between 0 and 35: <B>" + num + "</B>.")
</SCRIPT>
```

The script's effect appears in Figure 6.4.

Figure 6.4
Generating a random number through math.

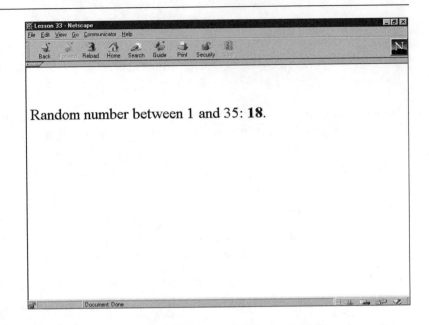

To see the effect on your own computer, click Lesson Thirty-Three Script's Effect in your download packet, or see it online at http://www.htmlgoodies.com/JSBook/lesson33effect.html.

Deconstructing the Script

It might not seem at first that there is a lot to this script, but it is quite useful. First, it's compact, and it always returns a positive integer starting at 0.

In addition, the fact that it runs without a function is also helpful.

Here's the line of code that does the trick:

```
var num = Math.round(35 * Math.random());
```

The line is set up as a variable assigned the name num. That enables you to post the result anywhere on the page.

The mathematics are done through two object.method statements.

Math is an object that alerts the browser that the methods which follow are to be used specifically to produce mathematical results. The Math object itself carries no value; it simply sets the course of the methods that follow to do math.

Math.round() is an object.method statement that takes whatever is in its argument and rounds it to the nearest integer.

`Math.random()` is an object method that returns a number between 0 and 1. Now, that might sound silly at first, but here's another thing about how JavaScript counts. It starts at 0 and goes up. Better than that, JavaScript has the capability to count in milliseconds.

There are actually 999 different responses this `Math.random` can return, from .001 up to .999.

The number 35 is in there because we put it there. It is known as the *upper limit*. The answer returns between 0 and 35 because it is mathematically impossible to go higher than what you're multiplying.

For example, `Math.random()` returns .234. 35 times .234 is 8.19. That rounds down because it's closer to 8 than it is to 9. Therefore, the random number produced is 8.

The line

```
document.write("Random number between 0 and 35: <B>" + num + "</B>.")
```

writes the random number to the document surrounded by text that explains to the user what the number represents.

But what if you do not want 0 as one of the random numbers? Well, you'll have to do two things:

- Add 1 to the output of the random number equation. Remember how we did that in the last lesson?
- Make the upper limit 34. If you leave it at 35, there's every chance that 35 will be the number returned and adding would make the number 36. That's bad.

Isn't this math stuff fun?

The Math Object

The `Math` object is amazing. Table 6.1 shows all the methods that can be attached to it. When using the `Math` object, think of it in the same way as you would the `Date.getSomething()` method. It functions in a similar fashion and returns numbers the same way.

Where you see *argument* in the table, I mean a mathematical equation.

For example, the first `Math.method()`—`Math.abs()`—could be written this way:

```
Math.abs((22*3) / 4)
```

Table 6.1   Math Object Methods

Method	Return Value
`Math.abs(`*argument*`)`	The absolute value of an argument
`Math.acos(`*argument*`)`	The arc cosine of the argument
`Math.asin(`*argument*`)`	The arc sine of the argument
`Math.atan(`*argument*`)`	The arc tangent of the argument
`Math.atan2(`*argument1, argument2*`)`	The angle of polar coordinates x and y
`Math.ceil(`*argument*`)`	The number one larger than or equal to the argument rounded up to the nearest integer
`Math.cos(`*argument*`)`	The cosine of the argument
`Math.exp(`*argument*`)`	A natural logarithm
`Math.floor(`*argument*`)`	The number 1 less than or equal to the argument rounded down to the nearest integer
`Math.E`	Base of natural logarithms, approximately 2.718
`Math.LN2`	Logarithm of 2 (appx: 0.6932), natural logarithm
`Math.LN10`	Logarithm of 10 (appx: 2.3026), natural logarithm
`Math.log`	Base-10 logarithm
`Math.LOG10E`	Base-10 logarithm of E
`Math.LOG2E`	Base-2 logarithm of E
`Math.max(`*arg1,arg2*`)`	The greater of the two arguments
`Math.min(`*arg1,arg2*`)`	The lesser of the two arguments
`Math.PI`	The value of pi, approximately 3.14159
`Math.pow(`*arg1, arg2*`)`	*arg1* raised to the *arg2* power
`Math.random`	A random number between 0 and 1, noninclusive of either 000 or 1
`Math.round(`*value*`)`	Rounds to the nearest integer
`Math.sin(`*argument*`)`	The sine of the argument
`Math.sqrt(`*argument*`)`	The square root of the argument
`Math.SQRT1_2`	The square root of 1/2
`Math.SQRT2`	The square root of 2
`Math.tan(`*argument*`)`	The tangent of the argument

Your Assignment

Set up the preceding script so that a prompt appears and asks the user for the upper limit number. The document should then read `Here is your random number between 1 and` `usersnumber`.

 You can see a possible answer to this assignment on your own computer by clicking Lesson Thirty-Three Assignment in your download packet, or see it online at `http://www.` `htmlgoodies.com/JSBook/assignment33.html`.

Lesson 34: Producing Random Statements and Images

As referenced in Lessons 32 and 33, producing random numbers is good, but by itself, the technique doesn't do much besides post a number. Here we start to take that concept of randomness and apply it to other items. In this case, one of three statements will pop up on the screen—which statement depends on which random number the computer comes up with.

In Lesson 21 in Chapter 4, "Flipping Images and Opening Windows with Mouse Events," you learned the concept of `if` and `else`. Here we use that concept once again to get the desired effect:

```
<SCRIPT LANGUAGE="JavaScript">
var0="An Apple A Day"
var1="A Stitch in Time"
var2="Bird in the Hand"
now=new Date()
num=(now.getSeconds() )%3
document.write("Random Number: "        + num + "<br>")
if (num == 0)
{cliche=var0}
if (num == 1)
{cliche=var1}
if (num == 2)
{cliche=var2}
document.write(cliche)
</SCRIPT>
<p>....as I always say.
```

You can see the script's effect in Figure 6.5.

 To see the effect on your own computer, click Lesson Thirty-Four Script's Effect in your download packet, or see it online at `http://www.htmlgoodies.com/JSBook/lesson34effect.` `html`.

Figure 6.5
Random statement.

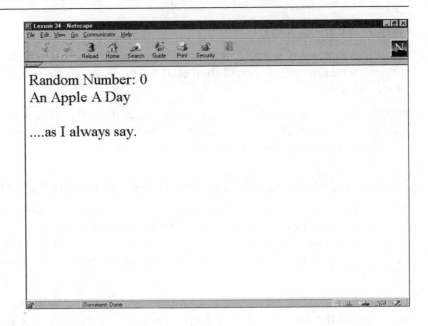

Deconstructing the Script

This one reads very nicely from the top down. Here we start by giving three lines of text three variable names var0 through var2:

```
var0="Apple a Day";
var1="A Stitch in Time";
var2="Bird in the Hand";
```

We could have started with 1, but that would have required setting the random number generator code to add 1. It's not worth the concern, so we're just starting with 0. Moving along:

```
now=new Date()
num=(now.getSeconds() )%3
```

Next, the script uses the two-line date code to draw a random number between 0 and 2. Note the number 3 after the % sign. Remember that means the numbers 0, 1, and 2 could come up.

The code has assigned the variable name now to the new date object and the variable num the result of the random number code.

Finally, this line writes the random number to the page through a document.write statement:

```
document.write("Random Number: "+ num + "<br>")
```

Getting the Random Statement

Now, let's look at the second section of the JavaScript:

```
if (num == 0)
        {cliche=var0}
if (num == 1)
        {cliche=var1}
if (num == 2)
        {cliche=var2}
document.write(cliche)
```

The code that assigned the variable and chose a random number is now used to choose one of these three statements. Let's take a look at just the first two lines of code:

```
if (num == 0)
        {cliche=var0}
```

This is a statement using the `if` method. Remember from Lesson 21 that any statement that follows `if` must be sitting inside parentheses.

Those two lines mean this: "If the number, `num`, created by the random number code is 0, set `cliche` equal to variable `var0`."

Notice the `cliche=` statement is within braces (`{}`). The reason is that it's actually a function of the `if` method.

But you remembered that from Lesson 21.

Double and Single Equal Signs

You might have caught this already, but it's very important, so we'll drive the point home. In JavaScript, a double equal sign actually means *is equal to*.

A single equal sign simply acts as the verb *is*. Remember that you use a single equal sign in assigning variable names. Think of that as meaning *is*. But, if you want to make the statement that something *is equal to* in JavaScript, you use the double equal signs.

Yes, we know it sounds backward, but that's the way it is.

We keep it straight by thinking that a double (`==`) means *is equal to*, and a single (`=`) means *is*.

Back to the Deconstruction

The code then sets two more cliché numbers to `var1` and `var2`, depending on whether 1 or 2 is chosen:

```
if (num == 1)
        {cliche=var1}
```

163

```
if (num == 2)
        {cliche=var2}
document.write(cliche)
```

Finally, a `document.write` statement is used to write the cliché to the page. Because there is no text surrounding `cliche`, no plus signs are necessary.

What's Happening?

The process is quite linear. First, three variable names are set, attaching three text strings to the variables `var0` through `var2`.

Next, a random number is chosen and written to the page.

Then, that number is looked at through a series of `if` statements. If the first statement isn't true, `num` does not equal 0, and the next `if` statement is looked at. If that statement isn't true, the script goes on to the next.

One of those statements will be true because only 0, 1, or 2 will be returned from the random number code.

Why Don't You Use an `else` with Your `if`?

It isn't necessary. One of those `if` statements will be true. You could just as easily have written this so that the last `if` statement was an `else`. It would have worked just the same way, but again, it's not necessary. Three `ifs` will do just fine.

Your Assignment

 We have three pictures for you at

- http://www.htmlgoodies.com/JSBook/pic1.gif
- http://www.htmlgoodies.com/JSBook/pic2.gif
- http://www.htmlgoodies.com/JSBook/pic3.gif

Modify this JavaScript program to display a random picture rather than text. Make the text under the image read `describes my mood today`.

 You can see a possible answer to this assignment on your own computer by clicking Lesson Thirty-Four Assignment in your download packet, or see it online at http://www. htmlgoodies.com/JSBook/assignment34.html.

Lesson 35: Introduction to `for` Loops

All programming languages have a branching method. The branching method in JavaScript is `if`, which we just looked at. It allows you to say, "If this is that, execute these statements."

In addition, all programming languages also have looping techniques. *Looping* is a fancy way of saying, "Run the script again and again, rather than just once."

JavaScript has two looping methods: for loops and while loops.

In general, you use for loops when you know how many times you want to perform a loop. In contrast, you use while loops when you are not sure how many times you want to perform a loop.

That probably didn't make a whole lot of sense, so let's get right to an example. We'll start with a for loop because we know how many times we want this script to loop (the next lesson discusses while loops):

```
We'll now count from one to five:
<script language="JavaScript">
for (i=1; i<=5; i=i+1)
{
document.write(i + "<BR>");
}
</SCRIPT>
...and we're done
```

The script's effect appears in Figure 6.6.

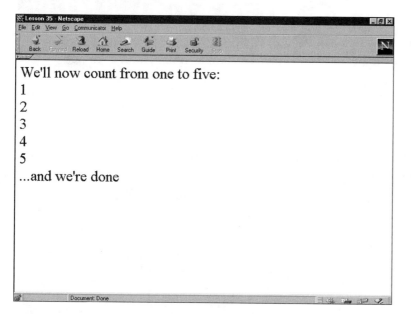

Figure 6.6
Results of a for *loop.*

 To see the effect on your own computer, click Lesson Thirty-Five Script's Effect in your download packet, or see it online at http://www.htmlgoodies.com/JSBook/ lesson35example.html.

Deconstructing the Script

First, look at how short this script is. It's a nice break, don't you think?

If you haven't noticed, the `for` statement is seen as a function. See the braces?

Let's look at the syntax of a `for` statement:

```
for(i=1; i<=5; i=i+1)
```

There are three parts separated by semicolons. We'll take each part in order:

```
i=1
```

This sets the starting value of the variable used to control the loop. In this case it's set to 1, but it could be set to 10 or 100. Think of it simply as a starting point for the loop. That starting point has now been assigned the variable i:

```
i <= 5
```

This is the condition controlling the number of times the loop will be repeated. In this example, the loop will be repeated while i is less than or equal to 5.

TIP

You're probably familiar with that less than sign from middle-school math. I was always able to keep the greater than and less than signs apart by thinking of it as an alligator's mouth. The alligator always wants to bite the biggest number. It's a good tip, compliments of Miss Scovern, my sixth-grade math teacher:

```
i=i+1
```

This defines the increment value. Every time the loop is run, the program adds 1 to i. The program can add any number you want; we just want it to add 1.

Finally, a `document.write` statement prints the number. Notice the `<BR>`. That makes each of the numbers break to the next line. You could just as easily have the numbers all in a row separated by commas, by just altering that section of text that appears after each number.

This JavaScript is triggered, or looped, five times. Therefore, it produces the numbers 1–5. We could have it count to 1,000,000 just as easily as 5, but that would take up too much Web page space.

Your Assignment

This is a great, and not so difficult, effect. You're going to use this for loop as a delay.

Write an HTML document that displays Counting Now with a white background. Then, use JavaScript to count to 10,000. Yes, that is 10,000. Do not use commas in for statements; otherwise, you'll get errors!

At the point the script is done counting, the background color should change to yellow, and an alert box should pop up that reads done.

Do not have the numbers print to the page. You do not want them to be seen because they are only there to count.

TIP

You might want to try writing the script setting the number to 10 rather than 10,000 to start with. You don't want to get stuck in a 10,000-number loop.

 You can see a possible answer to this assignment on your own computer by clicking Lesson Thirty-Five Assignment in your download packet, or see it online at http://www. htmlgoodies.com/JSBook/assignment35.html.

Lesson 36: Introduction to while Loops

This example looks at the while loop. You usually use for loops when you know how many times you want to perform a loop; you use while loops when you are not sure how many times you want to perform a loop.

Look at this code to see how to use variables to count iterations in a loop and to help you get ready for your assignment:

```
<SCRIPT LANGUAGE="JavaScript">
var usernum = prompt("How many times should I write Happy?","0")
loops=usernum
num=1
while (num <= loops)
{
document.write("Happy ")
num=num+1
}
document.write("Birthday")
</SCRIPT>
```

You can see the script's effect in Figures 6.7 and 6.8.

Figure 6.7
Getting information for the
while *loop.*

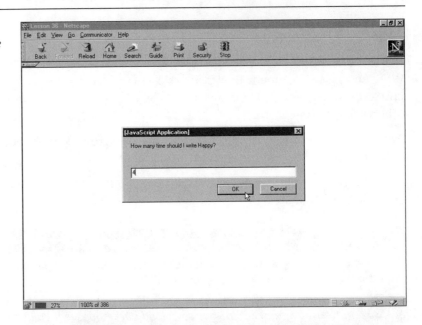

Figure 6.8
Results of a while *loop.*

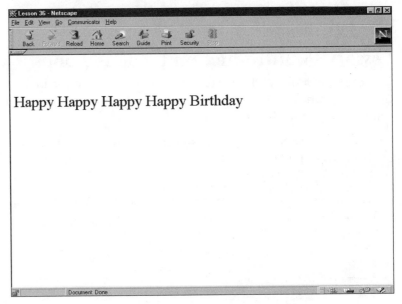

 To see the effect on your own computer, click Lesson Thirty-Six Script's Effect in your down-load packet, or see it online at http://www.htmlgoodies.com/JSBook/lesson36example. html.

The while *Condition*

The while loop is similar to the for statement in syntax. The difference is that in the for loop, you set the beginning index number and increment in the for statement.

The while statement just contains a condition, and you wait for input from the user to get the loop underway.

The script in this example uses the statement while(num <=loops).

The condition is actually just the <=. It stands for *less than or equal to*. Table 6.2 shows the other conditions JavaScript recognizes.

Table 6.2   Conditions JavaScript Recognizes

Condition	What It Means
==	Equal to
!=	Not equal to
<	Less than
>	Greater than
<=	Less than or equal to
>=	Greater than or equal to
?:	Conditional statement

The conditional statement is a pretty fancy item. It assigns a variable name depending on the outcome of one of the other conditions in the table. Here's an example:

```
YearsWithCompany = (ywc >=45) ? "retire" : "notretire"
```

If the person has been with the company equal to or more years than 45, the value retire is attached to it. Conversely, if the years value is less than 45, the notretire variable is attached.

Deconstructing the Script

Here's another short script. We'll whip right through it.

It starts with a basic prompt asking the user for a number. Notice that a 0 appears in the second set of quotation marks. That's done so that if the user simply clicks OK without entering a number, the script will still run without errors. You always need to be conscious of any move the user can make and code for it in the script.

That number is assigned the variable name usernum. The variable loops is set to represent the number the user enters.

The while(num<=loops) statement tells the program to do the loop over and over while the variable num is less than or equal to loops entered by the user. See the use of the <= condition?

It might seem that the variable num just came out of nowhere—basically, it did. We needed a number equal to 0. We could have set num to 0 but didn't need to. JavaScript counts everything and starts counting at 0. num is a new variable, so by default, it gets the value of 0.

If the user enters the number 7, the loop will roll seven times.

Each time the program goes through the loop, it writes Happy plus a space and adds 1 to num. The following code in the function does that:

```
document.write("Happy ")
num=num+1
```

Let's say the user enters the number 7. The loop rolls, and 1 is added to num. The script then rolls again and checks to see whether the new number meets the criteria. This looping continues until the number 7—the number the user entered—is met. After that's done, the looping stops.

The finishing touch is the addition of Birthday at the end through a document.write statement.

So Happy, Happy, Happy, Happy, Happy, Happy, Happy Birthday to you.

Your Assignment

Here's another challenge. Set up this lesson's script so that the prompt asks how long a random number the user wants. Then, take the number the user enters and create a random number that long.

TIP

You can't create the number as a whole; you must create it one number at a time.

 You can see a possible answer to this assignment on your own computer by clicking Lesson Thirty-Six Assignment in your download packet, or see it online at http://www. htmlgoodies.com/JSBook/assignment36.html.

Lesson 37: End-of-Chapter Review—A Browser-Detect Script

It's the end of a chapter, and that means review and do.

Look over the commands you have learned so far, shown in Table 6.3, and think about how you can use them to create useful and functional JavaScripts for your site. You've also been introduced to these JavaScript concepts:

- The `alert()`, `confirm()`, and `prompt()` methods
- The `if/else` conditional statement
- These event handlers: onBlur, onChange, onClick, onDblClick, onFocus, onKeyDown, onKeyPress, onKeyUp, onLoad, onMouseDown, onMouseMove, onMouseOut, onMouseOver, onMouseUp, and onSubmit
- These arithmetic operators: +, -, *, /, and %
- These conditions: ==, !=, <, >, =<, =>, and ?:
- The HTML 4.0 flag `<SPAN>`
- Creating variable names
- Creating a function
- `for` loops
- HTML form items
- The form item attribute `NAME=`
- These form item properties: `length`, `value`, and `selectedIndex`
- These form item methods: `toLowerCase` and `toUpperCase()`
- `while` loops

Table 6.3 Object-Related JavaScript Commands Demonstrated in Chapters 1–6

Object	Methods	Properties
date	getDate(), getDay(), getHours(), getMinutes(), getMonth(), getSeconds(), getYear()	
document	write()	alinkColor, bgColor, fgColor, linkColor, lastModified, location, referrer, title, vlinkColor

Table 6.3   continued

Object	Methods	Properties
history	go()	length
location		host, hostname, href
Math	random(), round()	
navigator		appCodeName, appName, appVersion, userAgent
window	close()	defaultstatus, directories, location, menubar, resizable, self, scrollbars, status, toolbar

Event Handlers

Here's the sample script:

```
<SCRIPT LANGUAGE="javascript">

if (navigator.appName == "Netscape")
{
location.href="nspage.html"
}
else
if (navigator.appName == "Microsoft Internet Explorer")
{
location.href="iepage.html"
}
else
if (navigator.appName != "Netscape")
{
location.href="textpage.html"
}
</SCRIPT>
```

The effect is difficult to show. Take a look, though, and if you don't get what's happening immediately, stop back and we'll describe it to you.

 To see the effect on your own computer, click Lesson Thirty-Six Script's Effect in your download packet, or see it online at http://www.htmlgoodies.com/JSBook/ lesson37effect.html.

This JavaScript is what is known as a browser-detect script. The purpose of the script is to view the user's browser and load a page made specifically for that browser. It's a script that is widely requested from the HTML Goodies site.

The script is set up to load `nspage.html` if the user's browser is Netscape Navigator, and to load `iepage.html` if the user's browser is Internet Explorer.

Finally, a statement acts as a catchall for users who are not running either browser. Those users are sent to `textpage.html`, a text-based version of the other two pages.

Deconstructing the Script

The script is made up of three `if` statements, but they really only check for two things.

The format of the script is set up to test for Netscape Navigator browsers first:

```
if (navigator.appName == "Netscape")
{
location.href="nspage.html"
}
```

The check is performed by asking whether the browser's `appName` is Netscape. If it is, that's the end of the script. The `nspage.html` is loaded, and all's well.

If the user is not running Navigator, however, the second `if` statement comes into play and checks to see whether the browser's `appName` is Internet Explorer. You'll notice an extra `else` in there between the two `if` statements. That's a good habit to get into because it breaks the script into multiple blocks of `if` statements. Moving along with the script ....

If the browser is MSIE, that's the end of the script. The `iepage.html` loads:

```
else
if (navigator.appName == "Microsoft Internet Explorer")
{
location.href="iepage.html"
}
```

> **NOTE**
>
> By the way, we found the return from the `navigator.appName` to use in the script by simply writing a very small script that returned the value to the page. Then, we ran the script in Netscape Navigator and Internet Explorer and wrote the values down.

If the browser is neither of those, the third `if` statement is checked:

```
else
if (navigator.appName != "Netscape")
{
location.href="textpage.html"
}
```

173

Notice again that an `else` is used before the third `if` statement.

The third statement might seem a bit silly. We already know that the browser is not Netscape. If it were, the script would have sent us to the Netscape page.

But that's the beauty of it all. We know the browser is not Netscape because the script would have never gotten this far if the browser were one of the other two.

By writing the code to check whether it is not Netscape, we are guaranteeing that this `if` statement is true; therefore, the browser goes to the `textpage.html`.

Pretty clever, huh?

Placement of the Script

Where you place this script is quite important. It should be on a page all by itself. External text will not display anyway and will probably slow the page's completion.

The user will never see this script. The reaction is usually so fast that all he sees is a fast blank page load, and then up comes the page for his browser.

So, make this a page unto itself and put the bells and whistles on the pages you write for the browsers.

Your Assignment

Your assignment, as it always is at the end of a chapter, is to create something you're proud to put on your Web pages. But we always make a suggestion.

Let's play the lottery, but not that silly three-number lottery; let's play the big six.

Set up a page with 12 small text boxes. Six of the boxes will be for the user to enter her six numbers between 1 and 47.

Then, there should be a button that randomly generates six numbers between 1 and 47.

Finally, a button should be created that pops up an alert box to tell the user whether she wins. (The win button is a bit of a ploy.)

 You can see a possible answer to this assignment on your own computer by clicking Lesson Thirty-Seven Assignment in your download packet, or see it online at http://www. htmlgoodies.com/JSBook/assignment37.html.

Chapter 7

Clocks, Counts, and Scroll Text

This chapter contains the following lessons and scripts:

The purpose of this chapter is to take what you have learned so far and create real-time effects with it. It's nice to be able to post the time the user arrived, but that's a static number. Here, you'll learn to create a digital clock that runs right in the browser window.

You'll also learn to post text depending on what time of day it is. It's a nice way to wish someone a good morning at the right time.

You'll also learn to create counts and countdowns to dates and events.

Finally, you'll learn one of the most popular events available through JavaScript—scrolling text.

Lesson 38: A Running Clock

In this lesson you'll set up a script that returns the hour, minute, and second the user arrives at the page. It's a format you should be quite familiar with at this point.

This lesson takes one more step by setting the script so that it runs again and again, giving the appearance that the clock is advancing on its own.

The script is displayed in full HTML document format to show the placement of each of the parts of code:

```
<HTML>
<HEAD>
<SCRIPT LANGUAGE="javascript">

function RunningTime() {

var RightNow = new Date()
var hr = RightNow.getHours() + 1
var min = RightNow.getMinutes()
var sec = RightNow.getSeconds()

var printIt = "Time: " +hr+ ":" +min+ ":" +sec

document.clock.clockface.value = printIt

var KeepItGoing=setTimeout("RunningTime()","1000")

}
</SCRIPT>
</HEAD>
<body bgcolor="ffffff" onLoad="RunningTime()">

<FORM NAME="clock">
<INPUT TYPE="text" name="clockface">
</FORM>

</body>
</html>
```

You can see the script's effect in Figure 7.1.

 To see the effect on your own computer, click Lesson Thirty-Eight Script's Effect in your download packet, or see it online at http://www.htmlgoodies.com/JSBook/lesson38example. html.

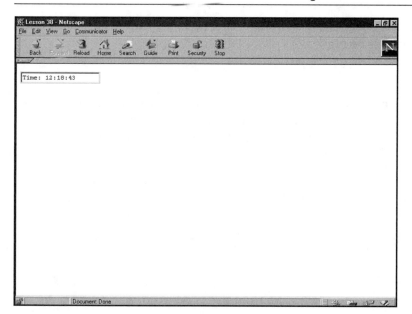

Figure 7.1
The digital clock.

Deconstructing the Script

We'll start from the bottom and then go over the JavaScript:

```
<FORM NAME="clock">
<INPUT TYPE="text" name="clockface">
</FORM>
```

You've seen this before. It's a basic HTML form text box meant to receive and display what is returned from the JavaScript.

The form itself is named clock, and the text box is named clockface.

Next up from the bottom is the onLoad= trigger that starts the script rolling when the page loads into the browser window. You'll find that in the BODY flag.

It would be best to explain what happens before going into each smaller section of the script.

The script is set up to return a basic *hour:minute:second* time format. The returns from the getSomething() methods display in a text box—you could probably figure that much out just by looking at the script.

The magic of this script is in the fact that it appears to be running, but it's not. Here's the deal: The script loads and posts the time to the text box. Then, the script waits one second and runs again. Then, it waits one second and runs again. Then, it waits one second

177

and ... you know the rest. The effect of the script updating every second is that the seconds are counting up and the clock is running.

No Loop!

Let me point out that this is not done with a for or a while loop. If we were to achieve the effect through a loop—and you can get the same effect—we would tie up the page to the point where you couldn't even click any links. The method used in this lesson is controlled; it runs one time every second.

If this were done with a loop, the loop might run 500 times per second or more. It would be all the browser could do to keep updating the page. It wouldn't have time for your users.

If you want a running clock, this is the way to go. Keep reading for the method.

Getting the Time

Now we move on to the script's parts. We'll work from the middle out. This is the code that returns the *hour:minute:second* time format:

```
var RightNow = new Date()
var hr = RightNow.getHours()
var min = RightNow.getMinutes()
var sec = RightNow.getSeconds()
```

The format is quite typical. The Date object is assigned the variable name RightNow. Then, the hour, minute, and second are assigned the variable names hr, min, and sec, respectively.

The Function

The entire script to this point is set up as a function. The format looks like this:

```
function RunningTime()
{
Everything mentioned so far is in here

setTimeout("RunningTime()","1000")
}
```

The function is titled RunningTime(). Each time RunningTime() is triggered, a new value from the Date object is returned and posted to the text box.

So, as mentioned earlier, we need to find a method of getting the function to run, wait a second, and then run again. As you might have already guessed, this is what does the trick:

```
setTimeout("RunningTime()","1000")
```

If you start to really get into writing JavaScript, this format will become very familiar. We're setting up a rest period. The `setTimeout()` method does just what its name implies: It sets a certain amount of time out. In this case, 1000/1000ths of a second, or one second.

The format to implement the `setTimeout()` method is the traditional format you would use to set up a variable.

The method `setTimeout()` is given two parameters: the name of the function, `RunningTime()`, and the number of milliseconds that the timeout should be.

Remember, JavaScript counts everything; it starts counting at 0, and it counts time in milliseconds. Thus, `1000` is equal to one second. If you want the script to count up in five-second intervals, set the number to `5000`.

The effect is that the script runs, waits a second, and then runs the function `RunningTime()`. Then, it waits a second and runs the function `RunningTime()`, and then waits a second ... you know the rest.

Just remember: The `setTimeout()` method command line is inside the function. In fact, it is the last line of code before the second curly brace that finishes off the function.

Placement is important—make sure `setTimeout()` is last.

Your Assignment

For this assignment, see whether you can get the running clock to display in the status bar.

 You can see a possible answer to this assignment on your own computer by clicking Lesson Thirty-Eight Assignment in your download packet, or see it online at `http://www. htmlgoodies.com/JSBook/assignment38.html`.

Lesson 39: A Fancy Digital Clock

Chapter 6, "Mathematics, Random Things, and Loops," discussed the `if` conditional statement. Here we're going to use those `if` conditions to redesign the clock in Lesson 38 so that it reads like a normal digital clock. It will read in normal time using only the hours 1–12 for the hour, rather than 1–24. In addition, we'll get the seconds to read 00 rather than 60 when the clock turns over to the new minute.

We'll even get an AM or PM to pop up at the end.

Here's the script:

```
<HTML>
<HEAD>
<SCRIPT LANGUAGE="javascript">

function RunningTime() {

var RightNow = new Date()

var ampm = RightNow.getHours()
if (ampm > 12)
 {nampm = "PM"}
else
 {nampm = "AM"}

var hr = RightNow.getHours()
if(hr >= 12)
 {nhr = hr -12}
else
 {nhr = hr}

if (hr == 0)
{nhr = "12"}
else
{nhr = nhr}
var min = RightNow.getMinutes()
if (min < 10)
 {nmin = "0" +min}
else
 {nmin = min}

var sec = RightNow.getSeconds()
if (sec < 10)
 {nsec = "0" +sec}
else
 {nsec = sec}

if (nsec >= 60)
 {nnsec = "00"}
else
   {nnsec = nsec}
```

```
var printIt = "Time: " +nhr+ ":" +nmin+ ":" +nnsec+ ":" +nampm

document.clock.clockface.value = printIt

setTimeout("RunningTime()","1000")

}
</SCRIPT>

</HEAD>

<BODY BGCOLOR="ffffff" onLoad="RunningTime()">

<FORM NAME="clock">
<INPUT TYPE="text" name="clockface">
</FORM>

</BODY>
</HTML>
```

The script's effect appears in Figure 7.2.

Figure 7.2
The fancy digital clock.

To see the effect on your own computer, click Lesson Thirty-Nine Script's Effect in your download packet, or see it online at http://www.htmlgoodies.com/JSBook/lesson39example. html.

Deconstructing the Script

By now, we're going to assume you understand the concept of returning the *hour:minute: second* time format by assigning the Date object a variable name and then assigning variables to the getHours(), getMinutes(), and getSeconds() methods to get the correct time.

In this script, that same format is followed; however, after each of the getSomething() methods, a series of if statements is set up to alter the number that is returned.

In addition, a series of if conditional statements is set up to assign text a variable name, depending on what number is being returned.

If this is all getting a little confusing, read on. We're going to take each new section in order.

The Hours

This is the code that returns the hour number and the if statements that alter it:

```
var ampm = RightNow.getHours()
if (ampm >= 12)
 {nampm = "PM"}
else
 {nampm = "AM"}

var hr = RightNow.getHours()
if(hr > 12)
 {nhr = hr -12}
else
 {nhr = hr}

if (hr == 0)
{nhr = "12"}
else
{nhr = nhr}
```

You might notice that the hour is called for twice. But also take note that the variable name in each call for the hour number is different. The reason is because the first small block of code is using the hour to assign a variable name to the text *AM* and *PM*. The second block of code ensures that the hour number returned is in the traditional 12-number format, rather than the 24-hour military time.

We'll look at the first small block of code first:

```
var ampm = RightNow.getHours()
if (ampm >= 12)
 {nampm = "PM"}
else
 {nampm = "AM"}
```

The number returned from the `RightNow.getHours()` `object.method` is assigned the variable `ampm`.

A basic `if/else` statement is set up that means, "If `ampm` is greater than 12, assign the variable `nampm` the text value of *PM*. If not, assign `nampm` the text value of *AM*." We chose the variable `nampm` to represent the new `ampm`. Get it?

Do you see what happened? The concept is that if the hour returned is after noon, the variable `nampm` is assigned `"PM"`; otherwise, it gets `"AM"`.

Now we have this variable in our hip pocket. Later, in a `document.write` statement, we can call for this text value and it will show up on the page. Got it? Good. You have to love this math stuff. Now the second small block of code:

```
var hr = RightNow.getHours()
if(hr > 12)
 {nhr = hr -12}
else
 {nhr = hr}
```

This works like the first block, except it actually alters the number that is returned from the `RightNow.getHours()` method.

The `if/else` reads, "If the variable `hr` is greater than 12, `nhr` (new hr, just like previously) is `hr` minus 12. If not, `nhr` equals `hr`."

The reason for subtracting 12 in the first instance is to lose the 24-hour format. If the script runs at 10 p.m., the number returned is 22. By subtracting 12, we get the more familiar 10.

But what if it's 0 o'clock? That can happen. If you remember, the `getHours()` method returns the numbers 0 (midnight) through 23 (11:00 p.m.). Thus, we run the risk of 0 being returned from midnight through 1:00 a.m. That's not good. So, let's set up yet another `if/else` statement that looks like this:

```
if (hr == 0)
{nhr = "12"}
else
{nhr = nhr}
```

The block of code tests the hour return. If the return is 0, the variable nhr is changed to 12 to represent the time between midnight and 1:00 a.m. Otherwise, we let nhr's value display as returned.

Yes, we could have created a new variable, but why bother? It's only going to come into play one twenty-fourth of the time anyway. We just kept the variable name the same. Besides, we liked nhr.

Now remember, this is set up so that nhr is the correct number—the number we want to post to the page. That's the variable you need to call for in the document.write statements, not hr. That hr variable was just used as a means to an end.

If this seems like a lot of worry over the hour number, it is. In Chapter 5, "Forms: A Great Way to Interact with Your Users," I talked about coding to cover every event that can take place. This is doing just that. We stopped and thought about how many different returns the hour can deliver and then how we could alter the hour return so that it would display correctly.

I think it's one of the more enjoyable parts of programming. Hopefully, you do, too, because we have to do it again for the minute and second returns. Here we go.

The Minutes

This code should be pretty easy for you to figure out after rolling through the hour code. Here it is:

```
var min = RightNow.getMinutes()
if (min < 10)
 {nmin = "0" +min}
else
 {nmin = min}
```

The minute is assigned the variable name min and is called for in the normal fashion. At this point, the number is correct, so there's no need to manipulate it more, right? Well, sharp-eyed readers have probably noticed that when the minute is less than 10, the return is just the single number. The display would look better if we could get a 0 in front when there is just that single digit. So that's what we're going to do.

The if/else statement reads, "If the variable min is less than 10, nmin (new min, remember?) will read 0 followed by the number. If not, make nmin equal to min."

Now we have that variable nmin in the correct form to be used in the clock.

The Seconds

Here's the code that creates the correct second return:

```
var sec = RightNow.getSeconds()
if (sec < 10)
  {nsec = "0" +sec}
else
  {nsec = sec}

if (nsec >= 60)
  {nnsec = "00"}
else
   {nnsec = nsec}
```

The first block of code is identical to what we just did with the minutes. If the second returned is less than 10, it makes the display two digits by writing a 0 in front of the single digit. If not, it lets nsec be equal to sec.

The second block of code comes into play only once a minute, but it's a great look. You know by adding 1 to the end of the RightNow.getSeconds() that the numbers 1–60 will be returned. But 60 is not a normal number to see on a digital clock. Usually, when the number gets to 59, the next number in line is 00. That's what the second block of code is doing. It reads, "If the number returned by nsec is greater than or equal to 60, make nnsec (new, new sec) equal to 00. If not, let nnsec equal nsec."

See how one variable is built off the value assigned to another? That's one of the cornerstones of JavaScript programming. You get a value returned and then manipulate it before displaying it for the viewer.

The Rest of the Script

The rest of the script is identical to the script in Lesson 38. The script gives the impression it is running through the use of the setTimeout() command:

```
setTimeout("RunningTime()","1000")
```

Finally, the output of the script is sent to an HTML form text box for display. It looks like this:

```
<FORM NAME="clock">
<INPUT TYPE="text" name="clockface">
</FORM>
```

It seems like a lot is going on again, and again, and again, and it is. But your computer's pretty smart—it can handle it.

Your Assignment

Rewrite a section of the script so that not only will the output of the script read AM and PM, but it should also read Good Morning between midnight and noon, Good Afternoon between noon and 6 p.m., and Good Evening after 6 p.m.

Tip

Set up the if statements with Good Evening as the result if the first if statement is true.

 You can see a possible answer to this assignment on your own computer by clicking Lesson Thirty-Nine Assignment in your download packet, or see it online at http://www. htmlgoodies.com/JSBook/assignment39.html.

Lesson 40: An Image-Driven Clock

This is a very popular effect. We'll use the template digital clock from Lesson 38 and set up a series of if statements so that the returns are images rather than text:

```
<SCRIPT LANGUAGE="javascript">

var RightNow = new Date()

var hr = RightNow.getHours()

if (hr == 0)
 {hrn = "<IMG SRC=1.gif><IMG SRC=2.gif>"}if (hr == 01)
 {hrn = "<IMG SRC=0.gif><IMG SRC=1.gif>"}
if (hr == 02)
 {hrn = "<IMG SRC=0.gif><IMG SRC=2.gif>"}
if (hr == 03)
 {hrn = "<IMG SRC=0.gif><IMG SRC=3.gif>"}
if (hr == 04)
 {hrn = "<IMG SRC=0.gif><IMG SRC=4.gif>"}
if (hr == 05)
 {hrn = "<IMG SRC=0.gif><IMG SRC=5.gif>"}
if (hr == 06)
 {hrn = "<IMG SRC=0.gif><IMG SRC=6.gif>"}
if (hr == 07)
 {hrn = "<IMG SRC=0.gif><IMG SRC=7.gif>"}
```

```
if (hr == 08)
 {hrn = "<IMG SRC=0.gif><IMG SRC=8.gif>"}
if (hr == 09)
 {hrn = "<IMG SRC=0.gif><IMG SRC=9.gif>"}
if (hr == 10)
 {hrn = "<IMG SRC=1.gif><IMG SRC=0.gif>"}
if (hr == 11)
 {hrn = "<IMG SRC=1.gif><IMG SRC=1.gif>"}
if (hr == 12)
 {hrn = "<IMG SRC=1.gif><IMG SRC=2.gif>"}
if (hr == 13)
 {hrn = "<IMG SRC=0.gif><IMG SRC=1.gif>"}
if (hr == 14)
 {hrn = "<IMG SRC=0.gif><IMG SRC=2.gif>"}
if (hr == 15)
 {hrn = "<IMG SRC=0.gif><IMG SRC=3.gif>"}
if (hr == 16)
 {hrn = "<IMG SRC=0.gif><IMG SRC=4.gif>"}
if (hr == 17)
 {hrn = "<IMG SRC=0.gif><IMG SRC=5.gif>"}
if (hr == 18)
 {hrn = "<IMG SRC=0.gif><IMG SRC=6.gif>"}
if (hr == 19)
 {hrn = "<IMG SRC=0.gif><IMG SRC=7.gif>"}
if (hr == 20)
 {hrn = "<IMG SRC=0.gif><IMG SRC=8.gif>"}
if (hr == 21)
 {hrn = "<IMG SRC=0.gif><IMG SRC=9.gif>"}
if (hr == 22)
 {hrn = "<IMG SRC=1.gif><IMG SRC=0.gif>"}
if (hr == 23)
 {hrn = "<IMG SRC=1.gif><IMG SRC=1.gif>"}


var min = RightNow.getMinutes() + 1

if (min == 01)
 {nmin = "<IMG SRC=0.gif><IMG SRC=1.gif>"}
if (min == 02)
 {nmin = "<IMG SRC=0.gif><IMG SRC=2.gif>"}
if (min == 03)
 {nmin = "<IMG SRC=0.gif><IMG SRC=3.gif>"}
if (min == 04)
```

```
 {nmin = "<IMG SRC=0.gif><IMG SRC=4.gif>"}
if (min == 05)
 {nmin = "<IMG SRC=0.gif><IMG SRC=5.gif>"}
if (min == 06)
 {nmin = "<IMG SRC=0.gif><IMG SRC=6.gif>"}
if (min == 07)
 {nmin = "<IMG SRC=0.gif><IMG SRC=7.gif>"}
if (min == 08)
 {nmin = "<IMG SRC=0.gif><IMG SRC=8.gif>"}
if (min == 09)
 {nmin = "<IMG SRC=0.gif><IMG SRC=9.gif>"}
if (min == 10)
 {nmin = "<IMG SRC=1.gif><IMG SRC=0.gif>"}


if (min == 11)
 {nmin = "<IMG SRC=1.gif><IMG SRC=1.gif>"}
if (min == 12)
 {nmin = "<IMG SRC=1.gif><IMG SRC=2.gif>"}
if (min == 13)
 {nmin = "<IMG SRC=1.gif><IMG SRC=3.gif>"}
if (min == 14)
 {nmin = "<IMG SRC=1.gif><IMG SRC=4.gif>"}
if (min == 15)
 {nmin = "<IMG SRC=1.gif><IMG SRC=5.gif>"}
if (min == 16)
 {nmin = "<IMG SRC=1.gif><IMG SRC=6.gif>"}
if (min == 17)
 {nmin = "<IMG SRC=1.gif><IMG SRC=7.gif>"}
if (min == 18)
 {nmin = "<IMG SRC=1.gif><IMG SRC=8.gif>"}
if (min == 19)
 {nmin = "<IMG SRC=1.gif><IMG SRC=9.gif>"}
if (min == 20)
 {nmin = "<IMG SRC=2.gif><IMG SRC=0.gif>"}

if (min == 21)
 {nmin = "<IMG SRC=2.gif><IMG SRC=1.gif>"}
if (min == 22)
 {nmin = "<IMG SRC=2.gif><IMG SRC=2.gif>"}
if (min == 23)
 {nmin = "<IMG SRC=2.gif><IMG SRC=3.gif>"}
```

```
if (min == 24)
 {nmin = "<IMG SRC=2.gif><IMG SRC=4.gif>"}
if (min == 25)
 {nmin = "<IMG SRC=2.gif><IMG SRC=5.gif>"}
if (min == 26)
 {nmin = "<IMG SRC=2.gif><IMG SRC=6.gif>"}
if (min == 27)
 {nmin = "<IMG SRC=2.gif><IMG SRC=7.gif>"}
if (min == 28)
 {nmin = "<IMG SRC=2.gif><IMG SRC=8.gif>"}
if (min == 29)
 {nmin = "<IMG SRC=2.gif><IMG SRC=9.gif>"}
if (min == 30)
 {nmin = "<IMG SRC=3.gif><IMG SRC=0.gif>"}

if (min == 31)
 {nmin = "<IMG SRC=3.gif><IMG SRC=1.gif>"}
if (min == 32)
 {nmin = "<IMG SRC=3.gif><IMG SRC=2.gif>"}
if (min == 33)
 {nmin = "<IMG SRC=3.gif><IMG SRC=3.gif>"}
if (min == 34)
 {nmin = "<IMG SRC=3.gif><IMG SRC=4.gif>"}
if (min == 35)
 {nmin = "<IMG SRC=3.gif><IMG SRC=5.gif>"}
if (min == 36)
 {nmin = "<IMG SRC=3.gif><IMG SRC=6.gif>"}
if (min == 37)
 {nmin = "<IMG SRC=3.gif><IMG SRC=7.gif>"}
if (min == 38)
 {nmin = "<IMG SRC=3.gif><IMG SRC=8.gif>"}
if (min == 39)
 {nmin = "<IMG SRC=3.gif><IMG SRC=9.gif>"}
if (min == 40)
 {nmin = "<IMG SRC=4.gif><IMG SRC=0.gif>"}

if (min == 41)
 {nmin = "<IMG SRC=4.gif><IMG SRC=1.gif>"}
if (min == 42)
 {nmin = "<IMG SRC=4.gif><IMG SRC=2.gif>"}
if (min == 43)
 {nmin = "<IMG SRC=4.gif><IMG SRC=3.gif>"}
```

```
if (min == 44)
 {nmin = "<IMG SRC=4.gif><IMG SRC=4.gif>"}
if (min == 45)
 {nmin = "<IMG SRC=4.gif><IMG SRC=5.gif>"}
if (min == 46)
 {nmin = "<IMG SRC=4.gif><IMG SRC=6.gif>"}
if (min == 47)
 {nmin = "<IMG SRC=4.gif><IMG SRC=7.gif>"}
if (min == 48)
 {nmin = "<IMG SRC=4.gif><IMG SRC=8.gif>"}
if (min == 49)
 {nmin = "<IMG SRC=4.gif><IMG SRC=9.gif>"}
if (min == 50)
 {nmin = "<IMG SRC=5.gif><IMG SRC=0.gif>"}

if (min == 51)
 {nmin = "<IMG SRC=5.gif><IMG SRC=1.gif>"}
if (min == 52)
 {nmin = "<IMG SRC=5.gif><IMG SRC=2.gif>"}
if (min == 53)
 {nmin = "<IMG SRC=5.gif><IMG SRC=3.gif>"}
if (min == 54)
 {nmin = "<IMG SRC=5.gif><IMG SRC=4.gif>"}
if (min == 55)
 {nmin = "<IMG SRC=5.gif><IMG SRC=5.gif>"}
if (min == 56)
 {nmin = "<IMG SRC=5.gif><IMG SRC=6.gif>"}
if (min == 57)
 {nmin = "<IMG SRC=5.gif><IMG SRC=7.gif>"}
if (min == 58)
 {nmin = "<IMG SRC=5.gif><IMG SRC=8.gif>"}
if (min == 59)
 {nmin = "<IMG SRC=5.gif><IMG SRC=9.gif>"}

document.write(hrn+ "<IMG SRC=sc.gif>" +nmin)
</SCRIPT>
```

You can see the script's effect in Figure 7.3.

 To see the effect on your own computer, click Lesson Forty Script's Effect in your download packet, or see it online at http://www.htmlgoodies.com/JSBook/lesson40example.html.

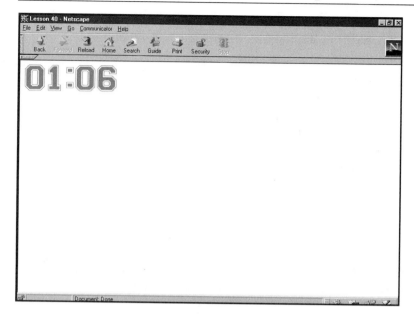

Figure 7.3
Clock displaying images.

Deconstructing the Script

To start with, let's create 11 images. They are the numbers 0–9 and a colon. The 11 images are shown in Figure 7.4.

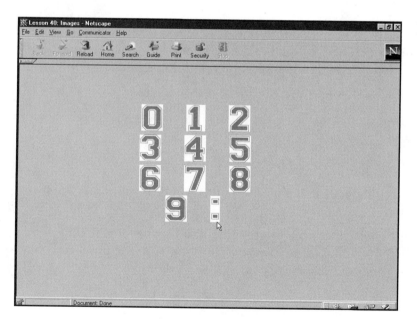

Figure 7.4
The clock images.

If you have grabbed the download packet from the HTML Goodies Web site, you already have the images on your computer. They are named 0.gif through 9.gif and sc.gif for the colon.

If you need to get them online, point your browser to http://www.htmlgoodies.com/JSBook/0.gif through http://www.htmlgoodies.com/JSBook/9.gif, as well as to http://www.htmlgoodies.com/JSBook/sc.gif for the colon.

The script is very long compared to the size of the scripts we've been working with up to this point. But if you take another look, you'll notice that the script is little more than the same *hour:minute* return format used in the previous two lessons with a whole lot of if statements underneath.

The Hour

The hour is returned using the basic RightNow.getHours() object.method statement and is assigned the variable name hr. We are dealing with the military time format here; 0–23 will be returned, so there's no need to add 1 to the getHours return. We'll just allow an if statement for a return of 0.

Then, the if statements start to roll. Here's the first one:

```
if (hr == 0)
  {hrn = "<IMG SRC=1.gif><IMG SRC=2.gif>"}
```

The first if statement deals with a getHours return of 0. That would be midnight. It reads, "If the hr variable, the number returned, is equal to 0, hrn (hour new is what we meant) is equal to these two images: <IMG SRC=1.gif><IMG SRC=2.gif>." That represents midnight.

Now we have the variable hrn set to return the 1 image and the 2 image.

Here's the second if statement that is enacted if the getHours return is equal to 01:

```
if (hr == 01)
  {hrn = "<IMG SRC=0.gif><IMG SRC=1.gif>"}
```

In this if statement, we're dealing with 1:00 a.m. The return will be 01, so we set the two numbers to display as 0 and 1.

We didn't have to use 0 and 1; we could have just returned the 1 image. It would have worked just as well, but we think it looks better to have all numbers in the time set to display double images. It's just personal preference.

The `if` statements roll on until all numbers, 0–23, are represented. Notice we have the 0 and the 1 image set to return for the number 13 so that the clock will display the traditional 1–12 hours.

An `else` statement isn't necessary at the end because we know that the number returned has to be 0–23. One of those `if` statements will come true every time.

The Minutes

Now this was a lot of coding. The concept is exactly the same as the earlier example, except we set 60 different `if` statements, one each for the numbers 1–59.

The code is the same except for one small difference. For the number 60, we set the images 0 and 0 to be returned. Clock readouts usually don't display 60, but rather 00, so we wanted to equal that.

The Display

This might be the shortest display since Lesson 1. The hour variable `hrn` is returned, the colon is placed, and then the minute variable `nmin` is returned. It looks like this:

```
document.write(hrn+ "<IMG SRC=sc.gif>" +nmin)
```

Because the variables are returning text representing four images—two for each—what you get is a series of five images across.

For example, if the time is 5:24, the `document.write` line will read as follows:

```
<IMG SRC=0.gif><IMG SRC=5.gif><IMG SRC=sc.gif>
➥<IMG SRC=2.gif><IMG SRC=4.gif>
```

Get it?

But I Want an Image Clock That Runs

And you shall have it. Contrary to what you might think, the format for getting a clock to run with images is a little more difficult than simply sticking a `setTimeout()` function at the end of this long script. The reason is that we're dealing with image code being written to a page, so it's quite involved.

That said, I do have an image-based clock for you in Script Tip 10, "A Digital Clock with Image Display." It's a bit involved and a little too much to put right here. After you finish the remainder of the lessons, take a look at the script. It's a big one, let me tell you.

Your Assignment

Add some code to the end of this script so that it also displays the seconds.

 You can see a possible answer to this assignment on your own computer by clicking Lesson Forty Assignment in your download packet, or see it online at http://www.htmlgoodies. com/JSBook/assignment40.html.

Lesson 41: Countdown to Date

How many days is it to your birthday, Christmas, the new year? You can figure it out automatically as long as you know how to set a date in the future. After you have that future point, you can perform mathematics to find out the number of days until the date you set.

Of course, you can also get the minutes and seconds, too, but first things first:

```
<SCRIPT LANGUAGE="javascript">

RightNow = new Date()

mil = new Date("January 1, 2005")
mil.setYear = RightNow.getFullYear;
day = (1000*60*60*24)
computeDay = (mil.getTime() - RightNow.getTime()) / day;
DayResult = Math.round(computeDay);

document.write("<center> "+DayResult+" days until
➥ January 1<sup>st</sup>, 2005</center>");

</SCRIPT>
```

The script's effect appears in Figure 7.5.

 To see the effect on your own computer, click Lesson Forty-One Script's Effect in your download packet, or see it online at http://www.htmlgoodies.com/JSBook/ lesson41example.html.

Deconstructing the Script

The concept of the script is pretty simple. We first set a date off in the distance. That's our ending point. We then grab the current date. Now that we have these two points, we can—through mathematics—figure out the number of days, minutes, or seconds from this point to the one we set way off in the future.

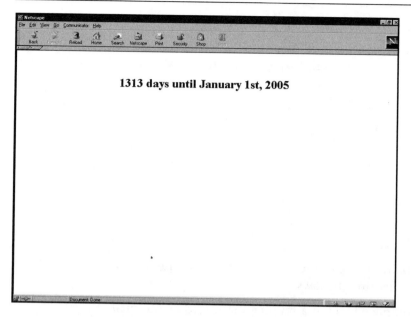

Figure 7.5
Display of days until January 1, 2005.

Here's script from the top down:

```
RightNow = new Date()

mil = new Date("January 1, 2005")
mil.setYear = RightNow.getFullYear;
```

The first three lines of the script set up the Date object and assign it the variable name RightNow.

Next, a new date is assigned to the variable mil because this is a script to figure out the days to the millennium. But take a second look. See how the instances now have a date in the middle, "January 1, 2005"? That's where we set a date off in the distance. Now we have our future point.

Set It!

Next, we permanently set the current year. mil.setYear is a method used to set a year point and not allow it to move.

When you use getSomething(), the number returned is ever-changing, especially the second. By changing the text get to set, we make it permanent. That works for hours, minutes, seconds, days, months, and as shown here, years.

JavaScript Counts by the Thousand

As if you didn't have enough to remember about how JavaScript counts, here's one more fact. 1000 is equal to one second. JavaScript counts time in 1/1000ths of a second (milliseconds).

Remember the `Math.random()` statement we used earlier to return a random number between 000 and 999? Well, that could be done because JavaScript counts in milliseconds.

So we move along.

What's a Day?

This is a day:

```
day = (1000*60*60*24)
```

Because we have set our point in the future, now we need to create some mathematical statements so we can start figuring the days.

1000 equals a second, multiplied by 60 is a minute, multiplied by 60 equals an hour, and multiplied by 24 equals a day. See how that works? Now we have a variable, day, that represents one 24-hour period.

Figuring the Days

Now let's do the math. We'll set a variable name, computeDay, to figure the days between the point we set in the future and the current date. It looks like this:

```
computeDay = (mil.getTime() - RightNow.getTime()) / day;
DayResult = Math.round(computeDay);
```

The variable `mil.getTime()` is new to this book. The method `getTime()` works under the object `Date`, just like any of the other get*Something*() or set*Something*() methods do.

Where `getTime()` differs is that it represents the current date. When this method is run, it grabs all the dates and times at once. This represents our second point in time—the present.

The math is performed by subtracting `rightNow` from our date in the future and dividing it by a day.

The number returned will most likely not be a round number, so we need to round it off using the `Math.round() object.method` statement.

The result is assigned the variable name `DayResult`.

Putting It on the Page

The result is put to the page through a basic `document.write` statement and use some fancy HTML coding to create the superscript *st*:

```
document.write("<center> "+DayResult+" days until
➥ January 1<sup>st</sup>, 2001</center>");
```

The script looks complicated at first, but after you break it down to its smallest parts, you can see it's a simple math problem where we display the results.

Your Assignment

Add some code to our script so it also displays the number of minutes until a set date.

(It's not as simple as multiplying the number of days by 60.)

 You can see a possible answer to this assignment on your own computer by clicking Lesson Forty-One Assignment in your download packet, or see it online at http://www. htmlgoodies.com/JSBook/assignment41.html.

Lesson 42: Scrolling Text

Scrolling, scrolling, scrolling. Keep those letters scrolling.

Setting up scrolling text is a little tricky. It's done by setting a line of text and then moving it a little to the left after a certain amount of time, again and again.

But after you get the scroll to roll, you can get it to scroll in the status bar, an HTML division, an HTML layer, or a text box, like we did here:

```
<HTML>
<HEAD>
<SCRIPT LANGUAGE="JavaScript">

var space = "                                    "
var scr = space + "This text is scrolling along..."

function ScrollAlong()
{

    temp = scr.substring(0,1);
    scr += temp
    scr = scr.substring(1,scr.length);
    document.Scroll.ScrollBox.value = scr.substring(0,55);
    setTimeout("ScrollAlong()",50);
```

```
   }
</SCRIPT>

</HEAD>

<BODY BGCOLOR="#FFFFFF" onLoad="ScrollAlong()">

<FORM NAME="Scroll">
<INPUT TYPE="text" size="50" name="ScrollBox" value="">
</FORM>

</BODY>
</HTML>
```

You can see the script's effect in Figure 7.6.

Figure 7.6
Scroll in text box.

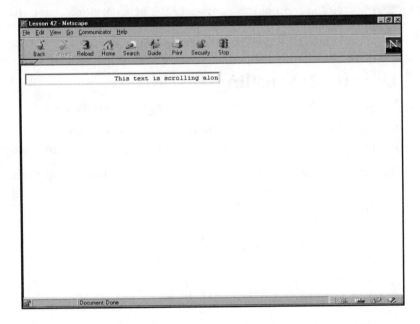

To see the effect on your own computer, click Lesson Forty-Two Script's Effect in your download packet, or see it online at http://www.htmlgoodies.com/JSBook/lesson42example.html.

Deconstructing the Script

The JavaScript that produces the scroll actually sits between the HTML <HEAD> flags. The script that creates the scroll is contained in a function named ScrollAlong() that is triggered by an onLoad= event handler in the <BODY> flag.

The output of the script is displayed in a text box that looks like this:

```
<FORM NAME="Scroll">
<INPUT TYPE="text" size="50" name="ScrollBox" value="">
</FORM>
```

The name of the entire form is Scroll, and the name of the text box that will receive the scrolling text is ScrollBox.

Now that you understand the setup and the names of all the external parts, let's concentrate on the script.

The Text That Scrolls

The first two lines of the script, before the function, set the text that will scroll:

```
var space = "                                                  "
var scr = space + "This text is scrolling along..."
```

If the first line looks a little strange, there's a good reason. It's meant to produce space before the scroll. The variable name space is assigned to around 50 spaces. Then, the variable name scr is assigned to space and the text "This text is scrolling along...".

Now we have a long set of spaces and then text. The reason is aesthetic. If we didn't put a bunch of space before, or after, the scrolling text, one scroll would just bump right into another.

Yes, we could have put all this on one line, but showing it this way was better because it gave us a chance to write this little section telling you to add a bunch of spaces before and after your scrolling text.

The Scrolling Script

This script, surrounded by the function ScrollingAlong(), actually creates the scroll. In reality, nothing is actually scrolling. The script is just taking all those spaces and text and moving them to the left a nudge, again and again. The effect is the appearance that the text is scrolling.

Let's break it down. First, the variable temp is assigned to scr.substring(0,1). scr, you'll remember, represents the text that will scroll along:

```
temp = scr.substring(0,1);
```

The substring(0,1) command is new. It returns a portion, or sub, of a text string depending on an index. The index is contained within the instance, 0 and 1. Basically, this command returns part of the text to the scroll when called on. At this point, it is set to return only one character. This is what actually creates the scroll.

Next, scr is given a new value. Here's the code:

```
scr += temp
```

The operator in the middle is what does the trick. That += operator means to add what is before the operator to what is beyond the operator. So, scr += temp could actually have been written as scr = scr + temp. The += is just a little shorthand we thought you'd like to know.

So what has happened? The substring scr is now the entire text string plus the entire text string one character in. If that happens again and again, the text builds, adding one more character from the string each time to the next letter or space in the string to create the next display. That gives the effect that the start point keeps moving one space to the left, eating away at the substring text. The text keeps displaying one letter to the right and gives the effect that it's actually scrolling out from the right side of the text box.

The script continues to build up again using scr as the variable of choice.

```
scr = scr.substring(1,scr.length);
```

Now, scr is assigned a value that's a substring of itself, working with the two indexes and the text string's length. This might seem a little confusing at this point, but what you are asking for here is a subset of the text string. If you enter a number, only that many letters will be returned. By setting the argument of the subset to the length of the substring, you can be assured the entire string will be returned, rather than just the string, each time missing one letter.

At this point, the code that came before is making the return keep moving one to the left. And then the following line, posting the text in full, is starting at that one space to the left again and again. That'll look like a scroll, right?

```
document.Scroll.ScrollBox.value = scr.substring(0,55);
```

The output of scr.substring is now being sent to the text box through the hierarchy statement document.Scroll.ScrollBox.value. The two numbers in the instance are, again, two arguments. Yet this time, we're not dealing with text, but rather that return space within the text box. This line is set up to provide 55 spaces of visible text in which the text will scroll.

You can prove that to yourself by setting the 55 to 25 and rerunning the script. The space in which the text scrolls will be cut almost in half.

Now you need to make the script keep repeating itself, because if it doesn't, this will be a one-character space scroll. That would be too quick and pretty boring. Here's what does it:

```
setTimeout("ScrollAlong()",50);
```

Here's that `setTimeout()` statement you've come to know and love. This time around, the variable name is `counts`, and it runs the next substring every 50/1000ths of a second.

Set the number higher to go slower, and set it lower to go faster. Just remember that you're not setting a speed here—you're setting the 1/1000ths of a second before the script runs again. The result is that the scroll appears faster or slower.

Scrolls are rough, but after you have the very basics of them, you should be able to scroll with the best of them.

Your Assignment

Alter the code in this lesson so that the text that scrolls is different, the scroll occurs in the status bar, and finally, it scrolls much faster than it is set to scroll now.

 You can see a possible answer to this assignment on your own computer by clicking Lesson Forty-Two Assignment in your download packet, or see it online at http://www.htmlgoodies.com/JSBook/assignment42.html.

Lesson 43: End-of-Chapter Review—Counting to an Event

Up until now, we have either had events that run consistently or figured out set times. Now let's get a countdown to roll in much the same fashion as we got the scroll to roll.

The script in this lesson is set up to count five seconds and then perform an event.

Table 7.1 shows the object-related JavaScript commands you've learned up to now. You've also been introduced to these JavaScript concepts:

- `string` and the `substring()` method
- The `alert()`, `confirm()`, and `prompt()` methods
- The `if/else` conditional statement

- These event handlers: onBlur, onChange, onClick, onDblClick, onFocus, onKeyDown, onKeyPress, onKeyUp, onLoad, onMouseDown, onMouseMove, onMouseOut, onMouseOver, onMouseUp, and onSubmit
- These arithmetic operators: +, -, *, /, and %
- These conditions: ==, !=, <, >, =<, =>, ?:, and +=
- The HTML 4.0 flag <SPAN>
- Creating variable names
- Creating a function
- for loops
- HTML form items
- The form item attribute NAME=
- These form item properties: length, value, and selectedIndex
- These form item methods: toLowerCase and toUpperCase()
- while loops

Table 7.1   Object-Related JavaScript Commands Demonstrated in Chapters 1–7

Object	Methods	Properties
date	getDate(), getDay(), getHours(), getMinutes(), getMonth(), getSeconds(), getTime(), setYear(), setDate(), setDay(), setHours(), setMinutes(), setMonth(), setSeconds()	
document	write()	alinkColor, bgColor, fgColor, linkColor, lastModified, location, referrer, title, vlinkColor
history	go()	length

Table 7.1   continued

Object	Methods	Properties
location		host, hostname, href
Math	random(), round()	
navigator		appCodeName, appName, appVersion, userAgent
window	close(),	defaultstatus, setTimeout() directories, location, menubar, resizable, self, scrollbars, status, toolbar

Here's a script that puts some of these concepts to work:

```
<HTML>
<HEAD>
<TITLE>Lesson 43</TITLE>

<SCRIPT LANGUAGE="JavaScript">

RightNow = new Date();
StartPoint = RightNow.getTime();

function StartTheCount()
{

 var RightNow2 = new Date();
        var CurrentTime = RightNow2.getTime();
        var timeDifference = CurrentTime - StartPoint;
        this.DifferenceInSeconds = timeDifference/1000;
        return(this.DifferenceInSeconds);
}

function TheSeconds()
{
        var SecCounts = StartTheCount();
        var SecCounts1 = " "+SecCounts;
SecCounts1= SecCounts1.substring(0,SecCounts1.indexOf(".")) + " seconds";

if (DifferenceInSeconds >= 6)
 {alert("done")}
else
{
        document.FormCount.CountBox.value = SecCounts1
       window.setTimeout('TheSeconds()',1000);}
```

```
    }
    </SCRIPT>

    </HEAD>

    <BODY BGCOLOR="FFFFFF" onLoad="window.setTimeout('TheSeconds()',1)">

    <FORM NAME="FormCount">
    <INPUT TYPE="text" size=9 NAME="CountBox">
    </FORM>

    </HTML>
```

The script's effect appears in Figure 7.7.

Figure 7.7
Alert box after countdown.

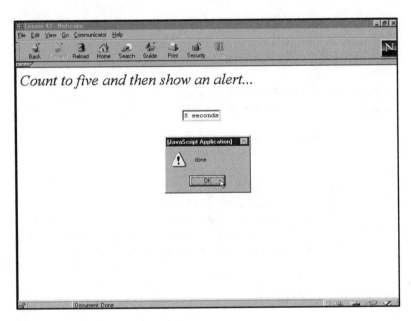

 To see the effect on your own computer, click Lesson Forty-Three Script's Effect in your download packet, or see it online at http://www.htmlgoodies.com/JSBook/ lesson43example.html.

Deconstructing the Script

For this chapter wrap-up, we'll use a rather large effect. The script is made up of objects you already know, but it has a lot of them. It also has two functions.

We'll start again from the bottom:

```
<FORM NAME="FormCount">
<INPUT TYPE="text" size=9 NAME="CountBox">
</FORM>
```

The preceding code creates an HTML form text box that receives the output of the script. The form itself is named `FormCount`, and the box that will receive the value is named `CountBox`. Now you know the names and can start tearing down the script.

The Script

The script begins in a familiar fashion, by assigning the value `RightNow` to the `Date` object:

```
RightNow = new Date();
StartPoint = RightNow.getTime();
```

Because we will be figuring out seconds until an event, we'll need to set a point in time. So, we assigned the variable `StartPoint` to the second in time the script runs—`RightNow.getTime()`.

The First Function

The first function is named `StartTheCount()`, appropriately enough. The code is similar to the code from Lesson 41 that figures the number of days until a set point:

```
function StartTheCount()
{

  var RightNow2 = new Date();
        var CurrentTime = RightNow2.getTime();
        var timeDifference = CurrentTime - StartPoint;
        this.DifferenceInSeconds = timeDifference/1000;
        return(this.DifferenceInSeconds);
}
```

The variable `RightNow2` is assigned to a brand-new `Date` object. Then, the variable `CurrentTime` is assigned to the exact point in time at which the script runs, as returned by `RightNow2.getTime()`.

The time difference in seconds between the `CurrentTime` and `StartPoint` is figured by subtracting one from the other. The answer is then divided by 1000—JavaScript's representation of a second. The result is assigned the variable name `DifferenceInSeconds`.

Now, we take our answer and run the second function.

The Second Function

The second function, named `TheSeconds()`, is actually a couple of events put together. The first event creates the count; the second event watches the numbers roll by and enacts an alert box when the count reaches 6.

The first event looks like this:

```
var SecCounts = StartTheCount()
var SecCounts1 = " "+SecCounts;

SecCounts1= SecCounts1.substring(0,SecCounts1.indexOf(".")) + " seconds";
```

The variable name `SetCount` is assigned to the output of the first function `DifferenceInSeconds`. Obviously, we didn't have to do this, but it seemed a good idea to assign a new name because we were in a whole new function.

The variable `SecCounts1` is assigned to a space plus the results of the first function. This is similar to how the scrolling script was put together, adding space to a value.

`SecCounts1` is then given a value, the substring of itself. A substring returns the greater of the two indexes in its instance. In the preceding code, the two indexes are 0 and the `indexOf()` `SecCounts1`.

Yes, that `indexOf()` is new. That command returns a count of what you point it toward. In this case, it points toward the results of the first script. That means the `indexOf()` starts to count from the point returned by the mathematics in the first function, probably 1 or less than 1.

However, now the substring will not return a letter as in the scroll script; instead it returns the number, and the `indexOf()` begins the count.

But how does it count up? Look at the last line of the second function:

```
window.setTimeout('TheSeconds()',1000);}
```

It's a basic `setTimeout()` method that reruns the function `TheSeconds()` every second. That's why the script counts; it is run again and again and again ....

Stopping the Count

One of the selling points of this script is that it counts up to a certain point and then throws an alert box, or whatever you set it to do.

The count is watched, and then the alert box is enacted by the following code:

```
if (DifferenceInSeconds >= 6)
 {alert("done")}
else
{
document.FormCount.CountBox.value = SecCounts1
window.setTimeout('TheSeconds()',1000);}
}
```

It is a simple `if/else` statement that says, "If the output of the first script, `DifferenceInSeconds`, is greater than or equal to 6, post an alert. If not, continue to post the output of `SecCounts1` to the text box `CountBox` in the form named `FormCount`."

Why Count from the First Function?

Ah, you noticed that. We're not relying on the count from the second function to set off the alert. You see, the second function is just a display—the first function is the one that is really keeping count. That's why we're using the result, `DifferenceInSeconds`, to count for the `if/else` statement.

It's a true count using that number. The count that displays is for show only.

Your Assignment

Set up a greeting for your users. This is a great effect. Get the text `Good Morning`, `Good Afternoon`, or `Good Evening`, to scroll in the status bar. The text should then be followed by the text `Welcome to my page`.

 You can see a possible answer to this assignment on your own computer by clicking Lesson Forty-Three Assignment in your download packet, or see it online at http://www. htmlgoodies.com/JSBook/assignment43.html.

Chapter 8

Arrays

This chapter contains the following lessons and scripts:

One of the staples of any programming language is the ability to create an indexed, ordered list of items for the program to use, manipulate, or display. That indexed list is called an *array*.

JavaScript offers two basic formats for presenting an array. Each works equally well, although after we get into the scripts in this chapter, you'll see how using one format or the other in particular cases is best, simply to keep it all straight in your own mind.

Setting up an array is a little tricky at first. You have to be concerned with the order of the items, whether the items are data or literal strings, and how the data will be used. Plus there's the concern that JavaScript counts everything, and the fact that it starts counting at 0.

But after you grasp the concept of setting up arrays, the possibilities of what you can do with them are endless.

Lesson 44: Two Different Array Formats

Sharp-minded readers might remember that way back in Lesson 15 (see Chapter 3, "Manipulating Data and the Hierarchy of JavaScript") we put together an array. The array was set up to present the day of the week. Here, we set up the exact same array and result—only this time we'll follow a different method of presenting the array.

Both formats are included for explanation purposes. We'll start with the format you haven't seen yet:

```
<SCRIPT LANGUAGE="JavaScript">

var dayName=new Array(7)
dayName[0]="Sunday"
dayName[1]="Monday"
dayName[2]="Tuesday"
dayName[3]="Wednesday"
dayName[4]="Thursday"
dayName[5]="Friday"
dayName[6]="Saturday"

var y=new Date();
var Today = y.getDay()

document.write("Today is "+dayName[Today] + ".");

</SCRIPT>
```

The script's effect appears in Figure 8.1.

 To see the effect on your own computer, click Lesson Forty-Four Script's Effect in your download packet, or see it online at http://www.htmlgoodies.com/JSBook/lesson44example. html.

Deconstructing the Script

Immediately following the <SCRIPT LANGUAGE=javascript> flag is the array that presents the days of the week. It looks like this:

```
var dayName=new Array(7)
dayName[0]="Sunday"
dayName[1]="Monday"
```

```
dayName[2]="Tuesday"
dayName[3]="Wednesday"
dayName[4]="Thursday"
dayName[5]="Friday"
dayName[6]="Saturday"
```

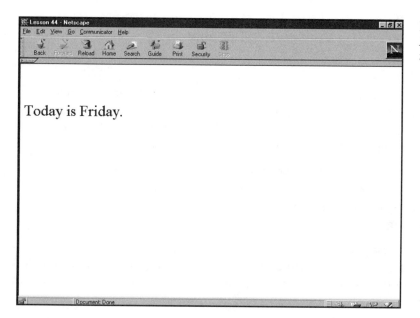

Figure 8.1
Day of the week posted through an array.

Notice the order. Remember that JavaScript counts everything and starts counting at 0. The order of the days in the previous code starts with 0 for Sunday. We chose to put Sunday first because, when you call for the dates of the week using the getDays() method, Sunday returns the number 0, Monday returns 1, and so on. So the order is not up for discussion.

The Format of a New Array

Look at the format of the array. The browser sees the array as a variable name. That's extremely handy because after the variable name is assigned, we can call on the array—and an index number—and just that piece of data or literal string is returned.

The array is assigned the variable name dayName. Notice the format used to set a new array. It is similar to the format used when setting a new Date object. You assign the variable name, specify that the assigned item is new, and then declare it as an array: new Array(7).

The number that appears in the array's instance (the parentheses) is the number of items in the array. Even though the array starts numbering items at 0, you still need to count the first item as a member of the array. Too frequently the author doesn't count the element because the first element in the array is listed as 0. JavaScript counts it, so you must count it, too.

Listing the Array Items

This format of listing array items is good in that the number assigned to the array item is right there for all the world to see. The first item looks like this:

```
dayName[0]="Sunday"
```

dayName is the variable name assigned to the entire array. To set apart an item as an element in the dayName array, you use the variable name and then the number that will be assigned by JavaScript, starting at 0 and simply counting up by 1. The number assigned to the indexed items in the array is referred to as the *index number*.

Notice the number is within square brackets. We always keep that usage straight because square brackets are all that's left. We can't use parentheses because they are used for parameters, and we can't use braces because they are used for enclosing functions. Okay, it's not a good method of remembering, but it sure works for us.

Next, the single equal sign is used to assign a value to the *variable[#]*. In this case, the value is a literal string, Sunday. It is text, nothing more. We do not want to manipulate this data or do anything with it other than display it if needed. Because it is only text, double quotation marks surround it.

Later in this chapter, we create arrays that consist of numbers and answers to a quiz. That numeric data is not to be returned. We want to manipulate it and return something else depending on the outcome; therefore, that numeric data does not appear within quotation marks. Here, though, we're using literal strings. They sit within the double quotation marks. Have we driven that point home?

To complete the array, you work down the line, assigning the same variable name and adding 1 to the number until you reach the end of your list. When all items have been listed, you've finished your array.

More than One in a JavaScript

It is more common to have multiple arrays in a JavaScript than it is to have only one. Your assignment today requires you to put more than one array in the script.

The format for each new script is the same as we've already described. However, each new array must be assigned a new variable name. Then, when you list the items in the array, you must assign them numbers using that new variable name.

However, every new array starts counting at 0.

Here's an example of three small arrays that could all go on the same page:

```
var tree=new Array(3)
tree[0]="Elm"
tree[1]="Pine"
tree[2]="Maple"

var NumberData=new Array(3)
NumberData[0]=15
NumberData[1]=30
NumberData[2]=45

var Cats=new Array(3)
Cats[0]="Fido"
Cats[1]="Chloe"
Cats[2]="Stimpy"
```

All three arrays have different variable names, and each list starts counting at 0. You can include 1,000 arrays on a page as long as you come up with 1,000 different variable names and number them all starting with 0.

Returning from the Array

Now that we have gone over the concept of setting up the array, we need to discuss how to get one of the items returned—and not just any item. Let's get the one we want. Here's the code that calls for the day of the week:

```
var y=new Date();
var Today = y.getDay()

document.write("Today is "+dayName[Today] + ".");
```

The first two lines should look familiar. The new `Date` object is assigned the variable name y. Then, the *object.method* statement `y.getDay()` is assigned the variable name `Today`. When all is said and done, `Today` will return the number representing the day of the week.

The `document.write` statement is where the magic happens. It starts off posting the text `Today is` , leaving the space for appearance. Then, a return is called for. Notice the plus signs. The return is the variable name we assigned to the array. We know that the string to be returned will come from that array, but which one?

Notice that within the square brackets is the output of y.getDay(), Today. That value is a number. If the number returned is 0, today must be Sunday. If the number returned is 4, today must be Thursday.

Whatever the number, the value is placed within the square brackets. That value is then used to go to the array and return the string attached to that number.

And the day of the week appears on the page.

But what about adding 1 to the y.getDate() statement to get the number up to snuff? It's not necessary. You added 1 when you were returning just a number. Because of the 0 being in the mix, you needed to add 1 because everything starts counting at 0. If you didn't, the month, year, hour, and so on would all be off by 1.

Here, there's no need to add 1. In fact, you'll mess things up by doing it. The array allows for 0 to be a correct answer. If you add 1, 0 will never be returned, and it will never get to be Sunday. And we can't have that.

A Different Type of Array

Now, let's look at the script we wrote in Lesson 15. It does the same thing as the script we've just discussed in this lesson, but the arrays are set up differently:

```
<SCRIPT LANGUAGE="JavaScript">
var dayName=new Array("Sunday","Monday","Tuesday",
➥"Wednesday","Thursday","Friday","Saturday")
var y=new Date();
var Today = y.getDay()
document.write("Today is "+dayName[Today] + ".");
</SCRIPT>
```

This is the line that creates the array:

```
var dayName=new Array("Sunday","Monday","Tuesday",
➥"Wednesday","Thursday","Friday","Saturday")
```

The same rules described earlier still apply. The array is assigned a variable name, and the array is noted as being new, just like setting up a Date object.

The difference between the two arrays is that in this format, we're allowing the JavaScript to assign the values for the array items, rather than doing it ourselves. Sunday is 0, Monday gets a 1, Tuesday gets 2, and so on.

The results will be the same, and both scripts will run just fine.

The main difference is that in this format, you can't tell at a glance which number is assigned to each element. I found myself counting more times than I wanted to.

When Do I Use One or the Other?

After writing the scripts in the chapter, we found that the format we use is as much personal preference as anything else. However, the straight-line format worked best when we were comparing two lines of arrays. That way, the arrays were listed on two lines, and we could quickly see which data went with which in the arrays.

When simply returning data based on the user's input, the vertical list is best.

But the choice is yours. Either one works, and both are useful. Just remember that strings are surrounded by double quotation marks, and when you use the all-in-a-row format—such as the script from Lesson 15—the items are separated by a comma and no spaces.

Your Assignment

Add a second array to the script, following the same pattern, to complete the phrase It is day in the month of month.

 You can see a possible answer to this assignment on your own computer by clicking Lesson Forty-Four Assignment in your download packet, or see it online at http://www. htmlgoodies.com/JSBook/assignment44.html.

Lesson 45: Combining User Input with Arrays

Joe is a huge fan of the *Rocky* movies. He wrote this script. The concept is pretty basic: There are five *Rocky* movies, and the user is asked to enter a number (1–5) in a text box and then click a button.

When the button is clicked, the title of the movie and a very brief plot summary appears in two other text boxes.

This script has two arrays. Depending on which number the user enters, that number in both arrays is returned. So here again, both arrays are locked into an order: One number, two arrays, and two returns.

While you read through the list, keep in mind that no *Rocky 0* exists. However, you have to make allowances for those users who try to be funny and enter a goose egg.

Here's the script:

```
<SCRIPT LANGUAGE="javascript">

function Balboa()
```

```
{
var num = document.RockyForm.RockyUser.value

var Movie = new Array(6)
Movie[0]="There was no Rocky 0"
Movie[1]="Rocky"
Movie[2]="Rocky II"
Movie[3]="Rocky III"
Movie[4]="Rocky IV"
Movie[5]="Rocky V"

var Outcome = new Array(6)
Outcome[0]="No Outcome"
Outcome[1]="Rocky Loses"
Outcome[2]="Rocky Wins"
Outcome[3]="Rocky Loses, then Wins"
Outcome[4]="Apollo Dies, Rocky Wins"
Outcome[5]="Rocky Wins Street Brawl"

document.RockyForm.RockyTitle.value=Movie[num]

document.RockyForm.RockyOutcome.value=Outcome[num]

}

</SCRIPT>

<FORM NAME="RockyForm">Enter a Rocky Movie Number (1-5):
<INPUT NAME="RockyUser" TYPE="text" SIZE="2">

<INPUT TYPE="button" Value="Tell Me What Happens"onClick="Balboa()"><P>

You chose: <INPUT NAME="RockyTitle" TYPE="text" SIZE="26"><BR>
The outcome was: <INPUT NAME="RockyOutcome" TYPE="text" SIZE="26">
</FORM>
```

You can see the script's effect in Figure 8.2.

 To see the effect on your own computer, click Lesson Forty-Five Script's Effect in your download packet, or see it online at `http://www.htmlgoodies.com/JSBook/lesson45example.html`*.*

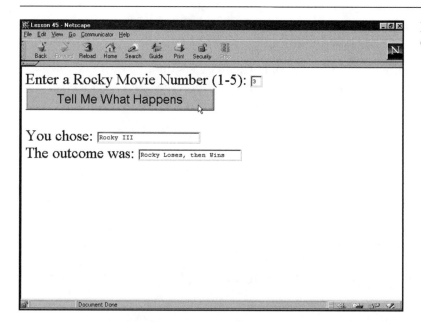

Figure 8.2
Output from user input.

Deconstructing the Script

As is often the case when the script includes a form element, we will start from the bottom:

```
<FORM NAME="RockyForm">Enter a Rocky Movie Number (1-5):
<INPUT NAME="RockyUser" TYPE="text" SIZE="2">

<INPUT TYPE="button" Value="Tell Me What Happens"
➥onClick="Balboa()"><P>

You chose: <INPUT NAME="RockyTitle" TYPE="text" SIZE="26"><BR>
The outcome was: <INPUT NAME="RockyOutcome" TYPE="text" SIZE="26">
</FORM>
```

This HTML form code is constructed to provide a box to accept data, a button to start the process, and then two text boxes to receive the output of the script. Let's take them in order.

The name of the entire form is `RockyForm`.

The box that receives the user's number is named `RockyUser`. Now we know enough to start creating hierarchy statements to represent this box. This particular text box is referred to as `document.RockyForm.RockyUser.value`.

217

Next, a form button reads Tell Me What Happened. When clicked, the button triggers a function named `Balboa()`.

The final two boxes receive the output of the script. The first gets the title of the movie, whose name is `RockyTitle`. The second box receives the brief plot line, whose title is `RockyOutcome`.

Okay, now that we know the players on the field, let's move on to the function.

The Function

The first three lines of the script play a very important role:

```
function Balboa()
{
var num = document.RockyForm.RockyUser.value
```

The first line sets the entire script into a function called `Balboa()`. Remember that from the button?

The second line has the opening brace to start encasing the script. Then, we get to the line that takes the information from the user.

In the preceding code, while identifying the text boxes, we stopped and wrote out the hierarchy of the box that receives the user's number. The line

```
var num = document.RockyForm.RockyUser.value
```

now assigns the variable `num` to whatever the user enters. That's important because later we will use that `num` value to call on a specific array object from both arrays.

The Arrays

Both arrays contain six elements. The titles of the films are assigned the variable name `Movie`, and the brief plot lines are assigned the variable name `Outcome`:

```
var Movie = new Array(6)
Movie[0]="There was no Rocky 0"
Movie[1]="Rocky"
Movie[2]="Rocky II"
Movie[3]="Rocky III"
Movie[4]="Rocky IV"
Movie[5]="Rocky V"

var Outcome = new Array(6)
Outcome[0]="No Outcome"
```

```
Outcome[1]="Rocky Loses"
Outcome[2]="Rocky Wins"
Outcome[3]="Rocky Loses, then Wins"
Outcome[4]="Apollo Dies, Rocky Wins"
Outcome[5]="Rocky Wins Street Brawl"
```

Notice that the two arrays are set in the same order. If you look at array item number three in each, the title and outcome line up. We'll use one number, represented by num, to pull from both arrays. If you don't have the two arrays in the same order, either the title or the outcome will be wrong.

Only five *Rocky* movies exist, but six items are in the array. The reason is that you simply can't ignore that 0 exists. JavaScript loves it; it has to have it. So, you make a point of offering it an array value. In this case, we simply specified that there was no *Rocky 0*, and there was no outcome.

Pulling from the Arrays

The following code enters information into the two text boxes when the button is clicked:

```
document.RockyForm.RockyTitle.value=Movie[num]

document.RockyForm.RockyOutcome.value=Outcome[num]
```

The first line returns the array item represented by the number the user entered from the Movie array.

The second line returns the array item represented by the number the user entered from the Outcome array.

Because both arrays are set up in the same order, the same number returns the same array item number, and the two results match up with each other. That means you won't get the title of *Rocky II* and the outcome of *Rocky IV*.

This type of script can be used to create numerous returns as long as the items being returned are in a set order. This technique could be used to create a listing of presidents, Super Bowl winners, World Series winners, or any other numeric rundown of items. It also could be set up as a great teaching tool.

Your Assignment

Add code to the sample script so that a third text box receives a rating. When the user clicks the button, he should see three things: the new rating, the name of the movie, and what happens.

You can see a possible answer to this assignment on your own computer by clicking Lesson Forty-Five Assignment in your download packet, or see it online at http://www. htmlgoodies.com/JSBook/assignment45.html.

Lesson 46: Random Quotes

One of the biggest selling points of JavaScript is how easily you can set up a random event. Arrays lend themselves to randomization very well.

In this lesson, we'll set up a script that returns one of ten quotes chosen at random.

Remember that even though we're using quotes, anything that you list in the array can be returned in a random fashion: Links, images, or a greeting are some of the more popular items.

So read through this lesson, think about how you could apply this concept of grabbing a random array item, and apply it to your own pages.

Here's the script:

```
<SCRIPT LANGUAGE="JavaScript">

var quote = new Array(10);
quote[0] = " Education is going to college to learn
➥to express your ignorance in scientific terms ";
quote[1] = "Chance favors the prepared mind";
quote[2] = "A stitch in time, saves nine.";
quote[3] = "The only difference between bravery and stupidity is the outcome";
quote[4] = "One should never let a formal education get in the way of learning";
quote[5] = "Happiness is two kinds of ice cream.";
quote[6] = "If you choose not to make a choice, you still have made a
➥decision.";
quote[7] = "Do, or do not. There is no try";
quote[8] = "Reality is merely an illusion, albeit a very persistent one.";
quote[9] = "No one ever said life would be easy.";

var now=new Date()
var num=(now.getSeconds())%10

document.write(quote[num])

</SCRIPT>
```

The script's effect appears in Figure 8.3. Note that we've added the text A Random Quote to the figure. The script does not post that text.

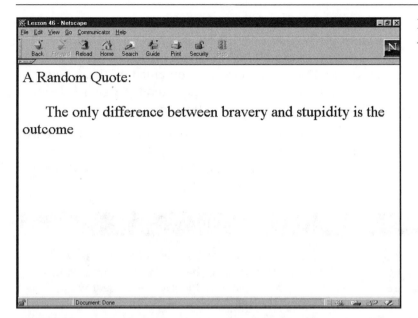

Figure 8.3
Random quote.

 To see the effect on your own computer, click Lesson Forty-Six Script's Effect in your down-load packet, or see it online at `http://www.htmlgoodies.com/JSBook/lesson46example.html`*.*

Deconstructing the Script

Do you like the quotes? If not, change them, or add more. Either way, let's get started tearing this script apart. Here's the array:

```
var quote = new Array(10);
quote[0] = " Education is going to college to learn to
➥express your ignorance in scientific terms ";
quote[1] = "Chance favors the prepared mind";
quote[2] = "A stitch in time, saves nine.";
quote[3] = "The only difference between bravery and stupidity is the outcome";
quote[4] = "One should never let a formal education get in the way of learning";
quote[5] = "Happiness is two kinds of ice cream.";
quote[6] = "If you choose not to make a choice, you still have made a deci-
sion.";
quote[7] = "Do, or do not. There is no try";
quote[8] = "Reality is merely an illusion, albeit a very persistent one.";
quote[9] = "No one ever said life would be easy.";
```

The format is the same as seen in the last lesson. But just to drive a point home, we could have used the array format in which all ten quotes were listed in a row, in quotation marks, and separated by commas (and no spaces). It would have worked just fine, but think of what it would have looked like. The line of code that contained the array items would have been a mile long and couldn't have been easily understood at a glance. Using the preceding format, you can quickly see each of the array items and its number.

Let's get back to the array. The array has been assigned the variable name `quote`. Ten items are in the array. Notice, though, that the array only goes up to 9. Again, that is because a 0 is in the count. We know we keep pointing it out, but it can be very confusing and very easy to overlook.

Tip

I have seen JavaScripts that use random arrays set up so that 0 never comes into play. The random number is set to return 1 as its lowest number. Still, the author had to make a point of putting a 0 array item in the run. It didn't have a useful value because it was never going to come up, but there had to be some value so the JavaScript wouldn't throw an error. Then, even though the author was working with only 10 items, he had to make a point of the array being listed as 11 items because even though the 0 item would never come into play, it still had to be counted. Ugh! What a pain. Follow the previous format and just remember that there has to be a 0 line. Your life and your math will be a whole lot easier.

The Random Number Code

We're using the same random number code found throughout the book. The `Date` object is assigned the variable name `now`:

```
var now=new Date()
var num=(now.getSeconds())%9
```

The variable `num` represents the random number produced by dividing the returned second by 10 and using the remainder. Did you remember that the % sign actually returns the remainder of the division? If not, now you will.

This code returns a number between 0 and 9. Of course, you know those are the same numbers we have set up in our array. See how all the pieces are coming together?

Putting It on the Page

Because we're dealing with only a returned value and no other text surrounding it, we don't need to use plus signs or quotation marks. What we want returned is one of the quote array items. Which item is returned is settled by entering the result of the random number code in the square brackets:

```
document.write(quote[num])
```

Depending on the number, that quote is returned to the page.

Random Anything

As long as the array is set up correctly and you set up the document.write statement in the correct fashion, just about anything can be returned randomly to the page. The HTML Goodies e-mail box receives a great deal of mail asking how to create random images, links, banners, and the like. This is how it's done. You'll have to play with the code a little to make it all display correctly, but we've shown you the base methodology and format.

So be random.

Your Assignment

Add five more quotes to the scripts. That might seem easy, but look closely. You have to do more than just add the text.

 You can see a possible answer to this assignment on your own computer by clicking Lesson Forty-Six Assignment in your download packet, or see it online at http://www. htmlgoodies.com/JSBook/assignment46.html.

Lesson 47: A Guessing Game Using Arrays

Let's play a game. In this example, the user is asked to guess the JavaScript's favorite state from a list of states. The prompt statement is repeated until the user guesses the state correctly. But it's not as easy as it seems. The user can't just keep guessing down the line until she gets it right by process of elimination. Each time the button is clicked, a new random state is selected.

This script uses the randomization you just read about and takes you in a new direction, testing user input against what is returned from the array:

```
<SCRIPT LANGUAGE="JavaScript">
var states=new Array()
states[0]="CT"
states[1]="PA"
states[2]="NJ"
states[3]="NY"
states[4]="RI"
```

```
function pickstate()
{
var now=new Date()
var num=(now.getSeconds())%5

var guess=prompt("What's my favorite state: CT, PA, NJ, NY, or RI?")
if (states[num] == guess.toUpperCase())
{alert("That's my favorite state!")}
else
{alert("No, Try again")}
}

</SCRIPT>

<FORM>
<INPUT TYPE="button" VALUE="Guess My Favorite State" onClick="pickstate()">
</FORM>
```

You can see the script's effect in Figure 8.4.

Figure 8.4
Random array game.

 To see the effect on your own computer, click Lesson Forty-Seven Script's Effect in your download packet, or see it online at http://www.htmlgoodies.com/JSBook/ lesson47example.html.

Deconstructing the Script

It might be more tradition at this point, but this script has form elements, so we'll start from the bottom:

```
<FORM>
<INPUT TYPE="button" VALUE="Guess My Favorite State" onClick="pickstate()">
</FORM>
```

The form element is simply a button to get the entire process under way. When the button is clicked, a function named `pickstate()` is triggered and run.

The Array

```
var states=new Array()
states[0]="CT"
states[1]="PA"
states[2]="NJ"
states[3]="NY"
states[4]="RI"
```

The array is the vertical format listing five possible favorite states. The state names are in double quotation marks, so they are simple literal strings that are returned later through a piece of random code.

The Game Function `pickstate()`

Now let's look at the `pickstate()` function:

```
function pickstate()
{
var now=new Date()
var num=(now.getSeconds())%5


var guess=prompt("What's my favorite state: CT, PA, NJ, NY, or RI?")
if (states[num] == guess.toUpperCase())
{alert("That's my favorite state!")}
else
{alert("No, Try again")}
}

</SCRIPT>
```

The random number is returned as it was in the last lesson. The Date object is assigned the variable now. Then, the variable num is assigned the returned number created by dividing the current second by 5 and using the remainder of the equation.

That means there is a possibility of five numbers being returned, 0–4. Those are the same five numbers represented in the array.

The game is played by first asking the user to name a favorite state:

```
var guess=prompt("What's my favorite state: CT, PA, NJ, NY, or RI?")
```

Notice that the prompt offers the choices the user can make. One of the five must be the choice. If the user does not enter one of those choices, the answer and the return from the array will simply match. The variable name guess is assigned to the user's entry.

Then, an if statement asks whether the array item returned by the random number generator is equal to the guess the user made:

```
if (states[num] == guess.toUpperCase())
```

We've tried to compensate for the fact that JavaScript sees lowercase and uppercase letters differently by adding the method toUppercase() to the end of the guess variable. (You might remember the toUpperCase() method from Chapter 5, "Forms: A Great Way to Interact with Your Users." It sets a literal string to all capital letters.) By using toUpperCase(), we ensure that the guess will always be uppercase and a user will not lose the game simply because he entered lowercase letters rather than the required uppercase letters.

Next, the if statement posts an alert box that reads That's my favorite state! if the user's state and the state returned from the random code are the same. If the two are not the same, an alert box pops up to say No, Try again:

```
{alert("That's my favorite state!")}
else
{alert("No, Try again")}
```

The game might seem simple at first, a basic one-in-five chance. Not so. At the start of every game, a new state is generated. Therefore, from game to game, the chance of choosing the winner stays the same. That means you just can't keep choosing the same state and winning by simple state elimination. That would be cheating.

Your Assignment

This one can be done a few different ways. Alter the script so that it produces a form button. When the user clicks the button, he will be sent to one of three randomly chosen links.

 You can see a possible answer to this assignment on your own computer by clicking Lesson Forty-Seven Assignment in your download packet, or see it online at http://www. htmlgoodies.com/JSBook/assignment47.html.

Lesson 48: A Password Script

Password protection is very popular on the Web. Whether what is being protected really requires protection is a matter of personal opinion. The thinking might be that if you need a password to see what is behind the curtain, it must be more important than what is just sitting out there for the world to see.

An array offers a fantastic method for setting up a password-protected page or directory.

The password script in this lesson offers an array of seemingly random letters. The user is asked to enter three numbers. Those numbers are checked against the array, and a page URL is created. The many number combinations make guessing at the name of the page being protected quite difficult.

But because you, the JavaScript author, know the page name, you can set up the script to return the correct three letters to form the protected page's address.

As you look down the script, I'll tell you that the page name being protected is joe.html and the password is 145:

```
<SCRIPT LANGUAGE="javascript">

function GoIn()
{
var Password = new Array("p","j","l","t","o","e","o","b","x","z")

function getNumbers()
{
return document.userInput.u1.value
return document.userInput.u2.value
return document.userInput.u3.value
}
```

```
var input1 = document.userInput.u1.value
var input2 = document.userInput.u2.value
var input3 = document.userInput.u3.value

var pw1 = Password[input1]
var pw2 = Password[input2]
var pw3 = Password[input3]

var pw = pw1 + pw2 + pw3
if (pw == pw1+pw2+pw3)
{location.href = pw+ ".html"}
}
</SCRIPT>
Put in Your Three-Number Password to Enter:
<FORM NAME="userInput">
<INPUT TYPE="text" Name ="u1" SIZE="2">
<INPUT TYPE="text" Name ="u2" SIZE="2">
<INPUT TYPE="text" Name ="u3" SIZE="2">
<INPUT TYPE="button" VALUE="Enter" onClick="GoIn()">
</FORM>
```

The script's effect appears in Figure 8.5.

Figure 8.5
Accepting the password.

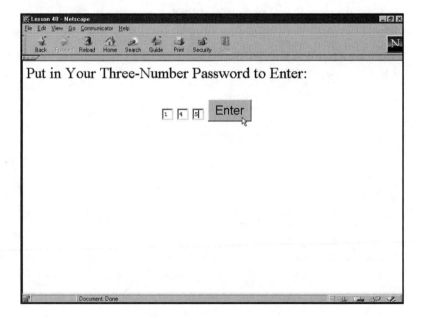

To see the effect on your own computer, click Lesson Forty-Eight Script's Effect in your down-load packet, or see it online at http://www.htmlgoodies.com/JSBook/lesson48example. html.

Deconstructing the Script

What's that? You say you didn't see the password in the script? Of course you didn't. What good would a password script be if all you had to do was look at the script and pull out the password? That's like writing the combination to a lock on the back of the lock. This script is a little hard to crack just by looking at the source code.

The Form Elements

This script contains form elements, so we will start from the bottom and meet the players:

```
Put in Your Three-Number Password to Enter:
<FORM NAME="userInput">
<INPUT TYPE="text" Name ="u1" SIZE="2">
<INPUT TYPE="text" Name ="u2" SIZE="2">
<INPUT TYPE="text" Name ="u3" SIZE="2">
<INPUT TYPE="button" VALUE="Enter" onClick="GoIn()">
</FORM>
```

The form itself is named userInput, which makes sense.

The first text box is named u1, the second is named u2, and the third is named u3.

Finally, a form button, when clicked, starts a function called GoIn().

Now you know the names and will understand the hierarchy statements, so let's go back to the top.

The Script

Here's the function GoIn() being created. The brace always comes right after the function name:

```
function GoIn()
{
var Password = new Array("p","j","l","t","o","e","o","b","x","z")
```

Next is the array. To the viewer, it looks like a run of random letters, which is what we want. It should look like there is no rhyme or reason to why the letters are set in the order they are. In reality, there is an order—at least an order we know—so that as the script pro-gresses, we can call for array letter number 1, number 4, and number 5, put them all together, and create joe.html.

Now, do you see a little pattern emerging? The other letters will never enter into it. We are interested only in the second letter in the list, which is represented by the number 1, so the letter is j.

The second number in the password script is 4. The letter represented by the number 4 is o. Remember, count up from 0!

The third number in the password is 5, and the letter represented by the number 5 is e.

By putting those three array items together and adding .html, we get the URL joe.html.

We made the order of the letters of joe correct. You can further attempt to confuse the reader by putting the letters out of order. Just make sure the numbers you call for are the numbers that coincide with the page name you are attempting to create.

Getting the Results into the Function

This is new. The purpose of this function is to ensure that the data the user entered in the three text boxes is in the function so we can work with it. It basically pulls the values into the script:

```
function getNumbers()
{
return document.userInput.u1.value
return document.userInput.u2.value
return document.userInput.u3.value
}
```

There was no need to do this in the game script in the last lesson because we were dealing with only one piece of data. Now, though, we have three. So, by setting up a function and calling for the return of the values found in the text boxes, we now have those three numbers in the function.

It is a good idea to do this anytime you have multiple input values from a user.

The following lines aren't necessary, but it is a good idea to assign a much simpler variable name to the data the user has entered in the text boxes. That way we don't have to write out those long hierarchy statements again and again:

```
var input1 = document.userInput.u1.value
var input2 = document.userInput.u2.value
var input3 = document.userInput.u3.value
```

Now, we start to build the page's URL from the data the user has entered. The three variable names pw1, pw2, and pw3 are assigned to the letters returned by taking the three numbers entered by the user and grabbing the corresponding letters in the array:

```
var pw1 = Password[input1]
var pw2 = Password[input2]
var pw3 = Password[input3]
```

For example, if the user entered the number 3 in the first box, pw1 would be equal to t. That happens two more times using the data in the second and third text boxes.

The variable name pw is created using the values pw1, pw2, and pw3:

```
var pw = pw1 + pw2 + pw3
```

Finally, an if statement asks whether pw is equal to pw1+pw2+pw3. Of course, it is—the variable pw was created by using those three pw# variables:

```
if (pw == pw1+pw2+pw3)
{location.href = pw+ ".html"}
}
```

Because pw always equals pw1+pw2+pw3, the script attempts to find a page with the URL made up of the three letters returned.

Unless the three letters are correct, the browser won't find the page. An error message will pop up saying the page made up of the three letters the user posted can't be found. Because the user is given no indication whether her answer is even close, every try is a random shot.

Ten letters exist, and three of them must be correct. That means the user has a 1-in-10 chance, times 3. Do the math; that's a pretty slim chance of just guessing the correct three numbers.

Now, those odds of guessing the password ring true only if you make your array out of purely random letters or groupings of letters. A smart person might be able to go into the previous code after seeing what it is looking for and pick out joe through a little brain power. But if I made the name of the protected page bjz, figuring it out would be much harder because that's just a group of letters that means nothing.

Toughening It Up

Try setting up the text array with multiple letters in each position.

Try setting up the script so that you require four numbers.

Try setting up the script so that each of the text boxes pulls from a different array, and make each array a different grouping of ASCII text characters.

You could make this JavaScript even more challenging by rewriting it so the script contains two arrays. The first is a series of random numbers, which coincide with letters in a second array. Use the number from the first array to pull a letter from the second.

For example, suppose the user enters the number 0. In the first array, the number in the 0 position is 4. Now, use that 4 to pull out the letter at the number 4 index position in the second array. I can't even begin to think of the odds of guessing that one correctly.

Your Assignment

This time around, you won't need to do much, but you will need to pay close attention to what you are changing. Take the script from this lesson, and alter it so that the new password is 364.

 You can see a possible answer to this assignment on your own computer by clicking Lesson Forty-Eight Assignment in your download packet, or see it online at http://www. htmlgoodies.com/JSBook/assignment48.html.

Lesson 49: End-of-Chapter Review—A Quiz

The purpose of this end-of-chapter review is the same as all the other ones. You are to take everything you have learned up to this point and create a new and useful script to place on your own pages.

Of course, we'll offer one ourselves and then make a suggestion or two.

Table 8.1 shows the object-related JavaScript commands you've been given up to now. You've also been introduced to these JavaScript concepts:

- string and the substring() method
- Arrays
- The alert(), confirm(), and prompt() methods
- The if/else conditional statement
- These event handlers: onBlur, onChange, onClick, onDblClick, onFocus, onKeyDown, onKeyPress, onKeyUp, onLoad, onMouseDown, onMouseMove, onMouseOut, onMouseOver, onMouseUp, and onSubmit
- These arithmetic operators: +, -, *, /, and %
- These conditions: ==, !=, <, >, =<, =>, ?:, and +=
- The HTML 4.0 flag <SPAN>
- Creating variable names
- Creating a function

- ⚫ `for` loops
- ⚫ HTML form items
- ⚫ The form item attribute `NAME=`
- ⚫ These form item properties: `length`, `value`, and `selectedIndex`
- ⚫ These form item methods: `toLowerCase` and `toUpperCase()`
- ⚫ `return`
- ⚫ `while` loops

Table 8.1   Object-Related JavaScript Commands Demonstrated in Chapters 1–8

Object	Methods	Properties
date	getDate(), getDay(), getHours(), getMinutes(), getMonth(), getSeconds(), getTime(), setYear(), setDate(), setDay(), setHours(), setMinutes(), setMonth(), setSeconds()	
document	write()	alinkColor, bgColor, fgColor, linkColor, lastModified, location, referrer, title, vlinkColor
history	go()	length
location		host, hostname, href
Math	random(), round()	
navigator		appCodeName, appName, appVersion, userAgent
window	close(),	defaultstatus, setTimeout() directories, location, menubar, resizable, self, scrollbars, status, toolbar

This lesson's script is a quiz. There are five form element drop-down boxes with three answers each. The user will choose the answers she feels are correct and click the button to see her score:

```
<SCRIPT LANGUAGE="javascript">

function Gradeit()
{

function getselectedIndex(){
return document.quiz.q1.selectedIndex
return document.quiz.q2.selectedIndex
return document.quiz.q3.selectedIndex
return document.quiz.q4.selectedIndex
return document.quiz.q5.selectedIndex
}

var Answers=new Array(1,2,2,3,1)
var UserAnswers = new Array(document.quiz.q1.selectedIndex,
➥document.quiz.q2.selectedIndex,document.quiz.q3.selectedIndex,
➥document.quiz.q4.selectedIndex,document.quiz.q5.selectedIndex)
var count0 = 0

if (Answers[0] == UserAnswers[0])
{count0 = count0 + 1}
else
{count0 = count0}

if (Answers[1] == UserAnswers[1])
{count1 = count0 + 1}
else
{count1 = count0}

if (Answers[2] == UserAnswers[2])
{count2 = count1 + 1}
else
{count2 = count1}

if (Answers[3] == UserAnswers[3])
{count3 = count2 + 1}
else
{count3 = count2}
```

```
if (Answers[4] == UserAnswers[4])
{count4 = count3 + 1}
else
{count4 = count3}

alert("You got " + count4 + "/5 right.")

}
</SCRIPT>

<FORM NAME="quiz">

<b>#1: What is 2 + 2?</b>
<SELECT NAME="q1">
<OPTION SELECTED>Choose One
<OPTION>4
<OPTION>2
<OPTION>22
</SELECT>
<P>

<b>#2: Trees have: </b>
<SELECT NAME="q2">
<OPTION SELECTED>Choose One
<OPTION>engines
<OPTION>leaves
<OPTION>dogs
</SELECT>
<P>

<b>#3: This book is about:</b>
<SELECT NAME="q3">
<OPTION SELECTED>Choose One
<OPTION>Nothing
<OPTION>JavaScript
<OPTION>Love and Romance
</SELECT>
<P>

<b>#4: Who sang "Yesterday"?</b>
<SELECT NAME="q4">
<OPTION SELECTED>Choose One
<OPTION>Van Halen
```

```
<OPTION>Metallica
<OPTION>The Beatles
</SELECT>
<P>

<b>#5 What color is blue?</b>
<SELECT NAME="q5">
<OPTION SELECTED>Choose One
<OPTION>blue
<OPTION>green
<OPTION>off-blue
</SELECT>
<P>

<INPUT TYPE="button" VALUE="Grade Me" onClick="Gradeit()">

</FORM>
```

The beauty of this script is that it uses two arrays to get the final score. The first array consists of the correct answers, whereas the second array consists of the answers given by the user.

One by one, the answers are checked against each other. If the answer is correct, 1 is added to the score. If not, the score remains the same.

The results of the script are then displayed in an alert box.

You can see the script's effect in Figure 8.6.

 To see the effect on your own computer, click Lesson Forty-Nine Script's Effect in your down-load packet, or see it online at `http://www.htmlgoodies.com/JSBook/lesson49example.html`*.*

Deconstructing the Script

Okay, this is a long script and it looks scary, but don't be put off. It's a lot of the same elements again, and again, and again.

This script has form elements, so we'll start at the bottom.

The Form Elements

Rather than display all five drop-down boxes, let's look at only the first one. The other four work exactly the same way. Hopefully, you can get the answer to this one:

```
<FORM NAME="quiz">

<b>#1: What is 2 + 2?</b>
<SELECT NAME="q1">
<OPTION SELECTED>Choose One
<OPTION>4
<OPTION>2
<OPTION>22
</SELECT>
<P>
```

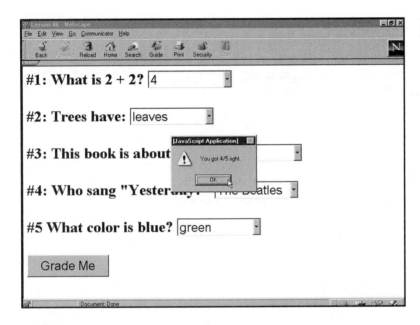

Figure 8.6
The results of the quiz.

The name of the entire form is quiz. Remember that the entire form contains all five drop-down menu boxes. You are seeing only the first one here. Look back at the full script if you need to.

The name of the first drop-down menu box is q1. We decided on that because it represented question one, which makes sense.

The next four drop-down menu boxes are set up the same, except they are named q2 through q5, respectively.

Remember: JavaScript counts everything and starts counting at 0. In each of these drop-down menu boxes, each selection is assigned a number by the JavaScript. The first is 0, and it counts up from there.

Notice that the first choice—the one that will receive the number 0—is not a viable answer. It simply displays Choose One, so the user knows to click to choose an answer.

Finally, there is a form button after the five drop-down menu boxes:

```
<INPUT TYPE="button" VALUE="Grade Me" onClick="Gradeit()">
```

That button triggers a function named Gradeit().

Still with us? Good.

The Script

The script is a little long, but there's nothing new in it, and its inner workings are pretty straightforward.

The script begins by being surrounded by the function Gradeit(). This is the function the HTML form button triggers when the user clicks:

```
function Gradeit()
{
```

You probably remember the next part from the last lesson. This function is making a point of bringing up the answers the user chose so that the data can be manipulated in this script. Notice the q1 through q5 names in the hierarchy statements:

```
function getselectedIndex(){
return document.quiz.q1.selectedIndex
return document.quiz.q2.selectedIndex
return document.quiz.q3.selectedIndex
return document.quiz.q4.selectedIndex
return document.quiz.q5.selectedIndex
}
```

Notice how I am not asking for the value the user entered because the input device is not a text box. It's a drop-down menu box, and the command used to return that value is selectedIndex. Remember that from Chapter 5?

Next come the answers. The array was created as a key:

```
var Answers=new Array(1,2,2,3,1)
```

The answers that are taken from the drop-down menu boxes are tested against these numbers. If the numbers returned from the menu boxes are the same, the user gets 5 out of 5. If not, the user gets a lower score.

Here are the results of the quiz as given by the user:

```
var UserAnswers = new
  Array(document.quiz.q1.selectedIndex,
➥document.quiz.q2.selectedIndex,document.quiz.q3.selectedIndex,
➥document.quiz.q4.selectedIndex,document.quiz.q5.selectedIndex)
```

Yes, the format for setting it up in the single-line array format is a little long, but the answers are in the single-line format, so we felt this should be, too.

We could have made this line shorter by assigning variable names to the long hierarchy statements. However, we're writing the statement only once, so assigning variable names is a step that just isn't required.

Grading the Test

Grading is achieved by comparing the Answers array and the UserAnswers array, one array item at a time. The 0 items in both arrays are compared. If they match, 1 is added. If not, nothing is done and it moves on to the next one.

Each time you grade another answer, you must change the variable name. It gets a little confusing, but follow it along.

First, a variable, count0, is created and assigned a 0 value:

```
var count0 = 0
```

You have to do this in case the user doesn't get any of the answers correct. Without setting the count to 0 to begin, the JavaScript would throw an error if the result was 0 out of 5.

Now we move to the grading itself. Let's look at only the first two questions being graded:

```
if (Answers[0] == UserAnswers[0])
{count0 = count0 + 1}
else
{count0 = count0}

if (Answers[1] == UserAnswers[1])
{count1 = count0 + 1}
else
{count1 = count0}
```

The first if statement compares the two numbers in the 0 position in the Answers and UserAnswers arrays.

If they are the same, count0 gets 1 added. If not, count0 remains the same value, 0.

The next two numbers in both arrays—the numbers in the 1 position—are now compared. If they are the same, count1, a new variable, equals count0 plus 1.

If not, count1 equals count0, or still 0.

The process continues this way, creating a new variable name to coincide with each new question's grading. It looks like this. Follow the new variable names along:

```
if (Answers[2] == UserAnswers[2])
{count2 = count1 + 1}
else
{count2 = count1}

if (Answers[3] == UserAnswers[3])
{count3 = count2 + 1}
else
{count3 = count2}

if (Answers[4] == UserAnswers[4])
{count4 = count3 + 1}
else
{count4 = count3}
```

When all is said and done, count4 will have the final score out of five. An alert box is set to pop up with count4's value displayed as a grade. It looks like this:

```
alert("You got " + count4 + "/5 right.")
```

Altering the Display

Okay, we agree that displaying the score on an alert box is a little cheesy. The point of showing you this script is to provide an example of getting a JavaScript to grade a quiz.

The display is up to you. You easily have enough knowledge at this point to take the count4 variable and post it all over the place.

In fact, look back through the script. You can pretty easily display the user's choices right along with her score. You can even make all that information pop up in a new browser window.

All we provided here was a way to get the math done. Now it's up to you to make it pretty. Think about it for a moment; there must be 50 ways to get this script to display the results.

Your Assignment

For this assignment, put together an entirely new script. The script should post a random image. Furthermore, the random image should have an URL attached to it. The URL should not be random—it should always be attached to that image when it displays.

 You can see a possible answer to this assignment on your own computer by clicking Lesson Forty-Nine Assignment in your download packet, or see it online at http://www. htmlgoodies.com/JSBook/assignment49.html.

Chapter 9

Putting It All Together

This chapter contains the following lessons and scripts:

All the way through this book, I've been pushing that you should always be thinking about building scripts that will be helpful to your users. You should be building scripts that do something that will be seen as a help to your Web site. This chapter is pretty much that idea wrapped up in six little scripts.

With only the JavaScript you know to this point, you have the ability to create rather large and involved scripts that can create some pretty great effects.

Because this is somewhat of a "wrap-up" chapter, allow me to talk about JavaScript usage for a short while.

As you've no doubt seen throughout this book, JavaScript can be rather flashy and intrusive. I find that when I teach HTML and Web design to new programmers, they tend to immediately jump on the flash and pizzazz of JavaScript. Alert boxes, pop-up windows, and prompt boxes pop up all over the pages. Is that good? Is it wise to use JavaScript in such a way to force a user to look at or do something?

Probably not.

Think about your own surfing habits. Do you enjoy when sites throw up elements without your input? Do you like to be slowed down to witness an effect that doesn't do much to help you? Case in point, would you like a site to pop up a prompt box that asks for your name just so that an alert box can pop up right after it proclaiming you are welcome into the site, calling you by the name you just entered?

I don't know that you would. JavaScript is fantastically helpful when used to interact with your users but also as an aid to the user. Scripts should help them along and do some of the work for them. Scripts also should put on little shows now and again.

But they shouldn't jump out and scream every time someone logs on to your site.

So, think about your own surfing. What is it that you've run into that you think a JavaScript could help you with? What script could you create that would be of assistance or add entertainment value to a Web site without throwing alert box confetti every time the user pops in?

It's said that necessity is the mother of invention. The following scripts are ones that I think offer assistance and a little pizzazz without going bonkers.

After all, this is what you want. You want a Web site that interacts with users and makes their stay within your domain a little more enjoyable. That way, they'll probably come back.

Let's look at some great little scripts you can incorporate … and maybe alter a bit to suit your own needs.

Lesson 50: JavaScript Animation

You already know about image flips that occur when the mouse passes over an image. Here you'll go one step farther. This script takes a series of 10 images and plays them one after another, like a movie.

The script acts as an animator so you can animate either GIF or JPEG images without the use of an animator software package.

We've simply counted our images from 0 to 9, but if you use images in the correct order, this script will play them at whatever speed you want to create a basic animation:

```
<SCRIPT LANGUAGE="JavaScript">

 var num=0

  img0 = new Image (55,45)
  img0.src = "0.gif"

  img1 = new Image (55,45)
  img1.src = "1.gif"

  img2 = new Image (55,45)
  img2.src = "2.gif"

  img3 = new Image (55,45)
  img3.src = "3.gif"

  img4 = new Image (55,45)
  img4.src = "4.gif"

  img5 = new Image (55,45)
  img5.src = "5.gif"

  img6 = new Image (55,45)
  img6.src = "6.gif"

  img7 = new Image (55,45)
  img7.src = "7.gif"

  img8 = new Image (55,45)
  img8.src = "8.gif"

  img9 = new Image (55,45)
  img9.src = "9.gif"


function startshow()
{

num=num+1

if(num==10)
{num=0}
```

```
document.mypic.src=eval("img"+num+".src")

setTimeout("startshow()","1000")
}
 </SCRIPT>



<IMG SRC="0.gif" NAME="mypic" BORDER=0>
 <p>

 <A HREF="javascript:startshow()">Display Animation</a>
```

You can see the script's effect in Figure 9.1.

Figure 9.1
The first cell of the animation count to 10.

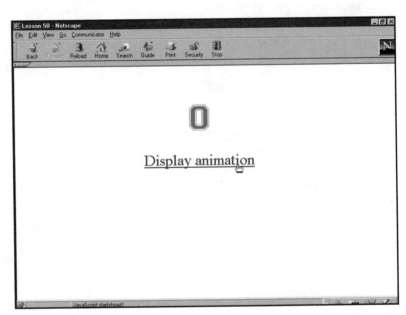

Deconstructing the Script

Let's begin by talking about the 10 small blocks of code that start the script:

```
Img0 = new Image (55,45)
  Img0.src = "0.gif"
```

```
Img1 = new Image (55,45)
Img1.src = "1.gif"
```

We're only showing the first two blocks of code here because the same format is followed again and again. Notice each of the small blocks of code calls for a new image, `0.gif` through `9.gif`.

The code is preloading the images. Remember what we're trying to do here. The latter portions of the script, which we'll get to in a moment, create an animation by showing 10 images in a row.

If you have to wait for the server to be contacted every time a new image is called for, it wouldn't be much of an animation. You want all 10 images in the cache and ready to go when the user clicks to start the animation show. That's why you need to preload all the images.

The format is pretty basic. It reads as if you were setting a new `Date` object. A variable name is assigned to a new `Image` object. The numbers in the parentheses are the height and width, in that order, of the image.

In the next line, the image source is offered in an `object.property` format: `img1.src = "0.gif"`. Note the double quotation marks. If you don't surround the name of the image in quotation marks, the script will think that the dot separates an object from a property or a method and cause an error. But by inserting double quotation marks, you set `"0.gif"` apart as a string.

And so it goes 10 times. Each time, a new object is set with a new variable name, and then a source is offered.

The result is a download of the image. Now, when the animation is called for, all the images are already in the browser cache—or at least on their way—and the viewer should get a good show.

The Animation

The basic concept here is that we're going to perform an image flip, but we're going to perform it 10 times in a row. After those 10 flips have occurred, we'll start from the top and do it all again.

The effect will be that 10 images flip by—one per second, or whatever timeframe you set—giving the impression of an animation. Here's the code that does the trick. It's not much, but it is powerful:

```
function startshow()
{
```

```
num=num+1

if(num==10)
{num=0}

document.mypic.src=eval("img"+num+".src")



setTimeout("startshow()","1000")
}
```

We'll start at the top. I mean the very top—look back at the very beginning of the script, right before the preload commands. See where I initiated a variable?

It looks like this:

```
var num=0
```

I set that above everything else so that the variable num would be available after the function started. Also, by setting it outside the function, I made it a global variable. Now let's look at the bottom of the script:

```
<IMG SRC="0.gif" NAME="mypic" BORDER=0>
```

Here's the HTML flag that places the first image on the page. Note that it has the name mypic set to it. That's going to be important when we look at the script's hierarchy statement shortly. Back to the function ....

Sorry to jump around, but I needed to get you all the parts to understand how this function works. We start by immediately increasing num by one:

```
num=num+1
```

That makes sense. 0.gif already is displaying on the page; we put it there through the HTML flag. We need 1.gif to appear now, so we add one to num.

Next, we need to check something. We don't have a 10.gif; however, if num keeps getting one added to it, sooner or later it will equal 10. That's a problem that easily can be fixed by telling the script that if num equals 10, just reset it to 0. Like so:

```
if(num==10)
{num=0}
```

The effect is a rollover from 9 to 0 and a count that starts all over again. Thus, the animation appears to loop. Cool, huh? Here's the code:

```
document.mypic.src=eval("img"+num+".src")
```

Now let's discuss the fancy stuff. We set the hierarchy statement to see the document, the specific image space `mypic`, and then to set a source. It's done just like an image flip, except now we use the preload commands.

The command `eval` evaluates what is inside the parentheses. For example, say that `num` is showing a count of 7. (I'm just pulling a number out of my head. There's no significance past that.)

The text within the parentheses will therefore read `img7.src`. See that? The `eval` command then evaluates what that means—the source for `img7` is `7.gif`.

How do I know that? Look at the preload commands. See how `img7.src` equals `7.gif`? That's it!

Therefore, image `7.gif` is placed in the image space `mypic`.

But how does it happen again and again? You should know this command by now:

```
setTimeout("startshow()","1000")
```

The function is called for repeatedly every second using `setTimeOut()`.

So, the function fires, it adds one to `num`, and then that number is checked to see whether it is `10`. If it's not, the function evaluates the image source requested by the hierarchy statement. It then posts the image to the space.

This happens repeatedly, each time raising `num` by one and then resetting it when it gets to `10`. The result is a 10-frame animation that loops again and again.

Calling for the Animation

Here's the code that starts the animation:

```
<A HREF="JavaScript:startshow()">Display animation</a>
```

Now, here's something new. Look at the format of the hypertext link that starts the animation. It points at `JavaScript:startshow()` rather than a hypertext link.

That's a quick way to put active text on a page to trigger a function. By putting `JavaScript:` in the hypertext formula, the browser knows that a function, contained within the document, will be enacted. The function name that follows tells the browser which to trigger. It's very clever.

Your Assignment

This one will take a bit of thought. Change the script so that the animation is no longer in it. Then, make it so that when you click, you get the next image in line, repeatedly, until you have rolled through the entire set of 10 images.

It should change to the next image only when you click. Basically, you should turn this animation script into a slideshow script.

 You can see a possible answer to this assignment on your own computer by clicking Lesson Fifty Assignment in your download packet or by viewing it online at `http://www.htmlgoodies.com/JSBook/assignment50.html`.

Lesson 51: Jumping Focus Between Form Elements

This is a fun little script that acts as an aid to the user. Let's say you set up a form that asks for information in a set structure. For example, you could ask for a phone number that is to be entered in three text boxes, a five- or nine-digit ZIP code, or a two-letter state abbreviation. After the user has filled in the information, why not set it up so that the cursor simply jumps right to the next text box?

You can get this effect by forcing the browser to put focus on the next element in line after the current element has reached its capacity.

I'll even go you one better. I've added a little piece of code that jumps the cursor to the first form element when the page loads. That way, the form is ready and waiting when your user starts to type.

Here's the script. It's a little long, so I've added a few comments to help you at each stage of the process. It's a tip you might want to think about when you get into writing bigger scripts. They can get confusing, even to the author. Here's the code:

```
<HEAD>

<SCRIPT LANGUAGE="javascript">

<!-- This code makes the jump from textbox one to textbox two -->
function check()
{
var letters = document.joe.burns.value.length +1;
if (letters <= 4)
{document.joe.burns.focus()}
else
{document.joe.tammy.focus()}
}
```

```
<!-- This code makes the jump from textbox two to textbox three -->
function check2()
{
var letters2 = document.joe.tammy.value.length +1;
if (letters2 <= 4)
{document.joe.tammy.focus()}
else
{document.joe.chloe.focus()}
}


<!-- This code makes the jump from textbox three to textbox four -->
function check3()
{
var letters3 = document.joe.chloe.value.length +1;
if (letters3 <= 4)
{document.joe.chloe.focus()}
else
{document.joe.mardi.focus()}
}


<!-- This code makes the jump from textbox four to the submit button -->
function check4()
{
var letters4 = document.joe.mardi.value.length +1;
if (letters4 <= 4)
{document.joe.mardi.focus()}
else
{document.joe.go.focus()}
}
</SCRIPT>

</HEAD>

<!-- The onLoad in the BODY flag puts focus in the first textbox -->
<BODY BGCOLOR="ffffff" onLoad="document.joe.burns.focus()">

<!-- This is the form -->
<FORM NAME="joe">
<INPUT TYPE="text" name="burns" size="10" MAXLENGTH="4" onKeyUp="check()"><BR>
<INPUT TYPE="text" name="tammy" size="10" MAXLENGTH="4" onKeyUp="check2()"><BR>
<INPUT TYPE="text" name="chloe" size="10" MAXLENGTH="4" onKeyUp="check3()"><BR>
<INPUT TYPE="text" name="mardi" size="10" MAXLENGTH="4" onKeyUp="check4()"><BR>
<INPUT TYPE="submit" VALUE="Click to Send" NAME="go">
</FORM>
```

251

You can see the script's effect in Figure 9.2.

Figure 9.2
After the first box was filled with four characters, focus jumped to the next box.

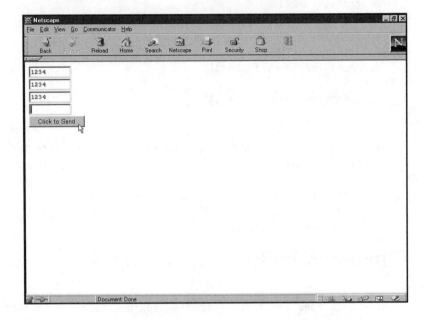

 To see the effect on your own computer, click Lesson Fifty-One Script's Effect in your download packet, or see it online at `http://www.htmlgoodies.com/JSBook/lesson51example.html`*.*

Deconstructing the Script

Okay, first things first.

Please understand that this works only with browser versions 4.0 and above—I'll tell you why in a moment. But don't let that stop you from installing this on your forms. Lower version browsers will not understand the event handler command and will not trigger the functions, which means no errors. Those users who have browser versions 4.0 or higher get the effect; those who don't just fill in the form as they normally would.

The reason the script works in only 4.0 and above actually has to do with the event handler onKeyUp rather than the script itself. Keep reading, and I'll tell you about my trial and error when writing the script and finally landing on the onKeyUp event handler.

The overall concept is this: There are four form elements, five if you count the submit button. A small piece of JavaScript places focus (denoted by the cursor appearance) on the first form element, the first text box.

Four JavaScript functions were created, and each is assigned to a text box. The JavaScript functions look at the number of characters within the text box. When the number reaches four, focus (again, the cursor) is placed on the next text box.

Each function can be changed around to your heart's content allowing as many or as few letters as you want.

By the way, I tried this with other form elements, radio buttons, check boxes, and select boxes. The effect works for them all. The form element becomes highlighted, but that's it. The user then has to use her mouse to complete the task. That's not at all a bad thing; I just wanted to make you aware of it. This format works best with text boxes and text area boxes.

Now let's break this code down, starting with the form elements.

The Form Elements

```
<FORM NAME="joe">
<INPUT TYPE="text" name="burns" size="10" onKeyUp="check()"><BR>
<INPUT TYPE="text" name="tammy" size="10" onKeyUp="check2()"><BR>
<INPUT TYPE="text" name="chloe" size="10" onKeyUp="check3()"><BR>
<INPUT TYPE="text" name="mardi" size="10" onKeyUp="check4()"><BR>
<INPUT TYPE="submit" VALUE="Click to Send" NAME="go">
</FORM>
```

This is a basic form whose name is joe.

After the form are four text boxes. Each box is given a name, size, and maximum length and is finally attached to a function triggered to work using the onKeyUp event handler.

Remember that from the previous code? That onKeyUp event handler is a relatively new command. This is where I ran into nothing but trouble when writing this script. The script must be set up so that every time someone enters a new character in a text box, the function must run to recount the number of characters the user has entered.

I tried everything—I mean everything. I tried onFocus and onClick; I even tried setting the function to a for loop and a while loop. I set up a setTimeout() function. Nothing worked. But as soon as I entered onKeyUp, I had success. Each time a key is released, the function runs.

So easy, yet so hard to find. You'll find that worrying over one little command will be one of your joys when writing JavaScript.

Now that you know the names of all the form elements, we can start to build some JavaScript hierarchy statements. For example, the first text box can be called on through the following statement:

```
document.joe.burns
```

Furthermore, the number of characters within the first text box can be returned through this hierarchy statement:

```
document.joe.burns.value
```

With those two concepts, the scripts basically build themselves. But wait! How did we get the focus to start in the first text box without any input from the user?

Getting the First Focus

That didn't just happen by default. We must "force" focus to the first text box. I did it in the BODY flag, like so:

```
<BODY BGCOLOR="ffffff" onLoad="document.joe.burns.focus()">
```

That focus() is what does the trick. By attaching it to the end of a hierarchy statement, focus is put on the form element. In this case, it's the first text box (burns) under the form (joe).

Keep that concept in mind. We'll do it again and again throughout the four functions.

From Box One to Box Two

The first two text boxes are named burns and tammy. If that seems odd to you, it isn't to me because I am using my own name and those of my family. I actually find that remembering my variable names is easier if I use common names I can remember. Because JavaScript doesn't worry about it, I don't. It helps me, so I use it.

You just learned that if you attach focus() to the end of the hierarchy statement, you can set focus on the form element. Let's put that concept to work.

The text box burns has its onKeyUp event handler set to a function named check(). It looks like this:

```
function check()
{
var letters = document.joe.burns.value.length +1;
if (letters <= 4)
{document.joe.burns.focus()}
else
```

```
{document.joe.tammy.focus()}
  }
```

The function first sets the number of characters found within the first text box (burns) to a variable and then adds one. The onKeyUp event handler is the trick. It forces the function to run **every time** something is entered.

Next, an if statement asks if the number of characters within the text box burns is less than or equal to four. If it is, focus remains on the text box burns.

We want the effect to allow four letters to appear in the text box, so to get that effect, we add one to the number of characters found in the box. That way, one equals two, two equals three, and so on. After the fourth letter is entered, the if statement is no longer true. Yes, you could get the same effect by not adding one and setting all the numbers up one, but that gets confusing. By adding one, you can set the if statement to the number of letters you want to appear in the box. It's much easier to follow.

After the if statement is no longer true (letters now equals 5, but only four letters are in the box), focus jumps to the next box, tammy.

Now that focus is on tammy, the function check2() is the one that runs each time a key is let up. See that in the form elements? The text box tammy has onKeyUp set to check2().

The function looks like this:

```
function check2()
{
var letters2 = document.joe.tammy.value.length +1;
if (letters2 <= 4)
{document.joe.tammy.focus()}
else
{document.joe.chloe.focus()}
  }
```

Does it look familiar? It should. It's the exact same format as before except that the function name has changed from check() to check2().

The variable name letters has been changed to letters2, and the hierarchy statements are now set to jump from text box two to text box three.

The reason for the changes is that you can't have the same variable names used twice to represent two different values within the same script.

After focus is on text box three, chloe, the function check3() takes over and performs the same tasks.

After focus is on the fourth text box, `mardi`, the function `check4()` takes over and does the same thing, except this time when four letters are entered, focus jumps to the submit button.

Don't expect the submit button to do anything—it won't.

Got it?

Do you see how the functions work? Each is doing the exact same thing. You just have to change some variable names so that you won't get JavaScript errors.

Cool, huh?

Your Assignment

Using what you know from this script, rewrite the script so that a user can enter a phone number into three separate text boxes. This is often done so that the company receiving the information can keep the phone numbers separated by area code and exchange. It's a fairly quick method of judging where groupings of customers are located.

 You can see a possible answer to this assignment on your own computer by clicking Lesson Fifty-One Assignment in your download packet, or see it online at http://www. htmlgoodies.com/JSBook/assignment51.html.

Lesson 52: Limiting Check Box Choices

Let's stay in the same vein regarding using a script to assist a person filling out a form.

Here's a fantastic effect. Multiple check boxes often are avoided in forms because users have a tendency to simply check all the boxes no matter what. Radio buttons have become the preferred element when a choice must be made. You typically see check boxes used as single items. I see them mostly at the end of larger forms asking whether I want to receive a newsletter or e-mail updates about a product I'm downloading.

But what if you want a user to choose two from, say, five elements?

Well, here's a script you can attach to your forms that enables you to limit the number of checks your users can make. You'll fall in love with check boxes all over again. I got the original idea for this script from an HTML Goodies reader. He has a similar script that works only in Internet Explorer, so I took the concept and rewrote it to work across browsers.

Here's the script:

```
<SCRIPT LANGUAGE="javascript">
function KeepCount() {
var NewCount = 0
if (document.joe.dog.checked)
{NewCount = NewCount + 1}
if (document.joe.cat.checked)
{NewCount = NewCount + 1}
if (document.joe.pig.checked)
{NewCount = NewCount + 1}
if (document.joe.ferret.checked)
{NewCount = NewCount + 1}
if (document.joe.hampster.checked)
{NewCount = NewCount + 1}
if (NewCount == 3)
{
alert('Pick Just Two Please')
document.joe; return false;
}
}
</SCRIPT>

<FORM NAME="joe">
<b>Pick Only Two Please!</b> <br>
<INPUT TYPE="checkbox" NAME="dog" onClick="return KeepCount()"> Dog<br>
<INPUT TYPE="checkbox" NAME="cat" onClick="return KeepCount()"> Cat<br>
<INPUT TYPE="checkbox" NAME="pig" onClick="return KeepCount()"> Pig<br>
<INPUT TYPE="checkbox" NAME="ferret" onClick="return KeepCount()"> Ferret<br>
<INPUT TYPE="checkbox" NAME="hampster" onClick="return KeepCount()"> Hampster
</FORM>
```

You can see the script's effect in Figure 9.3.

 To see the effect on your own computer, click Lesson Fifty-Two Script's Effect in your download packet, or see it online at *http://www.htmlgoodies.com/JSBook/lesson52example.html*.

Give it a try. I know it says to choose only two, but to see the effect, you'll need to pick a third option.

Go ahead! Break the rules! Try to pick three!

You can even make different choices, unclick choices, and change things around. As long as you have only two, you're good to go. But select three, and you get the alert.

Figure 9.3
Stop picking three!

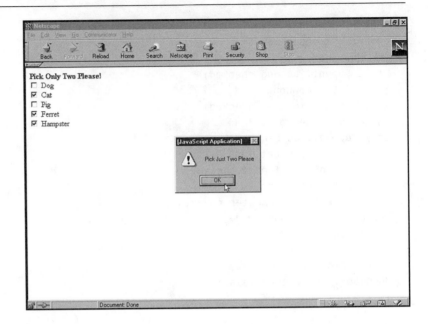

Deconstructing the Script

The example has only check boxes, but you can surround them with any number of extra form elements. I just singled out the form check boxes for demonstration purposes. The code looks like this:

```
<FORM NAME="joe">
<b>Pick Only Two Please!</b> <br>
<INPUT TYPE="checkbox" NAME="dog" onClick="return KeepCount()"> Dog<br>
<INPUT TYPE="checkbox" NAME="cat" onClick="return KeepCount()"> Cat<br>
<INPUT TYPE="checkbox" NAME="pig" onClick="return KeepCount()"> Pig<br>
<INPUT TYPE="checkbox" NAME="ferret" onClick="return KeepCount()"> Ferret<br>
<INPUT TYPE="checkbox" NAME="hampster" onClick="return KeepCount()"> Hampster
</FORM>
```

These are basic check boxes. The form is named joe, and each check box is then given a NAME. The NAME is equal to what the check box represents—that's pretty basic form stuff.

The trick is the onClick() inside each of the check boxes.

Notice that the onClick() asks for a return from a function named KeepCount(). That return function enables you to disallow the third box (or whichever you choose) to be checked.

258

Make a point of following that format; otherwise, this JavaScript won't give you the desired effect.

Got it? Super. Moving along ....

The Script

It's a fairly simple little script that looks like this:

```
<SCRIPT LANGUAGE="javascript">
function KeepCount() {
var NewCount = 0
if (document.joe.dog.checked)
{NewCount = NewCount + 1}
if (document.joe.cat.checked)
{NewCount = NewCount + 1}
if (document.joe.pig.checked)
{NewCount = NewCount + 1}
if (document.joe.ferret.checked)
{NewCount = NewCount + 1}
if (document.joe.hampster.checked)
{NewCount = NewCount + 1}
if (NewCount == 3)
{
alert('Pick Just Two Please')
document.joe; return false;
}
}
</SCRIPT>
```

The script works because it's set up to inspect every check box every time. That's how you're able to check, uncheck, and check again as long as only two are selected. The script counts the number of check marks every time you click.

We start with the function, which I called KeepCount() for fairly obvious reasons. You'll remember that this function triggers every time your user selects a check box. We need to give the JavaScript somewhere to keep a count, so I set it up as a variable named NewCount.

Now we get to the magic. Notice the script checks each check box right in a row, every time. Here's just the first blip of code:

```
if (document.joe.dog.checked)
{NewCount = NewCount + 1}
```

If the first check box (dog) is checked, NewCount gets one added to it. If not, it moves along to the next check box.

Following the script down, if cat is checked, one is added. If not, we go to the next blip.

Each check box is tested in order. The script keeps count again and again each time the user clicks. But what if three are checked?

```
if (NewCount == 3)
{
alert('Pick Just Two Please')
document.joe; return false;
}
```

If NewCount is equal (==) to 3, up pops the alert box and the user is returned to the form; therefore, the third check box is false. It deselects.

The function bracket and the end-script flag round out the script.

The reason the script is capable of counting the boxes repeatedly is at the top of the function. Every time the function triggers, the NewCount value is set back to 0.

You can set this to as many check boxes as you want and as many choices from those boxes as you want. If you use the effect more than once on a page, though, please remember that you must change the NAME of the check boxes, so you must also change those names in the script.

You'll need a blip of code for every check box you have for the check boxes to count each time. Just make sure that your script equals your check boxes both in number and in NAMEs. My suggestion is if you're going to use this more than one time on the page, paste an entirely new script with a new function name and new count name (other than NewCount).

Just be sure to keep the return command in the check boxes themselves. That's what makes the magic in this little script.

Your Assignment

I'll bet at least one of you noticed that this script has an alert in it. The first text in this chapter warned against using them. Well, actually it warned against using a lot of them.

Let's take that to heart. Rewrite this script so that an alert no longer exists, but rather the entire run of check boxes becomes unchecked.

Here's a hint: The change is quite minimal. Think about what command you would use when constructing an HTML form to create a button to clear the contents. After you have that, you'll know the command to uncheck every box.

When you get the command, remember that it is now going to act on the form, so add the two parentheses after the command.

Wow, I practically gave it to you.

Just remember that if you use this method as part of a larger form, it resets the entire thing.

 You can see a possible answer to this assignment on your own computer by clicking Lesson Fifty-Two Assignment in your download packet, or see it online at http://www. htmlgoodies.com/JSBook/assignment52.html.

Lesson 53: Positioning a New Window

In Lesson 19 (see Chapter 4, "Flipping Images and Opening Windows with Mouse Events") I discussed how to open a new window. If you remember, numerous methods are available for altering the look of that window, but there's more.

In this lesson, I'll show you a couple of neat tricks to working with a pop-up window. First, we'll start with a basic script that enables you to position the window when it pops up. After you have a handle on that, I'll give you one more line of code that will change your pop-up window to a pop-under window. That means the window pops up behind the parent window rather than resting on top, as new windows normally do.

We'll start with the script that enables you to position a new window.

I want to point out that I am triggering this new window through a button. Often, new windows are triggered simply through onLoad event handlers. I'll quickly discuss that also before the end of the lesson. I just want to use the button to show the code so it's a more controlled method to start with.

Here's the script:

```
<SCRIPT LANGUAGE="JavaScript">
function goNewWin() {

// Place the window
var NewWinPutX=100;
var NewWinPutY=210;

//Get what is below onto one line

TheNewWin =window.open("untitled.html",'TheNewpop',
'height=200,width=200,fullscreen=yes,toolbar=no,location=no,directories=no,
status=no,menubar=no,scrollbars=no,resizable=no');
```

```
//Get what is above onto one line

TheNewWin.moveTo(NewWinPutX,NewWinPutY);
}
</script>

<CENTER>
<FORM>
<input type="button" VALUE="click me!" onClick="goNewWin()">
</FORM>
</CENTER>
```

You can see the script's effect in Figure 9.4.

Figure 9.4
100 in and 210 down from the top.

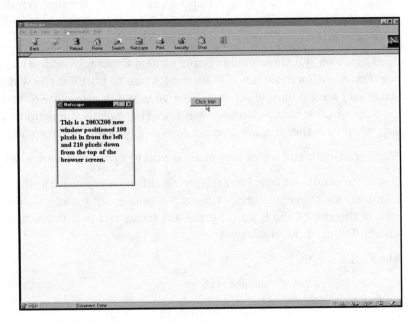

 To see the effect on your own computer, click Lesson Fifty-Three Script's Effect in your download packet, or see it online at http://www.htmlgoodies.com/JSBook/lesson53example.html.

Deconstructing the Script

Here's the basic thinking. To apply an effect to a new window, you must make that new window be seen as a single entity. The easiest method of that in JavaScript is to assign the new window to a variable name.

After you have that, you can then apply JavaScript commands to the variable name and affect the entire window. With me? Good.

We start by setting the entire script into a function. That enables us to call on the new window however and whenever we want using event handlers or some other command. Like so:

```
function goNewWin() {
```

We start this script by setting a couple of parameters in terms of placement. We create two new variables: NewWinPutX denotes where along the X (or horizontal) axis the window should be placed, and NewWinPutY denotes where along the Y (or vertical) axis the window will sit. Here's the code:

```
// Place the window
var NewWinPutX=100;
var NewWinPutY=210;
```

If you're wondering how the window is actually placed, the coordinates we just set are applied to the new window's upper-left corner. Using this script, that corner is at exactly 100 and 210.

Now let's assign the entire new window to a variable name all its own:

```
//Get what is below onto one line

TheNewWin =window.open("untitled.html",'TheNewpop',
'height=200,width=200,fullscreen=yes,toolbar=no,location=no,directories=no,
status=no,menubar=no,scrollbars=no,resizable=no');

//Get what is above onto one line
```

The window code is exactly what you read in Lesson 19; I just have it set to the variable TheNewWin.

Now we'll position it:

```
TheNewWin.moveTo(NewWinPutX,NewWinPutY);
```

The command that does the trick is moveTo.

Notice how moveTo has been set to affect the entire window by attaching it to the variable name representing the entire window—NewWin.

The moveTo command understands where to place the window because we have given it the parameters we set up previously: NewWinPutX,NewWinPutY.

After you get a new window set apart and attached to a variable name, you can have a great time playing with the window as a whole.

Now, you might be wondering why I set up the script so that I am calling for parameters from outside the `moveTo` command. I could have just as easily entered the numbers I wanted rather than going through the trouble of setting up `NewWinPutX,NewWinPutY`.

Good question. I did it that way specifically so I could break out the height and width. I design these scripts so that many people can use them, and I like to make them as easy as possible to manipulate, even for a beginner. By breaking out the positions, I can set aside a piece of code, title it like I did in the previous example, and make it rather blatant where to set the position coordinates. It's a help to another user, nothing more than that.

Here's another example, popping the window up and under.

Making a Pop-Under Window

For a new window to fall behind the parent window, you must do what's known as *blurring* the focus on that new window. We'll use the `blur` you learned about in Chapter 2, "Popping Up Text with Mouse Events."

You might have noticed in your own surfing that a pop-under window quickly shows up as an outline and then falls back behind the main window. That quick appearance is the new window coming to focus. After that focus is on the window, the code immediately blurs that window's focus, and it falls behind.

The effect is rather easy to get. We'll just add one line to the previous script:

```
TheNewWin.blur();
```

You most likely could have guessed that one, huh? We know we needed to blur the entire window, so we set the command with the variable representing the entire new window.

Placement within the script is really our only concern. I put the line last in my function. The new script would look like this:

```
<SCRIPT LANGUAGE="JavaScript">
function goNewWin() {

// Place the window
var NewWinPutX=100;
var NewWinPutY=210;

//Get what is below onto one line
```

```
TheNewWin =window.open("untitled.html",'TheNewpop',
'height=200,width=200,fullscreen=yes,toolbar=no,location=no,directories=no,
status=no,menubar=no,scrollbars=no,resizable=no');

//Get what is above onto one line

TheNewWin.moveTo(NewWinPutX,NewWinPutY);

TheNewWin.blur();
}
</script>
```

Using the onLoad Event Handler to Trigger the New Window

As I said before, a button seems a silly method of using this format. You'll most likely want the effect to fire as soon as the page loads.

To get that, you simply delete the previous HTML button code and fire the function using the onLoad event handler in the BODY flag. It'll look something like this:

```
<BODY BGCOLOR="FFFFFF" onLoad="goNewWin()">
```

Your Assignment

Let's see whether you can break out another set of parameters, other than the positioning X and Y numbers.

Alter this script so two new variables are set up that alter the new window's height and width. That means you'll need to pull those parameters out of the window code, of course. You'll also need to write a line of code that resizes the window—try using resizeTo().

Oh, and make the new window open via the onLoad event handler.

I know it's coding overkill, but it just might help a less knowledgeable coder down the line. Plus, it's a pretty good assignment, if I do say so myself.

 You can see a possible answer to this assignment on your own computer by clicking Lesson Fifty-Three Assignment in your download packet, or see it online at http://www. htmlgoodies.com/JSBook/assignment53.html.

Lesson 54: Self-Typing Typewriter

This is a fantastic effect. A text box shows up and the computer appears to be typing into it. Its uses can range from a simple greeting, to page instructions, to simply keeping a viewer's attention.

If you like to put scrolls on your page, this is a type of scroll but with a little twist. I also don't see it as being as intrusive as a scroll. Let's take a look.

Here's the script:

```
<SCRIPT LANGUAGE="javascript">
var i = 0
var typeString= "All work and no play makes Jack a dull boy."
+" All work and no play makes Jack a dull boy.
➥All work and no play makes Jack a dull boy. "
+" All work and no play makes Jack a dull boy.
➥All work and no play makes Jack a dull boy. "
+" All work and no play makes Jack a dull boy.
➥All work and no play makes Jack a dull boy. "

function type()
{
var typeLength= typeString.length
document.typewriterScreen.typepage.value=
➥document.typewriterScreen.typepage.value + typeString.charAt(i)
i++
setTimeout("type()",70)
}
</SCRIPT>


<BODY onLoad= "type()">
<FORM NAME="typewriterScreen">
<TEXTAREA ROWS=6 COLS=45 WRAP="virtual" NAME="typepage"></TEXTAREA>
</FORM>
```

The script's effect appears in Figure 9.5.

 To see the effect on your own computer, click Lesson Fifty-Four Script's Effect in your download packet, or see it online at `http://www.htmlgoodies.com/JSBook/lesson54example.html`.

What's Happening?

Here's the scoop on how the typing effect is created.

Each time the JavaScript is run, the script posts the value of the TEXTBOX with the next letter in the string, chosen by i. It works similarly to a scroll, working one letter into the string each time it runs.

266

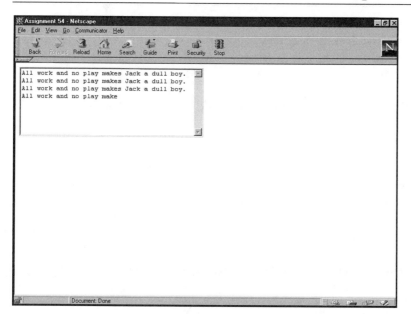

Figure 9.5
Typewriter typing.

The first time the JavaScript runs, the return is a blank TEXTBOX and the letter A from the string. That return is posted.

The next time it runs, the return from the TEXTBOX is A with the next letter in the string, 1, added. That return is also posted.

The next time the script runs, the return from the TEXTBOX is A1 and the next letter in the string, *1*, is added. That is posted.

If this happens again and again, the effect is the letters typing themselves to the screen. Now, let's dig into the script.

Deconstructing the Script

Usually, we would start by naming the HTML form elements, but not this time. The form elements actually play a role in the effect, so we will discuss them last after you understand the typing effect.

This script begins by setting up a variable i and setting it to one. Then, a very long literal string is given the variable name typeString. It looks like this:

```
var i = 0
var typeString= "All work and no play makes Jack a dull boy."
+" All work and no play makes Jack a dull boy.
➥All work and no play makes Jack a dull boy. "
```

```
+" All work and no play makes Jack a dull boy.
➥All work and no play makes Jack a dull boy. "
+" All work and no play makes Jack a dull boy.
➥All work and no play makes Jack a dull boy. "
```

Notice that each statement in quotation marks is connected by a plus sign so that one will just follow the other in one long line of text.

The Typing Function

The function is named `type()`:

```
function type()
{
var typeLength= typeString.length
document.typewriterScreen.typepage.value=
➥document.typewriterScreen.typepage.value + typeString.charAt(i)
i++
setTimeout("type()",70)
}
```

It is triggered to run through an `onLoad=` event handler in the BODY flag.

First, the variable `typeLength` is created and given the value of the number of letters in the literal string, `typeString.length`.

Next, the TEXTBOX of the following HTML form is set up to receive the output of the script. You can probably guess just from this line of code that the form itself is named `typewriterScreen` and the TEXTBOX is named `typepage`. They are.

The typing effect is created by taking the value of the TEXTBOX and adding the first character of `typeString`. That's done with the following code:

```
= document.typewriterScreen.typepage.value + typeString.charAt(i)
```

Remember that `i` is equal to one.

After that occurs, `i` starts to move incrementally up. Notice the double plus signs.

Finally, the code `setTimeout(type(),70)` sets a timeout for the script of 70/1000 of a second before it runs through the function again.

The HTML Form Elements

As I said earlier, the name of the form is `typewriterScreen` and the name of the TEXTAREA box is `typepage`. You can see that in the following code:

```
<FORM NAME="typewriterScreen">
<TEXTAREA ROWS=6 COLS=45 WRAP="virtual" NAME="typepage"></TEXTAREA>
</FORM>
```

This form element differs from the others we've used because this one plays a part in the effect. Notice the attribute WRAP="virtual". That forces the text to wrap at the edge of the TEXTBOX rather than continue going off to the right.

But it's the size that gets the look. The COLS attribute is set two letters longer than the text *All work and no play makes Jack a dull boy*. By doing that, we were able to create what appear to be carriage returns right where we want them. Without each new line of text appearing on a new line, a great deal of the effect would be lost.

Your Assignment

Add some code to the preceding script so that after the entire string of text has posted, an alert box pops up.

Hint: It should happen when the count is equal to the number of characters in the string.

 You can see a possible answer to this assignment on your own computer by clicking Lesson Fifty-Four Assignment in your download packet, or see it online at http://www. htmlgoodies.com/JSBook/assignment54.html.

Lesson 55: Scrolling Credits

When you go to the movies, do you stick around and watch the credits? Wouldn't it be great to get that kind of scroll on a Web page credit list?

That's what this script does—it scrolls the page rather than the text. It's a great effect, and a fitting end to the book's last lesson:

```
<SCRIPT LANGUAGE="javascript">

var I = 0;
function scrollit() {
if (I == 1000) {stop = true}
else {
self.scroll(1,I);
I = eval(I + 1);
setTimeout("scrollit()", 20);
}
}
```

```
</SCRIPT>

<BODY OnLoad="scrollit()">

<CENTER>

<BR><BR><BR><BR><BR><BR><BR><BR><BR><BR><BR>
<BR><BR><BR><BR><BR><BR><BR><BR><BR><BR><BR>

<font size="+5" color="008000" FACE="arial"><b>JavaScript Goodies</b></font>
<P>

<font size="+2" color="FFFFFF">by</font><P>

<font size="+3" color="ff00ff">Joe Burns, Ph.D.</font> <BR>

<font size="+2" color="ffffff">&</font><BR>

<font size="+3" color="ff00ff">Andree Growney</font> <BR><BR><BR>

</CENTER>
```

The script's effect appears in Figure 9.6.

Figure 9.6
Credits scrolling.

To see the effect on your own computer, click Lesson Fifty-Five Script's Effect in your down-load packet, or see it online at `http://www.htmlgoodies.com/JSBook/lesson55example.html`.

Deconstructing the Script

Okay, first off, let me explain what this is all about:

```
<BR><BR><BR><BR><BR><BR><BR><BR><BR><BR><BR>
<BR><BR><BR><BR><BR><BR><BR><BR><BR><BR><BR>
```

Do you see that code, right below the BODY flag and right above the HTML that will appear in the document window? It's there to add space before the text. If there is no space above the text, the page can't scroll.

Now remember, when you use this script, either make the page that will scroll longer than the browser's viewing area or add a bunch of breaks above the text so that the page is long enough to scroll.

Plus, if you create enough space so that the text is pushed down out of the browser screen, you get the effect of the text scrolling up and out of the bottom, like during a movie's credits.

The script starts again by setting the variable I to 0 outside a function.

The function is then set and named `scrollit()`:

```
var I = 0;
function scrollit() {
```

The function starts by setting up an `if` condition that states when I equals 1000, the scroll is to stop:

```
if (I == 1000) {stop = true}
```

Because that won't be true for 1,000 cycles of the script, something else has to happen.

The following code sets the scroll of the page, denoted by `self.scroll`, to scroll up one line:

```
else {
self.scroll(1,I);
```

Then one is added to I:

```
I = eval(I + 1);
```

271

Notice the `eval()` method. You should remember that it is used to set the results of the items within the parentheses to a numeric value.

Finally, the script is given a rest for 20/1000 of a second and the function is run again:

```
setTimeout("scrollit()", 20);
```

The process occurs repeatedly until I reaches 1000, or until the end of the page is reached and it can't scroll anymore.

The rest of the code is basic HTML to make the page long enough to actually have something to scroll.

Here's a hint about using this script: It looks best if the script starts the scroll on a blank page. That way, the text pops up from the bottom of the browser screen like normal movie credits.

To get that effect, you must either add enough blank lines of code above the first line of text to literally push the text off the screen or set up some other method of pushing the text off the bottom of the screen. Maybe a transparent 1×1 image set to a height of 400 or 600 would work well. I got the effect in the example by simply adding lines.

Now, take this code and make some credits. Be sure to remember Andree and me. Heck, we showed you how to do all this stuff; the least you could do is give us a credit.

Your Assignment

The assignment is to create your site's own scrolling credits, plus one more thing—create good and useful scripts.

 You can see a possible answer to this assignment on your own computer by clicking Lesson Fifty-Five Assignment in your download packet, or see it online at http://www. htmlgoodies.com/JSBook/assignment55.html.

Rainbow Text

If you've ever attempted to create a run of text where each letter is a different color, you know how unbelievably time-consuming it can be. Setting all those FONT COLOR flags can take weeks.

Well, FONT no more. This script is set up to create those multicolored runs of letters with little or no work on your part—aside from entering the text, of course. I mean … you have to do something, right?

This script was sent to me to use as a tip. I really liked it the first time I saw it. Yeah, I'm 37 (at least I was when I wrote this text), but bright lights and lots of color still make me happy. The script itself is a lot more interesting than the effect suggests. The coding is compact and gets the job done quickly.

You might want to test this script in a Netscape Navigator browser. It's not that the coding is Navigator-specific; it's just that if you look at the source code in IE, all you see is the script. In Navigator, you see the entire run of letters and the colors attached to them.

Here's the script:

```
<HTML>
<HEAD>

<TITLE>Put Some Colors Into The Text</TITLE>

<SCRIPT language=JavaScript>
<!-- Start hiding
var i

function ColoredText() {
var argLen = ColoredText.arguments.length;
if (argLen == 0)
{argLen = 1}

var text = ColoredText.arguments[0];
var textLen = ColoredText.arguments[0].length;
var defClrsArray = new Array("red","purple","cyan","green","blue",
➥ "magenta"); //default colors, change as needed

for (i=0; i<textLen; i++) {
charColor = text.charAt(i);

if (argLen == 1)
{
colorCode = Math.floor(Math.random() * defClrsArray.length);
tempStr = charColor.fontcolor(defClrsArray[colorCode])
}

else
{
colorCode = i % (argLen - 1);
tempStr = charColor.fontcolor(ColoredText.arguments[colorCode+1])
}
document.write(tempStr)
}
}
// Stop hiding -->

</SCRIPT>
</HEAD>
```

```
<BODY bgcolor="ffffcc">

<SCRIPT language=JavaScript>

<!-- Start hiding

ColoredText("This is a text sample written using the function
➥ ColoredText");

document.write ("<BR>")

ColoredText("Another text sample, this time only with red and orange
➥ repeatedly","red","orange");

document.write ("<BR><H1>")

ColoredText("Another sample with shades of
green","#006000","#007000","#008000","#009000","#00A000","#00B000");

document.write ("</H1><BR><BR><CENTER><FONT FACE=courier SIZE=+2>")

ColoredText("Try refreshing the page a couple of times!");

document.write ("</FONT></CENTER>")

// Stop hiding -->

</SCRIPT>

</BODY>

</HTML>
```

The effect is shown in Figure ST1.1. Of course, this is in black and white, so you should go see it online (see the following link).

 To see the effect on your own computer click Script Tip 1 in your download packet or see it online at http://www.htmlgoodies.com/stips/scripttip81effect.html.

The code is available for copy and paste at http://www.htmlgoodies.com/stips/ scripttip81script.html or by viewing the source of the page in your download packet.

275

Figure ST1.1
The letters are really colorful ... really. I know the shot is in black and white, so just take my word for it.

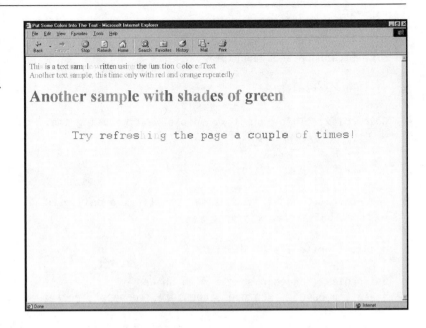

This is actually two scripts in one. Let's begin with the bottom script—that's the one that has all the display text:

```
<SCRIPT language=JavaScript>
<!-- Start hiding
ColoredText("This is a text sample written using the function
➥ ColoredText");
document.write ("<BR>")
ColoredText("Another text sample, this time only with red and orange
➥ repeatedly","red","orange");
document.write ("<BR><H1>")
ColoredText("Another sample with shades of
green","#006000","#007000","#008000","#009000","#00A000","#00B000");
document.write ("</H1><BR><BR><CENTER><FONT FACE=courier SIZE=+2>")
ColoredText("Try refreshing the page a couple of times!");
document.write ("</FONT></CENTER>")
// Stop hiding -->
</SCRIPT>
```

I can't stress enough that the previous code is truncated. See how some of the long lines break into two lines? When you run this on your system, the lines must all be on one line as it shows in the script.

What is on this page is for display purposes only.

Okay, you can see that this is both the text on the page and a script. Notice that the text that appears on the page is enclosed in the argument to the function. The concept is that the text within the instance will be displayed on the page only after the function `ColoredText()` has had the opportunity to act upon it.

Notice also that the HTML commands that alter the text are not included with the text. Those HTML tags are contained within `document.write` commands. They had to be because this is a script. Without the `document.write`, the script wouldn't know what to do with the text and you'd get an error.

If you tried to put the tags inside the `ColoredText()` instance, the script wouldn't see them as tags but rather as text to be altered. The concept of tags outside the text is pretty easy to follow. Notice all the beginning tags are in the `document.write` before the text, and all the end tags are in the `document.write` after the text.

No big deal. Moving along ....

If you look at the first `ColoredText()` line of text, you see that it's just text with nothing following it. Yet, the next two lines of text do have something following them. It might seem odd at first, but the text that had nothing following it is the most colorful.

The second line has `"red"` and `"orange"` after it. Note the displayed text is only red and orange.

The next line has a series of green hex codes; thus the text is in shades of green.

Here's a good rule of thumb: The more colors you offer after the text, the more colorful your text will be. The more shades of the same color you offer, the more smoothly your text will appear to flow. If you put in 50 different shades of green from lightest to darkest, your text will roll through that spectrum.

What Are Those Colors?

They're arguments. See the format? First, you have text in double quotation marks and then a list of elements, in this case colors, in double quotation marks one after the other.

That's JavaScript shorthand. You could get the exact same effect if you simply created an array of all the greens and called for one after the other, as is shown in Chapter 8, "Arrays." It would be a lot of typing, though. This way, the browser understands that what follows are arguments, thanks to the format. What's more, the arguments are turned into an array for you.

Now, that's helpful.

You now have four lines of text, two of which have arguments, so you know what color they're going to be. But how does that code that has no arguments get to be so darn colorful?

Putting Color to the Text

Now on to the fun part. Let's get to acting on those lines of text. First off, let's look at the really colorful ones, those without arguments:

```
function ColoredText() {
var argLen = ColoredText.arguments.length;
if (argLen == 0)
{argLen = 1}
var text = ColoredText.arguments[0];
var textLen = ColoredText.arguments[0].length;
var defClrsArray = new Array("red","purple","cyan","green","blue",
➥"magenta");
//default colors, change as needed
for (i=0; i<textLen; i++) {
charColor = text.charAt(i);

if (argLen == 1)
{
colorCode = Math.floor(Math.random() * defClrsArray.length);
tempStr = charColor.fontcolor(defClrsArray[colorCode])
}
else
{
colorCode = i % (argLen - 1);
tempStr = charColor.fontcolor(ColoredText.arguments[colorCode+1])
}
document.write(tempStr)
}
}
// Stop hiding -->
</SCRIPT>
```

Again, the script is a little out of order. You'll need to make a point of getting it into the same format as the display in the script.

The function isn't overly long, but it does get goofy at times, so let's examine it in two parts. First, I'll discuss the variables and how the non-argument text is created.

The name of the function is `Coloredtext()`. That's the same name as the function that wrote the text to the page. Actually, it was the same function. By placing the text inside the function instance, you literally pass the text to the function. It's after the text is given color that it's written to the page.

Let's start at the top.

The variable `argLen` is given the value of the argument's length. Remember, I previously said that the color names that follow the display text are arguments. The JavaScript knows they're arguments because of the format in which they are presented.

Obviously, the first line of text does not have any arguments. That would make the argument equal to zero. You can't have that, so the next blip of code asks whether the argument is equal to zero. If it is, the variable `argLen` is given the value of 1. That will still enable you to separate it from those that have at least two arguments, in the second line of text.

JavaScript has already turned those arguments into an array, so you need to get some hierarchy statements into array format to deal with them. That's these two:

```
var text = ColoredText.arguments[0];
var textLen = ColoredText.arguments[0].length;
```

The first line enables you to pull out a specific argument by calling for its array number. The second tells you the length of the array, meaning the number of items in the array.

The next line is a default list of colors. This is where the color in the non-argument text comes from. If there isn't a set of arguments, use these:

```
var defClrsArray = new Array("red","purple","cyan","green","blue",
➥"magenta");
```

Remember I said the script gets a little goofy? Here it comes. The next little section deals with attaching color to each of the letters in the display text:

```
for (i=0; i<textLen; i++) {
```

It starts with a `for` loop. The loop is set up with three conditions, each separated by a semicolon. The first condition sets a value to a variable; the second condition determines how often the loop should occur. In this case, the loop continues only as long as there are letters. See that? As long as `i` is less than the length of the text, it keeps looping.

Finally, the third condition does something to the variable if the loop isn't finished. In this case it adds one. The double plus sign does the adding. The effect is that each letter in the run of text is looked at one after the other until there's no more text. The following code sets a variable name to the character represented by `i`:

```
charColor = text.charAt(i);
```

Remember, this loops through again and again, so each time it loops, `charAt(i)` is different. The command `charAt()` pulls a specific letter out of a run of text. In this case, the letter it pulls is the letter equal to the number represented by `i`. As the loop rolls, `i` increases.

The following actually sets color:

```
if (argLen == 1)
{
colorCode = Math.floor(Math.random() * defClrsArray.length);
tempStr = charColor.fontcolor(defClrsArray[colorCode])
}
```

An `If` statement starts it off testing whether `argLen` is equal to 1. We know it is in the first line of text because I set it that way earlier. Remember that? If there are no arguments, `argLen` is equal to 1. In this case, it's equal to 1.

The variable `colorCode` is given a specific value through a little math. Just like algebra class, let's start inside the parentheses. `Math.random` generates a random number between 0 and 1 without choosing either 0 or 1. It could be .334 or .562 or anywhere in that range of numbers. That random number is then multiplied by the length of the default color array.

The number resulting from that equation is then floored by `Math.floor`. The `floor` takes whatever number is inside the parentheses and drops it to the lower whole number. For example, if the answer in the parentheses was 2.6, `Math.floor` would turn it into 2.

Yes, there's an equal to that going the other way. `Math.ceil` pushes the number to the ceiling, or the next higher full number. The number 2.6 would therefore become 3.

Here's an interesting thing to keep in mind: Notice how some arrays are set and some are random? If you refresh the example a few times, you'll notice that the lines with set arrays remain static and display the same color scheme. Those that use random colors, however, change.

Keep that in mind: Use this script either for random or a set color scheme.

And speaking of color ....

Assigning Color

The next line is a hierarchy statement that uses the default array of colors, represented by the variable `charColor`, and assigns the color as a `fontcolor` to what's inside the parentheses. The command `fontcolor` works just like `<FONT COLOR>` in HTML. If you look at the source code of this script in Netscape Navigator, you'll see letter after letter written with individual font color tags.

If the previous line generated the number 2, cyan would be the color plucked from the array. Remember, JavaScript starts counting at 0. That cyan color would be set into a `fontcolor` by the array statement inside the parentheses.

From the default color array, `defClrsArray`, pluck out the number represented by `colorCode`.

Next, assign it all to a variable named `tempStr`.

Now you have the colors yanked from the default list. But what about those texts that actually have arguments? And how does that text get written to the page?

We've already used up just about the entire function. Now we're interested in just this:

```
else
{
colorCode = i % (argLen - 1);
tempStr = charColor.fontcolor(ColoredText.arguments[colorCode+1])
}
document.write(tempStr)
}
}
```

See how it starts with `else`? That's because I cut it off in the middle of an `if` statement. If the display text carries an argument with it, this `else` statement is brought into play.

The variable `colorCode` is given a numeric value through a fairly fancy equation.

The value of `i` is `%` against the argument length minus one. For example, say you have six arguments. It would be six colors in this case. Let's say the `for` loop has rolled a few times and is now equal to 5.

The percent sign is a mathematical operator that returns the remainder of an equation. So let's do the math.

5 % (6–1) produces 5 % 5. There is no remainder, so 0 is returned. That is equal to the first element in the array created through the argument. The loop rolls again, and now `i` is equal to 6.

6 % (6–1) results in 6 % 5, which equals 1.2. The remainder, 2, is returned. The third color in the array is therefore returned (JavaScript starts counting at 0).

The next line works just like its partner. The `charColor.fontcolor` is given the value represented by the array of arguments plucked out by whatever number is returned by the line we just discussed plus one. That value is assigned to the variable `tempStr`.

Again, in the world of JavaScript, `fontcolor` is equal to `<FONT COLOR>` in HTML. Look at the source code in Navigator to see them all.

That's pretty slick, eh?

Lastly, a basic `document.write` puts `tempStr` on the page and we're done.

Full Text Date Script

A reader wanted to post a date that goes beyond the basic number returns. He wanted the date to display in text. I am the author of the following script, which I wrote to present the day and the month in text.

As an added bonus, the script adds the "th", "st", "nd", or "rd" depending on the day of the month. I also used a new method to extract a four-digit year, rather than a two-digit year. It's a bit long, but it works pretty well. It looks like this:

```
<SCRIPT LANGUAGE="JavaScript">

DaysofWeek = new Array()
DaysofWeek[0]="Sunday"
DaysofWeek[1]="Monday"
DaysofWeek[2]="Tuesday"
DaysofWeek[3]="Wednesday"
DaysofWeek[4]="Thursday"
DaysofWeek[5]="Friday"
DaysofWeek[6]="Saturday"
```

```
Months = new Array()
Months[0]="January"
Months[1]="February"
Months[2]="March"
Months[3]="April"
Months[4]="May"
Months[5]="June"
Months[6]="July"
Months[7]="August"
Months[8]="September"
Months[9]="October"
Months[10]="November"
Months[11]="December"

RightNow = new Date()

var day = DaysofWeek[RightNow.getDay()]
var date = RightNow.getDate()
var Month = Months[RightNow.getMonth()]
var Year = RightNow.getFullYear()

if (date == 1 || date == 21 || date == 31)
{ender = "<SUP>st</SUP>"}

else
if (date == 2 || date == 22)
{ender = "<SUP>nd</SUP>"}

else
if (date == 3 || date == 23)
{ender = "<SUP>rd</SUP>"}

else
{ender = "<SUP>th</SUP>"}

document.write("Today is " +day+ " " +Month+ " " +date+ ender+ ",
➥" +Year+ ".")
</SCRIPT>
```

The script produces the result shown in Figure ST2.1. I've made it a little bigger in the screen capture than it will come out on your page simply so you can better see the format.

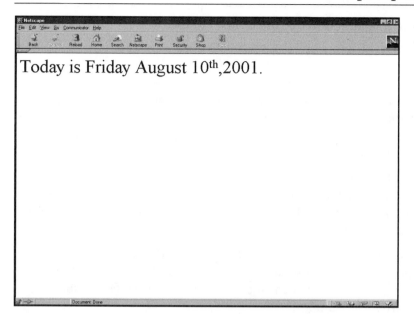

To see the effect on your own computer, click Script Tip Two in your download packet or see it online at *http://www.htmlgoodies.com/stips/scripttip31.html*.

The code is available for copy and paste at *http://www.htmlgoodies.com/stips/ scripttip31script.html* or by viewing the source of the page in your download packet.

Let's start from the top. This script relies on two arrays. The first array lists the days of the week, and the second array lists the months of the year. Here's the first array, the days of the week:

```
DaysofWeek = new Array()
DaysofWeek[0]="Sunday"
DaysofWeek[1]="Monday"
DaysofWeek[2]="Tuesday"
DaysofWeek[3]="Wednesday"
DaysofWeek[4]="Thursday"
DaysofWeek[5]="Friday"
DaysofWeek[6]="Saturday"
```

An array is just what you see—a listing of things the JavaScript can refer to later. This specific array is made up of text strings. Note that each day of the week is surrounded by double quotation marks. Those double quotation marks tell the browser that what is contained within should be treated as just text. However, arrays can contain just about any text, command, number, or combination of the three you want.

Each array starts with a line that announces to the browser that an array is starting. That line looks like this:

```
DaysofWeek = new Array()
```

The format is similar to setting up a new `Date()`, which you'll actually do later. The line announces a `new Array()` and gives the array a name. In this case, the name is `DaysofWeek`. I made the name up just like I would a variable name because, in reality, it is a variable name. It's just that this variable has multiple values.

Notice that the seven days of the week are numbered 0–6. It's what's called an *index number*. The format is to offer the name of the array, square brackets around the index number, and then the item that is being indexed. In this case it's a text string, so the double quotation marks surround the text.

The `getDay()` method returns the day of the week, but it returns that day as a numeric value, 0–6 representing Sunday through Saturday. Now do you see the reason for the order of days? We've set up an array of days that is equal to the returns that `getDay()` will return. A little later, we'll get into why this is important.

Now that you're somewhat familiar with the format of an array, let's take a look at the second one. This one deals with the months of the year:

```
Months = new Array()
Months[0]="January"
Months[1]="February"
Months[2]="March"
Months[3]="April"
Months[4]="May"
Months[5]="June"
Months[6]="July"
Months[7]="August"
Months[8]="September"
Months[9]="October"
Months[10]="November"
Months[11]="December"
```

The name of the array is `Months`, and the months are arranged in order 0–11 because those are the numbers returned by using the `getMonth()` method.

Okay, now you're up to speed with the concept and structure of an array. You can begin calling for the array index through the `getDay()` and `getMonth()` methods.

Taking Elements from the Arrays

Here's the code you're worried about right now:

```
RightNow = new Date()
var day = DaysofWeek[RightNow.getDay()]
var date = RightNow.getDate()
var Month = Months[RightNow.getMonth()]
var Year = RightNow.getFullYear()
```

The first line should be very near and dear to your heart by now. The variable name RightNow is assigned to a new Date() object. That new date()object contains all the information regarding the current date and time. Next, you'll use a couple of methods to extract from that Date() object the day, date, month, and year.

Let me explain this first line because, after you get this line down, the rest just falls into place:

```
var day = DaysofWeek[RightNow.getDay()]
```

The line starts by assigning the variable name day to the result of what follows.

What follows is the variable name of the first array, DaysofWeek. Now you know that this line will act on the first array, which is the one that lists the days of the week.

The format is the same as one of the DaysofWeek array items. Square brackets immediately follow the array name, and inside those brackets is the code that returns the day of the week: RightNow.getDay().

So what's going to happen is the RightNow.getDay() will return a number, 0–6, representing the day of the week. Let's say the number returned is 4. In the DaysofWeek array, 4 means Thursday. Thus, the variable day now represents Thursday. When you call on the variable day, the text Thursday is returned.

The next line of code

```
var date = RightNow.getDate()
```

follows a similar format but is not attached to an array. This is the number day of the month, and you want that to remain a number.

The next line follows the array format exactly, except this time around you're looking for the month of the year:

```
var Month = Months[RightNow.getMonth()]
```

Let's say it's May. `RightNow.getMonth()` would therefore return the number 4. That's equal to the text string May in the Months array. Thus, when you call on the variable name Month, you'll get the text string May.

The last line of code might be new to you:

```
var Year = RightNow.getFullYear()
```

In the past, I've used the older `getYear()` method to extract the year from the `Date()` object. Well, that works, but it returns only a two-digit year. That created some problems when Y2K came and went. Because we're past the year 1999, you should start to use only the `getFullYear()` method because it returns the full four-digit year. You should start using it across the board when you want a year displayed.

Now you have all the returns ready to go. You have the day in text, the number date, the month in text, and a four-digit year. All you need to do now is decide which two-letter extension should print after the day number. Of course, it has to be the correct two letters; you don't want your text to read Tuesday, May 11rd, 1999.

That would be bad.

Adding Those Two Letters

After you write a computer language for a while, you start to find sections of commands you really enjoy using. In HTML, I really like tables. I think they're great. In JavaScript, it's the `if/else` conditional statements. I'm amazed at how flexible and powerful they really are. I used another one in this script—you've probably seen it by now. It looks like this:

```
if (date == 1 || date == 21 || date == 31)
{ender = "<SUP>st</SUP>"}
else
if (date == 2 || date == 22)
{ender = "<SUP>nd</SUP>"}
else
if (date == 3 || date == 23)
{ender = "<SUP>rd</SUP>"}
else
{ender = "<SUP>th</SUP>"}
```

The purpose of the previous conditional statements is to look at the number returned from the `RightNow.getDate()` object.method statement. Remember that you assigned that number to return the variable name date.

The purpose of these lines of code is to look at the number and decide which two-letter extension should follow. Let's think it through logically. Yes, you could set up a condition for every number 1–31, but that's really going overboard.

There are only three times when the "st" is needed.

There are only two times when the "nd" is needed.

There are only two times when the "rd" is needed.

The rest of the numbers get the "th".

So, you should set up the conditions as follows:

```
if (date == 1 || date == 21 || date == 31)
{ender = "<SUP>st</SUP>"}
```

The first statement reads, "If the date is equal to 1 or equal to (notice the double equal signs) 21 or equal to 31, then the variable ender equals st". That would help produce "1st", "21st", and "31st".

You probably already know that the HTML <SUP> makes text appear as the smaller letters up high. You can also set that to <SUB> if you want, but I don't think the effect is quite as nice.

Did you catch that double vertical lines mean "or"? That's a great way of adding multiple conditions that have the same result all in one line of code rather than writing each condition out on its own. If you don't know, you'll find that vertical line on the same keyboard button as the backslash, usually just above the Enter key.

As with all if statements, if the first condition does not apply, the script rolls over to the next one in line. It looks like this:

```
else
if (date == 2 || date == 22)
{ender = "<SUP>nd</SUP>"}
```

This tests whether the date number is either 2 or 22. If so, ender is equal to nd. If not, you move along:

```
else
if (date == 3 || date == 23)
{ender = "<SUP>rd</SUP>"}
```

Is the date 3 or 23? If so, ender is equal to rd. If not, you move on:

```
else
{ender = "<SUP>th</SUP>"}
```

This is a catchall. You set up a conditional system that tests the date number return over three sets of if statements: If the number meets none of the statements, this else statement handles it. If the number gets this far—and it's a darn good bet it will because "th" is the most frequently used text—ender is equal to th.

Now that you have all the parts, use a basic document.write() statement to get it onto the page for all the world to see:

```
document.write("Today is " +day+ " " +Month+ " " +date+ ender+ ", " +Year+ ".")
```

Got it? Good.

Random Banner Ad Script

Again, this one was by request. It's a random banner script. I wrote this one, so feel free to use it. The script uses two arrays and five images to get its effect. The script posts a random banner. What's more, the banner is active. You can click it to go where the banner reads. It's a quick script that can be used in myriad ways.

I have every intention of doing this entire script quickly. It's all review:

```
<SCRIPT LANGUAGE="javascript">

banners = new Array()
banners[0]="<IMG BORDER=0 SRC=banner0.gif>"
banners[1]="<IMG BORDER=0 SRC=banner1.gif>"
banners[2]="<IMG BORDER=0 SRC=banner2.gif>"
banners[3]="<IMG BORDER=0 SRC=banner3.gif>"
banners[4]="<IMG BORDER=0 SRC=banner4.gif>"
```

```
GoTo = new Array()
GoTo[0]="http://www.htmlgoodies.com"
GoTo[1]="http://www.developer.com"
GoTo[2]="http://www.mtv.com"
GoTo[3]="http://www.vh1.com"
GoTo[4]="http://www.whitehouse.gov"

var Number = Math.round(4 * Math.random());

var TheLink = GoTo[Number]
var TheImage = banners[Number]

document.write("<CENTER><A HREF=" +TheLink+ ">" +TheImage+ "</A>
➥</center>")
</SCRIPT>
```

 To see the effect on your own computer, click Script Tip Three in your download packet or see it online at http://www.htmlgoodies.com/stips/scripttip34.html.

The code is available for copy and paste at http://www.htmlgoodies.com/stips/ scripttip34script.html or by viewing the source of the page in your download packet.

The Arrays

```
banners = new Array()
banners[0]="<IMG BORDER=0 SRC=banner0.gif>"
banners[1]="<IMG BORDER=0 SRC=banner1.gif>"
banners[2]="<IMG BORDER=0 SRC=banner2.gif>"
banners[3]="<IMG BORDER=0 SRC=banner3.gif>"
banners[4]="<IMG BORDER=0 SRC=banner4.gif>"

GoTo = new Array()
GoTo[0]="http://www.htmlgoodies.com"
GoTo[1]="http://www.developer.com"
GoTo[2]="http://www.mtv.com"
GoTo[3]="http://www.vh1.com"
GoTo[4]="http://www.whitehouse.gov"
```

The script starts off with two arrays. The first array, named banners, is a series of five images. Those are our banners. Figure ST3.1 shows what banner0.gif through banner4.gif look like.

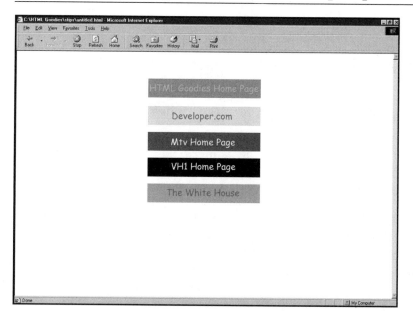

Figure ST3.1
The five images you'll need for this script.

You can grab each of the four images at `http://www.htmlgoodies.com/stips/banner0.gif` through `http://www.htmlgoodies.com/stips/banner4.gif`.

Notice that double quotation marks surround each indexed item so you know each is to be handled as if it were just simple text. Notice also that no quotation marks are around the zero or the name of the image. That would mess up the script by stopping the line too early and result in an error.

The second array contains the URLs that will match the banners. Note that the URLs are in the same order as the banners. That way, you can use the same number to call for an element from each array. For example, the first banner reads "HTML Goodies Home Page." The first `GoTo` array item is the URL for HTML Goodies. Now you can use the number 0 to return both the Goodies banner and the Goodies URL. With me?

The Random Number

```
var Number = Math.round(4 * Math.random());
```

The variable number is assigned a random number between 0 and 4.

That number is created by multiplying 4 times a random point between .001 and .999 created by the `Math.random` commands. The numbers returned can be 0, 1, 2, 3, or 4. The `Math.round` object.method statement ensures that the number is rounded off so there are no remainders in the result.

Calling for the Array Index

```
var TheLink = GoTo[Number]
var TheImage = banners[Number]
```

Two new variable names are created. TheLink represents the text return from the GoTo array, whereas the variable TheImage represents the return from the banners array.

In both cases, the same number—the random number created earlier—is used to choose the item from both arrays. That way you know all the banners/URLs will line right up.

Writing It to the Page

Next, you'll use JavaScript to build a line of HTML. Because this HTML creates something on the page, remember to place this script wherever on the page you want the effect to appear:

```
document.write("<CENTER><A HREF=" +TheLink+ ">" +TheImage+ "</A>
➥</center>")
```

You're using a document.write() statement to get it to the page. Notice that the A HREF command is fully built—you're just filling in the blanks. The two text strings from the arrays are placed, and the entire line of HTML is centered.

When the page displays, the banner is centered on the page and is active to the URL it is representing.

See how we've taken parts from other scripts and built something new? You can do that. Using just what's on this page, you could make a random line of text come up on your page or use a function to enact the script so it offers random fortunes, like the Magic 8-Ball. You can do it.

Frames Script

If you ever have trouble writing code for frames, like I do, then this is the script for you.

All you do is ask for a certain number of frames in rows and columns, and the script writes it out for you.

On top of its functionality, it offers some new JavaScript coding to look at. Plus, it is easily understandable when you start to break it down.

Here it is:

```
<HTML>
<HEAD>
<TITLE>Frame Maker</TITLE>

<SCRIPT language=JavaScript>
```

```
//Below are Variables that will be used in each paste function
var top="<HTML>" + "\r" + "<TITLE>My Frame Page</TITLE>" + "\r" +
➥"<HEAD></HEAD>"
var nf="<noframes>" + "\r" + "You need a frames-capable browser to
➥view this page." + "\r" + "</noframes>" + "\r" + "</HTML>"
var f="</frameset>"
var bc="bordercolor=blue"
var MW="marginwidth=0"
var MH="marginheight=0"
//Below are six functions that produce frame code in the TEXTAREA box
function framesa()
{
document.Framer.Fillit.value=top
+ "\r" + "<frameset cols=50%,* "
+ " " + bc + "\r" + "<frame src=w.htm" +" " + "name=One"
+ "\r" + "scrolling=auto" + " " + MW + " " + MH + " " +
➥"noresize=yes>"
+ "\r" + "<frame src=x.htm" +" " + "name=Two"
+ "\r" + "scrolling=auto" + " " + MW + " " + MH + " " +
➥"noresize=yes>"
+ "\r" + f
+ "\r" + nf
}

function framesb()
{
document.Framer.Fillit.value=top
+ "\r" + "<frameset rows=50%,* "
+ " " + bc + "\r" + "<frame src=w.htm" +" " + "name=One"
+ "\r" + "scrolling=auto" + " " + MW + " " + MH + " " +
➥"noresize=yes>"
+ "\r" + "<frame src=x.htm" +" " + "name=Two"
+ "\r" + "scrolling=auto" + " " + MW + " " + MH + " " +
➥"noresize=yes>"
+ "\r" + f
+ "\r" + nf
}

function framemixa()
{
document.Framer.Fillit.value=top
+ "\r" + "<frameset cols=30%,* " + bc + " " + "noresize=yes>"
+ "\r" + "<frame src=w.htm" + " " + "name=One" + " " + "scrolling=yes"
```

```
+ "\r" + MW + " " + MH + " " + "noresize=yes>"
+ "\r" + "<frameset rows=50%,*>"
+ "\r" + "<frame src=x.htm" + " " + "name=Two" + " " + MW
+ "\r" + MH + " " + "scrolling=yes>"
+ "\r" + "<frame src=y.htm" + " " + "name=Three" + " " + "scrolling=no"
+ "\r" + MW + " " + MH + " " + "noresize=no>"
+ "\r" + f
+ "\r" + f
+ "\r" + nf
}


function frames3v()
{
document.Framer.Fillit.value=top
+ "\r" + "<frameset cols=33%,33%,*" + " " + bc
+ "\r" + "<frame src=w.htm name=One" + " " + "scrolling=auto"
+ "\r" + MW + " " + MH + " " + "noresize=yes>"
+ "\r" + "<frame src=x.htm" + " " + "name=Two" + " " +
➥"scrolling=auto"
+ "\r" + MW + " " + MH + " " + "noresize=yes>"
+ "\r" + "<frame src=y.htm" + " " + "name=Three" + " " +
"scrolling=auto"
+ "\r" + MW + " " + MH + " " + "noresize=yes>"
+ "\r" + f
+ "\r" + nf
}


function frames3h()
{
document.Framer.Fillit.value=top
+ "\r" + "<frameset rows=33%,33%,*" + " " + bc
+ "\r" + "<frame src=w.htm name=One" + " " + "scrolling=auto"
+ "\r" + MW + " " + MH + " " + "noresize=yes>"
+ "\r" + "<frame src=x.htm" + " " + "name=Two" + " " +
➥"scrolling=auto"
+ "\r" + MW + " " + MH + " " + "noresize=yes>"
+ "\r" + "<frame src=y.htm" + " " + "name=Three" + " " +
"scrolling=auto"
+ "\r" + MW + " " + MH + " " + "noresize=yes>"
+ "\r" + f
+ "\r" + nf
}
```

```
function framemixb()
{
document.Framer.Fillit.value=top
+ "\r" + "<frameset cols=30%,* " + bc + " " + "noresize=yes>"
+ "\r" + "<frameset rows=50%,*>" + "\r" + "<frame src=w.htm" + " " +
"name=One"
+ " " + "scrolling=no" + " " + MW + "\r" + MH + " " + "noresize=yes>"
+ "\r" + "<frame src=x.htm" + " " + "name=Two" + " " + MW
+ "\r" + MH + " " + "scrolling=yes>"
+ "\r" + f
+ "\r" + "<frameset rows=50%,*>" + "\r" + "<frame src=y.htm" + " " +
"name=Three"
+ "\r" + "scrolling=no" +" " + MW + " " + MH + " " + "noresize=no>"
+ "\r" + "<frame src=z.htm" +" " + "name=Four" + " " + "scrolling=yes"
+ "\r" + MW + " " + MH + " " + "noresize=yes>"
+ "\r" + f
+ "\r" + f
+ "\r" + nf
}
//Below is the function that copies text from one box to the other
function Copy()
{
if (document.Framer.Fillit.value=="")
{ alert ('The top box is empty. Please enter a script by clicking
➥one of the frames buttons.') }
else
{ document.Framer.Pastebox.value=document.Framer.Fillit.value }
}
//Below is the function that displays the code in a new window
function view()
{
if (document.Framer.Pastebox.value=="")
{ alert ('The paste box is empty. Please enter a script by clicking
➥the Copy/Edit button.')
return false;
}
else
{ alert('If you like the results, remember to paste it to a text
➥editor!')
boat = open ("","DisplayWindow")
see = parent.document.Framer.Pastebox.value
boat.document.write (see)
return true;
```

```
}
}

</SCRIPT>


</HEAD>

<BODY aLink=#ff0000 bgColor=#c0c0c0 link=#0000ee text=#000000
➥vLink=#551a8b>

//Below is the FORM and TABLE code that creates the look on the page
<FORM name=Framer>
<TABLE border=1>
<TBODY>
<TR>
<TD WIDTH="150">

<b>1.</b> Choose One:<P>
<INPUT onClick=framesa() type=button value="2 Vertical"><BR>
<INPUT onClick=frames3v() type=button value="3 Vertical"><BR>
<INPUT onClick=framesb() type=button value="2 Horizontal"><BR>
<INPUT onClick=frames3h() type=button value="3 Horizontal"><BR>
<INPUT onClick=framemixa() type=button value="3 Mixed"><BR>
<INPUT onClick=framemixb() type=button value="4 Mixed"><BR> </TD>
<TD vAlign=top>
<TEXTAREA cols=56 name=Fillit rows=15></TEXTAREA>
<CENTER>
</TD></TR>
<TR>
<TD>

<b>2.</b> Paste it in:<P>
<INPUT onClick=Copy() type=button value=Copy/Edit><p>
<INPUT onClick="alert('Misfire? No problem, a new copy will be pasted to
➥the bottom box. Good Luck!');Copy()" type=button value="Start Over"><BR>
<INPUT onClick=reset() type=button value="Clear All"><BR> </TD>
<TD vAlign=top>
<TEXTAREA cols=56 name=Pastebox rows=15></TEXTAREA>

<CENTER>
<b>3.</b> Then: <INPUT onClick=view() type=button value=" View It! ">
</CENTER>
```

```
       </TD>
       </TR>
       </TBODY>
       </TABLE>

       <P>
       </FORM>
       </P>

       </BODY>

       </HTML>
```

Now that's a script! In this case bigger does mean better. Figure ST4.1 is what you get with that code.

Figure ST4.1
This script creates quite an interface and helps with frames code.

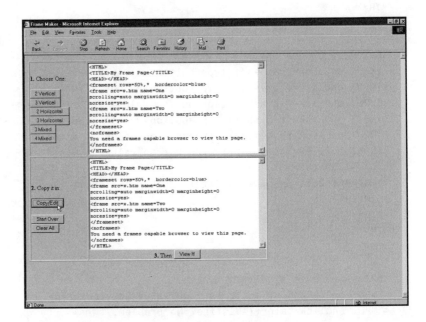

To see the effect on your own computer, click Script Tip Four in your download packet or see it online at http://www.htmlgoodies.com/stips/scripttip49effect.html.

The code is available for copy and paste at http://www.htmlgoodies.com/stips/ scripttip49script.html or by viewing the source of the page in your download packet.

Normally, when FORM commands are involved, I go after those first. Not this time. I want to start by talking about how the frame code is created.

If you were going to create a script like this, you might find yourself writing the same things again and again. Every frame code requires the HTML and TITLE flags. You'd also write the NOFRAMES code again and again. Yes, you could write it again and again, but it would be a whole lot easier if you simply assigned a short variable name to the code; then you could call it all up with just a couple of letters.

That's what was done in the first block of code:

```
var top="<HTML>" + "\r"
+ "<TITLE>My Frame Page</TITLE>"
+ "\r" +"<HEAD></HEAD>"

var nf="<noframes>" + "\r" + "You need a frames-capable browser to
➥view this page."
+ "\r" + "</noframes>" + "\r" + "</HTML>"

var f="</frameset>"
var bc="bordercolor=blue>"
var MW="marginwidth=0"
var MH="marginheight=0"
```

You get to pick out what each of the variables represent, so I'll just discuss a couple of them. With this, all you need to do is call for "top" and you'll get the entire text string:

```
<HTML>
<TITLE>My Frame Page</TITLE>
<HEAD></HEAD>
```

Won't that make life a little easier? Now, you might notice the code \r stuck in there. Look again and notice where it's stuck. It's put in as if it were text (double quotation marks are around it). See what it does? It produces a line break when the text string is displayed. How's that for a good trick? Just make sure the slash is a backslash—a forward slash does not make the line break.

So, now you have top for the header information, nf for the noframes text, f for the end frameset flag, bc for the body's background color, MW for the marginwidth, and MH for the marginheight.

The First Frame Function

Moving down the script, let's look at the first, and easiest, frame function. This is the function that produces the text for two vertical frames:

```
function framesa()
{
```

```
document.Framer.Fillit.value=top
+ "\r" + "<frameset cols=50%,* "
+ " " + bc + "\r" + "<frame src=w.htm" +" " + "name=One"
+ "\r" + "scrolling=auto" + " " + MW + " " + MH + " " +
➥"noresize=yes>"
+ "\r" + "<frame src=x.htm" +" " + "name=Two"
+ "\r" + "scrolling=auto" + " " + MW + " " + MH + " " +
➥"noresize=yes>"
+ "\r" + f
+ "\r" + nf
}
```

It really looks cryptic, huh? Well, let's break it down. When the function is called for, the first thing you'll get is top. That's the header information. Then you get a line break and then the frameset flag. The background color (bc) then is added and a line break. The first frame window's source is next, adding a NAME, a line break, the scrolling=auto text, the marginwidth (MW), marginheight (MH), and finally the noresize=yes text.

You'll notice a lot of blank spaces were created by using the code (" "). That's the author's preference. I always add spaces by putting a space on the end of the text inside the double quotation marks. This is another method that works just as well.

That format is followed again for the next frame window source: a line break, the end frameset flag (f), and another line break. Then the noframes text (nf) is added.

Put it all together and you get the following display:

```
<HTML>
<TITLE>My Frame Page</TITLE>
<HEAD></HEAD>
<frameset cols=50%,* bordercolor=blue>
<frame src=w.htm name=One
scrolling=auto marginwidth=0 marginheight=0 noresize=yes>
<frame src=x.htm name=Two
scrolling=auto marginwidth=0 marginheight=0 noresize=yes>
</frameset>
<noframes>
You need a frames-capable browser to view this page.
</noframes>
</HTML>
```

That format was followed six times until the author created the six FRAME code functions: framesa(), framesb(), framemixa(), frames3v(), frames3h(), and framemixb(). Read them through—go slowly because they get confusing. I was impressed the first time I went through it. It's a pretty nice bit of coding.

The Buttons

Let's jump to the bottom again to get a handle on the buttons. You've probably noticed by now that this script has many of the same function types again and again. A bunch of buttons display, but they all work pretty much the same way. Each has an onClick event handler that triggers a function found farther up the page.

First, here are a few names. Take a look at the code toward the bottom. You see that multiple FORM elements are used. The NAME of the form itself is Framer. The top TEXTAREA box is named Fillit, and the bottom box is named Pastebox.

When I spoke about the six frame functions last time, I neglected the code document.Framer.Fillit.value that starts each one. That code points to the first TEXTAREA box, setting its value. That's why the text appears where it does.

That's easy enough, but how does the text get pasted from the top box to the bottom box? Again, a button is involved, triggering the paste. The button's purpose is to fire the function Copy(). It looks like this:

```
function Copy()
{
if (document.Framer.Fillit.value=="")
{ alert ('The top box is empty.') }
else
{ document.Framer.Pastebox.value=document.Framer.Fillit.value }
}
```

The function is an if/else conditional statement. If the top box (document.Framer.Fillit.value) is empty (""), throw up an alert that says so. Otherwise, what is in document.Framer.Fillit.value should now go into document.Framer.Fillit.value.

So far, so good, but there are two more buttons to deal with.

The Start Over button is similar to the one you just looked at. In fact, it fires the same Copy() function. The only difference is that it first launches an alert box that is intended to put you at ease. The button code looks like this:

```
<INPUT onClick="alert('Misfire? No problem.');Copy()"
type=button value="Start Over">
```

See how it's done? The alert code is followed by a semicolon and then the function name. Nice effect.

The `Clear` All button fires another function named `reset()`. Don't bother looking for it; it isn't there. Reset is a function built into the browser. When you make Guestbook forms, you create a `reset` button through this code:

```
<INPUT TYPE="reset">
```

In this case, the coding is just a little different to allow you to put text on the reset button. Here's how the author did it:

```
<INPUT onClick=reset() type=button value="Clear All">
```

One click and everything goes away! Just remember that for this effect, every FORM element must be between the same FORM and /FORM flags; otherwise, only those elements within the reset's FORM flags will erase.

All that's left to do is open the new window and display it.

Showing the Code

The button that displays the frame code in a new window looks like this:

```
<INPUT onClick=view() type=button value=" View It! ">
```

The `function view()` looks like this:

```
function view()
{
if (document.Framer.Pastebox.value=="")
{ alert ('The paste box is empty.')
return false;
}

else
{ alert('If you like the results, paste it to a text editor!')
boat = open ("","DisplayWindow")
see = parent.document.Framer.Pastebox.value
boat.document.write (see)
return true;
}
}
```

The function is again set up as an `if/else` conditional statement. The purpose is to post an alert box if the user attempts to view when nothing is there to view:

```
if (document.Framer.Pastebox.value=="")
{ alert ('The paste box is empty.')
```

```
   return false;
   }
```

If the bottom TEXTAREA box is empty (""), the alert goes up and the return is false. That means the script dies right there. It doesn't go any further.

Otherwise, the following occurs:

```
else
{ alert('If you like the results, paste it to a text editor!')
boat = open ("","DisplayWindow")
see = parent.document.Framer.Pastebox.value
boat.document.write (see)
return true;
```

Assign the code ("","DisplayWindow") to the variable boat. Why boat? I don't know; ask the author. Notice the empty quotation marks at the beginning. That is where a page URL would normally sit. Because it's empty, it's forcing the script to look at itself for the information to display.

Next, the variable see is assigned the value of what is in the bottom TEXTAREA box (parent. document.Framer.Pastebox.value). Now the command parent sits in front because you're dealing with two windows and you want the information taken from the window that spawned the new one—the parent.

Into boat (the new window), you document.write see, the contents of the bottom TEXTAREA box found on the parent window. Then, it returns true, which completes the event.

There you go. I'll bet the first time you saw this one, you thought it was going to take 10 tips to complete. That's part of the beauty of JavaScript programming. You can use the same format again and again in the same script to get different results. I only had to show you one frame code function, and you could get them all.

PROTECT YOUR VALUABLES

Do not leave your personal items unattended and available for someone to steal (backpacks, purses, textbooks, cell phones, etc.)

Report problems to the Campus Police. Call 299-2311 for an officer to assist you. Call 741-2092 to make a report.

Search Multiple Search Engines

When I started HTML Goodies, oh so long ago, I was sent a lot of scripts that were posted straightaway. I needed to fill space at first. As the months went on, I became more selective in what should be posted. I guess the two biggest criteria in posting a script were these: Is it original, and is it functional?

I received a bunch of scripts that would change the background of a page using everything from event handlers to a person's name to make the change. It's clever, but not overly useful. After you have the basic concept of changing the background color, you pretty much can take it from there.

I received the following multiple search engine script right in the middle of all those background-color–changing scripts. The script was much larger than you see it here. I've cut it down a bit for this series of Script Tips. It used to search ten different engines, now it only searches five. Of course, by the end, you'll know it well enough to add as many searches as you'd like.

The script is quite functional in that it allows many searches from one page. Results are posted in a new window so you never leave the search page. Plus, you don't have to perform each search individually. You could put in a keyword (or keywords, cleverly enough) and five search engines will return their results in five separate windows.

It's a very helpful, and involved, script. People have been asking that I get into some more advanced JavaScript. Well, this should fit the bill.

Here's the code:

```
<SCRIPT LANGUAGE="JavaScript">

function wordsplit(items)
{
var charect = "";
for (var n = 1 ; n <= items.length ; n++)
{
if (items.substring(n-1,n) == " ")
{ charect+="+"; }
else
{ charect+=items.substring(n-1,n); }
}
return charect;
}

function search()
{
var keywords=document.searching.query.value;
var search1;
var search2;
var search3;
var search4;
var search5;

key=wordsplit(keywords);

if(document.searching.yahoo.checked)
{
search1= document.searching.yahoo.value;
search1+=key;

wind=window.open(search1,"newwindow1","width=700,height=200,
➥scrollbars=yes");

}
```

```
else

if(document.searching.altavista.checked)
{
search2 = document.searching.altavista.value;
search2+=key;

wind=window.open(search2,"newwindow2","width=700,height=200,
➥scrollbars=yes");

}
if(document.searching.webcrawler.checked)
{
search3 = document.searching.webcrawler.value;
search3+=key;

wind=window.open(search3,"newwindow3","width=700,height=200,
➥scrollbars=yes");

}
if(document.searching.lycos.checked)
{
search4 = document.searching.lycos.value;
search4+=key;

wind=window.open(search4,"newwindow4","width=700,height=200,
➥scrollbars=yes");

}
if(document.searching.excite.checked)
{
search5 = document.searching.excite.value;
search5+=key;

wind=window.open(search5,"newwindow5","width=700,height=200,
➥scrollbars=yes");

}


}

</SCRIPT>
```

```
<FORM NAME="searching">
Enter the Key word : <INPUT TYPE="text" NAME="query" SIZE=20><BR><BR>
<b>Select the Search Engine(s):</b><br>

<INPUT TYPE="checkbox" NAME="yahoo"
➥VALUE="http://search.yahoo.com/search?p="> Yahoo<br>

<INPUT TYPE="checkbox" NAME="altavista "VALUE="http://www.altavista.digital.com/
➥cgi-bin/query?pg=q&what=web&fmt=.&q=">Altavista<br>

<INPUT TYPE="checkbox" NAME="webcrawler" VALUE=" http://search.excite.com/
➥search.gw?c=web&lk=webcrawler&onload=&s=j >WebCrawler<br>

<INPUT TYPE="checkbox" NAME="excite"
➥VALUE="http://www.excite.com/search.gw?trace=a&search=">Excite<br>

<INPUT TYPE="checkbox" NAME="lycos"
➥VALUE="http://www.lycos.com/cgi-bin/pursuit?query=">Lycos<br>

<INPUT TYPE="button" VALUE="Search" onClick="search()">
<INPUT TYPE="reset" VALUE=" Clear ">
</FORM>
```

Put in your keyword and search away. It'll look like Figure ST5.1.

Figure ST5.1
*The search interface is
"framed" by the three
windows that pop up from
each of the three chosen
search engines.*

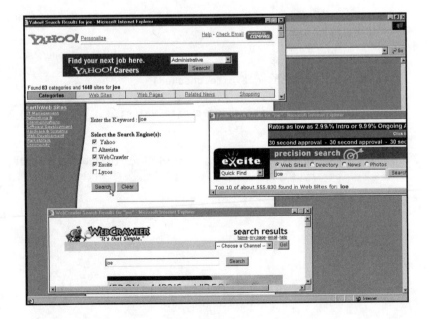

To see the effect on your own computer, click Script Tip Five in your download packet, or see it online at http://www.htmlgoodies.com/stips/scripttip42.html.

The code is available for copy and paste at http://www.htmlgoodies.com/stips/ scripttip42script.html or by viewing the source of the page in your download packet.

As with most scripts that include FORM elements, I want to start with them. If you're a regular Script Tip reader, you're probably familiar with NAMEs and VALUEs. Still, read this over. You'll find this form used in a different way from what you're used to.

The form code looks like this:

```
<FORM NAME="searching">

Enter the Keyword :
<INPUT TYPE="text" NAME="query" SIZE=15>

<b>Select the Search Engine(s):</b>


<INPUT TYPE="checkbox" NAME="yahoo"
VALUE="http://search.yahoo.com/search?p="> Yahoo

<INPUT TYPE="checkbox" NAME="altavista"
VALUE="http://www.altavista.digital.com/cgi-bin/query?pg=q&what=
➥web&fmt=.&q=">Altavista

<INPUT TYPE="checkbox" NAME="webcrawler"
VALUE=" http://search.excite.com/search.gw?c=web&lk=webcrawler&onload=&s=j ">
➥WebCrawler

<INPUT TYPE="checkbox" NAME="excite"
VALUE="http://www.excite.com/search.gw?trace=a&search=">Excite

<INPUT TYPE="checkbox" NAME="lycos"
VALUE="http://www.lycos.com/cgi-bin/pursuit?query=">Lycos


<INPUT TYPE="button" VALUE="Search" onClick="search()">
<INPUT TYPE="reset" VALUE=" Clear ">
</FORM>
```

Okay, you have three things to look for here. First is the text box in which the user enters the keyword to be searched. The second is the code that allows the choice of search engines, and the third is the button that triggers the function to search.

311

NAMEs

The name of the FORM itself is searching, and the text box name is query. Each of the check boxes is given the name of the search engine it represents.

Finally, the button triggers a function called search().

Now you know enough to start constructing hierarchy statements, but unlike other forms you've dealt with here, this has multiple hierarchy statements depending on what the user chose. We'll get into how the JavaScript knows which has been clicked later.

The Check Boxes

Yes, this could have also been done with radio buttons and, with some special coding, a drop-down menu. The reason the author chose check boxes is because that enables the user to check as many as desired. It doesn't limit the choice. Let's look at the first check box code:

```
<INPUT TYPE="checkbox" NAME="yahoo
➥"VALUE="http://search.yahoo.com/search?p="> Yahoo
```

It's a basic INPUT TYPE="checkbox" format. This check box represents Yahoo!, so that's the NAME. Now, here's the trick: see the VALUE? That VALUE is the URL that attaches to the Yahoo! search engine. If you attached the keywords entered by the user to the end of that URL, you'd get a search performed.

It's the same with the other four check boxes. Each VALUE is equal to the URL required to perform a search on that particular engine. The code is pretty easy to find. You just go to the search page of the engine and look at the source code; I'm sure that's where the author got it.

So, you have a text box that assigns the variable query to keywords. You also have check boxes that return URLs of search engines. Put the two together, and you get a full search string. Seeing the process yet?

Replacing the Space with a Plus Sign

I have found that one of the hardest things about writing a JavaScript is trying to set up code so that every possible thing a user could do is handled in one way or another. I always forget something.

Many of you know that when using a search engine, a plus sign (+) between words is a good idea to help to search. Let's look at the code that searches the keywords entered in this script. If a space is found, a plus sign replaces it.

I am worried about the code that makes up the first function, wordsplit(items). It looks like this:

```
function wordsplit(items)
{
var charect = "";
for (var n = 1 ; n <= items.length ; n++)
{
if (items.substring(n-1,n) == " ")
{ charect+="+"; }
else
{ charect+=items.substring(n-1,n); }
}
return charect;
}
```

Now, this is not the function that performs the search. That function is called search(), and it's coming later. This function is one that is called upon as part of search. Rather than going back and forth, I'll tell you what this does so that you can just plug it in later.

Notice the function has the parameter items in the instance. That means that items is returned to the function to be acted on.

The function begins with a variable, charect, being set and assigned the value of nothing. See the empty quotation marks? That means "no space".

Next a loop is created with this code:

```
for (var n = 1 ; n <= items.length ; n++)
```

The loop's format follows this pattern: A variable, n, is created and given the value of 1. Then a condition is set, which states that n is less than, or equal to, the length of characters in the item. Finally, the third element of the loops states what should happen as long as the condition is not met. The code n++ means that n should move upward incrementally. Double minus signs mean moving downward in the same fashion.

So, what in the world does this do? It looks at each character in the item one by one. Again, this is a little out of order. The item is given the same value as what the user writes into the text box. Stay with me; that will happen soon. For now, just take my word that that's what it means.

Each time a new character is looked at, an if/else statement is employed. If the character is a space, that space is replaced with a plus sign (+). If it is not a space (else), the character stays the same and the loop fires up again, checking the next character.

This happens as long as n is less than the length of characters in the text entered by the users. Every character is checked, and every empty space is given the new value of (+).

Then, after all the characters have been checked, the loop shuts down and the new text is returned. That means the script now has it stored for later use. And you will use it later.

Doing the Search

You've set up search URLs and created something that will check the entered text for spaces. Now, you'll do the search.

Because five search engines are represented, I really need to show you only one section of the function because the other four follow the same format. Here's the top of the function triggered by the button and the first search, Yahoo!:

```
function search()
{
var keywords=document.searching.query.value;
var search1;
var search2;
var search3;
var search4;
var search5;
key=wordsplit(keywords);
if(document.searching.yahoo.checked)
{
search1= document.searching.yahoo.value;
search1+=key;
wind=window.open(search1,"newwindow1","width=700,height=200,
➥scrollbars=yes");
```

The function traditionally starts with function search() and then the curly bracket.

Next a variable, keywords, is set and assigned the value of what was written in the text box:

```
document.searching.query.value.
```

Next, five new variables are set, search1 through search5. They are not assigned any value yet; they are just being created now so that they will be available later to receive values.

Next, you attach the output of the text box with the previous function that checked for spaces:

```
key=wordsplit(keywords);
```

Here, the variable key is created and assigned the value of wordsplit(keywords). Get what just happened? keywords represents what was written into the text box. Because that variable name is within the instance of the function, it is given over to it. Thus, what was written into the text box is handed to the function wordsplit() to be checked for spaces.

Remember that the results of that handing off are assigned the variable name key. That means that key is now the text entered by the user with any spaces changed to plus signs. It's ready to be used in a search.

Next are the if statements. Five of them are used because the user had five search engines to choose from:

```
if(document.searching.yahoo.checked)
{
search1= document.searching.yahoo.value;
search1+=key;

wind=window.open(search1,"newwindow1","width=700,height=200,
➥scrollbars=yes");
```

It reads as follows: If the check box Yahoo! is checked, search1 (remember creating that?) is to have the VALUE found in the check box representing Yahoo! (that's the search URL).

Next, search1 is to have the variable key added to it. Remember that key is the text entered by the user. The addition takes place because of this operator: +=. See that? It means to *concatenate* or build together the strings you're working with.

So now search1 represents the entire URL plus the text to be searched. Now you need to open that URL in a new window:

```
wind=window.open(search1,"newwindow1","width=700,height=200,
➥scrollbars=yes");
```

A new window opens using search1 as its URL. That performs the search. The new window has the name of newwindow1, is 700×200, and will have scrollbars.

The second curly bracket ends this particular if statement.

But what if Yahoo! is not checked?

Then this particular if statement is not true and is ignored. The script goes on to the next, and the next, and the next until one is correct.

But what if no check boxes are checked?

Then none of the if elements are true and nothing happens. The script just sits there looking back at you.

Can I put up an alert saying to post?

Using the format here, it's a bit rough. Here's the catch 22: If you put an alert as a final `else` statement, that alert will pop up every time, regardless of whether the user checked a box.

To prevent that `else` from being called on every time, you need to put an `else` between every `if` statement. Then the alert pops up only when no other boxes are checked; however, this limits the search capabilities because the user can't choose multiple engines. As soon as the script runs into an `if` statement that is true, it stops.

I played around with some code, checking all the `if`s in one shot, and it started to be too much code for what it produced. I'm happy with the page just sitting still if no search engines are checked.

So, there you go! It's a multiple search engine script.

Image Proportion Script

If you've ever attempted to guess at the correct height and width when attempting to resize an image in HTML code, you know it can be pretty rough guessing.

Sure, you could open an image editor, but I like to stay inside the browser. This script solves those problems. You can stay in the browser and still get those proportions and get a look at the image before choosing the numbers.

I received this "Proportional" script from Ann Evans. It was a great idea. You enter the height and width of an image you want to resize. Then, by entering a new height, the script figures the new width, keeping the same proportions the image original had.

I really liked the script, but thought it asked too much of the user. I knew you could grab the image's height and width straight from the image. Then, after setting the new height and width, it seemed logical to show the image in its new dimensions.

So, using Ann's original calculations and table structure, I rewrote and added on until I got this:

```
<!-- The following creates the prompt and displays the image -->
<SCRIPT LANGUAGE="javascript">

var path = prompt("Where will I find the image? Put in full URL or Hard Drive
➥Path and Image Name For example: C:/directory/image.jpg","Only image name
➥ required if in same directory")

if(path == "Only image name required if in same directory")
{
alert('Come on, put in an image name')
javascript:location.reload()
}

if(path == null)
{
alert('Do not click Cancel')
javascript:location.reload()
}

else
{document.write("<IMG NAME=thepic SRC=" +path+ ">");}

</SCRIPT>


<!-- The following contains the two resize functions and two new
➥window functions -->

<SCRIPT LANGUAGE="javascript">

var high = document.thepic.height;
var wide = document.thepic.width;

function newW()
{
    a = high;
    b = wide;
    c = document.calc.h2.value;
    d = (b*c)/a;
    document.calc.width2.value = Math.round
}
```

```
function newH()
{
a = high;
b = wide;
e = document.calc.wb2.value;
f = (a*e)/b;
document.calc.height2.value = Math.round(f)
}



function newWin()
{
var OpenWindow=window.open("", "newwin", "height=500,width=500");
OpenWindow.document.write("<HTML>")
OpenWindow.document.write("<TITLE>Image</TITLE>")
OpenWindow.document.write("<BODY BGCOLOR='000000'>")
OpenWindow.document.write("<CENTER>")
OpenWindow.document.write("<IMG SRC=" +path+ " HEIGHT=" +c+ "
➥WIDTH=" +d+ ">")
OpenWindow.document.write("</CENTER>")
OpenWindow.document.write("</HTML>")
}

function newWin2()
{
var OpenWindow=window.open("", "newwin2", "height=500,width=500");
OpenWindow.document.write("<HTML>")
OpenWindow.document.write("<TITLE>Image</TITLE>")
OpenWindow.document.write("<BODY BGCOLOR='000000'>")
OpenWindow.document.write("<CENTER>")
OpenWindow.document.write("<IMG SRC=" +path+ " HEIGHT=" +f+ "
➥WIDTH=" +e+ ">")
OpenWindow.document.write("</CENTER>")
OpenWindow.document.write("</HTML>")
}

</SCRIPT>

<!-- The following contains the two tables on the page -->

<h2>Resize It</h2>

<FORM NAME="calc">
```

```
<TABLE border="12" cellspacing="0" cellpadding="4" bgcolor="#fdf99d">
<TR>
    <TD align="center">Height:<BR><SCRIPT
LANGUAGE="javascript">document.write("<B>"+high+"</B>")</SCRIPT></TD>
    <TD align="center">Width:<BR><SCRIPT
LANGUAGE="javascript">document.write("<B>"+wide+"</B>")</SCRIPT></TD>
    <TD align="center">Enter New Height:<BR><INPUT TYPE="text" SIZE=5
➥ NAME="h2"></TD>
    <TD align="center"><INPUT TYPE="button" VALUE="Solve" onClick=
➥"newW()"></TD>
    <TD align="center">New Width Equals<BR><INPUT TYPE="text" NAME=
➥"width2" SIZE=10></TD>
    <TD align="center"><INPUT TYPE="button" onClick="newWin()"
➥VALUE="Let Me See It"></TD>
</TR>

</TABLE>

<TABLE border="12" cellspacing="0" cellpadding="4" bgcolor="#fdf99d">
<TR>
    <TD align="center">Height:<BR><SCRIPT
LANGUAGE="javascript">document.write("<B>"+high+"</B>")</SCRIPT></TD>
    <TD align="center">Width:<BR><SCRIPT
LANGUAGE="javascript">document.write("<B>"+wide+"</B>")</SCRIPT></TD>
    <TD align="center">Enter New Width:<BR><INPUT TYPE="text" SIZE=5
➥NAME="wb2"></TD>
    <TD align="center"><INPUT TYPE="button" VALUE="Solve" onClick=
➥"newH()"></TD>
    <TD align="center">New Height Equals<BR><INPUT TYPE="text"
➥NAME="height2" SIZE=10>
    <TD align="center"><INPUT TYPE="button" onClick="newWin2()"
➥VALUE="Let Me See It">
</TD>
</TR>
</TABLE>
</FORM>
```

Figure ST6.1 shows the script in action.

 To see the effect on your own computer, click Script Tip Six in your download packet, or see it online at http://www.htmlgoodies.com/stips/scripttip45example.html. *When you are prompted for an image name, enter* **angel.jpg**. *Of course, you can always enter the full URL to one of your own images, too, if you're connected to the Internet.*

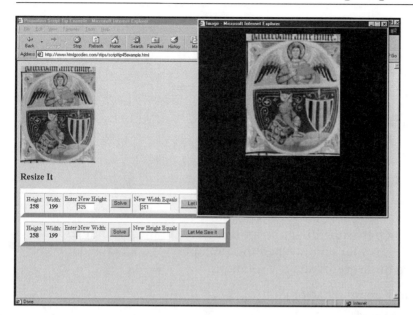

Figure ST6.1
This is the interface of the image proportion script with a second window showing the new proportions of the image entered into the text boxes.

I should point out that the system has a little bug. Because the image you call for might not be in cache, sometimes the incorrect height and width are displayed. Don't worry, though, because you can fix that by simply refreshing the page.

However, even if the displayed height and width are incorrect, the results created from your entering a new height or width will be correct.

The code is available for copy and paste at http://www.htmlgoodies.com/stips/ script-tip45script.html or by viewing the source of the page in your download packet.

The script uses a series of steps to complete the effect. Let's start with the first thing you see on the page, the prompt. The blip of prompt code asks for the path to the image. Yes, I know it's a little wordy and long to read.

After the prompt has the path and name of the image, it uses that to create an image flag that posts the image to the page. Let's look at it. Please understand that I have greatly reduced the amount of text in the prompt box for this example:

```
<SCRIPT LANGUAGE="javascript">

var path = prompt("Text on the gray","Text in the box")

if(path == "Text in the box")
{
alert('Come on, put in an image name')
```

```
javascript:location.reload()
}

if(path == null)
{
alert('Do not click Cancel')
javascript:location.reload()
}

else
{document.write("<IMG NAME=thepic SRC=" +path+ ">");}
</SCRIPT>
```

One of the hardest things to do when writing a script is to guess all the possibilities that could occur when someone uses your script. When this prompt pops up, I saw four events that could happen. Here are those events and my solutions:

1. The user enters a correct image name or path.

   Solution: The image is posted.

2. The user clicks OK to display the image.

   Solution: Create an alert box telling user to enter the image name.

3. The user clicks Cancel.

   Solution: Create a prompt box asking for image name.

4. The user enters incorrect information.

   Solution: I can't predict incorrect information, so that results in a broken image, which gives a 40×40 height and width.

I wrote the previous prompt to cover each of those concerns. If you'd like to go back to the example and try each event, click here. Otherwise, let's take it in order:

```
var path = prompt("Text on the gray","Text in the box")
```

This is the basic format of a prompt. Again, I have greatly reduced the text used in the original, so you'll get the idea. Whatever the user types in the box is assigned the variable name path:

```
if(path == "Text in the box")
{
alert('Come on, put in an image name')
javascript:location.reload()
}
```

The first if statement is used if the user simply clicks OK without changing the information in the box.

If the "path" equals "Text in the box" (note the double quotation marks so that 'Text in the box' is seen as a text string rather than code), an alert pops up that reads Come on, put in an image name. After the user clicks OK in the alert box, javascript:location.reload() reloads the page and the prompt pops up again.

Here are two things you should notice: the curly brackets around the alert, and the reload. These are important so that the script understands it should do both if the statement is true. Also, note that the text string is the same as what is in the text box on the prompt. Be sure those two are the same when you use the script; otherwise it won't work.

Here's the second if statement. The script goes to this one if the first isn't found to be true. This is triggered if the prompt data is null. That means the user simply clicked Cancel. Notice that null is not in quotes. It is not a text string, but rather a literal:

```
if(path == null)
{
alert('Do not click Cancel')
javascript:location.reload()
}
```

The same basic format is used if this if statement is true. An alert pops up, the page is reloaded, and the prompt pops up again. Consider this next bit of code:

```
else
{document.write("<IMG NAME=thepic SRC=" +path+ ">");}
```

If both of the if statements are false, which is what you're hoping for, a document.write statement is used to create a basic image flag posting the picture the user has entered.

See the NAME=thepic in the flag? That will become important in the next section of this Script Tip.

Grabbing and Displaying the Dimensions

You might have noticed that after the prompt, I have placed four functions inside one set of <SCRIPT LANGUAGE="javascript"> and </SCRIPT> flags. That's common; there's no need to create a separate set of flags for each function. As long as they don't share any variable names, you can just line them up one after the other.

I am concerned with the first two lines, before the functions begin lining up:

```
var high = document.thepic.height;
var wide = document.thepic.width;
```

Each line assigns a variable name to a dimension of the image. The variable `high` is produced from the hierarchy statement `document.thepic.height`.

See `thepic`? That's the name of the image space. That name was put into the image flag created from the prompt code. That way these lines of code understand that the height returned should be from that image space.

The same format is followed to get the width. So, now `high` and `wide` represent the image's height and width. You want to post that in the table that appears below the image:

```
<FORM NAME="calc">

<TABLE border="12" cellspacing="0" cellpadding="4" bgcolor="#fdf99d">

<TR>

<TD align="center">Height:<BR>
<SCRIPT LANGUAGE="javascript">
document.write("<B>"+high+"</B>")
</SCRIPT>
</TD>

<TD align="center">Width:<BR>
<SCRIPT LANGUAGE="javascript">
document.write("<B>"+wide+"</B>")
</SCRIPT>
</TD>

<TD align="center">Enter New Height:<BR>
<INPUT TYPE="text" SIZE=5 NAME="h2">
</TD>

<TD align="center">
<INPUT TYPE="button"
VALUE="Solve" onClick="newW()">
</TD>

<TD align="center">New Width Equals<BR>
<INPUT TYPE="text" NAME="width2" SIZE=10>
</TD>

<TD align="center">
<INPUT TYPE="button"
onClick="newWin()" VALUE="Let Me See It">
```

```
</TD>

</TR>

</TABLE>
</FORM>
```

What you see in this code is the first table. This is the one that enables you to enter a new height and get the new width.

This is a table, but it also uses FORM elements so that text can be entered by the user. Therefore, you need to get a handle on the FORM NAMEs.

The FORM itself is called calc. The first text box, the one that will accept the new height, is named h2. The second text box, the one that will display the new width, is named width2. Those two text boxes can now be given attention through hierarchy statements such as document.calc.width2.value.

There are also two buttons. The first fires a function called newW(). That creates the new width value. The second triggers a function called newWin(), which produces the new window showing the image with the new dimensions.

We're interested in the displays, first off. Here's the first table cell that displays the image height:

```
<TD align="center">Height:<BR>
<SCRIPT LANGUAGE="javascript">
document.write("<B>"+high+"</B>")
</SCRIPT>
</TD>
```

Notice an entire script format is used to get the job done. This is common. It adds up to a bit of text, but you get the display you need. The return from +high+ is bold just for display purposes. The format is followed again to display the width in the next table cell.

To perform any calculations, you're going to need three numbers: The old height and width (you already have that), a new height or width from the user (you can see the box that will receive that value), and a function that will do the math for you. In this case, that function is called newW().

New Width

The first table has a button that fires a function named newW(). It looks like this:

```
function newW()
{
```

```
a = high;
b = wide;
c = document.calc.h2.value;
d = (b*c)/a;
document.calc.width2.value = Math.round(d)
}
```

To make the math equation that will figure the new width a little easier, a is assigned to the image's current height, which is represented by `high`. Then, b is assigned to the current width, represented by `wide`.

Next, the new height value entered by the user—`document.calc.h2.value` (the text box)—is assigned the variable c.

The calculation for the new width is (b*c)/a, and the result of that equation is assigned the variable d.

Now, you need to display it in the text box `document.calc.width2.value`. However, very seldom do numbers calculate perfectly, so you need to take d and round it off. You do that using `Math.round(d)`.

Now the new width displays in the text box. But what of the second table and figuring the new height? The function is very similar, except for where user input comes from and the equation. It is called `newH()` and looks like this:

```
function newH()
{
a = high;
b = wide;
e = document.calc.wb2.value;
f = (a*e)/b;
document.calc.height2.value = Math.round(f)
}
```

Now the information from the viewer is coming from a text box called `wb2`. If you look at the code for the second table, you'll see that text box. The calculation for the new height is (a*e)/b, and that value is sent to a text box named `height2`. Again, look at the second table code and you'll see it.

Because you're dealing with new numbers here, you must assign new variable names to the new height and width. Notice that e equals the new width, and f equals the new result. Notice also that the variable names were changed in the equation. You must make these changes; otherwise, both equations will use the same numbers, which is not good.

So far, you've grabbed the image's current height and width and, using that information plus one value from the user, created a new height or new width. That's pretty good, but it's better if you can then take those values and show the user what the image will look like.

Let Me See It

In the two table codes, the last button is used to pop up the new window to display the image with the new height and width. Just as with the two functions that perform the number calculations, these two display functions are very similar. I'll walk you through the first and quickly show you the changes in the second.

Here's the first display function:

```
function newWin()
{
var OpenWindow=window.open("", "newwin", "height=500,width=500");
OpenWindow.document.write("<HTML>")
OpenWindow.document.write("<TITLE>Image</TITLE>")
OpenWindow.document.write("<BODY BGCOLOR='000000'>")
OpenWindow.document.write("<CENTER>")
OpenWindow.document.write("<IMG SRC=" +path+ " HEIGHT=" +c+ "
➥WIDTH=" +d+ ">")
OpenWindow.document.write("</CENTER>")
OpenWindow.document.write("</HTML>")
}
```

Because of width concerns, a couple of the lines have been truncated. Please be aware that each line starts with `OpenWindow.document.write`, and all that comes before the next should go on one line.

You should notice immediately that this is the basic format for opening a new window using a function. The window opens through the `window.open`, `object.method` format.

The effect is achieved by assigning the variable `OpenWindow` to the new window. Notice the empty quotation marks just inside the parentheses. That forces the script to look to itself for what will appear in the new window.

Next, the name `newwin` is assigned to the new window. It will never come into play in this script, but the format requires you to have it.

Then, the height and width of the new window is offered. I thought about setting up the script so that the height and width would conform to the new image size, but decided against it. It was a lot of coding for very little event. Besides, if the user creates an image that is too large for the 500×500 window, he can always click the maximize button.

Now, you begin lining up lines of HTML code to go into the new window. These lines of code are written to the new window through document.write statements assigned to the new window through the variable OpenWindow. Each is a new line of code.

As you can see, it's about as simple an HTML document as you can get. It offers a title, background color, and centered image. The image is what you're concerned with now.

I used three variables to create the new image. The first is path. Remember that from way back in the prompt code? That's the name and path of the image. Then, c is the new height, and d is the new width. When the document.write statement writes it to the page, it appears as inline image code and the image displays in the dimensions set by the math function from the last tip.

If you recall, you needed to change a couple of variable names to do the math for the second table's results. Well, to get that second table's results to display, you must use those new variable names in a new function set up to display the image:

```
function newWin2()
{
var OpenWindow=window.open("", "newwin2", "height=500,width=500");
OpenWindow.document.write("<HTML>")
OpenWindow.document.write("<TITLE>Image</TITLE>")
OpenWindow.document.write("<BODY BGCOLOR='000000'>")
OpenWindow.document.write("<CENTER>")
OpenWindow.document.write("<IMG SRC=" +path+ " HEIGHT=" +f+ "
➥WIDTH=" +e+ ">")
OpenWindow.document.write("</CENTER>")
OpenWindow.document.write("</HTML>")
}
```

It looks similar, but a few changes have been made. The name of the function is newWin2(), so it can be called on by the second button. Notice that the name of the window has changed—it is now newwin2. You can't have two windows with the same name on the same page. Because you figured the new height and width using e and f, those are the variable names used to create the new image.

So, there you go, multiple scripts working together to create one nice effect. I don't know that this script is good to put online for others to play with; I see it more as something to help you when creating your own pages.

A Calculator

Here we go with a script that has been requested time and time again—a calculator. Here's the code. It's a little long, but after you get into it, you'll see it could have been three times as long if it weren't for some fancy coding tricks:

```
<HTML>
<HEAD>

<SCRIPT LANGUAGE="JavaScript">
<!-- start hiding

function getPi()
{return Math.PI}
```

```
function getRandom()
{return Math.random()}

function change()
{
var temp = document.calculator.text.value;

if (temp.substring(0,1) == "-")
{document.calculator.list.value = "";
document.calculator.text.value = 0 - document.calculator.text.value
➡ * 1}

if (temp.substring(0,1) != "-")
{document.calculator.list.value ="";
document.calculator.text.value = "-" + temp.substring(0,temp.length)}
}

function recip(x)
{document.calculator.text.value = (1/(x))}
function raisePower(x)
{

var y = 0

y = prompt("What is the exponent?", "")

document.calculator.text.value = Math.pow(x,y)
}

// end hiding -->
</SCRIPT>


<!-- Visible Table Starts Here -->

</HEAD>

<BODY>

<TABLE BORDER=1 CELLSPACING=2 CELLPADDING=3%>
<TR>
<FORM NAME="calculator">
<TD COLSPAN=5 BGCOLOR=RED>
```

```
<CENTER>
<INPUT NAME="list" TYPE=HIDDEN>
<INPUT TYPE=TEXT NAME="text" VALUE="">
</TD>
<TD COLSPAN=2 BGCOLOR=RED>
<CENTER>
<INPUT TYPE=BUTTON VALUE=" Backspace " NAME="backspace" onClick="
➥document.calculator.text.value = document.calculator.text.value.substring
➥ (0,document.calculator.text.value.length*1 -1)">
</TD>
<TD COLSPAN=2 BGCOLOR=RED>
<CENTER>
<INPUT TYPE=BUTTON VALUE=" Clear " NAME="clear"
onClick="document.calculator.text.value=''">
</TD>
</TR>
<TR>
<TD BGCOLOR=BLUE>
<CENTER>
<INPUT TYPE=BUTTON VALUE=" 7 " NAME="but7" onClick="
➥document.calculator.text.value+='7'">
</TD>
<TD BGCOLOR=BLUE>
<CENTER>
<INPUT TYPE=BUTTON VALUE=" 8 " NAME="but8" onClick="
➥document.calculator.text.value+='8'">
</TD>
<TD BGCOLOR=BLUE>
<CENTER>
<INPUT TYPE=BUTTON VALUE=" 9 " NAME="but9" onClick="
➥document.calculator.text.value+='9'">
</TD>
<TD BGCOLOR=YELLOW>
<CENTER>
<INPUT TYPE=BUTTON VALUE=" + " NAME="add" onClick="
➥document.calculator.text.value+='+'">
</TD>
<TD BGCOLOR=YELLOW>
<CENTER>
<INPUT TYPE=BUTTON VALUE=" - " NAME="subtract" onClick="
➥document.calculator.text.value+='-'">
</TD>
<TD BGCOLOR=LIME>
```

331

```
<CENTER>
<INPUT TYPE="BUTTON" VALUE=" 1/x " NAME="reciprocal" onClick="
➥recip(document.calculator.text.value)">
</TD>
<TD BGCOLOR=LIME>
<CENTER>
<INPUT TYPE="BUTTON" VALUE=" x^y " NAME="power" onClick="
➥raisePower(document.calculator.text.value)">
</TD>
<TD BGCOLOR=LIME>
<CENTER>
<INPUT TYPE=BUTTON VALUE=" sin " NAME="sin" onClick="
➥document.calculator.text.value= Math.sin(document.calculator.text.value*
➥3.141592653589793/180)">
</TD>
</TR>
<TR>
<TD BGCOLOR=BLUE>
<CENTER>
<INPUT TYPE=BUTTON VALUE=" 4 " NAME="but4" onClick="
➥document.calculator.text.value+='4'">
</TD>
<TD BGCOLOR=BLUE>
<CENTER>
<INPUT TYPE=BUTTON VALUE=" 5 " NAME="but5" onClick="
➥document.calculator.text.value+='5'">
</TD>
<TD BGCOLOR=BLUE>
<CENTER>
<INPUT TYPE=BUTTON VALUE=" 6 " NAME="but6" onClick="
➥document.calculator.text.value+='6'">
</TD>
<TD BGCOLOR=YELLOW>
<CENTER>
<INPUT TYPE=BUTTON VALUE=" * " NAME="multiply" onClick="
➥document.calculator.text.value+='*'">
</TD>
<TD BGCOLOR=YELLOW>
<CENTER>
<INPUT TYPE=BUTTON VALUE=" / " NAME="divide" onClick="
➥document.calculator.text.value+='/'">
</TD>
<TD BGCOLOR=LIME>
```

```
<CENTER>
<INPUT TYPE=BUTTON VALUE=" | x | " NAME="absolute"
➥onClick="document.calculator.text.value=Math.abs(
➥document.calculator.text.value)">
</TD>
<TD BGCOLOR=LIME>
<CENTER>
<INPUT TYPE=BUTTON VALUE=" exp. " NAME="exp" onClick="
➥document.calculator.text.value+='E'">
</TD>
<TD BGCOLOR=LIME>
<CENTER>
<INPUT TYPE=BUTTON VALUE=" cos " NAME="cos"
➥onClick="document.calculator.text.value=Math.cos(
➥document.calculator.text.value*3.141592653589793/180)">
</TD>
</TR>
<TR>
<TD BGCOLOR=BLUE>
<CENTER>
<INPUT TYPE=BUTTON VALUE=" 1 " NAME="but1" onClick="
➥document.calculator.text.value+='1'">
</TD>
<TD BGCOLOR=BLUE>
<CENTER>
<INPUT TYPE=BUTTON VALUE=" 2 " NAME="but2" onClick="
➥document.calculator.text.value+='2'">
</TD>
<TD BGCOLOR=BLUE>
<CENTER>
<INPUT TYPE=BUTTON VALUE=" 3 " NAME="but3" onClick="
➥document.calculator.text.value+='3'">
</TD>
<TD BGCOLOR=YELLOW>
<CENTER>
<INPUT TYPE=BUTTON VALUE=" ( " NAME="leftbracket" onClick="
➥document.calculator.text.value+='('">
</TD>
<TD BGCOLOR=YELLOW>
<CENTER>
<INPUT TYPE=BUTTON VALUE=" ) " NAME="rightbracket" onClick="
➥document.calculator.text.value+=')'">
</TD>
```

```
<TD BGCOLOR=LIME>
<CENTER>
<INPUT TYPE=BUTTON VALUE=" x? " NAME="square" onClick="
➥document.calculator.text.value= document.calculator.text.value
➥* document.calculator.text.value">
</TD>
<TD BGCOLOR=LIME>
<CENTER>
<INPUT TYPE=BUTTON VALUE=" round " NAME="round"
➥onClick="document.calculator.text.value=Math.round(
➥document.calculator.text.value)">
</TD>
<TD BGCOLOR=LIME>
<CENTER>
<INPUT TYPE=BUTTON VALUE=" tan " NAME="tan"
➥onClick="document.calculator.text.value=Math.tan(
➥document.calculator.text.value*3.141592653589793/180)">
</TD>
</TR>
<TR>
<TD BGCOLOR=BLUE>
<CENTER>
<INPUT TYPE=BUTTON VALUE=" 0 " NAME="but0" onClick="
➥document.calculator.text.value+='0'">
</TD>
<TD BGCOLOR=BLUE>
<CENTER>
<INPUT TYPE=BUTTON VALUE=" . " NAME="decimal" onClick="
➥document.calculator.text.value+='.'">
</TD>
<TD BGCOLOR=BLUE>
<CENTER>
<INPUT TYPE=BUTTON VALUE=" +|- " NAME="sign" onClick="change()">
</TD>
<TD COLSPAN=2 BGCOLOR=BLACK>
<CENTER>
<INPUT TYPE=BUTTON VALUE=" = " NAME="equals"
➥onClick="document.calculator.text.value=eval(
➥document.calculator.text.value)">
</TD>
<TD BGCOLOR=LIME>
<CENTER>
<INPUT TYPE=BUTTON VALUE=" x? " NAME="sqrt"
```

```
➥onClick="document.calculator.text.value=Math.sqrt(
➥document.calculator.text.value)">
</TD>
<TD BGCOLOR=LIME>
<CENTER>
<INPUT TYPE=BUTTON VALUE=" rand " NAME="random" onClick="
➥document.calculator.text.value = getRandom()">
</TD>
<TD BGCOLOR=LIME>
<CENTER>
<INPUT TYPE=BUTTON VALUE=" pi " NAME="pi" onClick="
➥document.calculator.text.value+= getPi()">
</TD>
</TR>
</TABLE>

</FORM>

</BODY>
</HTML>
```

You can see it in action in Figure ST7.1.

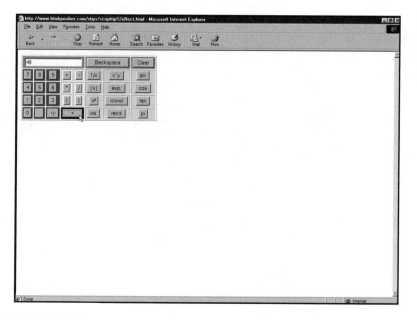

Figure ST7.1
The calculator after figuring a stunningly difficult equation that apparently added up to 48.

To see the effect on your own computer, click Script Tip Seven in your download packet or see it online at http://www.htmlgoodies.com/stips/scripttip52effect.html.

The code is available for copy and paste at http://www.htmlgoodies.com/stips/ scripttip52script.html or by viewing the source of the page in your download packet.

Okay, the overriding first concern is the display. The calculator face is nothing more than a big table, five cells tall by eight cells across. You'll notice that some of the cells span multiple cells. The display, for instance, rolls across five cells. The Backspace and the Equals buttons both span two. See that?

You'll find as you get into the calculator that the vast majority of the calculations are done inside the table using onClick event handlers. Only a few functions are involved for some of the larger returns.

Let's get into it and attack the first line of cells in the table. This is the line that includes the display, backspace, and clear buttons. This line is quite different from the others, so let's examine it by itself:

```
<TABLE BORDER=1 CELLSPACING=2 CELLPADDING=3%>
<TR>

<FORM NAME="calculator">

<TD COLSPAN=5 BGCOLOR=RED>

<INPUT NAME="list" TYPE=HIDDEN>
<INPUT TYPE=TEXT NAME="text" VALUE="">
</TD>
<TD COLSPAN=2 BGCOLOR=RED>

<INPUT TYPE=BUTTON VALUE=" Backspace " NAME="backspace" onClick="
➥document.calculator.text.value = document.calculator.text.value.substring(
➥0,document.calculator.text.value.length*1 -1)">
</TD>
<TD COLSPAN=2 BGCOLOR=RED>
<INPUT TYPE=BUTTON VALUE=" Clear " NAME="clear"onClick="
➥document.calculator.text.value=''">
</TD>
</TR>
```

The Display

The display is created through the use of form commands that create a simple text box. The code looks like this:

```
<FORM NAME="calculator">
<TD COLSPAN=5 BGCOLOR=RED>
<INPUT NAME="list" TYPE=HIDDEN>
<INPUT TYPE=TEXT NAME="text" VALUE="">
```

Wait! There are two text boxes, but I only see one!

That's because one is hidden. See how the TYPE is set to HIDDEN? That's a great way to have a couple of boxes and display only one. Later in the script, we'll talk about the button that changes the number in the display from positive to negative, or back again. To do that, you must exchange data back and forth. By using this hidden text box, you have a place to set the data before you move it back. Stay tuned; we'll get to that button soon enough.

The name of the form itself is calculator, and the name of the display text box is text. In addition to a name, the box is also given a value set to nothing. See the empty quotation marks? That's to ensure there's nothing in the display to start with.

Now, you know that any time you want to send something to the display, you use the hierarchy document.calculator.text.value.

The Backspace Button

The backspace button is next. The code looks like this:

```
<INPUT TYPE=BUTTON VALUE=" Backspace " NAME="backspace"
➥onClick="document.calculator.text.value =
➥document.calculator.text.value.substring(
➥0,document.calculator.text.value.length*1 -1)">
```

This button is a bit of a code monster. Before getting into it, let's stop and think about what it's supposed to do. By clicking the Backspace button, you want the last number in the display to be eliminated. To do that, you need to make the JavaScript see that what is in the display text box is individual numbers in a string. If you do that, you can then set it so the last number of the string is eliminated with a click of the button.

Notice the button has a name and then a value so that it displays correctly, but it's the onClick event handler that does the dirty work. When clicked, the value found in the display (document.calculator.text.value) is set to a substring. See how the command substring is added after the equal sign? In the instance (the parentheses) then, a comparison is set up. Remember that in a substring instance, the larger of two elements is performed. In this case, there's zero and then a calculation.

The calculation is the length of what appears in the display, times one, minus one. It's that minus one that does the trick. By taking one away, you clip off the last item in the sub-string (that's the last number); then by clicking the Backspace button, you clip off the last number. Clever, no?

The Clear Button

This works much the same way as the Backspace button using an onClick to enact an effect upon the display:

```
<INPUT TYPE=BUTTON VALUE=" Clear " NAME="clear"
➥onClick="document.calculator.text.value=''">
```

This has a name, then a value attached for display, and then the magic of the onClick. By clicking the button, you're setting the value of the display box to … well, nothing. See the empty single quotation marks? No matter what has come before or what is presently in the display text box, by clicking the Clear button, you set it to nothing, thus you clear it.

Next, let's start on the numbers and the calculator functions. From here on, the buttons all pretty much work the same way. The hard part is keeping them in the correct order so the table display is correct.

The Other Buttons

Let's get into the buttons you find past the top row. Each of these buttons works in basically the same onClick way. It's the format of the table that will probably be most confusing.

If you've looked at the code, you might wonder why the keypad numbers are not all in a row. This is because the author has opted for this calculator to sit inside a table, so he had to set up all the buttons in the order that would display them in the table. If you follow it along, it goes something like this:

Numbers 7, 8, 9, plus, minus, reciprocal, power, sine

Numbers 4, 5, 6, times, divide, absolute, exponent, cosine

Numbers 1, 2, 3, left par., right par., square, round, tangent

Zero, decimal, +/- sign, equals, square root, random, Pi

Let's examine that first line. It's a good representation of the next two lines:

```
<TD BGCOLOR=BLUE>
<CENTER>
<INPUT TYPE=BUTTON VALUE=" 7 " NAME="but7" onClick="
➥document.calculator.text.value+='7'">
```

```
</TD>

<TD BGCOLOR=BLUE>
<CENTER>
<INPUT TYPE=BUTTON VALUE=" 8 " NAME="but8" onClick="
➥document.calculator.text.value+='8'">
</TD>

<TD BGCOLOR=BLUE>
<CENTER>
<INPUT TYPE=BUTTON VALUE=" 9 " NAME="but9" onClick="
➥document.calculator.text.value+='9'">
</TD>

<TD BGCOLOR=YELLOW>
<CENTER>
<INPUT TYPE=BUTTON VALUE=" + " NAME="add" onClick="
➥document.calculator.text.value+='+'">
</TD>

<TD BGCOLOR=YELLOW>
<CENTER>
<INPUT TYPE=BUTTON VALUE=" - " NAME="subtract" onClick="
➥document.calculator.text.value+='-'">
</TD>

<TD BGCOLOR=LIME>
<CENTER>
<INPUT TYPE="BUTTON" VALUE=" 1/x " NAME="reciprocal" onClick="
➥recip(document.calculator.text.value)">
</TD>

<TD BGCOLOR=LIME>
<CENTER>
<INPUT TYPE="BUTTON" VALUE=" x^y " NAME="power" onClick="
➥raisePower(document.calculator.text.value)">
</TD>

<TD BGCOLOR=LIME>
<CENTER>
<INPUT TYPE=BUTTON VALUE=" sin " NAME="sin" onClick="
➥document.calculator.text.value= Math.sin(document.calculator.text.value*
➥3.141592653589793/180)">
</TD>
```

It's fairly obvious that the lines are a bit convoluted due to the space restrictions on this page. Please make a point of following the form shown in the code link for this script; otherwise, you're sure to get errors.

Let's discuss them one at a time, but let's do it by only showing the button code. There's no need to continue displaying all the table code. This is a JavaScript Script Tip, right? Right.

Seven

This button represents the number 7:

```
<INPUT TYPE=BUTTON VALUE=" 7 " NAME="but7" onClick="
➥document.calculator.text.value+='7'">
```

The Value " 7 " is on the face of the button, and the Name given is "but7" (as in button seven). When the button is clicked, a 7 is placed in the display window denoted by document.calculator.text.value. See that in the previous onClick statement?

Please note: The operator += acts to add or *concatenate* two text strings. By using the +=, the display is not replaced with the number, but rather the number is placed at the end of the display. So, when you click 7, a 7 displays. If you then click again, the += places the next 7 after the first rather than simply replacing it. That way, every time you click, that value is added to the display rather than replacing what is already in the display. Later, after all the numbers and operators are lined up, you'll figure the equation.

Got it? Good. Moving along ....

Eight

The same holds true for the number 8. An onClick puts the number 8 in the display window:

```
<INPUT TYPE=BUTTON VALUE=" 8 " NAME="but8" onClick="
➥document.calculator.text.value+='8'">
```

Nine

The same goes for the number 9:

```
<INPUT TYPE=BUTTON VALUE=" 9 " NAME="but9" onClick="
➥document.calculator.text.value+='9'">
```

Add

Now we get into the actual format of how the calculator works. This is the addition button:

```
<INPUT TYPE=BUTTON VALUE=" + " NAME="add" onClick="
➥document.calculator.text.value+='+'">
```

Note the format is the same as the number buttons except this button places a plus sign in the display window. This button simply sets a plus sign in place so that an addition can occur; it doesn't actually do the addition. That occurs when the equal button comes into play.

Subtract

Take a look at this:

```
<INPUT TYPE=BUTTON VALUE=" - " NAME="subtract" onClick="
➥document.calculator.text.value+='-'">
```

Look familiar? Again, the button does not perform any subtraction. It simply places a minus so that later, when the equal button is clicked, a subtraction can occur.

Reciprocal

Here's an interesting piece of code:

```
<INPUT TYPE="BUTTON" VALUE=" 1/x " NAME="reciprocal" onClick="
➥recip(document.calculator.text.value)">
```

Do you know what this is? Me neither, so I looked it up. It is a function that figures a pair of numbers that has 1 as its product. That is, what number, when divided into the number in the display, produces the number 1?

Okay, I don't really get it either, but if you're a math person I'm sure it makes perfect sense to you. I'm only here to show you how to do it. This is the first button in this row that actually must have a number posted in the display to function.

When the onClick is enacted, it appears as if a JavaScript command called recip is enacted. Nope. recip is actually the name of a function found between the HEAD commands. It looks like this:

```
function recip(x)
{document.calculator.text.value = (1/(x))}
function raisePower(x)
```

```
{
var y = 0
y = prompt("What is the exponent?", "")
document.calculator.text.value = Math.pow(x,y)
}
```

When you click, the x is replaced with the value inside the display. See that in the previous `onClick: recip(document.calculator.text.value)`? That value is then set into a fraction with 1 as the denominator.

Next, another function named `raisePower()` is brought into work. A variable—y—is set to 0. Then, y gets a value from the user through a prompt. That value acts as the exponent or power. Finally, the display receives the number it originally had raised to the power the user offered through the use of the `Math.pow(#,#)` format. The first # is the number, and the second # is the power it will be raised to.

If nothing is written inside the display then the math acts on nothing and nothing is returned.

Power

The code for the power button is as follows:

```
<INPUT TYPE="BUTTON" VALUE=" x^y " NAME="power" onClick="
➥raisePower(document.calculator.text.value)">
```

It uses the same format as the previous code, except here the JavaScript command `raisePower` is set to act on what is inside the display and raise it to the first power.

Sine

Sine is the ratio of the side opposite the angle of the hypotenuse. Here is the code:

```
<INPUT TYPE=BUTTON VALUE=" sin " NAME="sin" onClick="
➥document.calculator.text.value=
 Math.sin(document.calculator.text.value*3.141592653589793/180)">
```

Now we get into another format of finding the answer. Again, a number must be shown in the display for this to work. When the button is clicked, the value of the display is created through the `Math` object setting a sine (`Math.sin`) by multiplying the number displayed by Pi (3.141592653589793) and then dividing that by 180. Even though you might not understand the math, do you see how it works?

The Next Two Lines

The next two lines of code are as follows:

> Numbers 4, 5, 6, times, divide, absolute, exponent, cosine
>
> Numbers 1, 2, 3, left par., right par., square, round, tangent

These work exactly the same way. The numbers post to the display using the same formats as shown previously. The multiply and divide do not perform the action; they simply place the correct character so that the math can be done later. The square, round, tangent, absolute, exponent, and cosine math is done basically the same way as shown previously, using JavaScript commands and short math equations just like the previous one. You might not understand the math, but you can understand this format:

```
Absolute: Math.abs(document.calculator.text.value)"

Exponent: onClick="document.calculator.text.value+='E'

Cosine: Math.cos(document.calculator.text.value*3.141592653589793/180)

Square: document.calculator.text.value * document.calculator.text.value

Round: Math.round(document.calculator.text.value)"
Math.tan(document.calculator.text.value*3.141592653589793/180)"
```

Next, let's get into actually how the calculator works and the final line of buttons. They get a little tricky.

The Last Row of Buttons

OK, we're on to the last line of buttons. This one gets a little tricky, so let's take it by itself.

The last line of buttons look like this:

> Zero, decimal, +/- sign, equals, square root, random, Pi

Here are the actual button codes without all the table coding:

```
<INPUT TYPE=BUTTON VALUE=" 0 " NAME="but0" onClick="
➥document.calculator.text.value+='0'">
<INPUT TYPE=BUTTON VALUE=" . " NAME="decimal" onClick="
➥document.calculator.text.value+='.'">
<INPUT TYPE=BUTTON VALUE=" +|- " NAME="sign" onClick="change()">
<INPUT TYPE=BUTTON VALUE=" = " NAME="equals"
➥onClick="document.calculator.text.value=eval(
```

```
➥document.calculator.text.value)">
<INPUT TYPE=BUTTON VALUE=" x¹/₂ " NAME="sqrt"
➥onClick="document.calculator.text.value=Math.sqrt(
➥document.calculator.text.value)">
<INPUT TYPE=BUTTON VALUE=" rand " NAME="random" onClick="
➥document.calculator.text.value = getRandom()">
<INPUT TYPE=BUTTON VALUE=" pi " NAME="pi" onClick="
➥document.calculator.text.value+= getPi()">
```

Allow me to discuss these a little out of order. You've seen some of the formats before, so I'll talk about them first.

Zero and Decimal

Does this look familiar:

```
<INPUT TYPE=BUTTON VALUE=" 0 " NAME="but0" onClick="
➥document.calculator.text.value+='0'">
<INPUT TYPE=BUTTON VALUE=" . " NAME="decimal" onClick="
➥document.calculator.text.value+='.'">
```

It should. Both of these buttons act like the other number buttons 1–9. You click, and a 0 is placed in the display. You click, and a decimal point is placed in the display.

Again, notice the use of += to add the number to the display rather than replacing what is already displayed.

Square Root

Here is the code for the Square Root button:

```
<INPUT TYPE=BUTTON VALUE=" x¹/₂ " NAME="sqrt"
➥onClick="document.calculator.text.value=Math.sqrt(
➥document.calculator.text.value)">
```

Just as before, the number displayed is acted on through the Math object and the command sqrt to create the result.

In case you're wondering, x&#189 is the ASCII code to display x1/2. Cool, huh?

Random

```
<INPUT TYPE=BUTTON VALUE=" rand " NAME="random" onClick="
➥document.calculator.text.value = getRandom()">
```

For this random button, and the Pi button that follows, the author decided to use a function. Note in the code how the display (document,calculator.text.value) is created by going to the function getRandom(), which looks like this:

```
function getRandom()
{return Math.random()}
```

The function simply returns (return) a random number (created through Math.random) to the display. It seems simple enough, but you might ask why not just follow the same format for putting it all in the onClick? I guess you could, but I would think the author set this aside as a function because the random number had nothing to do with the display. By setting it in a function, he separated it from any other numbers, which is probably a good idea.

Pi

This is the same as the previous one:

```
<INPUT TYPE=BUTTON VALUE=" pi " NAME="pi" onClick="
➥document.calculator.text.value+= getPi()">
```

The number for Pi is returned from a function that looks like this:

```
function getPi()
{return Math.PI}
```

Again, could the author have simply done it inside the button itself? Yes. This, I think, is just a cleaner method of doing it. Plus, pi has a decimal point in it, and that's tough to get into a simple display. Doing this solved that problem pretty quickly.

Equals

Ah, now you get to the meat of the calculator function—the equal button. If you click this one, you get the answer. How you get the answer is a matter of how the author set up the script:

```
<INPUT TYPE=BUTTON VALUE=" = " NAME="equals"
➥onClick="document.calculator.text.value=eval(
➥document.calculator.text.value)">
```

Remember earlier in the script, the majority of the buttons simply set numbers or operators (+, -, /, *) into the display? You clicked the numbers and they displayed one right after the other so that when you were done putting in all your numbers, the equation you entered appeared there in the display.

The equal button simply says "Do it!" after you've entered the numbers. There in the display is a math equation. Click the equal button, and that equation is evaluated (eval) and the result is placed in the display. Poof! Your answer! And you thought it was hard ....

There's one more button to worry about. It's the one that changes a number from negative to positive or the other way around. It's clever and is a Script Tip unto itself.

Positive to Negative

There's one more thing to worry about in this calculator script—the button that changes numbers from negative to positive. At the beginning of this Script Tip, you saw two text boxes, one of which was hidden. Now that hidden text box comes into play.

Three codes are used here. The first is the button that triggers the function that changes a number from positive to negative or back again. It has the value of +|- on the front, and the code looks like this:

```
<INPUT TYPE=BUTTON VALUE=" +|- " NAME="sign" onClick="change()">
```

The button itself isn't all that hard to understand; all it does is enact a function called change(). That function looks like this:

```
function change()
{
var temp = document.calculator.text.value;

if (temp.substring(0,1) == "-")
{document.calculator.list.value = "";
document.calculator.text.value = 0 - document.calculator.text.value
➡ * 1}

if (temp.substring(0,1) != "-")
{document.calculator.list.value ="";
document.calculator.text.value = "-" + temp.substring(0,temp.length)}
}
```

Now, remember, that the previous display is a little cramped. Make sure the function is in the format shown in the script code.

Let's take a look at what happens. When the button is clicked, the value that appears in the display (document.calculator.text.value) is assigned the variable name temp.

Next, the script tests to see whether the value is already negative. An if statement asks if the text.substring's first character is equal to the minus sign. Remember that any time you set a substring, you must set up a comparison where the larger number wins. In this case the two numbers are 0 and 1. The one is bigger, so it wins and the first character in the substring is checked.

Notice the two equal signs: That means "is equal to."

If the first character is equal to the minus sign, the hidden text box comes into play. Here's that code:

```
<INPUT NAME="list" TYPE=HIDDEN>
<INPUT TYPE=TEXT NAME="text" VALUE="">
```

I have listed the hidden box and then the display text box. Both of them come into play here. The hidden text box is given the name list. Now you can get at the box using the hierarchy statement document.calculator.list.value.

So, back to "If the first character is the minus sign." If it is, the hidden text box is given a value of nothing. By doing that, it brings it into play. That hidden box is then set to 0, the value in the display is taken away, and the result is multiplied by 1. That sets the same number to a positive value.

If the first character is not a minus sign, the second if statement comes into play. This statement asks if the first character is *not* equal to a minus sign. (!= is the operator for "is not equal to").

If this if statement is true then, again, the hidden box is given a value of nothing to bring it into play. The value of the hidden box is then set to a minus sign plus the full length of the temp variable substring.

I know that seems a bit much, but by adding the value through a substring, the value remains the same. Rather than the entire thing being seen as one entity, which it is not, it remains a string of characters, which it is.

And that wraps up the calculator. It is quite involved and sometimes a little rough to get hold of, but now that you're through it, I think you'll agree it was a manageable project.

Placing a Cookie

Ever since HTML Goodies was created, the cookie has been the one thing that people either hated or couldn't wait to get on their Web pages. I have a tutorial on what a cookie actually is on the HTML Goodies site at `http://www.htmlgoodies.com/tutors/cookie.html`. It's a lot of reading, but basically a cookie is a text file—less than 4K—a server places on your computer to track or remember things for you.

Whatever you think about cookies, there's no denying they're popular. In this Script Tip, we'll get into how you can set, and retrieve, cookies for your visitors.

The script was originally sent to be posted on HTML Goodies by Giedrius. Usually, I alter the scripts for these tips a bit. Not this one; I barely touched it, except to change a display. I like it just how the author put it together. I also made a point of keeping his name in the code as author. I would ask you do the same.

First, let's get into how this specific script works; then we'll talk about how you can use the format to create larger, more useful effects. For instance, I altered the script to show two separate messages depending on whether this is the user's first time receiving a cookie. One reads Nice to meet you, and the other reads, Welcome back. I'll show you how to do that after you get through the script in its current state.

Here's the script:

```
<SCRIPT language="JavaScript">
<!--
//This script was made by Giedrius
cookie_name = "NameCookie2010";
var GuestName;

function putCookie()
{
if(document.cookie)
{ index = document.cookie.indexOf(cookie_name);
}
else { index = -1;}

if (index == -1)
{
GuestName=window.prompt("Hello! What's your name?","Nobody");
if (GuestName==null) GuestName="Nobody";
document.cookie=cookie_name+"="+GuestName+"; expires=Tuesday,
➥05-Apr-2010 05:00:00 GMT";
}
else
{
namestart = (document.cookie.indexOf("=", index) + 1);
nameend = document.cookie.indexOf(";", index);
if (nameend == -1) { nameend = document.cookie.length;}
GuestName = document.cookie.substring(namestart, nameend);
if (GuestName=="Nobody")
{
GuestName=window.prompt("Hello again!!!"+"\n"+"Last time you didn't
➥tell me your name. Maybe you want to do it now?","Nobody");
if ((GuestName!="Nobody")&&(GuestName!=null))
{document.cookie=cookie_name+"="+GuestName+"; expires=Tuesday,
➥05-Apr-2010 05:00:00 GMT";}
if (GuestName==null) GuestName="Nobody";
}
}
```

```
}

function getName()
{
if(document.cookie)
{
index = document.cookie.indexOf(cookie_name);
if (index != -1)
{
namestart = (document.cookie.indexOf("=", index) + 1);
nameend = document.cookie.indexOf(";", index);
if (nameend == -1) {nameend = document.cookie.length;}
GuestName = document.cookie.substring(namestart, nameend);
return GuestName;
}
}
}

putCookie();
GuestName=getName();

//STOP HIDING THE SCRIPT-->
</script>

<!-- What is below will appear on the page itself -->
<SCRIPT>
document.write("Hello, "+GuestName+", nice to meet you!!!");
</SCRIPT>
```

You'll feel better if you have a cookie, which is shown in Figure ST8.1.

 To see the effect on your own computer, click Script Tip Eight in your download packet, or see it online at http://www.htmlgoodies.com/stips/scripttip60effect.html. Please note that you will get the prompt only the first time you use it. Past that, there's already a cookie set, so there's no need to ask for your name again.

The code is available for copy and paste at http://www.htmlgoodies.com/stips/ scripttip60script.html or by viewing the source of the page in your download packet.

The script, actually *scripts*, isn't very threatening in the present form. The code first checks to see whether it has already set a cookie. If not, it sets one. It then checks to see whether the person entered her name the last time. If not, it requests the name again. If a cookie has already been set, it simply displays the name. All these checks means you're bound to have quite a few conditional statements checking things for you.

Figure ST8.1
The prompt is asking for the user's name. That information is sent to a cookie by the script.

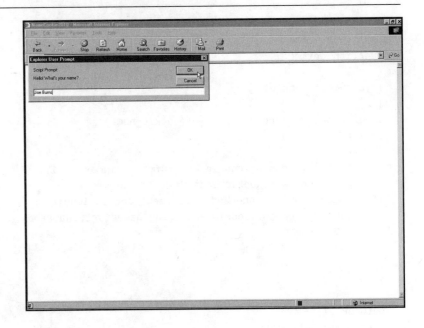

There's no simple way to attack this script, so let's just get started from the top down. First, you set a couple of variables and check to see whether a cookie exists:

```
cookie_name = "NameCookie2010";
var GuestName;

function putCookie()
{
if(document.cookie)
{
index = document.cookie.indexOf(cookie_name);
}
else { index = -1;}
```

The first line sets a text string value to the variable name cookie_name. Usually, I put var before each of these types of statements, but not now. I left it out to be able to make the point that when setting variable names, the command var isn't necessary because the single equal sign implies that that one item is to be representative of the other.

Yes, you could write this as

```
var cookie_name = "NameCookie2010";
```

but you don't have to. As the author wrote it is sufficient.

The next line does use the var command because in this case, the variable name is only being brought into play for later, but as of yet it does not have a value assigned to it. You just want to have it in the JavaScript's memory for when you need it later. The function putCookie() is actually a little mis-named. This function does not *put* any cookie; it checks to see whether a cookie already exists:

```
if(document.cookie)
```

The if statement asks for the document.cookie. Although the text is confusing, remember that cookie is actually a property of document. Yes, I know that the cookie does not reside in the document, but rather in a file in another part of the hard drive. That doesn't matter to JavaScript. cookie is a property and simply saying document.cookie starts the process of looking for one. For once, something that should be difficult is easy. Go figure. So, is there a cookie? You need to find out.

Now, here's the rest of the if statement:

```
{
index = document.cookie.indexOf(cookie_name);
}
else { index = -1;}
```

It attempts to set index (a property, the index of something) to equal document.cookie.indexOf(cookie_name). Remember that cookie_name is NameCookie2010. You set that first thing in the script, remember?

Notice how you grabbed the cookie. You know that cookie is a property of document just as any form elements would be. That's why you get to use a hierarchy statement format when going after the cookie.

The command indexOf() is a method that returns the location of a text string. Basically, the line looks to see whether a text string named NameCookie2010 appears on this computer. If it does appear, the statement is already true. So, nothing needs to be set because index is already equal to NameCookie2010. Let's move on to what follows in the else statement.

The else statement says to set the index to -1 if the other can't be found. You might remember that -1 is used in JavaScript to indicate a string is not found because JavaScript counts 0 as a viable number. This command sets the cookie index to null.

Why? Why not set the cookie right then and there?

Because it's not that easy. Besides, the author is not really going to set the index to -1—he set it there to indicate that the named cookie has not yet been set for this document.

Setting the Cookie

Okay, this is a little backward so I'm going to describe how it runs. In the previous code you set up a test that looked for a cookie named `NameCookie2010`. If the cookie was found then the variable `index` was given the value of the location of the cookie. If there was no cookie, `index` was given the value of -1. So what happens if `index` is -1? Well, this:

```
if (index == -1)
{
GuestName=window.prompt("Hello! What's your name?","Nobody");
if (GuestName==null) GuestName="Nobody";
document.cookie=cookie_name+"="+GuestName+"; expires=Tuesday,
➥05-Apr-2010 05:00:00 GMT";
}
else
{
namestart = (document.cookie.indexOf("=", index) + 1);
nameend = document.cookie.indexOf(";", index);
if (nameend == -1) { nameend = document.cookie.length;}
GuestName = document.cookie.substring(namestart, nameend);
{
```

It's yet another `if` statement, but look at how it's constructed. If there is not a cookie, or if there is not but one of the named value, the first part is enacted and a cookie is set. If there is, the cookie is read and a certain part of it is assigned to the variable `GuestName`.

It's backward from the first `if` statement that checks first and then sets to place a cookie. This `if` statement places first, and if it doesn't need to place, it reads the cookie. Let's place it first:

```
if (index == -1)
{
GuestName=window.prompt("Hello! What's your name?","Nobody");
if (GuestName==null) GuestName="Nobody";
document.cookie=cookie_name+"="+GuestName+"; expires=Tuesday,
➥05-Apr-2010 05:00:00 GMT";
}
```

Let's say `index` is equal to -1. First, the variable `GuestName` is given the value of a prompt. As you can see, the prompt pops up and asks for a name. In the text box, though, is the text `Nobody`. See that in the previous code? It's important.

The next line checks the variable value. If `GuestName` equals (double equal sign) `null`, meaning nothing, `GuestName` is set to `Nobody`. Now you have a safety net in case the user just simply presses Enter, thus entering `Nobody`. You also have it set up so that if the user blanked the text box and pressed Enter, the variable is set to `Nobody` anyway.

Finally, you actually set the cookie. The hierarchy statement `document.cookie` followed by an equal sign sets. You have the text of the cookie to be set first with the name of the cookie itself, then the text the user entered, and then an expiration date. Notice the format for the date. You must follow that just as you see it.

Here's the text as it appears in the cookie set on my system: `NameCookie2010`. Here's the code:

```
Joe
~~local~~/E:\HTML Goodies\Scripttips\
0
3625486336
30069884
1906963680
29301170
*
```

First is the name of the cookie and then the word I entered, `Joe`. Next is the location—notice it's `local`. Last is the expiration date in milliseconds because JavaScript counts time in milliseconds.

So the cookie is set; at least what you wrote to the cookie is set. But what if there already is a cookie? Well, you need to grab what the user wrote. You already know by looking that the text the user wrote is second in the run of text. So, you need to grab just that. Here's the code that does it:

```
}
namestart = (document.cookie.indexOf("=", index) + 1);
nameend = document.cookie.indexOf(";", index);
if (nameend == -1) { nameend = document.cookie.length;}
GuestName = document.cookie.substring(namestart, nameend);
{
```

As you can see, the `document.cookie` is acted on by using the method `indexOf`. That command returns a location of a string depending on two arguments within the instance (parentheses). In this case, you are interested in the text string set by the cookie.

First, the variable `namestart` is assigned the index of an equal sign and the text of the string. Remember that in this case, a text string's first character is always given the value of `0` and the last character is given the value of `-1`. If you think about it for a moment, you'll realize that that's JavaScript for beginning and end, and JavaScript sees `0` as a viable number.

So, you have a method of grabbing the beginning of the string plus one (the +1). The equal sign is not shown in the string, but it's implied as the name jumps to the next line; therefore, you're looking for something that starts with an equal sign in the length of the text string. That's the word Joe in the previous code.

Next in the script, nameend is given the index of a semicolon and the length of the text string. A semicolon is seen as the end of a line in JavaScript, so this denotes the end of the line after the word Joe.

The next line states that if the end of the text is the end of the line of text (nameend = -1) then make nameend equal to the entire remainder of the text string. This would come into play if no expiration date were in place and Joe ended the line of text.

Finally, the variable GuestName is given the value of what is contained between namestart and nameend. That's the text entered by the user. That text is assigned as a text string to a variable and can be used and posted anywhere on the page, or any other page for that matter because the cookie never goes away.

Next, let's look into what happens if GuestName actually represents the default—Nobody. We can't just let that lie now, can we?

What About Nobody?

If a user comes to your page and doesn't play nice with this script, allowing it to simply read Nobody by pressing Return, you should make a point of showing that person the error of his ways and give him a second chance.

Here's the code you're interested in:

```
if (GuestName=="Nobody")
{
GuestName=window.prompt("Hello again!!!"+"\n"+"Last time you didn't
➥tell me your name. Maybe you want to do it now?","Nobody");
if ((GuestName!="Nobody")&&(GuestName!=null))
{document.cookie=cookie_name+"="+GuestName+"; expires=Tuesday, 05-Apr-2010
➥05:00:00 GMT";}
if (GuestName==null) GuestName="Nobody"; }
```

This little blip of code is the annoyer. It comes into play only if a cookie has been set and the person is returning. The script never incorporates this code if there is no cookie because of the code's placement. Let's see how it works.

Let's start with another familiar if statement asking if the value of GuestName is equal to Nobody. If so, a prompt is fired up and the user is again asked to put in his name.

Notice the \n in the window.prompt. That represents a new line to JavaScript, so this won't all be run together.

Again, the default is set to Nobody.

Now you need to set the cookie off of what the user did. The next line tests for that. The double ampersands (&&) means "and". So, you're testing whether the value of GuestName is not equal (!=) to Nobody and not equal to nothing (null). If that's the case—meaning at least something was put in the text box—then it is set to a cookie.

The next line is the catchall if the user blanks the text box and goes on. The code tests if GuestName is equal to null. If it is, the value is reset to Nobody. You can now be pretty sure that the user will get this warning again when he stops back.

That's the extent of what you need to do to set the cookie. Next, we talk about grabbing it and posting it to the page.

Displaying Cookie Contents

The cookie is set, so now you need to use coding to go get it. In the case of this script, the display is immediately after setting the cookie. Keep in mind that that doesn't always have to be the case. You easily can split this code and set on one page but grab and display on another. That's the purpose of these cookies—to carry information across pages.

This blip of code looks very similar to the one you looked at previously. The reason is because the two perform the same duties, except the first one grabs the text string from the cookie to assign it to the variable GuestName, whereas this one grabs it so it can be displayed. Here's the code:

```
function getName()

{
if(document.cookie)
{
index = document.cookie.indexOf(cookie_name);
if (index != -1)
{
namestart = (document.cookie.indexOf("=", index) + 1);
nameend = document.cookie.indexOf(";", index);
if (nameend == -1) {nameend = document.cookie.length;}
GuestName = document.cookie.substring(namestart, nameend);
return GuestName;
}
}
}
```

```
   putCookie();
   GuestName=getName();
```

This is a function, so there has to be something to trigger it. Look at the last line of the script. `GuestName` is equal to the function `getName`—that's what starts it. The entire script must be put into the browser memory; then the last line fires this function by calling for its output.

So here we go. If there is a `document.cookie` (which you know exists, at least in this format), `index` equals what is contained in the cookie `NameCookie2010`.

If the index is non-existent (`-1`), `namestart` is equal to the equal sign plus one to the length.

Consequently, `nameend` is equal to the rest of that line until the end, which is represented by the semicolon. Remember all of this two tips ago?

If there is no end to the string (`nameend==-1`) then `nameend` is equal to the full length of the cookie. This occurs if no expiration date is set. `GuestName` then must be given the value of what is between `namestart` and `nameend`, which is what the user entered.

Finally, the script is told to return that value.

The next line is what started the entire process in the first place, triggering the first function you looked at, `putCookie()`. You know the next line—it fires up the function you just looked at.

Displaying It

After `GuestName` is given the value of what is contained in the cookie, you can place it anywhere on the page using `document.write` statements. Here's what the author used:

```
<SCRIPT>
document.write("Hello, "+GuestName+", nice to meet you!!!");
</SCRIPT>
```

The text appears and the name is displayed.

So, there you go: A cookie is set and retrieved. It's a great script, but I do see one problem with it. After a cookie is set, the text always reads `Nice to meet you`. Well, after 10 visits, you're not "meeting" your user anymore.

I took the script, altered it a bit, and got it to display the `Nice to meet you` greeting the first time it displayed. Each time after that, it reads `Welcome back`. Here's how.

Two Different Welcomes

If you want to see this new coding in action, point your browser to http://www.
htmlgoodies.com/stips/scripttip64effect.html.

The new code, including the text denoted in the following, can be found at
http://www.htmlgoodies.com/stips/scripttip64script.html.

When I set out to do this, I knew the answer was going to be a conditional statement of
some kind. I also knew it would say something such as, if the user is a first-timer,
use this greeting. If not - use this.

The question then becomes what would you use to check? The answer is a new variable I
named FirstTime. The variable is inserted into the script in specific places so that if the
user receives a cookie for the first time, her FirstTime variable is set to "y". All times after
that, the variable is set to "n". Then, you could do a simple check to see whether the variable is "y" or "n" and set the document.write as you see fit.

Notice the n and y are in quotes. That sets them aside as text strings rather than values.

Placing the Variable

Here's the top of the script. Look for the FirstTime variable:

```
cookie_name = "NameCookie2010";
var GuestName;
var FirstTime

function putCookie()
{
if(document.cookie)
{
index = document.cookie.indexOf(cookie_name);
FirstTime = "n"
}

else

{
FirstTime = "y"
index = -1;
}
```

Notice first that var FirstTime is set so it will be recognized the rest of the way through the
script. I often refer to this as *putting the variable into play.*

Strange as it might seem, the first thing you check is whether a cookie exists; therefore, the first setting `FirstTime` could receive is `"n"`, meaning it isn't the user's first time. See the placement? It's just after the index of the cookie is found and set to a variable name.

The reason for the placement is because after that point in the script, the majority of things are meant to set new cookies, right? If that's true, somewhere in the new cookies you need to insert the line that sets `FirstTime` to `"y"`. Look at the previous code, and you'll see it. It's in the first `else` function.

It's there because of the structure of the script. You want the placement so that when `FirstTime` is given a value, at no other time in the script would the value change. By putting it in the first `if` and `else` statements, you can be assured that if there is a cookie, `FirstTime` will be set to `"n"`. Also, because `else` is skipped if the original statement is `true`, you know you can safely place the second `FirstTime` there.

If there is a cookie, the script sets it to `"n"` and skips the `else`. If not, the `else` comes into play and sets `FirstTime` to `"y"`.

That's the hard part; now we get to the fun. This little piece of code posts a greeting depending on which value was assigned:

```
<SCRIPT LANGUAGE="JavaScript">
if (FirstTime == "y")
{document.write("Hello, "+GuestName+", nice to meet you!!!");}
else
{document.write("Hello, "+GuestName+", welcome back!!!");}
</SCRIPT>
```

It's another `if` statement that tests only whether `FirstTime` is equal to `"y"`. If it isn't then you know it has to be `"n"` and the `else` statement will take it from there.

You should be able to take it from here. If it's `"y"` then the greeting reads Nice to meet you. But if it's `"n"` then the greeting reads, Welcome back.

A 16.7 Million-Color Script

Please Note! This script was written specifically to work on MSIE browsers. If you try to run this on Netscape, it will throw errors. After going through this script, you'll rewrite it and get it to work on Netscape Navigator.

Take a look at the code, and we'll get started. I know, it's a long code so we've shortened it here. Be sure to check out the entire version online:

```
<SCRIPT LANGUAGE="javascript">

// This javascript is property of the Silicon Valley Garage.

function mix()
{
if (document.all)
```

```
{
document.all("box").style.background =
➥"#"+document.ColorMix.red.options[document.ColorMix.red.selectedIndex]
➥.value+document.ColorMix.green.options[document.ColorMix.
➥green.selectedIndex].value+document.ColorMix.blue.options[
➥document.ColorMix.blue.selectedIndex].value;
➥document.ColorMix.code.value = "#"+document.ColorMix.red.options[
➥document.ColorMix.red.selectedIndex]
➥.value+document.ColorMix.green.options[
➥document.ColorMix.green.selectedIndex].value+document.ColorMix.blue.
➥options[document.ColorMix.blue.selectedIndex].value;
}
else
{
alert("Sorry, your browser does not support the programming needed to run this
➥script.");
}
}

if (document.all)
{
var menu = "
<OPTION VALUE=\"ff\">255</OPTION>
<OPTION VALUE=\"fe\">254</OPTION>
<OPTION VALUE=\"fd\">253</OPTION>
<OPTION VALUE=\"fc\">253</OPTION>
<OPTION VALUE=\"fb\">252</OPTION>
<OPTION VALUE=\"fa\">251</OPTION>
<OPTION VALUE=\"f9\">250</OPTION>
<OPTION VALUE=\"f8\">249</OPTION>
<OPTION VALUE=\"f7\">248</OPTION>
<OPTION VALUE=\"f6\">247</OPTION>
<OPTION VALUE=\"f5\">246</OPTION>
<OPTION VALUE=\"f4\">245</OPTION>
<OPTION VALUE=\"f3\">244</OPTION>
<OPTION VALUE=\"f2\">243</OPTION>
<OPTION VALUE=\"f1\">242</OPTION>
<OPTION VALUE=\"f0\">241</OPTION>
<OPTION VALUE=\"ef\">240</OPTION>
<OPTION VALUE=\"ee\">239</OPTION>
<OPTION VALUE=\"ed\">238</OPTION>

...
```

```
<OPTION VALUE=\"12\">018</OPTION>
<OPTION VALUE=\"11\">017</OPTION>
<OPTION VALUE=\"10\">016</OPTION>
<OPTION VALUE=\"0f\">015</OPTION>
<OPTION VALUE=\"0e\">014</OPTION>
<OPTION VALUE=\"0d\">013</OPTION>
<OPTION VALUE=\"0c\">012</OPTION>
<OPTION VALUE=\"0b\">011</OPTION>
<OPTION VALUE=\"0a\">010</OPTION>
<OPTION VALUE=\"09\">009</OPTION>
<OPTION VALUE=\"08\">008</OPTION>
<OPTION VALUE=\"07\">007</OPTION>
<OPTION VALUE=\"06\">006</OPTION>
<OPTION VALUE=\"05\">005</OPTION>
<OPTION VALUE=\"04\">004</OPTION>
<OPTION VALUE=\"03\">003</OPTION>
<OPTION VALUE=\"02\">002</OPTION>
<OPTION VALUE=\"01\">001</OPTION>
<OPTION SELECTED VALUE=\"00\">000</OPTION>";
document.write("<TABLE BORDER=\"0\" CELLPADDING=\"0\" CELLSPACING=\"0\" WIDTH=\
➥"100%\">");
document.write("<FORM NAME=\"ColorMix\">");
document.write("<TD BGCOLOR=\"#000000\" HEIGHT=\"25\" ID=\"box\"
➥COLSPAN=\"4\"></TD><TR>");

document.write("<TD WIDTH=\"25%\"><FONT COLOR=\"#ffffff\"
➥FACE=\"arial, geneva, times new roman\" SIZE=\"2\"><B>Red:
➥ </B></FONT><SELECT NAME=\"red\" ONCHANGE=\"mix();\" SIZE=\"1\">"
➥+menu+"</SELECT></TD><TD WIDTH=\"25%\"><FONT COLOR=\"#ffffff\"
➥FACE=\"arial, geneva, times new roman\" SIZE=\"2\"><B>Green:
➥</B></FONT><SELECT NAME=\"green\" ONCHANGE=\"mix();\" SIZE=\"1\">"
➥+menu+"</SELECT></TD><TD WIDTH=\"25%\"><FONT COLOR=\"#ffffff\"
➥ FACE=\"arial, geneva, times new roman\" SIZE=\"2\"><B>Blue:
➥</B></FONT><SELECT NAME=\"blue\" ONCHANGE=\"mix();\"
➥SIZE=\"1\">"+menu+"</SELECT></TD><TD WIDTH=\"25%\">
➥<INPUT NAME=\"code\" MAXLENGTH=\"7\" SIZE=\"10\"
➥TYPE=\"text\" VALUE=\"#000000\"></TD><TR>");
document.write("</FORM>");
document.write("</TABLE>");
}
</SCRIPT>
```

Figure ST9.1 shows the script in action.

Figure ST9.1

Set each of the Red, Green, and Blue sections to a stronger or weaker setting; the bar across the top shows the color.

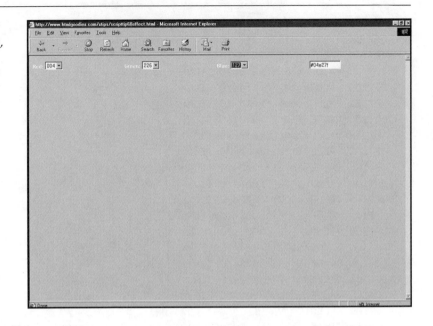

Click Here *To see the effect on your own computer, click Script Tip Nine in your download packet, or see it online at http://www.htmlgoodies.com/stips/scripttip65effect.html.*

The code is available for copy and paste at http://www.htmlgoodies.com/stips/scripttip65script.html or by viewing the source of the page in your download packet.

If you didn't take it from the code, this is a table format. The table is four cells wide with one cell spanning across all four. That spanning cell is the one that receives the color.

The red, green, and blue settings are all drop-down select box form elements. As you have probably noticed, there are 256 choices in each drop box, 000–255.

What the script does is offer the viewer the ability to choose the RGB values and in turn changes them to the more Web-friendly hex values. It does this through the three drop-down boxes. Let's start with those.

The drop-down box code looks like this:

```
<OPTIONVALUE=\"ff\">255</OPTION>
<OPTIONVALUE=\"fe\">254</OPTION>
<OPTIONVALUE=\"fd\">253</OPTION>
<OPTIONVALUE=\"fc\">253</OPTION>
<OPTIONVALUE=\"fb\">252</OPTION>
<OPTIONVALUE=\"fa\">251</OPTION>
<OPTIONVALUE=\"f9\">250</OPTION>
```

Many items have been deleted here to save space:

```
<OPTION VALUE=\"05\">005</OPTION>
<OPTIONVALUE= \"04\">004</OPTION>
<OPTIONVALUE= \"03\">003</OPTION>
<OPTIONVALUE= \"02\">002</OPTION>
<OPTIONVALUE= \"01\">001</OPTION>
<OPTION SELECTEDVALUE=\"00\">000</OPTION>
```

It's a little backward from how I do my boxes. I always have the option selected choice first. This author decided to go the opposite way and put it at the bottom. No problem, it works just as well.

Now, let's talk a little about colors so you get the concept of this box. You probably know that in Hex code, FFFFFF equals white and 000000 equals black.

The concept of a hex code is two characters representing a level of red, green, and blue. The levels are 1–9 and A–F. The higher the number or letter, the more intense the color. So, FF is the highest saturation of color, and 00 is the lowest saturation.

In the case of white, FF FF FF means the highest saturation of red, green, and blue. That's white. When you're dealing with light, mixing all the colors together gives you white. Don't believe me? Grab a crystal glass and shine white light into it. All the colors contained in that white light will show on the wall.

In the case of black, 00 00 00 means no saturation of color at all because black is the absence of color. If I wanted red, I could set the hex to FF 00 00. That's a ton of red, no green, and no blue. Are you getting my drift here?

Now let me throw a monkey wrench into the mix. That hex code I was just talking about is actually a representation of a three-digit, or *decimal*, code used to make color. It works the very same way. 000 is equal to no color saturation at all, and 255 is equal to complete saturation.

Now at the code for the drop-down menu, previously in the chapter. Start at the bottom. You can see that the choice 000 has a value of 00 in hex. The next choice is 001, which has a value of 01 in hex. If you continue up the menu, you'll see the hex gradually getting stronger as the three-digit number increases. Basically, what you have here is all 256 numbers in a drop-down box and their hex counterparts as the values for the choices.

With that in mind, we can begin to describe how this script functions. When the script first loads, zero values are shown in the R, G, and B drop boxes. That's equivalent to black, so black is shown in the table cell. In addition, the hex #000000 is shown in the text box.

Each time a new value is selected, both the table cell and the text box are updated, so a function that alters them both must be involved.

If you've looked at the code, you can see the table being constructed in the `document.write` statements, but you might also have noticed that only one drop-down box is in the code, yet three show up on the page. It's a clever trick we'll get to as the tip goes on.

What Are All Those Back Slashes for?

So glad you asked. The backslash is what's known as an *escape sequence*. It basically enables you to type in data that shows as text or that alters the text around it. In this case, the author is using (\"):

```
<OPTION VALUE=\"05\">
```

That backslash followed by a double quotation mark allows a double quotation mark to appear on the page. You could probably guess that if you stuck a double quotation mark in there, the script would think you were ending the line and errors would fall all over the place. The author could have simply written the code without any quotation marks, but he wanted quotation marks around the attribute when the page compiled, so the backslash, double quotation mark combination was used to get them.

You'll see this all the way through the script. Don't think it means anything more than a simple double quotation mark.

Building the Table

The code for the table is written to the page through JavaScript `document.write` commands. It looks like this:

```
document.write("<TABLE BORDER=\"0\" CELLPADDING=\"0\"
➥CELLSPACING=\"0\" WIDTH=\"100%\">");

document.write("<FORM NAME=\"Color\">");

document.write("<TD BGCOLOR=\"#000000\" HEIGHT=\"25\" ID=\"box\"
➥COLSPAN=\"4\"></TD><TR>");

document.write("<TD WIDTH=\"25%\"><FONT COLOR=\"#ffffff\"
➥FACE=\"arial, geneva, times new roman\" SIZE=\"2\"><B>Red:
➥ </B></FONT><SELECT NAME=\"red\" ONCHANGE=\"mix();\" SIZE=\"1\">"
➥+menu+"</SELECT></TD><TD WIDTH=\"25%\"><FONT COLOR=\"#ffffff\"
➥FACE=\"arial, geneva, times new roman\" SIZE=\"2\"><B>Green:
➥</B></FONT><SELECT NAME=\"green\" ONCHANGE=\"mix();\" SIZE=\"1\">"
```

```
➥+menu+"</SELECT></TD><TD WIDTH=\"25%\"><FONT COLOR=\"#ffffff\"
➥ FACE=\"arial, geneva, times new roman\" SIZE=\"2\"><B>Blue:
➥</B></FONT><SELECT NAME=\"blue\" ONCHANGE=\"mix();\"
➥SIZE=\"1\">"+menu+"</SELECT></TD><TD WIDTH=\"25%\">
➥<INPUT NAME=\"code\" MAXLENGTH=\"7\" SIZE=\"10\"
➥TYPE=\"text\" VALUE=\"#000000\"></TD><TR>");

document.write("</FORM>");
document.write("</TABLE>");
```

You see how messed up it looks. But let's take it step-by-step, and you'll quickly see how it works.

To begin with, the table is created:

```
document.write("<TABLE BORDER=\"0\" CELLPADDING=\"0\" CELLSPACING=\"0\" WIDTH=\
➥"100%\">");
```

The table has no border, has no cell padding or spacing, and spans the width of the page (100%).

Next, a form is started. Remember that you're going to use drop-down boxes and they are form elements, so you need a form:

```
document.write("<FORM NAME=\"ColorMix\">");
```

The name of the form is Color.

Next, the first table cell—the one that will span the others—is written to the page:

```
document.write("<TD BGCOLOR=\"#000000\" HEIGHT=\"25\" ID=\"box\"
➥COLSPAN=\"4\"></TD><TR>");
```

The cell has a black background, is 25 pixels high, has the ID name box, and spans the next four columns. Now let's look at the three drop-down menus.

You might notice that the next line is much longer than it has to be. This could be written with multiple document.write statements, but the author chose to put it all on one line. No sweat. It works just the same. Let's take just the first part of it:

```
<TD WIDTH=\"25%\"><FONT COLOR=\"#ffffff\" FACE=\"arial, geneva,
➥times new roman\" SIZE=\"2\">
<B>Red: </B></FONT>
<SELECT NAME=\"red\" onChange=\"mix();\"SIZE=\"1\">"+menu+"
➥</SELECT></TD>
```

This is the first of four table cells. The background color is white, the font face is Arial, and it will contain the Red drop-down menu. Now for the clever part.

Notice that contained within the table cell are the beginning commands for a select box. The NAME will be red, and when something changes within the box (onChange), a function named mix() will be called into play.

Then, a variable named mix is called for, and the select box is ended. But what is mix?

Look at the full script again. Menu is a text string made up of the entire drop-down menu discussed in Script Tip 8, "Placing a Cookie." That's the reason you see only one drop-down menu in the code, but three pop up in the browser window. The author set the box to a variable name and then called for it three times. Why not? All three menus are the same, and it saves typing time.

If you continue through the table code, you'll see the next two cells being created exactly the same way, except the next one has the NAME "green" and the third has the NAME "blue".

The last blip of code in that long run creates the text box that will receive the hex code. It looks like this:

```
<TD WIDTH=\"25%\"><INPUT NAME=\"code\" MAXLENGTH=\"7\" SIZE=\"10\"
➥TYPE=\"text\" VALUE=\"#000000\"></TD><TR>");
```

The text box is given the name code and a value of #000000 that displays when the page is first loaded. That's what the three drop-down menus will read, so that's what is displayed.

Finally, a /FORM and a /TABLE are written to complete the table.

Now you have a table with parts you can grab through hierarchy statements. The text box is reachable through document.ColorMix.code.value, and each drop-down menu reads the same, except the color appears where "code" is in the statement:
document.ColorMix.red.value, document.ColorMix.blue.value, and
document.ColorMix.green.value.

The box that receives the color is a little different; it carries an ID and is affected by a function discussed in the next section.

The mix() Function

The engine that makes this script run is a simple function named mix().

The mix() function performs the same maneuver twice sending the same result to two different places. One result goes to the table cell to display the color, while the other goes to the text box to display the hex code. The function looks like this:

```
function mix()
{
if (document.all)
{
document.all("box").style.background =
"#"+document.ColorMix.red.options[document.ColorMix.red.selectedIndex]
➥.value+document.ColorMix.green.options[document.
➥ColorMix.green.selectedIndex].value+document.
➥ColorMix.blue.options[document.ColorMix.blue.selectedIndex]
➥.value;

document.ColorMix.code.value = "#"+document.ColorMix.red.options[
➥document.ColorMix.red.selectedIndex].
➥value+document.ColorMix.green.options[
➥document.ColorMix.green.selectedIndex]
➥.value+document.ColorMix.blue.options[
➥document.ColorMix.blue.selectedIndex].value;
}
else
{
alert("Sorry, your browser does not support the programming
➥needed to run this script.");
}
}
```

The function begins like all other functions do, but the command function, the name of the function, mix, the instance, and then a curly bracket encase what the function will do.

The first line of the function is the reason this will not run on Netscape Navigator browsers. The if statement begins with the command if(document.all).

That is a proprietary command understood by IE4 and above browsers. By attaching all to a document, you basically set it up to be a representation of all the elements in the HTML document. It helps you attach style attributes to elements of the page.

For now, its usage in the if statement basically asks if the browser can support the command all. If it can't, an alert pops up telling the user he doesn't have a browser powerful enough to run the script. Bummer.

But let's stick with what happens if the document.all is recognized and the mix() function runs.

Remember that each of the drop-down menus carries with it an onChange event handler. That way, any time the user alters the display of the menu, the function is triggered to run. No matter what change is made, the script responds. Pretty slick.

The first item you're interested in altering is the long table cell. This is the line that attaches the function to it:

```
document.all("box").style.background =
```

Now `document.all` is carrying arguments. See the parentheses after `all`? In this case, `all` is being used as an array representing all the elements on the page. What is in the instance is `box`—the ID name given to the table cell. So now you're focusing right on that specific element of the page.

But what will you do to it? You'll work with the background style. See the format? You're going to set a background style color for that specific element, `box`.

This is the reason the script doesn't function properly in Netscape Navigator. This format is MSIE only.

Next, you need to set the background style to some color. That color is formed by taking the value selected by the user from the Red, Green, and Blue drop-down menus. Here's the first blip of code:

```
"#"+document.ColorMix.red.options[document.ColorMix.red.selectedIndex]
```

The color code begins with a pound sign (#). It's in quotation marks and is attached to the front of the hex code. Next, you grab the red code. The item comes from the first drop-down box denoted by `document.ColorMix.red.options`. Exactly what hex was chosen is represented by `[document.ColorMix.red.selectedIndex]`.

`selectedIndex` is the value of the item chosen; those values are hex codes. So, if the user selects `255`, the value `FF` is returned to this run.

Now look at the code again. The same thing happens when grabbing the value from the Green and then the Blue drop-down menus. When those three hex values are put together, you get a hex code. That hex code is assigned to the table cell, and the background color changes. In the next full line of the function, the exact same thing occurs. The choices the user made are pulled together to create a hex code; however, in this line of code, the hex is sent to the text box for display:

```
document.ColorMix.code.value =
```

So, each time a new value is selected in any of the boxes, the `mix()` function is triggered. That function firsts tests the browser; then it grabs the choices the user made, changes the table cell background, and sends the hex to a text box for display.

It's a great script, but as I said, it works only in MSIE 4.0 and above. I took some time to play with the code and got it to work in Netscape (and of course MSIE also).

Making It Work in Netscape

Okay, let's just stop and think it through. For this script to run in Netscape Navigator (NN), you must eliminate all the commands NN doesn't understand. Therefore, `document.all` and `document.all("box").style.background` must be eliminated.

You have to flip the script upside down for NN to run it. For NN to run hierarchy statements, the elements must already be loaded into the browser memory. In the case of the MSIE-only script, the commands came first and then the table was built. It's opposite here: First, you have to build the table, and then you can post the function.

Finally, in NN, table cells are not seen as individual items. You can't change a specific cell in a dynamic fashion. You can, however, change the page background. You'll do that next.

Changing that background is shown in Figure ST9.2.

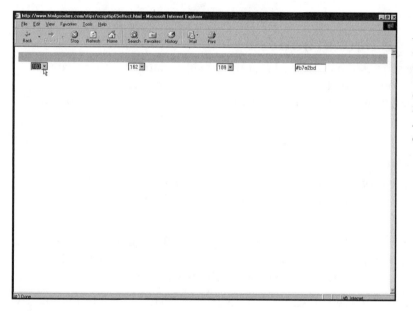

Figure ST9.2
It's basically the same script, except the entire background changes rather than just a bar of color. I actually like the effect much better because I can see a bigger patch of the color.

 To see the effect on your own computer, click Script Tip NineB in your download packet, or see it online at http://www.htmlgoodies.com/stips/scripttip68effect.html.

The code is available for copy and paste at http://www.htmlgoodies.com/stips/script-tip68script.html or by viewing the source of the page in your download packet. I don't know that such a long script needs to be reposted here for just a few changes.

Losing the MSIE-Only Commands

The biggest thing is to find an equivalent to the way the original author worked with docu-
ment.all. It was basically a line of code that had to be true for the function to work. So, I
set up an `if` statement that will always be true. The code is at the top of the script:

```
var zork = 1
if (zork==1)
```

I created a variable named zork and set it to 1. Next, I asked if zork was equal to 1. It is, of
course, so the script goes on. The drop-down menu is assigned the entire run of hex codes.

Flipping the Table and Function

Note the script. I just copied and pasted the document.write statements above the function.
It was a simple cut and paste.

Changing the Page Background

Step three is to set up the script so that the background is being changed rather than the
table cell. The first line of code in the function is now set up to alter document.bgColor—
the background of the page. The user's choices are gathered just the same way as before; I
didn't change that at all.

One More Slight Change

Instead of having the page background appear white, I had it appear black because that's
what the drop-down menus read when the page is first loaded. I did that by adding a
BGCOLOR attribute in the <BODY> flag.

Now the script will run in Netscape as well as MSIE. This is actually a good way to help you
learn JavaScript. Find a script that will run only in one browser or another; then take the
time to find out why and alter the script so it will run in both.

Because of the makeup of the browsers, I wasn't able to get the effect exact, but I got pretty
close, don't you think?

A Digital Clock with Image Display

In lesson 40 in Chapter 7, "Clocks, Counts, and Scroll Text," I told you that I had a digital clock that runs displaying numbers. This is it. You need a lot of little parts to make in run. First, let me show you the code; then we'll get to where you can grab the parts you'll need.

Here's the script:

```
<HTML>
<HEAD>
<SCRIPT LANGUAGE="JavaScript">
<!--

var d=new Array();
for(i=0;i<10;i++) {
d[i]=new Image();
d[i].src="dgt"+i+".gif";
}
var pm=new Image;
pm.src="dgtp.gif";
```

```javascript
var am=new Image;
am.src="dgta.gif";
var dates,min,sec,hour;
var amPM="am";

function clock() {
dates=new Date();
hour=dates.getHours();
min=dates.getMinutes();
sec=dates.getSeconds();
if(hour < 12) {
amPM=am.src;
}
if(hour > 11) {
amPM=pm.src;
hour=hour-12;
}
if(hour == 0) {
hour=12;
}
if(hour < 10) {
document["tensHour"].src="dgtbl.gif";
document["Hour"].src=d[hour].src;
}
if(hour > 9) {
document["tensHour"].src=d[1].src;
document["Hour"].src=d[hour-10].src;
}
if(min < 10) {
document["tensMin"].src=d[0].src;
}
if(min > 9) {
document["tensMin"].src=d[parseInt(min/10,10)].src;
}
document["Min"].src=d[min%10].src;
if(sec < 10) {
document["tensSec"].src=d[0].src;
}
if(sec > 9) {
document["tensSec"].src=d[parseInt(sec/10,10)].src;
}
document["Sec"].src=d[sec%10].src;
document["amPM"].src=amPM;
```

```
setTimeout("clock();",100);
}
//-->
</SCRIPT>
</HEAD>
<BODY BGCOLOR="ffffff" onload="clock();">
<center>

<img src="dgtbl.gif" name="tensHour"><img src="dgtbl.gif" name="Hour">
➥<img src="dgtcol.gif"><img src="dgtbl.gif" name="tensMin">
➥<img src="dgtbl.gif" name="Min"><img src="dgtcol.gif">
➥<img src="dgtbl.gif" name="tensSec">
➥<img src="dgtbl.gif" name="Sec"><img src="dgtbl.gif">
➥<img src="dgtbl.gif" name="amPM">

</CENTER>
</body>
</HTML>
```

Here's the clock. You'll get something that looks similar to Figure ST10.1.

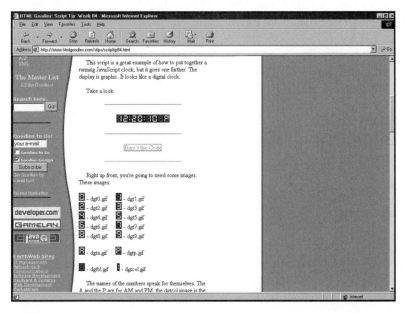

Figure ST10.1
A screen capture from the Script Tip showing the clock and the images you must download to install the clock on your page.

 To see the effect on your own computer, click Script Tip Ten in your download packet or see it online at http://www.htmlgoodies.com/stips/scripttip84.html.

The code is available for copy and paste at `http://www.htmlgoodies.com/stips/scripttip84script.html` or by viewing the source of the page in your download packet.

The images you'll need are available through a Zip file found in your download packet or online at `http://www.htmlgoodies.com/JSBook/digitalclockface.zip`.

You also can grab the images individually if you want. They are online at

- `http://www.htmlgoodies.com/stips/dgt0.gif` through
  `http://www.htmlgoodies.com/stips/dgt9.gif`
- `http://www.htmlgoodies.com/stips/dgta.gif`
- `http://www.htmlgoodies.com/stips/dgtp.gif`
- `http://www.htmlgoodies.com/stips/dgtbl.gif`
- `http://www.htmlgoodies.com/stips/dgtcol.gif`

They are also in the download pack under the previously mentioned names without the domain and directory.

The names of the numbers speak for themselves. The A and the P are for a.m. and p.m., respectively, and the `dgtcol` image is the colon column. The `dgtbl` is the blank image that shows up when nothing is called for—it's also the default image. It shows up even if the script doesn't run. You'll see that in the image code.

And speaking of that code, here it is:

```
<img src="dgtbl.gif" name="tensHour">
<img src="dgtbl.gif" name="Hour">
<img src="dgtcol.gif">
<img src="dgtbl.gif" name="tensMin">
<img src="dgtbl.gif" name="Min">
<img src="dgtcol.gif">
<img src="dgtbl.gif" name="tensSec">
<img src="dgtbl.gif" name="Sec">
<img src="dgtbl.gif">
<img src="dgtbl.gif" name="amPM">
```

Now, you might have noticed that I have listed them vertically, but in the code on the page they're all in one long line. When you put this on your page, use the long line. The reason is that browsers often mistake a carriage return for a space. If that happens, a space will exist between each number and the effect will die.

You'll notice I've broken out the `dgtcol` images. They never change, so at this point, you need not worry about them.

The two hour numbers are broken down into tensHour and Hour. The minutes are done the same way (tensMin and Min), as are seconds (tensSec and Sec).

The final digit is the amPM image.

Now that you have the image code down, let's load them.

Loading All the Images

One of the main concerns about running a digital clock like this one is getting all those images into the browser's memory cache. If you have to wait for a download every time a new number is needed, the effect will die. You want all those images loaded when they're called for, so you should preload them. Here's the code that does it:

```
var d=new Array();
for(i=0;i<10;i++) {
d[i]=new Image();
d[i].src="dgt"+i+".gif";
}
```

This is a very clever piece of script. Ten images must load: the numbers 0–9. There are other images, yes, but it's the numbers we're concerned with right now.

You begin by setting up an array, but the array doesn't exist yet. You'll build it in a moment, and it will be named d.

This code forms a loop. Remember that from lesson 35 in Chapter 6, "Mathematics, Random Things, and Loops?" In this case it's a for loop with three conditions, and i equals 0. As long as i is less than 10, it will loop through. If i isn't yet 10, you add 1 to it (++). Therefore, i will eventually equal 10 and the loop will stop.

Whatever is between the curly brackets ({ }) following the loop is done every time the loop flows through.

Notice the square brackets ([ ]). That's JavaScript for a number replacement. The variable i is sitting in there. Each time the script loops through, i is replaced with the number it represents set by the previous loop.

So, the first time the loop executes, this is created:

```
d0=new Image();
d0.src="dgt0".gif";
```

The next time, you get this:

```
d1=new Image();
d1.src="dgt1".gif";
```

Following the process through, the script runs 10 times. Recognize the format? The codes it's creating are preloads. By looping through, the digit images are preloaded.

What about the other images? Here you go:

```
var pm=new Image;
pm.src="dgtp.gif";
var am=new Image;
am.src="dgta.gif";
var dates,min,sec,hour;
var amPM="am";
```

Okay, they're in the cache. Let's post them, correctly, to the page.

Displaying the Images

Let's begin playing around with replacing those image tags with the correct numbers, depending on what time it is.

The time is grabbed from the user's browser, so there's no need to worry about daylight savings time or time zones. As long as the viewer has her browser set correctly, you're good to go. If she doesn't, well, you can't help that.

Let's start at the top of the script just below the loading loop and code:

```
function clock() {
dates=new Date();
hour=dates.getHours();
min=dates.getMinutes();
sec=dates.getSeconds();
if(hour < 12) {
amPM=am.src;
}
if(hour > 11) {
amPM=pm.src;
hour=hour-12;
}
if(hour == 0) {
hour=12;
}
if(hour < 10) {
document["tensHour"].src="dgtbl.gif";
document["Hour"].src=d[hour].src;
}
if(hour > 9) {
```

```
document["tensHour"].src=d[1].src;
document["Hour"].src=d[hour-10].src;
}
if(min < 10) {
document["tensMin"].src=d[0].src;
}
if(min > 9) {
document["tensMin"].src=d[parseInt(min/10,10)].src;
}
document["Min"].src=d[min%10].src;
if(sec < 10) {
document["tensSec"].src=d[0].src;
}
if(sec > 9) {
document["tensSec"].src=d[parseInt(sec/10,10)].src;
}
document["Sec"].src=d[sec%10].src;
document["amPM"].src=amPM;
setTimeout("clock();",100);
}
```

Don't get put off by its size. It's basically the same thing again and again after you get to the numbers.

Now ... from the top!

The function is named clock(). You might have noticed that it's called for by an onLoad event handler in the <BODY> tag. If you didn't notice, well, it is.

First, you get to some basic clock-building JavaScript. Hopefully, you remember this from Chapter 7:

```
dates=new Date();
hour=dates.getHours();
min=dates.getMinutes();
sec=dates.getSeconds();
```

The variable dates is given the value new Date(). Date() is a JavaScript method that contains all the elements of the current date and time. Remember?

See all the separate elements? Now, you need to use some more code to simply suck out the parts you want. In this case, you want the hour (getHours()), minutes (getMinutes()), and seconds (getSeconds()).

The three items are assigned the variable names hour, min, and sec, respectively.

379

Now that you have the elements, let's test them:

```
if(hour < 12) {
amPM=am.src;
}
if(hour > 11) {
amPM=pm.src;
hour=hour-12;
}
if(hour == 0) {
hour=12;
}
```

Let's start with the hour: If it's less than 12, the image tag named amPM receives the am.src. If you remember the preload commands, that would be dgta.gif.

If the hour is greater than 11, you put the pm.src (dgtp.gif) into the tag amPM, and you take the number represented by hour and subtract 12. That's because JavaScript works in military time. If the time is 20, you take away 12, and get 8 p.m. Get it?

Finally, what if hour is equal to 0 (midnight)? The code says to make hour 12. Now that that's all fixed, let's place the hour:

```
if(hour < 10) {
document["tensHour"].src="dgtbl.gif";
document["Hour"].src=d[hour].src;
}
if(hour > 9) {
document["tensHour"].src=d[1].src;
document["Hour"].src=d[hour-10].src;
}
```

You're worried about two numbers here: If the hour is 10 or greater, you need to place a 1 in the first image and then whatever the hour is in the next. If the hour is 9 or less, you need a blank in the first digit space and whatever the number is below.

It works through a series of if statements. You start by asking whether the hour is less than 10. If so, the tenHour image tag gets the dgtbl.gif—that's the blank image. The second image, Hour, gets the digit equal to the hour (1–9). It's done by using the square brackets and allowing the variable inside the square brackets to be replaced by the variable value. Make sense?

If the hour is greater than 10, the first image (tensHour) gets the number one image and the second number is created by the hour minute ten. Remember that the hour returned is in military time, but in the previous code, you took 12 away from any number greater than

12. If the hour returned is 2300 hours, you subtracted 12, resulting in 11. Then, you took away 10 here, resulting in 1. 1 is then used to post the image.

The minutes and seconds are also done through some fancy mathematical fun.

Minutes and Seconds

You're in the home stretch now. You've grabbed the time, configured the returns into numbers you can play with, and used those numbers to post the a.m./p.m. image and the two hour images. Now, you'll set the minutes and seconds.

Here's the code:

```
if(min < 10) {
document["tensMin"].src=d[0].src;
}
if(min > 9) {
document["tensMin"].src=d[parseInt(min/10,10)].src;
}
document["Min"].src=d[min%10].src;
if(sec < 10) {
document["tensSec"].src=d[0].src;
}
if(sec > 9) {
document["tensSec"].src=d[parseInt(sec/10,10)].src;
}
document["Sec"].src=d[sec%10].src;
document["amPM"].src=amPM;
setTimeout("clock();",100);
```

The script plays with the minutes and seconds in the same way it did the hours, through `if` conditional statements.

If the minute returned is less than tensMIN (the first minute image), it is set to d0.src. If you look at the previous script, you'll see that is the dgt0.gif.

If the minute is more than 9, you must get the correct 10 number in the tensMin position. You already know that the minute returned is 10 or above, so you need 1, 2, 3, 4, or 5. The little math equation parseInt(min/10,10) does the trick.

parseInt is a JavaScript function that turns a text string into an integer and returns that integer. Let's say that the minute returned is 43. If you divide 43 by 10, you get 4.3. The second number allows you to set the base of the integer returned. In this case, 10 is the base. That gets rid of whatever comes after the decimal point (3 in this example). The number returned is therefore 4.

Now that you have the first minute image, you need the second. That is done, again, by a quick mathematic equation. The value assigned to Min is arrived at by taking the minute returned, dividing it by 10, and returning the remainder. That's what the percentage sign does.

For example, say the minute returned is 36. If you divide that by 10, you get 3.6. The remainder is 6, which is what's returned.

The seconds are done exactly the same way, following the same math and using the seconds returned.

Finally, the amPM flag is given the value represented by the variable amPM from the previous code. Remember that? It was almost the first thing you set in the script.

Okay, you've posted all the images. The problem is that the second changes, well, every second. You need to get this script to run again and again to repost again and again. The effect is a running digital clock.

The setTimeout() method does that; it's set to run the function clock() every 100/1000ths of a second.

That should do it.

JavaScript Basic Concepts

This appendix contains the following:

- Literals
- Boolean Literals
- Comments
- Document Object Model
- Event Handlers
- Literal Integers
- Methods
- Objects
- Operators
- Properties
- String
- Variable

Literals

A *literal* is a name assigned to a variable. It is an unchanging title that remains throughout the script. Here's an example:

```
var browser = navigator.Appname
```

This has created a variable called `browser` that is now equal to the browser name.

A *literal string* is any set of characters with quotation marks around it. This set of characters doesn't change. For example, in this code

```
document.write("Hello there")
```

`"Hello there"` is a literal string.

Boolean Literals

Boolean literals are literals that have only two values, 1 and 0. The Boolean literal often is used to represent true (1) and false (0). It helps to think of the true and false as yes and no. Consider this example:

```
window.open("" NAME="newwindow" HEIGHT=300,WIDTH=300,TOOLBAR=1;)
```

The `toolbar=1` is a Boolean literal that means yes, you want a toolbar.

Comments

Comments are lines of text that are written to the page but do not affect the script's workings. The most common use is to add lines into a script along the way as a description of what is happening:

```
<SCRIPT>
//This prompt requests user name and assigns it the variable 'username'
var username = prompt("What is Your Name?")
</SCRIPT>
```

In the previous code you see the double slash comment command. The double slash (//) comments out everything that follows it as long as it stays on the same line. If you allow the text to go to another line without another set of double slashes, the script will think the comment is part of the code and will most probably throw an error.

Multiple-line comments can be created using this format:

```
/*In between the slash and star, you can have
    multiple lines of text.  As long as the code is surrounded
    it will all comment out.*/
```

Rule of thumb: Keep the asterisk on the side of the slash closest to the text.

Document Object Model

The concept of hierarchy is of the utmost importance to JavaScript. An example is writing a line to denote a specific text box HTML form element. Let's say the form itself is named FormA and the text box is named Tbox.

The HTML code would look like this:

```
<FORM NAME="FormA">
<INPUT TYPE="text" NAME=Tbox">
</FORM>
```

If you were to write a line of JavaScript representing the text that a user might type into that text box, the code would look like this:

```
window.document.FormA.Tbox.value
```

That statement shows the hierarchy of the page. The browser window, window, is the largest overriding element in the statement. All events will happen within the browser window. The document (document) is the next largest, and then the form itself (FormA). Next is the text box (Tbox), and finally value, which represents what the user has typed into the text box.

The concept of hierarchy is consistent throughout JavaScript and is known as the *Document Object Model (DOM)*.

The name DOM, however, is not very descriptive. So, throughout this book, the term *hierarchy statement* is used to represent the DOM in any JavaScript.

Event Handlers

An *event handler* is a command that sits inside an HTML flag and does not require the beginning <SCRIPT> flag to work. An example is using an onClick event handler inside the HTML code for a button. When the mouse clicks on the button, the event handler performs the event it's set up to do. Here's an example:

```
<FORM>
<INPUT TYPE="button" VALUE="Click For An Alert"
onClick="alert("Thanks for clicking!")">
</FORM>
```

When the button is clicked, the alert button pops up. You can get a complete list of event handlers in Appendix B, "JavaScript Command Reference."

Literal Integers

A *literal integer* is any whole number. For instance, 9 is a literal integer, whereas 9.23 is not. Literal integers can also be hexadecimal notation employing the numbers 1–9 and the letters a–f. This hex color code for purple is an example of a literal integer: 800080.

Methods

A *method* is any function that acts on an object. The command window.open() is used to open a new browser window. In this case, window is the object and open() is the method acting on the object.

Methods can be easily recognized by the two parentheses immediately following them. Sometimes those parentheses are given certain parameters by putting those parameters between the parentheses. When the parentheses are empty, the method acts fully on the object it follows.

Objects

Objects are items that already exist to JavaScript, such as Math or Date or are created through JavaScript code. Objects are items that either can be acted on or have certain properties or characteristics attached to them.

Operators

Think of an *operator* as something that connects or works between two literals. The binary operators shown in Table A.1 are the most common.

Table A.1   Binary Operators

Operator	Meaning
+	Add
-	Subtract
*	Multiply
/	Divide
%	Divide and return remainder

The operators in Table A.2 test the relationships between literals.

Table A.2   Operators Testing Relationships Between Literals

Operator	Meaning
<	Less than
>	Greater than
<=	Less than or equal to
>=	Greater than or equal to
=	Assignment
==	Equal to
!=	Not equal to
||	Or
&	And (adding JavaScript commands together)
&&	And (literal)
?:	Conditional

The operators in Table A.3 are used to separate and end JavaScript commands and lines.

Table A.3   Operators That Separate and End JavaScript Commands

Operator	Meaning
,	Separates commands
;	Ends a line of JavaScript

Properties

A *property* is a characteristic or portion of a larger object. An example of a property is the status bar of the browser window written this way: `window.status` (*object.property*).

String

A *string* is any number of characters inside double or single quotation marks. Here's an example:

```
document.write("This is a string")
```

This example simply writes that string to the HTML document.

Variable

The ability to assign variable names to lines of code is paramount in JavaScript. Except for JavaScript commands themselves and an additional short list of unacceptable variable names in Appendix C, "JavaScript Reserved Variable Words," a *variable* can be any series of letters or numbers, or a combination of both.

JavaScript allows for two levels of variables, local and global.

Local variables are variables that are viable only within a function. JavaScript understands that whenever a variable is encased within a function, that variable name is viable only inside that function. That way, if you copy and paste a script onto a page that already has a script on it, any variables that are equally named will not clash as long as that variable name is found within a function.

Global variables are variables that are not found within functions, and therefore they *can* clash with the variables on the same page.

Here's an example:

```
<SCRIPT LANGUAGE="javascript">
var joe = 12
function writeit()
{
var joe = "Joe Burns"
document.write(joe)
}
</SCRIPT>
```

The variable joe is used twice, but because one occurrence is found outside the function—the global variable—and one is found inside the function—the local variable—the two will not clash.

Now, with all that said, it is not a good idea to follow this format and use similar variable names within your scripts. The purpose of the local variables being hidden is far more for protection against clashes with other scripts on the same page than with variable names within the same script.

JavaScript Command Reference

This appendix is arranged in alphabetical order. It covers the commands found in this book, plus commands that can be substituted in some of the scripts in this book.

Please note that JavaScript is case sensitive. The capitalization pattern used in this appendix is how the commands must appear in your scripts; otherwise, they will not work.

action **Property**

An action works with the return of an HTML form. It works the same as the value you assign to the ACTION attribute when you define a form, and it's primarily used to call server-side CGI scripts. It's used to actually do something with the form information. Let's say you have a form you have named forma. It would look like this:

```
<FORM NAME="forma">
<INPUT TYPE="text" NAME="Tbox">
</FORM>
```

You could send the output of that form to an e-mail address by using the following command:

```
<FORM NAME="forma">
<INPUT TYPE="button"onClick="forma.action='mailto:jburns@htmlgoodies.com'">
</FORM>
```

alert **Method**

The `alert` method displays a JavaScript modal dialog box containing the text noted in the command. The alert box offers only an OK button—unlike the confirm box, which offers both an OK and a Cancel button. Follow this format to have an alert box open upon the loading of the page:

```
<BODY onLoad="alert("This is an Alert Box!")">
```

The alert box is shown in Figure B.1.

Figure B.1
An alert box.

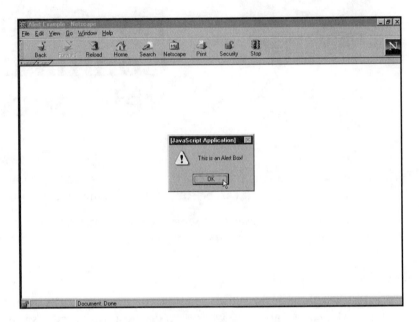

You can find `alert` used as part of a JavaScript example in Lesson 6 in Chapter 2, "Popping Up Text with Mouse Events."

See also: `confirm` and `prompt`

alinkColor **Property**

You use `alinkColor` to return the active link color using a `document.write` statement:

```
<SCRIPT LANGUAGE="javascript">
document.write("The active link color " +document.alinkColor+ ".")
</SCRIPT>
```

You can find `alinkColor` used as part of a JavaScript example in Lesson 3 in Chapter 1, "The Basics."

See also: `bgColor`, `fgColor`, `linkColor`, and `vlinkColor`

appCodeName **Property**

The `appCodeName` property returns the codename string of the browser. The command uses this format:

```
<SCRIPT LANGUAGE="javascript">
document.write("You are using " +navigator.appCodeName+ ".")
</SCRIPT>
```

You can find `appCodeName` used as part of a JavaScript example in Chapter 1, Lesson 3.

See also: `appName`, `appVersion`, `navigator`, and `userAgent`

appName **Property**

This returns the official name of the browser string:

```
<SCRIPT LANGUAGE="javascript">
document.write("You are using " +navigator.appName+ ".")
</SCRIPT>
```

You can find `appName` used as part of a JavaScript example in Chapter 1, Lesson 3.

See also: `appCodeName`, `appVersion`, `navigator`, and `userAgent`

appVersion **Property**

This command returns the browser version number string:

```
<SCRIPT LANGUAGE="javascript">
document.write("You are using " +navigator.appVersion+ ".")
</SCRIPT>
```

You can find `appVersion` used as part of a JavaScript example in Chapter 1, Lesson 3.

See also: `appCodeName`, `appName`, `navigator`, and `userAgent`

array **Method**

Arrays are variables. For the most part, variables have only one value. However, an array is a variable with multiple values. An array can be an ordered collection of many numbers, letters, words, or objects, or a combination of those four.

When you create an array, the items are assigned a number, starting at 0 and counting up:

```
var NewArray=("item0", "item1", "item2", "item3")
```

You can also set up arrays of literals by numbering them in this fashion:

```
var dayName=new Array(7)
dayName[0]="Sunday"
dayName[1]="Monday"
dayName[2]="Tuesday"
dayName[3]="Wednesday"
dayName[4]="Thursday"
dayName[5]="Friday"
dayName[6]="Saturday"
```

After creating an array, you can call for only one item of the array by calling for the item by number. Using the previous array of the days of the week, this code would return `Friday`:

```
<SCRIPT LANGUAGE="javascript"
document.write(dayName[5])
</SCRIPT>
```

You can find `array` first used as part of a JavaScript example in Lesson 15 in Chapter 3, "Manipulating Data and the Hierarchy of JavaScript." Chapter 8, "Arrays," is devoted to arrays.

back **Method**

The `back` method is used in conjunction with the `history` object to move throughout the browser's history list:

```
<SCRIPT LANGUAGE="javascript">history.back()   //one page back in history
history.back(-3)  //moves three pages back in history
</SCRIPT>
```

You can set the number so the `back` command moves as many pages as you want. Be careful, though, that the user actually has as many pages in his history as you call for.

Please note that if `back` is used within a frameset, the entire frameset will not reload. Each frame that was changed loads the page that came before it.

You can find `back` used as part of a JavaScript example in Chapter 2, Lesson 9.

See also: `forward`, `go`, and `history`

bgColor **Property**

This sets or returns the document background color. Here, bgColor is used inside an HTML radio button and the onClick event handler to set the background color:

```
<FORM>
<INPUT TYPE="radio" onClick="document.bgColor = green">
</FORM>
```

You can find bgColor used as part of a JavaScript example in Chapter 1, Lesson 3.

See also: alinkColor, fgColor, linkColor, and vlinkColor

big **Method**

The big method is used to alter a text string. It sets the string to print to the document one font size bigger than the default:

```
<SCRIPT LANGUAGE="javascript">
var textString = "Hello there!"
document.write(textString.big())
</SCRIPT>
```

See also: blink, bold, fixed, fontcolor, fontsize, italics, small, and strike

blink **Method**

The blink method sets a text string to blink on and off in the browser window:

```
<SCRIPT LANGUAGE="javascript">
var textString = "Hello there!"
document.write(textString.blink())
</SCRIPT>
```

This is a Netscape Navigator–only command. Internet Explorer will not recognize it. Besides, this is an unwelcome command. For the most part, people do not like blinking text, so use it sparingly if at all.

See also: big, bold, fixed, fontcolor, fontsize, italics, small, and strike

bold **Method**

The `bold` method sets a text string to appear in bold text font:

```
<SCRIPT LANGUAGE="javascript">
var textString = "Hello there!"
document.write(textString.bold())
</SCRIPT>
```

See also: `big`, `blink`, `fixed`, `fontcolor`, `fontsize`, `italics`, `small`, and `strike`

close **Method**

The `close` method acts on its object—`window` or `self`—to close the window. The following code shows how a button can close the main window using an `onClick` event handler:

```
<FORM>
<INPUT TYPE="button" VALUE="Close the Window" onClick="self.close()">
</FORM>
```

See also: `clear`, `open`, `window`, `write`, and `writeln`

confirm **Method**

The `confirm` method displays a dialog box that offers both an OK and a Cancel button. Refer to the section "The `alert` Method" earlier in this appendix for a different type of box. This script uses a function to offer a confirm box as a test when entering a page. The `confirm` method returns either `true` or `false`, depending on the user's choice of button:

```
<SCRIPT LANGUAGE="javascript">
function confirmit()
{if (!confirm ("Are you sure you want to enter?"))
history.go(-1);return " "}
</SCRIPT>
```

The confirm box is shown in Figure B.2.

You can find `confirm` used as part of a JavaScript example in Lesson 21 in Chapter 4, "Flipping Images and Opening Windows with Mouse Events."

See also: `alert` and `prompt`

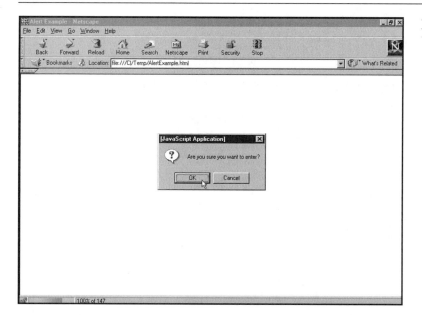

Figure B.2
The confirm box.

Date **Object**

Date is an object that contains all date and time information, allowing for the return of both specific date and time strings. This is the simplest use of the object to return a full date and time string:

```
<SCRIPT LANGUAGE="javascript">
var  dayandtime = new Date()
document.write("It is " +dayandtime+ ".")
</SCRIPT>
```

You can find Date used as part of a JavaScript example in Chapter 3, Lesson 12.

See also: getDate, getDay, getFullYear, getHours, getMinutes, getMonth, getSeconds, getTimezoneOffset, and getYear

defaultStatus **Property of** window

The defaultStatus property of the window object is used to display a string message in the browser's status bar. You use defaultStatus when you want an event to occur in the status bar requiring no loading. For example, a scroll would be placed in the status bar through a defaultStatus. A text rollover, which requires loading, should use "status" (covered later in the Appendix):

```
<SCRIPT LANGUAGE="javascript">
defaultStatus = "This page's title is " +document.title+ "."
</SCRIPT>
```

You can find defaultStatus used as part of a JavaScript example in Chapter 3, Lesson 14.

See also: status and window

document **Object**

The document object represents the current HTML document loaded into the browser. Here, document is acted on by a write method to post text to the page:

```
<SCRIPT LANGUAGE="javascript">
document.write("Hello there!")
</SCRIPT>
```

You can find document used as part of a JavaScript example in Chapter 1, Lesson 1.

See also: write and writeln

document **Property**

document is both an object and a property. The document property is part of the window object. You don't see window a great deal because the window object is often implied, as it is in this example:

```
document.bgColor = red
```

The technically correct method of writing the previous line is

```
window.document.bgcolor = red
```

However, because window is the overriding, highest-level object in JavaScript, window is not required at the beginning of hierarchy statements. It is simply implied.

See also: alinkColor, anchor, bgColor, cookie, fgColor, lastModified, linkColor, location, referrer, title, and vlinkColor

eval **Method**

eval is a method that forces a string value to evaluate to a string expression. Here's an example:

```
<SCRIPT LANGUAGE="javascript">
document.mypic.src=eval("img"+num+".src")
</SCRIPT>
```

You can find `eval` used as part of a JavaScript example in Lesson 36 in Chapter 6, "Mathematics, Random Things, and Loops."

fgColor **Property**

The `fgColor` property represents the foreground color (actually the text color) of the current HTML document. You could return the `fgColor` color (text color) using a `document.write` statement:

```
<SCRIPT LANGUAGE="javascript">
document.write("The text color " +document.fgColor+ ".")
</SCRIPT>
```

You can find `fgColor` used as part of a JavaScript example in Chapter 1, Lesson 3.

See also: `alinkColor`, `bgColor`, `linkColor`, and `vlinkColor`

fixed **Method**

The `fixed` method sets a string to a font much like the typewriter text `<TT>` font in HTML:

```
<SCRIPT LANGUAGE="javascript">
var textString = "Hello there!"
document.write(textString.fixed())
</SCRIPT>
```

See also: `big`, `bold`, `fontcolor`, `fontsize`, `italics`, `small`, and `strike`

fontcolor **Method**

`fontcolor` works similarly to the `<FONT COLOR>` flag in HTML. It sets a string to a specific color:

```
<SCRIPT LANGUAGE="javascript">
var textString = "this will be red text"
document.write(textString.fontcolor("red"))
</SCRIPT>
```

See also: `big`, `bold`, `fixed`, `fontsize`, `italics`, `small`, and `strike`

`fontsize` **Method**

`fontsize` sets a text string to a relative sized font much like the <FONT SIZE> HTML flag:

```
<SCRIPT LANGUAGE="javascript">
var textString = "this will be red text"
document.write(textString.fontsize("4"))
</SCRIPT>
```

See also: `big`, `bold`, `fixed`, `fontcolor`, `italics`, `small`, and `strike`

`for` **loop**

The `for` loop is used to run a group of code statements repeatedly, by setting a series of parameters that have to be true for the looping to stop. Traditionally, `for` loops are used when you know how many times you want a loop to run. This is the format for a `for` loop:

```
<SCRIPT LANGUAGE="javascript">
for (i=1; i<=5; i=i+1)
{
JavaScript event
}
</SCRIPT>
```

The event loops as long as `i` is less than or equal to 5. Notice that each time the loop runs, `i` has one added to it; therefore, this script loops five times.

You can find the `for` loop used as part of a JavaScript example in Chapter 6, Lesson 35.

See also: `while`

`forward` **Method**

`forward` is used with the `history` object to move through the browser's history list:

```
<SCRIPT LANGUAGE="javascript">
history.forward()      //moves one page forward in the history
history.back(-3)   //moves three back in the history
</SCRIPT>
```

You can set the number of pages higher or lower than 1, but remember that the user might not have visited enough pages for the button created by this code to work. It's best to just use 1.

You can find `forward` used as part of a JavaScript example in Chapter 2, Lesson 9.

See also: `back`, `go`, and `history`

frame **Property**

The frame property is used to denote a specific frame window, usually in terms of a hypertext link. Frames are given a numeric order, starting with 0, in the order they appear on the HTML document. This example loads page.html into the second frame in the list of frame commands:

```
<FORM>
<INPUT TYPE="BUTTON" OnClick="parent.frames[1].location='page.html'">
</FORM>
```

frame can also be written as an object representing a portion of the browser window set aside through HTML FRAMESET flags. The frame itself is named in the HTML as shown in the following code:

```
<FRAMESET COLS="50%,50%">
<FRAME SRC="page1.html" NAME="frame1">
<FRAME SRC="page2.html" NAME="frame2">
</FRAMESET>
```

After it is named, each frame window is an object and can be targeted to receive a hypertext link output through JavaScript, as shown in the following code:

```
parent.frame1=page3.html
```

function **Object**

The purpose of the function command is to both combine and name a group of JavaScript events specifically to create a single event. By assigning a function name to a set of JavaScript commands, the entire group of events can be called later in the script by using just the function name.

The format for creating a function is shown in the following code. This function will be named bob:

```
<SCRIPT LANGUAGE="javascript">
function bob()
{
JavaScript commands and statements
}
</SCRIPT>
```

The function can be triggered to run in different ways. The following format calls the function when the HTML document loads into the browser window. Note the parentheses following the function name. It's the same format used with a method to act on an object—that's because a method is a function applied to an object.

```
<BODY onLoad="bob()">
```

You can find `function` first used as part of a JavaScript example in Chapter 3, Lesson 14.

getDate Method

The `getDate` method returns the numeric integer of the day of the month (1–31, if the month has that many days):

```
<SCRIPT LANGUAGE="javascript">
RightNow = new Date();
document.write("Today's day is " + RightNow.getDate()+ ".")
</SCRIPT>
```

You can find `getDate` used as part of a JavaScript example in Chapter 3, Lesson 12.

See also: `getDay`, `getFullYear`, `getHours`, `getMinutes`, `getMonth`, `getSeconds`, `getTimezoneOffset`, and `getYear`

getDay Method

The `getDay` method returns the numeric integer of the day of the week, where Sunday is 0 and Saturday is 6:

```
<SCRIPT LANGUAGE="javascript">
RightNow = new Date();
document.write("Today's day is " + RightNow.getDay()+ ".")
</SCRIPT>
```

This numeric representation is not very helpful. You'll need to write a script to change the number into a day text string using an array.

You can find `getDay` used as part of a JavaScript example in Chapter 3, Lesson 12.

See also: `getDate`, `getFullYear`, `getHours`, `getMinutes`, `getMonth`, `getSeconds`, `getTimezoneOffset`, and `getYear`

getFullYear Method

The `getFullYear` method returns a four-digit integer (rather than two) representation of the current year:

```
<SCRIPT LANGUAGE="javascript">
RightNow = new Date();
document.write("The hours is " + RightNow.getFullYear()+ ".")
</SCRIPT>
```

This command was created as a repair to the Y2K bug.

You can find `getFullYear` used as part of a JavaScript example in Chapter 3, Lesson 12.

See also: `getDate`, `getDay`, `getHours`, `getMinutes`, `getMonth`, `getSeconds`, `getTimezoneOffset`, and `getYear`

getHours **Method**

The `getHours` method returns the numeric integer of the current hour in military format, 0–23:

```
<SCRIPT LANGUAGE="javascript">
RightNow = new Date();
document.write("The hours is " + RightNow.getHours()+ ".")
</SCRIPT>
```

You can find `getHours` used as part of a JavaScript example in Chapter 3, Lesson 12.

See also: `getDate`, `getDay`, `getFullYear`, `getMinutes`, `getMonth`, `getSeconds`, `getTimezoneOffset`, and `getYear`

getMinutes **Method**

The `getMinutes` method returns the numeric integer of the current minute, 0–59:

```
<SCRIPT LANGUAGE="javascript">
RightNow = new Date();
document.write("The minute is " + RightNow.getMinutes()+ ".")
</SCRIPT>
```

You can find `getMinutes` used as part of a JavaScript example in Chapter 3, Lesson 12.

See also: `getDate`, `getDay`, `getFullYear`, `getHours`, `getMonth`, `getSeconds`, `getTimezoneOffset`, and `getYear`

getMonth **Method**

The `getMonth` method returns the numeric integer of the current month. In one of the more interesting JavaScript quirks, this method is actually always off by 1 because it sees

January as 0. To fix that, you should always add 1 to the output of the method. Here's the format:

```
<SCRIPT LANGUAGE="javascript">
RightNow = new Date();
NewMonth = [RightNow.getMonth+1]
document.write("The Month is " + NewMonth + ".")
</SCRIPT>
```

You can find getMonth used as part of a JavaScript example in Chapter 3, Lesson 12.

See also: getDate, getDay, getFullYear, getHours, getMinutes, getSeconds, getTimezoneOffset, and getYear

getSeconds Method

The getSeconds method returns the numeric integer of the current second, 0–59:

```
<SCRIPT LANGUAGE="javascript">
RightNow = new Date();
document.write("The seconds are " + RightNow.getSeconds()+ ".")
</SCRIPT>
```

You can find getSeconds used as part of a JavaScript example in Chapter 3, Lesson 12.

See also: getDate, getDay, getFullYear, getHours, getMinutes, getMonth, getTimezoneOffset, and getYear

getTimezoneOffset Method

The getTimezoneOffset method returns the number of minutes difference between your user's computer and Greenwich mean time (GMT):

```
<SCRIPT LANGUAGE="javascript">
RightNow = new Date();
document.write("The minutes offset is "+ RightNow.getTimezoneOffset()+ ".")
</SCRIPT>
```

See also: getDate, getDay, getFullYear, getHours, getMinutes, getMonth, getSeconds, and getYear

getYear Method

The getYear method returns a two-digit representation of the year, created by taking the current year and subtracting 1900:

```
<SCRIPT LANGUAGE="javascript">
RightNow = new Date();
document.write("The year is " + RightNow.getYear()+ ".")
</SCRIPT>
```

You can get the full four-digit year representation by using the `getFullYear` method or by re-adding the 1900.

For years after 1999, `getYear` returns a three-digit value instead of a two-digit value.

You can find `getYear` used as part of a JavaScript example in Chapter 3, Lesson 12.

See also: `getDate`, `getDay`, `getFullYear`, `getHours`, `getMinutes`, `getMonth`, `getSeconds`, and `getTimezoneOffset`

`go` Method

`go` works with the `history` object to load pages from the user's history file:

```
<SCRIPT LANGUAGE="javascript">
history.go(-2)   // Go back two pages in the history
</SCRIPT>
```

You can find `go` used as part of a JavaScript example in Chapter 2, Lesson 9.

See also: `forward` and `history`

`history` Object

`history` is an object representing the browser's history file, which is the list of pages the viewer has visited during the current session. The following example returns the number of items listed in the history file. The command `value` is used to retrieve the number:

```
<SCRIPT LANGUAGE="javascript">
document.write("You've been to " + history.length + "pages.")
</SCRIPT>
```

You can find `history` used as part of a JavaScript example in Chapter 1, Lesson 3.

See also: `back` and `forward`

`host` Property

The `host` property returns the name of the user's host and the port being used to connect to the Internet. If no port is specified, just the host name is returned:

```
<SCRIPT LANGUAGE="javascript">
document.write("You're from " +location.host+ ".")
</SCRIPT>
```

The line might return www.joe.com:80.

You can find host used as part of a JavaScript example in Chapter 1, Lesson 3.

See also: hostname, href, location, and protocol

hostname **Property**

The hostname property returns the user's host in the same manner as host, but without the port number attached:

```
<SCRIPT LANGUAGE="javascript">
document.write("You're from " +location.hostname+ ".")
</SCRIPT>
```

The line might return www.joe.com.

You can find hostname used as part of a JavaScript example in Chapter 1, Lesson 3.

See also: host, href, location, and protocol

href **Property of** location

href is used to denote a string of the entire URL of a specified window object. Using this property, you can open a specified URL in a window:

```
<FORM>
<INPUT TYPE="button" onClick="location.href='page.html'">
</FORM>
```

You can find href used as part of a JavaScript example in Chapter 2, Lesson 6.

See also: host, hostname, location, and protocol

if/else

The if/else structure is a conditional statement. The format states that if something is true, enact a specified JavaScript event. If not, enact a different JavaScript event.

The format follows this pattern:

```
<SCRIPT LANGUAGE="javascript">
if (condition to be met)
{JavaScript event}
```

```
else
{some other JavaScript event}
</SCRIPT>
```

If the condition following the if condition is met, the function in the first set of braces is enacted. If not, the function in the second set of braces runs.

In addition, you can set up a series of if conditions with no else. You would write one if statement after another, as shown in the following code:

```
<SCRIPT LANGUAGE="javascript">
if (condition to be met)
{JavaScript event}
if (condition to be met)
{some other JavaScript event}
if (condition to be met)
{some other JavaScript event}
if (condition to be met)
{some other JavaScript event}
</SCRIPT>
```

However, if you follow this format, you should ensure that one of the if statements will be true every time, even if it means adding a condition that acts as a catchall if all your conditions are false. By setting up your if/else statements so that each time the script runs, at least one of them is true, you have control over whatever input the user or the script itself offers.

You can find if/else first used as part of a JavaScript example in Chapter 4, Lesson 21.

indexOf **Method**

The method indexOf returns the numeric location of a specific string or character. Because JavaScript counts everything and begins counting at 0, every string has an ordered set of letters.

In addition, indexOf can be used to check whether something does not appear in a string through the use of the -1 condition. Here's an example:

```
<SCRIPT LANGUAGE="javascript">
if (document.TheForm.email.value.indexOf("@")==-1)
{alert("there's no @, this is not a valid email address")}
else
{alert("Go on")}
</SCRIPT>
```

This code checks to see whether the text string entered in the text box e-mail includes an @. You use -1 because 0 is actually an index number in the mind of JavaScript. Therefore, you can't ask whether there are 0 instances of @. If an @ appears in the text box, there is a 0 index number. The -1 format checks for no instances.

You can find `indexOf` used as part of a JavaScript example in Lesson 43 in Chapter 7, "Clocks, Counts, and Scroll Text."

`italics` **Method**

The `italics` method is used to make a string print to a document in italics:

```
<SCRIPT LANGUAGE="javascript">
var textString = "Hello there!"
document.write(textString.italics())
</SCRIPT>
```

See also: `big`, `bold`, `fontcolor`, `fontsize`, `small`, and `strike`

`lastModified` **Property**

When a document is altered and saved, or placed on a server, a date is recorded. The `lastModified` method returns that date to the current document:

```
<SCRIPT LANGUAGE="javascript">
document.write("I updated this page on " +document.lastModified+ ".")
</SCRIPT>
```

But remember that `lastModified` depends on the server's records. It isn't always accurate, so use it as a guide, rather than as an end-all for the last updated date.

You can find `lastModified` used as part of a JavaScript example in Chapter 1, Lesson 3.

See also: `alinkColor`, `anchor`, `bgColor`, `cookie`, `fgColor`, `lastModified`, `linkColor`, `location`, `referrer`, `title`, and `vlinkColor`

`length` **Property**

The `length` property returns a number representing the number of items that appear within the object it is attached to. The following example returns the number of pages the user has visited by returning the length of the `history` object:

```
<SCRIPT LANGUAGE="javascript">
document.write("You've been to " +history.length+ "pages")
</SCRIPT>
```

This property can also be used to return the number or characters in a string or HTML form text box.

You can find `length` used as part of a JavaScript example in Lesson 24 in Chapter 5, "Forms: A Great Way to Interact with Your Users."

See also: `array` and `history`

linkColor **Property**

The `linkColor` property denotes or returns the color of the links within the current document.

You could return the `linkColor`, in hexadecimal form, using a `document.write` statement:

```
<SCRIPT LANGUAGE="javascript">
document.write("The link color " +document.linkColor+ ".")
</SCRIPT>
```

You can find `linkColor` used as part of a JavaScript example in Chapter 1, Lesson 3.

See also: `alinkColor`, `fgColor`, and `vlinkColor`

location **Object**

`location` represents Internet address information about the current HTML document. You can use the current location to jump to another location. The event will look similar to a simple hypertext link being clicked:

```
<FORM OnSubmit="location.href = 'page.html'">
<INPUT TYPE="text">
<INPUT TYPE="submit">
</FORM>
```

You can find `location` used as part of a JavaScript example in Chapter 2, Lesson 6.

See also: `host`, `hostname`, `href`, `location`, `pathname`, `port`, and `protocol`

location **Property**

The `location` property represents the location of the current document. Use it to return the page's URL:

```
<SCRIPT LANGUAGE="javascript">
document.write("You're looking at " +document.location+ ".")
</SCRIPT>
```

You can find `location` used as part of a JavaScript example in Chapter 1, Lesson 3.

`Math` Object

Note the capitalization: The *M* is uppercase. `Math` is an object, but by itself it means nothing other than that it represents mathematics. But after you attach a method to `Math`, it can represent a number or a method of manipulating numbers. Table B.1 lists many of the `Math` object's methods and properties. You'll be able to tell the methods because they are followed by parentheses—the properties are not. Again, notice the capitalization.

Table B.1   `Math` Object Methods

Method	Return Value
`Math.abs(argument)`	The absolute value of an argument
`Math.acos(argument)`	The arc cosine of the argument
`Math.asin(argument)`	The arc sine of the argument
`Math.atan(argument)`	The arc tangent of the argument
`Math.atan2(argument1, argument2)`	The angle of polar coordinates x and y
`Math.ceil(argument)`	The number 1 larger than or equal to the argument
`Math.cos(argument)`	The cosine of the argument
`Math.exp(argument)`	A natural logarithm
`Math.floor(argument)`	The number 1 less than or equal to the argument
`Math.E`	Base of natural logarithms
`Math.LN2`	Logarithm of 2 (appx. 0.6932)
`Math.LN10`	Logarithm of 10 (appx. 2.3026)
`Math.log`	Logarithm of positive numbers greater than 0
`Math.LOG10E`	Base-10 logarithm of E
`Math.LOG2E`	Base-2 logarithm of E
`Math.max(arg1,arg2)`	The greater of the two arguments
`Math.min(arg1,arg2)`	The lesser of the two arguments
`Math.PI`	The value of pi
`Math.pow(arg1, arg2)`	*arg1* raised to the *arg2* power
`Math.random`	A random number between 0 and 1
`Math.round`	Rounds to the nearest number

Table B.1   continued

Method	Return Value
Math.sin(*argument*)	The sine of the argument
Math.sqrt(*argument*)	The square root of the argument
Math.SQRT1_2	The square root of 1/2
Math.SQRT2	The square root of 2
Math.tan(*argument*)	The tangent of the argument

The previous arguments are put together using these mathematics operators:

- +: Add
- –: Subtract
- *: Multiply
- /: Divide

For example

```
<SCRIPT LANGUAGE="javascript">
Math.square(2*2)   //will return 2, the square root of four (2*2)
</SCRIPT>
```

Many of the preceding Math.*methods* that represent numbers can be used together to create mathematical equations. This code returns a random number between 1 and 50:

```
<SCRIPT LANGUAGE="javascript">
Math.round(50 * Math.random());
</SCRIPT>
```

You can find Math, and some of the preceding methods, used as part of a JavaScript example in Chapter 6, Lesson 33.

navigator **Object**

navigator is the object containing all the information regarding the user's browser:

```
<SCRIPT LANGUAGE="javascript">
document.write("You're using " +navigator.appName+ ".")
</SCRIPT>
```

You can find navigator used as part of a JavaScript example in Chapter 1, Lesson 3.

See also: appCodeName, appName, appVersion, and userAgent

onBlur **Event Handler**

onBlur is enacted when the form item loses focus, meaning cursor attention has moved away from the element:

```
<FORM>
<INPUT TYPE="text"onBlur="alert('Stop!  Did you fill in your name?')">
</FORM>
```

You can find onBlur used as part of a JavaScript example in Chapter 2, Lesson 6.

onChange **Event Handler**

onChange occurs when data in a form item is changed and focus is moved off that item:

```
<FORM>
<TEXTAREA onChange="alert('Something wrong?')"></TEXTAREA>
</FORM>
```

You can find onChange used as part of a JavaScript example in Chapter 2, Lesson 6.

onClick **Event Handler**

When the mouse is clicked on a particular element identified by the event handler, onClick is enacted:

```
<FORM>
<INPUT TYPE="submit" onClick="location.href='page.html'">
</FORM>
```

You can find onClick used as part of a JavaScript example in Chapter 2, Lesson 6.

onDblClick **Event Handler**

onDblClick is new to the HTML 4.0 code and can be used in a range of elements, including forms, tables, and the <SPAN> command that can encompass any item. The event handler is performed when the mouse is clicked twice. This example shows the use of the <SPAN> flag:

```
<SPAN onDblClick="function()"><IMG SRC="image.gif"></SPAN>
```

The <SPAN> command is only there to carry the onDblClick. It alters the image in no other way.

You can find onDblClick and <SPAN> used as part of a JavaScript example in Chapter 2, Lesson 8.

410

onFocus **Event Handler**

onFocus occurs when focus is placed on a form item, meaning it was clicked or moved to by pressing the Tab key:

```
<FORM>
<INPUT TYPE="text" onFocus="window.status='Fill in your name'"
</FORM>
```

You can find onFocus used as part of a JavaScript example in Chapter 2, Lesson 6.

onKeyDown **Event Handler**

onKeyDown is enacted when the user presses a key:

```
<FORM>
<INPUT TYPE="text" onKeyDown="alert('Filling in the form yet??')">
</FORM>
```

onKeyUp **Event Handler**

When the user releases the key, onKeyUp is enacted:

```
<FORM><INPUT TYPE="text" onKeyUp="alert('Thanks, that hurt.')">
</FORM>
```

onLoad **Event Handler**

onLoad appears in the BODY flag of the HTML document:

```
<BODY onLoad="function()">
```

Its purpose is to act as a trigger for a function, or the JavaScript code that is attached to it, when the page loads.

You can find onLoad used as part of a JavaScript example in Chapter 2, Lesson 6.

onMouseDown **Event Handler**

onMouseDown is new with HTML 4.0, so not all browsers support it yet. This event occurs when the mouse button is clicked down:

```
<IMG SRC="image.gif" onMouseDown="document.pic1='image2.gif'">
```

You can find onMouseDown used as part of a JavaScript example in Chapter 2, Lesson 8.

onMouseMove **Event Handler**

onMouseMove occurs when the user moves the mouse:

```
<BODY onMouseMove="function()">
```

onMouseOut **Event Handler**

onMouseOut is usually used in conjunction with the onMouseOver event handler to create an image flip effect:

```
<A HREF="http://www.cnn.com"
onMouseOver="document.pic1.src='menu1on.gif'"
➥onMouseOut="document.pic1.src='menu1off.gif'">
<IMG SRC="menu1off.gif" BORDER=0 NAME="pic1"></a>
```

You can find onMouseOut used as part of a JavaScript example in Chapter 2, Lesson 7.

onMouseOver **Event Handler**

When the mouse passes over the top of the item, onMouseOver occurs:

```
<A HREF="http://www.cnn.com"
onMouseOver="document.pic1.src='menu1on.gif'"
onMouseOut="document.pic1.src='menu1off.gif'">
<IMG SRC="menu1off.gif" BORDER=0 NAME="pic1"></a>
```

You can find onMouseOver used as part of a JavaScript example in Chapter 2, Lesson 5.

onMouseUp **Event Handler**

onMouseUp takes place when the user releases the mouse button and is often used in conjunction with onMouseDown to create an effect of two events with one mouse click:

```
<A HREF="http://www.cnn.com"
onMouseDown="document.pic1.src='menu1on.gif'"
onMouseUp="document.pic1.src='menu1off.gif'">
<IMG SRC="menu1off.gif" BORDER=0 NAME="pic1"></a>
```

You can find onMouseUp used as part of a JavaScript example in Chapter 2, Lesson 8.

onSelect **Event Handler**

onSelect is enacted when some, or all, of the form element is highlighted:

```
<FORM>
<INPUT TYPE="text" onSelect="alert('function()')">
</FORM>
```

onSubmit **Event Handler**

The onSubmit event occurs when the form is submitted. This event handler goes best in the submit-button portion of the HTML form:

```
<FORM>
<INPUT TYPE="submit" onSubmit="document.bgColor='red'">
</FORM>
```

You can find onSubmit used as part of a JavaScript example in Chapter 2, Lesson 6.

onUnload **Event Handler**

Like the onLoad event handler, onUnload is often found in the BODY flag:

```
<BODY onLoad="function()" onUnload="alert('bye!')">
```

It is enacted when the user moves to another page or unloads the current page.

You can find onUnload used as part of a JavaScript example in Chapter 2, Lesson 6.

open **Method**

You can use open to open a new browser window, in which you can load a whole new HTML document, or to create a second window from the original page. This code opens a new browser window and loads page.html into it:

```
<SCRIPT LANGUAGE="javascript">
window.open('page.html')
</SCRIPT>
```

This example creates a new browser window and fills it with the text from the document.write statements:

```
<SCRIPT LANGUAGE="javascript">
function openWindow()
```

413

```
{
OpenWindow=window.open("", "newwin", "height=250,width=250")
OpenWindow.document.write("<HTML>")
OpenWindow.document.write("<TITLE>Welcome</TITLE>")
OpenWindow.document.write("<BODY BGCOLOR='pink'>")
OpenWindow.document.write("<H1>Welcome to my page!</H1>")
OpenWindow.document.write("</BODY>")
OpenWindow.document.write("</HTML>")
}
</SCRIPT>
```

This code sets the new window's HEIGHT and WIDTH to 250 pixels. The open method also allows you to set the window elements shown in Table B.2.

Table B.2   Window Elements That Can Be Set with the open Method

Window Element	Can Be Set to...
Toolbar	Yes or no
Menu bar	Yes or no
Scrollbars	Yes or no
Resizable	Yes or no
Location	Yes or no
Directories	Yes or no
Status	Yes or no

You can find open, and the commands listed previously, used as part of a JavaScript example in Chapter 4, Lesson 19.

See also: window

parent **Property of** frame **and** window

parent is used in hierarchy statements to denote the document in a frame situation or the document that spawned the new window:

```
<FORM>
<INPUT TYPE="button" onClick="parent.location.href='page.html'">
</FORM>
```

See also: frame and window

pathname **Property**

The `pathname` method is used to return the path portion of a URL without the root of the server:

```
<SCRIPT LANGUAGE="javascript">
document.write("You're at www.joe.com/" +location.pathname+ ".")
</SCRIPT>
```

See also: `host`, `hostname`, `href`, `port`, and `protocol`

port **Property**

`port` returns the port the user is attached to during her Internet session:

```
<SCRIPT LANGUAGE="javascript">
document.write("You're using port: " +location.port+ ".")
</SCRIPT>
```

See also: `host`, `hostname`, `href`, `pathname`, and `protocol`

prompt **Method**

`prompt` is used to display a JavaScript dialog box in order to gather information from the user. The prompt is always assigned a variable. The information offered by the user then takes on that variable name. If the user offers no information, the value for the variable is entered as null.

In the following example, the text in the first set of quotation marks appears on the prompt box. The text in the second set of quotation marks appears in the text area on the prompt box. If you do not want text in the text area, leave the quotation marks empty:

```
<SCRIPT LANGUAGE="javascript">
var name =  prompt("This is a Prompt Box", "write your name here")
</SCRIPT>
```

Figure B.3 shows what the prompt box looks like.

You can find `prompt` used as part of a JavaScript example in Chapter 3, Lesson 11.

See also: `alert` and `confirm`

Figure B.3
The prompt box.

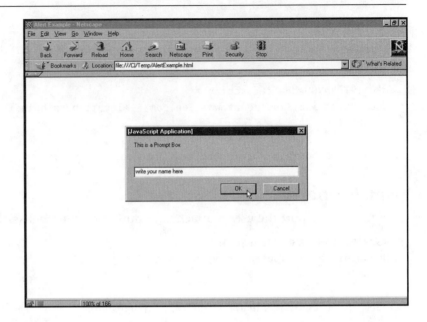

protocol **Property**

protocol is the set of rules used by the browser to deal with the currently loaded page or the file the hypertext link is pointing at:

```
<SCRIPT LANGUAGE="javascript">
document.write("This document is displayed using "+location.protocol+ ".")
</SCRIPT>
```

Returned strings might include http, ftp, mailto, news, file, or JavaScript.

See also: host, hostname, href, pathname, and port

referrer **Property**

referrer returns the URL of the document visited just before the current document:

```
<SCRIPT LANGUAGE="javascript">
document.write("You just came from " +location.referrer+ ".")
</SCRIPT>
```

You can find referrer used as part of a JavaScript example in Chapter 1, Lesson 3.

See also: document

self **Property**

self denotes the current window. This example creates a button that closes the current window:

```
<FORM>
<INPUT TYPE="button" onClick=" self.close()">
</FORM>
```

selectedIndex **Property**

selectedIndex is used to return the number representing the index of a select item. For example, the following HTML form drop-down menu box is a series of select items:

```
<FORM NAME="FormA">
<SELECT NAME="SelectBox">
<OPTION> Red
<OPTION> Green
<OPTION> Blue
</SELECT>
</FORM>
```

The options Red, Green, and Blue are numbered 0, 1, and 2, respectively. To return that index number to a JavaScript, you would use this hierarchy statement:

```
document.FormA.SelectBox.selectedIndex
```

You can find selectedIndex used as part of a JavaScript example in Chapter 5, Lesson 27.

setDate **Method**

The method setDate is used to set a number representing the day of the month, 1–31, through the Date object:

```
<SCRIPT LANGUAGE="javascript">
var Millenium = new Date ()
var pointintime = Millenium.setDate("January 1, 2005")
</SCRIPT>
```

The date January 1, 2005 is now a set point in the future and can be used to figure the amount of time between a point in time and January 1, 2005.

See also: setHours, setMinutes, setMonth, setSeconds, setTime, setTimeout, and setYear

setHours **Method**

setHours is used to set the current hour from 0 (midnight) through 23 (military format) as a specific point in time. The format is

```
<SCRIPT LANGUAGE="javascript">
var Millenium = new Date ()
var pointintime = Millenium.setHours("January 1, 2001")

</SCRIPT>
```

The format can be used to figure the number of hours until the specified date.

See also: setDate, setMinutes, setMonth, setSeconds, setTime, setTimeout, and setYear

setMinutes **Method**

setMinutes is used to set the minute, 0–59, as a specific point in time. The format is

```
<SCRIPT LANGUAGE="javascript">
var Millenium = new Date ()
var pointintime = Millenium.setMinutes("January 1, 2001")

</SCRIPT>
```

The format can be used to figure the number of minutes until the specified date.

See also: setDate, setHours, setMonth, setSeconds, setTime, setTimeout, and setYear

setMonth **Method**

setMonth is used to set the current month, 0 (January) through 11 (December), as a specific point in time. The format is

```
<SCRIPT LANGUAGE="javascript">
var Millenium = new Date ()
var pointintime = Millenium.setMonth("January 1, 2001")

</SCRIPT>
```

The format can be used to figure the number of months until the specified date.

See also: setDate, setHours, setMinutes, setSeconds, setTime, setTimeout, and setYear

setSeconds **Method**

setSeconds is used to set the current second, 0–59, as a specific point in time. The format is

```
<SCRIPT LANGUAGE="javascript">
var Millenium = new Date ()
var pointintime = Millenium.setSeconds("January 1, 2001")

</SCRIPT>
```

The format can be used to figure the number of seconds until the specified date.

See also: setDate, setHours, setMinutes, setMonth, setTime, setTimeout, and setYear

setTime **Method**

setTime is the base of the Date object. It returns the number of milliseconds since January 1, 1970 until the point in time set by you. The format is as follows:

```
<SCRIPT LANGUAGE="javascript">
var Millenium = new Date ()
var pointintime =  Millenium.setTime("January 1, 2001")

</SCRIPT>
```

The format can be used to figure the total time until the specified date.

See also: setDate, setHours, setMinutes, setMonth, setSeconds, setTimeout, and setYear

setTimeout **Method**

The setTimeout method is used to fire a function after a set amount of down time. The method should be used inside the function it will affect. The format is

```
<SCRIPT LANGUAGE="javascript">
function joe()
{
JavaScript events

var timer = setTimeout("joe()", 1000)
}
</SCRIPT>
```

This format loops the function joe repeatedly, waiting 1 second before starting the loop the next time. Remember that JavaScript counts time in milliseconds, so 1000 is equal to 1 second.

You can find setTimeout used as part of a JavaScript example in Chapter 7, Lesson 42.

setYear **Method**

setYear is used to set the current year, minus 1900, as a two-digit representation. The format is

```
<SCRIPT LANGUAGE="javascript">
var Millenium = new Date ()
var pointintime = Millenium.setYear("January 1, 2001")
</SCRIPT>
```

The format can be used to figure the number of years until the specified date.

See also: setDate, setHours, setMinutes, setMonth, setTime, and setTimeout

You can find setYear used as part of a JavaScript example in Chapter 7, Lesson 41.

small **Method**

small is used to alter text strings to display one size smaller than the browser default:

```
<SCRIPT LANGUAGE="javascript">
var textString = "Hello There"
document.write("textString.small()")
</SCRIPT>
```

See also: big and fontsize

status **Property**

The status area is the lowest portion of the browser window. It's where Document Done appears when a page has finished loading. You can direct and alter the display in this space using this format:

```
<A HREF="page.html" onMouseOver="window.status='Click Here!'">link</A>
```

You can find status used as part of a JavaScript example in Chapter 2, Lesson 5.

strike **Method**

`strike` is used to create a strikethrough effect on a text string:

```
<SCRIPT LANGUAGE="javascript">
var textString = "Hello There!"
document.write(textString.strike())
</SCRIPT>
```

See also: `big`, `bold`, `italic`, and `small`

sub **Method**

`sub` is used to create a subscript, such as the *2* in *H₂O*:

```
<SCRIPT LANGUAGE="javascript">
var textString = "2"
document.write("H")
document.write(textString.sub())
document.write("O")
</SCRIPT>
```

See also: `big`, `bold`, `italic`, `small`, and `sup`

substring **Method**

The method `substring` is used to return a portion of a text string between two indexes. Here's an example:

```
<SCRIPT LANGUAGE="javascript">
var TextString = "Merry Christmas"
var TheString = TextString.substring(1,0)
</SCRIPT>
```

This JavaScript returns the first letter of the text string because the number 1 is the greater of the two indexes.

sup **Method**

`sup` works the same way as the `sub` method. It's used to create superscript text, such as the *st* in *1ˢᵗ*:

```
<SCRIPT LANGUAGE="javascript">
var textString = "st"
```

```
document.write("1")
document.write(textString.sup())
</SCRIPT>
```

See also: big, bold, italic, small, and sub

title **Property**

title refers to the title of the HTML document. Used with document, you can return the page's title:

```
<SCRIPT LANGUAGE="javascript">
document.write("The Title is " +document.title+ ".")
</SCRIPT>
```

You can find title used as part of a JavaScript example in Chapter 1, Lesson 3.

toLowerCase **Method**

toLowerCase is used to change a text string to all lowercase letters:

```
<SCRIPT LANGUAGE="javascript">
var textString = "Hello There!"
document.write(textString.toLowerCase())
</SCRIPT>
```

You can find toLowerCase used as part of a JavaScript example in Chapter 5, Lesson 24.

See also: toUpperCase

toUpperCase **Method**

toUpperCase is used to change a text string to all uppercase letters:

```
<SCRIPT LANGUAGE="javascript">
var textString = "Hello There!"
document.write(textString.toUpperCase())
</SCRIPT>
```

The toUpperCase and toLowercase methods are good for case-insensitive string comparisons.

You can find toUpperCase used as part of a JavaScript example in Chapter 5, Lesson 24.

See also: toLowerCase

userAgent **Property**

userAgent returns the HTTP protocol header used to load the current HTML document:

```
<SCRIPT LANGUAGE="javascript">
document.write("The header reads " +document.userAgent+ ".")
</SCRIPT>
```

You can find userAgent used as part of a JavaScript example in Chapter 1, Lesson 3.

See also: appCodeName, appName, and appVersion

value **Property**

value represents the text that is written, or given, to an HTML form item. The value of a text box or text area is the text the user has typed in. The value of a radio button or check box is a simple 1 (yes) or 0 (no), depending on whether the user has clicked the element.

In the following code

```
<FORM NAME="FormA">
<INPUT TYPE="text" NAME="Tbox">
</FORM>
```

the text a user typed into the form's text box is represented by

```
document.FormA.Tbox.value
```

You can find value used as part of a JavaScript example in Chapter 5, Lesson 23.

var **Variable**

var is used to assign a variable name to a string or set of JavaScript commands. The traditional method follows this pattern:

```
<SCRIPT LANGUAGE="javascript">
var navapp = navigator.appName
document.write(navapp)</SCRIPT>
```

Now you can call for navigator.appName throughout the remainder of the script with just the variable name navapp.

Actually, the single equal sign is enough to set a variable name. The var isn't required, but it's still a good idea to use it to help yourself when writing scripts.

You can find var first used as part of a JavaScript example in Chapter 3, Lesson 11.

See also: the descriptions of local and global variables in Appendix A, "JavaScript Basic Concepts"

`vlinkColor` Property

`vlinkColor` is used to return the current HTML document's visited link color:

```
<SCRIPT LANGUAGE="javascript">
document.write("The link color is " +document.vlinkColor+ ".")
</SCRIPT>
```

You can find `vlinkColor` used as part of a JavaScript example in Chapter 1, Lesson 3.

See also: `alinkColor`, `bgColor`, `fgColor`, and `linkColor`

`while` Loop

The `while` loop is a format that enables a JavaScript—or a set of JavaScript statements—to run again and again as long as a condition has not been met. Traditionally, `while` loops are used when you do not know how many times the script will loop. This is a possible format for a `while` loop:

```
<SCRIPT LANGUAGE="javascript">
var loops=input from a prompt or other method within the script
var num=1
while (num <= loops)
{
JavaScript event
}
</SCRIPT>
```

Because the number that will be assigned to the `loops` variable is unknown, a `while` loop is used with a condition so that when the loop's variable number equals the number returned from the script (`num <= loops`), the looping will stop.

You can find the `while` loop used as part of a JavaScript example in Chapter 6, Lesson 36.

See also: `for` loop

`window` Object

The `window` is the browser window. This is the highest-level object accessible in the JavaScript hierarchy (DOM).

You can find `window` used as part of a JavaScript example in Chapter 2, Lesson 5.

For examples of its use, see the frame, parent, self, status, and top properties.

See also: alert, close, confirm, open, prompt, and write methods, and the onLoad and onUnload event handlers

write **Method**

write is used with the document object to write lines of text to an HTML document. Those lines appear on the pages just as written, carrying no effects from the script. In this instance, the command is simply a delivery device:

```
<SCRIPT LANGUAGE="javascript">
document.write("Hello There!")
</SCRIPT>
```

You can find write used as part of a JavaScript example in Chapter 1, Lesson 1.

See also: writeln

writeln **Method**

The writeln method works much the same way as the write method. Using writeln affects how the document looks in its source code, breaking lines where the next writeln method starts. It does not alter the look of a document in the browser window—only in the source code:

```
<SCRIPT LANGUAGE="javascript">
document.writeln("Hello There!")
</SCRIPT>
```

You can find writeln used as part of a JavaScript example in Chapter 1, Lesson 1.

See also: write

JavaScript Reserved Variable Words

When naming variables or functions, you must be careful not to use a word that already exists in the JavaScript language. The command words found in Appendix A, "JavaScript Basic Concepts," and Appendix B, "JavaScript Command Reference," are all off-limits.

You'll do yourself a world of good if you start following a variable-naming convention. For example, you could start naming all your variables starting with your initials or your first name. I use the names of my family. I never run into trouble that way.

In addition, here is a list of off-limits words. Although they might not be currently in use in the JavaScript language, they are reserved for later versions of JavaScript:

abstract	default	goto	native
break	do	if	new
byte	double	implements	null
case	extends	import	package
catch	false	in	private
char	final	instanceof	protected
class	finally	int	public
const	float	interface	return
continue	for	long	short

static	this	transient	void
super	throw	true	while
switch	throws	try	with
synchronized			

And, of course, `var` and `function` are off-limits.

Scripts Available on htmlgoodies. com

This appendix contains the following scripts:

- Alert Scripts
- Button, Links, and E-mail Scripts
- The Three Cs: Clocks, Calendars, and Calculator Scripts
- Color Scripts
- Game Scripts
- HTML and Developer Scripts
- Image Scripts
- Scrolling Scripts
- Text-Based Scripts
- Miscellaneous Scripts

The `http://www.htmlgoodies.com/JSBook/` site offers more than 500 JavaScripts from many great authors. Each script is available for you to test, download, and use. Try your hand at altering some of these scripts. Make them better, change where the output appears in the browser window, or just use them as they are. They're ready to go.

The scripts are loosely broken into the following categories:

- **Alert scripts**—Such as button, link, and e-mail scripts; these all produce alert, prompt, or confirm boxes.
- **Buttons and e-mail scripts**—These deal with buttons and e-mail scripts.
- **Clocks, calculators, and calendar scripts**—These deal with numbers, times, or dates.
- **Color scripts**—These deal with color.
- **Game scripts**—These either play games or deal with them as their topics. Also, some scripts deal with leisure activities, such as music.
- **HTML and developer scripts**—These deal with HTML and the development of Web pages. A lot of these scripts work "behind the scenes" to create a look or an event to help your Web pages or Web site. This is also where you'll find all the password-protection scripts.
- **Image scripts**—These deal with, display, manipulate, or create image animation.
- **Scrolling scripts**—These scroll text in the document window, text boxes, and the status bar, among other places.
- **Text-based scripts**—These all have one thing in common: They produce text and manipulate text on the HTML document.
- **Miscellaneous scripts**—These don't fit anywhere else.

Without further ado, here's the list of scripts.

Alert Scripts

These scripts all use alert, prompt, or confirm boxes.

No Clicking!: This script disables the user's ability to click the page. *Requires Microsoft Internet Explorer 4.0.*

Alert Page Verification Form: This script posts a new page when a part of the form has not been filled out or has not been filled out correctly.

How Long Load?: How long did it take your page to load? This script tells you.

Screen Rez: Do you have the correct screen settings for this page? Use this script to alert your users.

800×600 Alert: This script pops up an alert box if the user has his settings at 800×600, but you can change it to whatever settings you want.

Web-TV User Alert: This script pops up an alert box when a Web TV user stops by.

Update Alert: When someone enters the page, this script pops up an alert with the date and time of the page's last update.

No Go IE: This script tells the user that he is not using Internet Explorer and that the following page has some IE-only elements. A choice to enter is then offered.

Multiple Alerts: That's what you get when you click.

Three Choices: This script provides an alert box that offers three choices to the viewer before entering your site.

Coming From?: This script produces an alert that welcomes the user from the page he just left.

Are You 18?: If the user is, he can enter—if he's not, he can't.

Chooser Script: This script gives you a list of pages to choose from. Choose one, and tell the browser what to do with it.

Yes, No Script: Do you enter? Yes or no.

Thank You Link: This one gets your name and then sends you to the link of your choice with an alert message.

Personalized Welcome: As is, this script asks for your domain and then gives you a nice greeting. You can change it to ask for anything, and then give the same greeting.

Pop-Up Box: When someone logs into your page, an alert box pops up. He sees the page no matter what button he clicks.

A Better Pop-Up Box: This script works the same way as the previous one, but it won't allow the viewer in the page if he clicks Cancel.

Insert Name: This script pops up a prompt box asking for the viewer's name. What he enters is posted throughout the page.

Coming and Going: This script posts an alert when the person enters and again when he leaves.

Anonymous Name: This script asks for the name the same as the previous script. However, this script enables the viewer to remain anonymous if he so chooses.

Mouse-Over Alert Box: This script produces an alert box when the mouse passes over a link.

Advanced Mouse-Over Alert Box: This script pops up a prompt box asking for the person's name. After the user types it in, an alert box pops up saying "Hi."

Click For Alert Box: Clicking the link brings up an alert box.

First/Last Name: This script pops up a prompt box that asks for the viewer's first and last names and then posts them where you want them in the document.

Answer to Page: This script pops up a prompt box and asks a question. Depending on the answer, the viewer is sent to a specific page.

A Confirm Box: This script works a lot like the previous ones, except this is a confirm box. It has a question mark rather than an exclamation point.

Button, Links, and E-mail Scripts

These scripts employ buttons, create links to other pages, or deal with e-mail.

Click N' Go #2: This is a basic, well-written, drop-down link menu.

Guest Book Prompt: This script prompts you for a name and then creates a guestbook for that name and associated e-mail address.

Rotating Text Links: Text links rotate in a text box.

HotMail Fetch: This script grabs your HotMail e-mail in the background while you do other things. (Contents are in a Zip file.)

E-mail Button with Subject: You get a button that asks for a subject line. You then get an e-mail with that subject.

A Drop-Down Menu Script: With a GO! button. Woohoo!

See Source: Here's a button that enables you to see the source of a page.

Link Message: This sends users a message when they click.

Link Search: This script enables the user to enter a word and then click a link to choose which search engine gets the honor.

Drop-Down Link Menu in Frames: This script is what many have been asking for—a drop-down link menu that works with frames. (Contents are in a Zip file.)

No Click Links: This script creates a link that works with no click; you just pass the mouse over it.

AOL Style Keyword: This script acts like the AOL keywords by taking a user to a new page depending on the word she enters.

Link of the Minute: Depending on the minute, you get a link.

Highlight Button: Pass your mouse over the button, and it lights up. *Requires Microsoft Internet Explorer 4.0.*

Menu Links: This is a combination script of image flips and `OnMouseOver` that creates a nice navigation panel. See it in action. (Contents are in a Zip file.)

Navigation Panel: This is a menu of links. Just click once to go.

Get a Cursor: This script is used with form commands. Use it and your first form element will get a cursor in the text box without having to be clicked.

Go Box: This is a great script. This one allows for a description of the link and then the ability to see the page code.

New Window Search: This script enables the search of multiple search engines. Results are posted on separate pages in new windows.

Mailto: Alerts: This script works with the basic mailto: forms. When the user clicks to send the mail, the script first asks whether everything is okay, and it then says thanks.

Total Cost Form: This script enables your users to choose from a list of priced items. The script tallies the items, adds the tax, and sends the information to you.

`MouseOver` Color Buttons: These are link buttons that change color when you move over them. *Requires Microsoft Internet Explorer 4.0.*

Search Box: This is a nice copy-and-paste item that enables your users to search multiple search engines from your page.

Linker: This script enables the user to select a series of links. It then creates a page using just those links.

& Script: This script tells you the & ASCII commands required to place nonletter and nonnumber characters on your page.

Layered Search Window: This script creates a layer window using a mouse-over. The new layer is the search window. *Requires 4.0 browsers.*

Three Step Go Window Link: You'll need to see it to understand the goofy title I gave it.

Scared Button: The button does not allow you to click it.

Radio Button Links: Clicking the radio buttons sends you to a new link.

Scrolling Buttons: This script enables you to list multiple buttons that scroll through—it's a neat effect.

Plug-In Script: This script tells which plug-ins a person has on her browser. *Requires Navigator 4 or better.*

Big Plug-In Script: This does the same as the previous script, but offers more information about the plug-ins. *Requires Navigator 4 or better.*

Running IE4 or better?!?!: Are you? This script tells you.

HREF Script: You enter the URL, and off you go.

Fill All for Guest Books: This script does not let the user submit the guestbook form without filling in all the offered fields.

Fill All with Alert: This is the same as the previous script, but it offers an alert on submit that asks for verification.

Multiple Form Check: This is a series of scripts that check guestbook form fields for many items, including all fields being filled in, letters or numbers, too many spaces, capitalization, and more.

Multiple Random E-mailing: One button chooses a random e-mail address to send a letter to.

Status Bar Button: This is a button that posts text in the status bar. It doesn't have much worth, but it's great fun.

Headliner!: This is a button with text scrolling across it. Each text scroll is different, and each scroll carries its own URL. It is currently set up to run with frames.

Go There Button: This is a menu of links with a button that activates the browser.

Link Info: This is a great, great script. When the mouse passes over the link, information is posted in form boxes. Check it out.

Great Place: Here's a two-step link taking you to a great place.

Info Mail: This script gathers the user's name, e-mail address, and URL and sends them to you with the click of a button.

E-mail Checker: This script works with the simple guestbook format.

Webring: This script allows you to start your own Webring using another site's power.

Targets in Pull-Down Menus: This is how you add TARGET commands to frame page pull-down menus so the links you offer can change specific frames.

Blinker Button: One link—blinking text.

Static Words Link Button: Four links, static words.

Scrolling Link Button: This is a link button that scrolls the text.

One Button—Many Links: This is a link button with four links.

Mailto: Script Verification: This script acts like a CGI-based guestbook sending the viewer to another page when she submits the form to your e-mail.

Check E-mail Address: This script allows you to enter an e-mail address and verify whether it is a true address.

I Sent It Already!: This script displays a personalized message telling the user that her mailto: guestbook data has been sent.

Random Link Pages: This script asks a couple of questions and takes you to a page based on your answers.

Browser Detector Buttons: This script tells all about the browser a viewer is using.

Scrolling Link Buttons: You get a scrolling list of links—choose one and click to go.

Random Link Generator: This script produces five random links.

Explorer Only!!!—Link Buttons: This script uses ActiveX technology to produce Explorer links.

Random Link Buttons: This script produces a random link.

Drop-Down Link Menu: This script does what the others do, but it flips around. Try it.

Two Images/Two Links: This script flips between two images. Depending on which one is up, that's the one that works when clicked.

Color Buttons: Click the button, and change the color.

New Window Button: This is a button that opens a new browser window with a new page.

BACK and FORWARD Buttons: These buttons act just like the buttons at the top of the browser.

Jump Buttons: These buttons enable you to jump around within a page.

Link Reads Along Bottom: This script enables you to change what text appears in the status bar when the mouse pointer passes over the link.

Erase Status Bar: When words appear in the status bar, they tend to stay there until new words are called for. This script sets it so the words erase within two seconds after appearing.

Questions, Then Send: This script asks questions. Depending on your answers, you are sent to an appropriate page.

Countdown to Page Change: This is a counter that counts until a preset time. At that time, that page changes.

Wait for Page Change: This script waits a preset amount of time and then changes to a page depending on your browser type.

Choose Link Destination: This script posts radio buttons underneath an HREF link. You click the button and the link becomes that destination.

Jump Box: This is a pull-down menu that enables you to choose a link and jump to it.

Another Jump Box: This is a different script version of the previous one.

Another Jump Box: Ditto above.

Another Jump Box: Ditto, ditto.

E-mail: This is a button that produces an e-mail window addressed to you.

E-mail with Subject and CC: This script creates an e-mail button with the subject box and the CC box already filled out.

E-mail with Subject: Ditto for the previous one, but only the subject line is filled out.

E-mail with CC: Ditto, but only the CC box is filled out.

E-mail Has Been Sent Alert: You attach this script to a simple guestbook form, and it alerts the viewer that the e-mail is being sent.

Button Box: This is a button that produces an alert box when clicked.

Reload Button: Here's a button that reloads the current page when clicked.

Auto Back and Forward: Using this script automatically sends people forward or backward one page, depending on how you set it up.

Radio Button Color Changer: Click the radio button, and the background changes color.

Color Button: Click the button, and the background changes color.

Question/Color Button: This button asks two questions. Depending on the answers, the background color changes.

The Three Cs: Clocks, Calendars, and Calculator Scripts

These scripts all deal with numbers, times, or dates.

Quadratic Equation: This script does just what it says. *Requires Microsoft Internet Explorer.* (Contents are in a Zip file.)

Time Zone Buttons: This script uses your computer's time to figure six other major time zones.

Calendar and Datebook: With one script, you get both. (Contents are in a Zip file.)

Today Calendar: This script gets the date and posts the current month's calendar. It's a great script.

Square Root in the Status Bar: This script figures a square root and posts the answer in the status bar.

Loan Amount: This is a great math script. Use this script to know what your payments will be before the guy at the bank tells you.

Digital Clock: This one is exactly what it says. (Contents are in a Zip file.)

Slope: You give this script four input points, and it figures the slope of the line.

The Areas: Need to find an area? This is your script.

DHTML Clock: It is what it says—in big blue letters no less. *Requires Microsoft Internet Explorer 4.0 or better.*

Tangent: All you triangle fans out there will love this one.

Sine: Ditto.

Cosine: Ditto. Ditto.

Count It!: You put in a number and the script counts up to it. It's useless but fun.

The Pythagorean Theorem: A squared plus B squared equals C squared. This little script will bear me out.

Circle Circumference: This one uses pi. Mmmmmm … pie.

Parameter of a Quadrilateral: Please have the width and length ready.

Area of a Quadrilateral: Ditto the same information—different equation.

Another Great Science Calculator: Enough said.

Digital Clock: Three items displayed—time, AM/PM, and date.

Number of Letters: This script is basically useless but fun. You put in a sentence, and it counts the number of letters.

Money Conversion Script: Pick from a long list of currencies. The conversion is done for you.

Area of a Triangle: Use this script to get through that math class.

Multiple Java Calendar: This script is a real work. Take a look at all the functions.

Running Calculator: How far—how fast?

World Clock—Daylight Savings Time: Just as it says ....

Circle Calculator: This script helps a great deal with finding the area and other measurements of a circle.

Math Check: How good are your math skills? This script checks you over four levels.

College Tuition Chooser: Choose a college based on the money you'll spend.

The Super Calculator: The author claims it's the greatest JS calculator yet! Please note, though, it will not work on Microsoft Internet Explorer. Maybe it isn't that great.

Percentage Calculator: Find the percentage of any number from another.

Power Calculator: Figure the power of any number.

Solve for X: This one will get you through high school algebra.

Nautical Calculator: This is a great script that figures a lot of stuff you'll need to know next time you take the boat out.

Celsius to Fahrenheit: And back again.

JavaScript Clock Fix: This is a fix for some JavaScript clocks that are displaying the wrong month.

Click Through Rate Calculator: This figures the percentage for you.

Another Calculator: This has plus, minus, and divide. You get the idea.

Another Calculator: Another version of the old favorite.

Graphic Enhanced Calculator: You have to see this script to believe it. You'll need to grab the script and a ton of little graphics to get it to function.

Another Calculator: This one has a pi key.

Celsius to Fahrenheit: That's what it does ... differently from the previous one.

Date and Time: This script puts up the date and time someone entered your page.

Tells Time, Begs You to Stay: That's what it does when you try to leave.

Java Alarm Clock: You tell the script when you want to be alerted. It keeps track of the time, and a box pops up when it's time.

Body Mass Calculator: Are you in good shape? Do you really want to know?

Simple Calculator(s): This can be one large calculator or four small ones. Take a look.

Your Age in Dog Years: Woof.

A Great GPA Calculator: This one recognizes + and –.

Basic Calendar: This script is just what it says.

Entire Year Calendar: It takes up space, but you get the entire year.

Entire Year Calendar: This script does what the previous one does, but it also highlights the current date.

Calendar/Datebook: This script displays a calendar-type datebook you can fill in with your appointments.

Entire Year Calendar: What sets this script apart is that every day is a link to a different page.

A Calculator: Figure out math equations to your heart's content.

Another Clock: This is a basic digital clock.

Java Clock: This is a digital clock that displays the time plus AM or PM inside a small frame.

Click Displays Date and Time: This script produces a button. Click it and you get the date and time.

Single Function Calculator: This script does only one function. You can change what that function is, but it still does only the one.

Equation Helper: This script takes just about any equation and solves for X.

Count Up: You set the length of time. This script then counts up and displays a message when time's up.

Count Down: Ditto, but this one counts down.

Countdown to Page Change: A timer is set up that changes the page when a predetermined time is reached.

GPA Calculator: Figure out your grade right from the Web. This script takes your final marks and shows you your all-important grade point average.

Conversion Calculator: This one deals with distances.

Conversion Calculator: This one deals with weights.

Conversion Calculator: This one deals with volume measurements.

A Stopwatch: This is nothing fancy. It just counts up until you say stop or reset.

Color Scripts

These scripts display or manipulate color in some fashion.

Color Box: You can see boxes of color, click boxes of color, and get hex!

Color Gradient Test: You choose the color, and this script shows it from dark to light and back again.

Show Color Cube: This is a great script! It lets you enter the word, hex, or RGB code of a color. It then posts a small cube showing the color.

Get the Lights: This is a simple game where clicking the correct radio button "turns on" the lights.

Red to Black ... and Back: This script is annoying. Maybe that's why I like it. It flashes red to black a few times—and then posts the page.

Light Switch: This script is useless but really fun. It goes from light to dark with a switch.

Lights Out!: Click the button and the lights go out.

Color Wait: This script rolls colors when someone logs in to the page—but what's more, it posts text along the bottom of the page while the person is waiting.

Background Roller: This script rolls through a series of colors again, and again, and again, until you go nuts.

Background Flasher: Go easy or go silly. This is a fun script.

Random Background Colors: This adds a little random color to your page.

Background Color Prompt: This allows your user to choose the background color before entering.

Hex to RGB and Back Again: Put in the hex code and get the red, green, and blue, and vice versa.

Background Table Color: Use the table to choose a color for the page depending on what mood you're in.

Color Change with Display: This script slowly fades in a background color. But while it is fading, the color codes display. Take a look. I like this one.

Color Start: This script tells you to wait for the page to load while you watch a color display.

Color Cube: You have to try it to believe it. You'll see many colors as you roll your pointer along.

Hex Coder: This is a great script. You type in the color name, and it gives you the hex code. It's great for page development.

Large Color Script: This is a very useful script. This script gives hex codes and color combinations.

All Colors: This one asks you about all the different things you can do with colors. It then posts your answers. It's great for seeing how colors work together before using them on your page. *Netscape Navigator browsers only.*

Color Code Verify: Enter a color code, and a window pops up showing you what it looks like.

Background Color Log: Try to get the last background color. This script plays along.

Background Color with Alert: That's what it does.

Chat Room Color Prompt: Do you go into chat rooms? Take this script with you.

Word = Background Color: A prompt box asks for a word and changes the background color by what you type. Any word seems to work.

Color = Hour: This script produces a different background color depending on the time of day.

Pull-Down Color Menu: Use the menu to change the background color.

New Color Every 5 Seconds: Enough said.

New Color Every Second: Ditto.

An Interview for a New Color: This one takes time, but it's fun.

Color Buttons: Click the button, and change the color.

Pull-Down Colors: This is a pull-down menu of colors.

Background Color Changer: Using this script will make your page's background roll through colors of your choice before posting the text.

B&W Background: This script fades the background from black to white before the text appears.

Mouse-Over Color Change: You will offer color names. When the mouse passes over the name, the background changes to that color.

Mouse-Over Color Changer: This script changes the page to blue when the mouse passes over.

Text Color Changer: This script changes color depending on what the viewer types to the page.

Radio Button Color Changer: Click the radio button, and change the color.

Button Color Changer: Click the button, and change the color.

Questions then Color: This button asks you two questions. Depending on your answers, it changes the background color.

Day/Night Script: During the morning hours, your page is black text on white; at night it turns to white text on black. It's a day/evening effect.

Game Scripts

These scripts either play or deal with games as their topics. Also, some scripts deal with leisure activities, such as music.

Ships at Sea: This is a two-player version of a sinking game.

Peg Solitaire: Jump over one, and take it out. You've played this before—now try it on your computer. (Contents are in a Zip file.)

Bridge: This script will help your game.

NBA Totals Projection: How will your favorite player do?

Magic Eightball: Remember that water-filled eight ball that would tell you your fortune? Here it is in Java form.

Magic Eightball Two: This is another version of the magic eight ball with a whole lot more graphical support.

Roundball: This is a basketball animation. You can play college or pro.

Field Goal: Line it up and hopefully kick it through. *Requires Netscape Navigator 4.0.*

The Right Button: Can you find the button that will light when you click it? No fair looking at the code.

Point Guard Stats: How's your favorite player doing? How are you doing? This script tells you.

Super Bowl Game: Can you tell me who won, and who lost, the last 31 Super Bowls? (Posted before Super Bowl XXXII.)

Chinese Zodiac: What was the Chinese animal zodiac sign the year you were born?

Frame-Based Quiz with Timer: You're under the gun on this one.

Basketball Champ Quiz: How well do you know the champs from seasons past?

Social Security State: Enter the first three numbers of your SS number, and this script will tell you the state that issued it. There is no concern about giving the number. The script is self-contained, and the first three numbers are basically worthless without the other six.

Jay's Game: Play this! It's a speed game where you try to check off numbers before time runs out. It's tougher than you think.

The Maze: You have to play it to believe it.

Text-Based Quiz: This quiz is more text-based than the other form-based quizzes.

Random Number Entry: The script picks a random number between 1 and 10. You guess at it. When you get it right—or after three tries—you get to enter.

Get to See Hanson: … or any other rock group. This is a game where you move forward to meet the group.

Graded Multiple Choice Quiz: This is a quiz that grades itself and places a check or an X if the answer is right or wrong. The only downfall is that the answers are pretty easy to locate before taking the quiz.

Slots: Play with someone else's money.

Insult Machine: Tell people what you think. Choose one of four insults, and the script delivers it.

Brick: This is a great copy of the old brick game.

Tic Tac Toe: This has two players and one screen.

Middle School Quiz: This is a simple quiz game. You can change it to include your own questions, answers, and responses.

Football: Play football online.

Baseball: Ditto with baseball.

French Translator: Use this script to translate a phrase from English to French.

A Quiz: This is a four-question quiz that grades you. Welcome to high school.

Find Me!: This is a fun game created by a 12-year-old JavaScript wizard. Find the only working link!

Blackjack-21: Play the game. I like this script because it calls the dealer "The Idiot." Ever played and felt that way?

Backspace Race: See whether you can get rid of the text before the computer does.

Find Mr. Hockey: This is a simple seek-and-find–type game.

Check's Out!: Try to get rid of all the checks. I couldn't do it.

What's Your Sign?: Enter your birthday, and you get your sign.

Lottery Number Picker: Why play birthdays—use this script!

Golf Handicapper: This script figures the USGA handicap index.

A Mad Lib Game: Try playing!

Russian Roulette: Someone wins—someone loses … with a bang.

HTML and Developer Scripts

These scripts deal with HTML and the development of Web pages. A lot of these scripts work "behind the scenes" to get a look or an event to help your Web pages or Web site. This is also where you'll find all the password-protection scripts.

Got Frames?: This script goes into your page's BODY command and performs a redirect if the user tries to look at the page outside of the frame setting.

Monitor Detect: This is a redirect script that deals with the monitor settings set by the user. (Contents are in a Zip file.)

Tag Pad: This is an HTML editor that works a lot like using Notepad.

Open C Drive: Click the button and get the contents of the C drive.

See Size Window: The user enters the height and width of a new window and clicks a button, then a new window pops up. It's great for page development.

PC/MAC Detect Script: Depending on which operating system the viewer is using, this script sends the user to a specific page best viewed with that type of system.

Every Other Password: This is a pretty good password script that takes every other letter of the password and creates the page name. See it for yourself. (Contents are in a Zip file.)

JavaScript Redirect: This script acts like a meta refresh in JavaScript.

The Same Size: This script opens a window the same size as the current window. *Navigator browsers only.*

A Good HTML Editor: Enough said ….

Please Wait Script: This script posts a message telling the user to wait because the page is being loaded.

Version 4 or Not: This script recognizes the user's browser version number. If it's version 4, a specific page is brought up. Anything else goes to another page.

Stay Alive: If your server kicks you off after a couple of minutes of inactivity, downloading gives you headaches, right? This script makes sure you have activity within the timeframe so you do not get kicked off.

Remote Control Window: The little one works the big one.

Password 33 Script: You can password-protect your pages. See it in action.

Immediate Page Load: This script enables the user to load two pages at once so the second comes in very quickly when called for.

Transport or Password: This script enables the person to type in a word. If the word is a page, the user is transported. It also works pretty well as a password script.

Page Depending on Browser: This script notes the browser and sends the viewer to the page best suited for him.

PageMaker Clone: Make your own page with this one.

Multiple Search Engines: Search multiple Internet search engines with one click.

Remote Surfs Four Sites: This script enables you to surf four sites at once.

Four Search: This script enables you to search four search engines at once, all on one screen.

onMouseOver Layers: This script uses layer commands with the onMouseOver commands. *Requires Netscape 4.0.*

onMouseOver Layers Menu: This script uses layer commands with the onMouseOver command to create a pull-down menu. *Requires Netscape 4.0.*

Layer Toggle: This script uses JavaScript to toggle between layers. *Requires Netscape 4.0.*

HTML Editor: This JavaScript helps with HTML page construction.

3-Step Password: This is a pretty good password script that does its best to protect the password and the link it is going to. It's tough to figure out from the script.

Password Script: This is yet another nice password script.

Remote Control Window: This script pops a window up that enables you to control the first window.

Page of the Day: This script sets up a page of the day. You get 31 at the most—until they invent a month with 32 days.

Random Page: This script posts a page stating that a random page is to come, and then it goes to the random page from the list you offer.

Two Number Password: This script is great because it is difficult to grab the password from the script. Give it a try.

Simple Password: It doesn't get easier than this one.

Searchable Database: This is a script that acts as a search engine. It basically searches itself, but if you take the time to enter all the titles and descriptions of your pages, it searches just like a personal search engine.

Who Came—And When: This script is a personalized counter.

Stops onMouseOver Text from Hanging Around: Use this script to ensure that the onMouseOver text you use doesn't stay on the status bar after the user has moved on.

Verification of Guestbook Data: This script posts a virtual page when someone uses your simple mailto: guestbook.

Random Image Plus Link: This script produces a random image plus a link associated with that image.

Stops New Browser Windows: This script enables you to target to the same browser window to stop new windows from opening in your image maps and frames.

A Great HTML Editor: What more can I say?

Password: This script requires a password be typed in to enter a specific page. The password is the page's name.

Keypad Password: This script produces a key pad. The viewer enters a password number to get to the next page. The password is the name of the page. You can change the password number.

A Counter: This is a simple counter that produces an alert box count each time you enter the page. It also administers a greeting depending on the number of times. However, it only counts up to 10.

Cookie Counter: This is a fully functioning counter that uses the viewer's cookie to post a count on the page.

An HTML Editor: Now you can create your HTML documents right to your browser window.

Another HTML Editor: Choose your favorite.

Image Scripts

These scripts deal with, display, or manipulate images, or set images into motion.

Smooth Stop: This is an animation than brings images to a smooth stop, as if on ice. *Netscape Navigator 4.0 only.*

Page Branding: This is a Geocities-style page brand.

Three to One Image Flip: This script is very clever. Three images sit on top of one another. When the mouse passes over one of them, it "blows up" to fill the space of all three. (Contents are in a Zip file.)

Triple Flip Button: This script is a triple image, image flip.

Show Active Channel: This script looks at the user's browser. If it's an Explorer browser, the Active Channel image is posted to the page.

Multiple Image Flip: Three images are used to create one pretty cool flip.

DHTML Christmas Countdown: This is a clock that counts down to Christmas with a flying Santa. *Microsoft Internet Explorer 4.0 only.*

Image Toggle: This is a basic image flip, except the flip is enacted by the user clicking buttons.

Image Browser: Use this script to enable users to scroll through a list of images.

Stay Flipped Image Flip: After it's flipped, it stays.

Dual Image Flip: Not only do you get an image flip, you also get a secondary image popping up. (Contents are in a Zip file.)

Image Option: Select an image from a pull-down list. Click the button and it displays.

Background Time: This script posts a different background color and image, plus a different image on your page, depending on what time of day it happens to be.

Flip Flap Image Script: This is a great multiplatform, image-flipping script.

Move the Image: This script enables you to make an image interactive. Your viewers can move it anywhere they want. *Microsoft Internet Explorer 4.0 only.*

An Image Depending on the Date: Want a specific image on only a certain date or dates? This script will do it for you.

Floating Apple: This script employs layering to enable the Apple logo to break apart and fly around the screen. *Netscape 4 versions only.*

Black Hole: An image MouseOver starts a multiple-page slide show.

447

Image Map Status Bar Message: This script uses mapping commands to make messages on different sections of an image map.

Multiple Image Flipping: This is a great script and great effect. Take a look.

Image Mover: This is another image-moving script using Netscape 4.0 layer commands. *Requires Netscape Navigator 4.0.*

Image Search: This employs multiple images with a flip script to enable your readers to search five different search engines.

Four Movers: This script enables four images to basically fly all over your page. *Requires Netscape Navigator 4.0.*

Image Mover: This is a great script. The active image rolls all over the screen no matter what text is in its way. *Requires Netscape Navigator 4.0.*

Image Display JavaScript: This script enables your user to click a link and see a picture pop up in a new, framing browser window.

Stop the Picture: If you have a large image downloading, this script enables your viewer to click a button and stop it.

Client-Side Image Map Script: This script works a lot like a client-side image map, except it displays sections in a text box rather than the status bar.

Image Flipping Link: People have been asking for this one. On the `MouseOver`, the image changes, plus different text appears in the status bar. Really slick.

`MouseOver` for Image Maps: This script enables you to place text in the status bar for your image maps.

New Image GIF: This script places a new `.GIF` image where you want it—what's more, it keeps an eye on the date. When you want the image to come down, it removes it for you.

Random Image Plus Link: This script produces a random image plus a link associated with that image.

Random Number Generator—with Images: This script produces a random number that is displayed with images.

Random Pictures: This is an improvement over my script.

Another Random Picture Script: Ditto above.

Picture in Black: This script displays a chosen image surrounded by black in its own window.

Picture Changer: This script produces a picture change when the mouse moves across. Use small images.

Random Picture Display: This is a random picture generator. You will need 60 pictures to make it work correctly.

New Image Each Month: Depending on the month, this script displays another picture.

New Image Each Hour: Depending on the hour, this script displays another picture.

New Image Each Day: Depending on the date, this script displays another picture.

Scrolling Scripts

Scrolling text is very popular. These scripts scroll text in the document window, text boxes, and the status bar, among other places.

Left Right Scroller: This script scrolls text in from the left and the right inside a text box.

Easy Status Bar Scroll: This script does just what it says.

Bounce Scroll: This script bounces scrolling text all over the page. It'll get attention if nothing else. *Netscape 4.0 required.*

Super Scroll: This is a scroll that sizes itself to your page and then gives the user a few options to play with.

Dual Scroll: Why did I post this script? I don't know—it just looked cool to me.

Letter by Letter Scroll: This script scrolls along letter by ... oh, you know the rest.

Multiline Scroll: This script posts a message depending on the time of day and then runs a multiple-line scroll message.

Active Scroll: This script produces a scroll that is also an active link.

Netscape Marquee: This is a Netscape version of the Microsoft Internet Explorer Marquee. *Requires Netscape 4.0.*

Scroll to the New Century: Here's a countdown scroll to the year 2000 ... or to whatever date you want.

Scroll in Spanish: This is a scrolling JavaScript—in Spanish.

Spanish Form Scroll: This is a form scroll—in Spanish.

Spanish Backward Scroll: This is a scroll that goes the wrong way. It's also written in Spanish.

Controlled Scroll: This is a scroll your viewers have some control over.

Four Scroll: This is a scroll employing four lines.

Ping Pong Visual: This is a ping pong visual you can control.

Prompting Scroll: This script asks you for some text and then scrolls it for you.

Replace Scroll: Take a look; this replaces letters in a scroll.

Flashing Words: This isn't exactly a scroll, but it's close. Words flash in the status bar along the bottom. It's useless but fun.

Little Scroll: This script produces a scroll along the bottom, but only a tiny one.

Pong Scroll: It's too hard to describe—just go see it.

Roll Scroll: The scroll comes in one letter at a time.

Scroll on Status Bar: This script produces a scroll down in the status bar, where it reads "Document Done."

A Basic Scroll: This script produces a scroll on the document window.

One-At-A-Time Scroll: One-letter-at-a-time scroll across the status bar at the bottom of the browser.

Small Scroll: Here is a quick, easy-to-understand, on-page scroll.

Another Small Scroll: Ditto above, but with different scripting.

A Large, Involved Scroll: This script is a big pup. It allows modification on every aspect of the text and the scroll. Detailed instructions are included.

Capital Scroll: This isn't a scroll per se, but it fits here. It takes a line of text and changes each letter from lowercase to uppercase. It looks like a wave.

Text-Based Scripts

These scripts all have one thing in common: They produce text on the HTML document.

Random Up to 50: This script produces a random number between 1 and 50, but you can set it to any upper limit you want.

Netscape Low Version: If your user is running Navigator version 2.0 or less, this script pops up text that offers a link to upgrade.

Status Scroll Count: The length of time you've been in a page just scrolls right by.

Add from Prompt: This script calls for information through a prompt and then enables you to post it in a text box through the use of a button.

Post Next Holiday: This script does what it says.

Hello in Bar: This throws up a prompt for the user's name and then offers a greeting in the status bar.

New Array Text Pages: This is a series of five scripts that create "… Of the Day" type events wherein something happens each day or at a specific time of day. Where this script is different is that it uses a new type of array programming to get the effect in a simpler fashion.

Fun Text: It's like a Mad Lib game that plays for you.

Meta Tags: This script uses a prompt command to gather information to create your page's meta tags.

Headline Linker Script: This script is a little hard to explain. The idea is that you can get three headlines in a text box. Each is its own location, too. You click the box to make it work. Go see it—it'll be easier than me explaining it.

Text Fader 1.3: This script is sooooo cool.

Transfer Data: Use this script to transfer data across pages. This is currently set up to transfer data from a form from one page to another.

Super Script Date: This script posts the date but also adds either the "st" or "th" after the day number.

Message Plus Date: This is two scripts in one. This script is offered in two formats.

Remind Me: This script sits quietly in your browser until a specific date. Then, it pops up telling you the time has come.

Tip Box: This script pops up a Tool Tip–style box when the mouse passes over text. (Contents are in a Zip file.) *Requires Microsoft Internet Explorer 4.0.*

Make Me a Password: This is a great script. Need a password? This script generates a random letter and number password at whatever length you require.

Mad Libber: This is a basic Mad Lib game.

Full Text Date: Just copy and paste, and it's all yours.

Just the Date: This script posts the month (in text form) and the day.

Color Gradient Text: This is a great script that "rainbows" your text.

Highlighter: This script enables an onMouseOver to highlight a link. *Requires Microsoft Internet Explorer 4.0.*

Text Fader: This script is great. You'll have to see it to get the full effect.

You Came in ...: This script tells the user something he already knew—when he came into the page. But it does so in such grand fashion that I had to post it. *Requires Microsoft Internet Explorer 4.0.*

The Updater: This script posts the date the page was last updated.

Pop-Up Tables: As your mouse passes over text, a table pops up to tell you more. It's DHTML and has to be seen to be believed. *Requires Microsoft Internet Explorer 4.0.*

Flashing Warning: Just what it says. *Requires Navigator 4.0.*

Proclaim It!: This script posts two large lines of text to tell the world ... something. *Requires Netscape Navigator 4.0.*

Personal Title Bar: This script prompts the user for a name and then uses that to post the title command for the page.

Date and Time in Status Bar: This script posts the date and time in the status bar.

Quote in New Window: This does just what it says.

Follow the Moving Mouse: This script creates a block of color and text that follows your mouse around the screen. Think of it as a pet. *Requires Netscape Navigator 4.0.*

Hello in the Status Bar: This script asks for the user's name and then posts it in the status bar.

Layer Click: Click and the text follows you—a great effect. *Requires Netscape Navigator 4.0.*

Place the Message: This is a great script for developers to have around. It enables you to enter coordinates and then see where they fall on the page. *Requires Netscape Navigator 4.0.*

Moving Block of Text: This script gives you a colored block of text that flies around your screen. And who wouldn't want that? *Requires Netscape Navigator 4.0.*

Count the Seconds: This script counts the seconds a user has been in your page. It also posts alerts at certain times.

Random Link Script: This script posts a random link to follow.

Age Update Script: This script posts an age and automatically updates it when the birthday passes.

Status Bar Clock: Tell your users what time it is—in the status bar.

Link Change: Run your mouse over the link, and it changes. *Requires Microsoft Internet Explorer 4.0.*

Get Back to Frames: This script displays a message that the page the viewer is looking at should be in a frame setting and will not run by itself.

Bigger Text: This makes text jump out when the mouse moves over it. *Requires Microsoft Internet Explorer 4.0.*

Flipping Burst: The text becomes much more brilliant when your mouse moves over it. *Requires Microsoft Internet Explorer 4.0.*

Multicolored Text: Every letter is a different color. It's very Saturday morning.

Copyright and Last Updated: This is a good, quick script you can paste onto your documents to provide a bit of good information.

Fade Out: This script fades text in and out. You have to see this! *Requires Microsoft Internet Explorer 4.0.*

Many, Many Quotes: 160 sayings to get you started on your day.

Random Fact: Useless knowledge finally has a home.

Everyday Script: You get a different color scheme and message every day of the week.

All About: This script tells the user all about her machine and browser.

Goodbye Window: This script posts a goodbye window with links when your user leaves the page.

Sesame Street: This script makes your page brought to you by a random letter and a random number.

Which President?: You need this script for high school. Pick a number between 1 and 42, and this script tells you which president it was.

World Time: This script displays the current time and times for multiple locations around the world.

Time Stamp: This time stamp is an update of earlier versions. Here you get a 12 at midnight instead of a 0.

How Many Days Until Christmas?: This script tells you.

Browser and More: This script posts your browser and operating system and tells you whether an update is available to you. If one is, you get a link to it.

Tips for the Day: This is a script that offers your viewers some tips. You choose the topic.

Lots of Stuff Script: Take a look at this one. It posts all kinds of stuff about your visit.

Pass the Text: This script is really silly, but you can't seem to stop doing it.

Date/Time in Spanish: This script posts the correct time and date in Spanish.

Rainbow Text: Enter your text, and this script makes it a rainbow color.

James Bond: Use this script, answer the questions, and you'll get the famous James Bond quote.

Update Message: This script displays the last time the page was updated and then a message to the viewer.

Day-to-Day Message: This script displays a different message depending on the day of the week.

Java or Not?: This script displays whether the browser is JavaScript-enabled.

Microsoft Explorer 4.0 Link Color: This script changes the link color on `MouseOver`. *Requires Microsoft Internet Explorer 4.0.*

Post the Date in Numbers: That's what it does.

Coming from Display: This script displays the page that referred the user to your page.

Who Came—and When?: This script prompts the viewer and then tells her how many times she has been to the page before.

Text in Status Bar Delay: This script enables the text in the status bar to stay for a short time—about a second—and then goes away.

Lose Text in Status Bar: This script makes status bar text go away quickly.

Text in Status Bar: This script puts text in the status bar when the mouse goes over a link. Use it to announce your home page.

Displays Date and Time of Arrival: Enough said.

Displays Family: This script is good for small children. It enables them to answer questions about their families and then posts their answers, equaling a happy family.

A Mad Lib Game: Try playing!

Stops `onMouseOver` Text from Hanging Around: Use this script to make it so that the `onMouseOver` text you use doesn't stay on the status bar after the user has moved on.

Last Modification: This script posts when the page was last modified.

Date Page: This is a great script that creates a link to a page depending on the date. You could write pages forever … but don't.

Blinking Greetings: This script posts a greeting depending on the time of day. Plus, it blinks! Woohoo!

Display a Message Depending on the Time: That says it all. You can change the messages displayed.

Displays the Browser Version: Post this script, and the user will see what type of browser (Netscape or Explorer) she is using.

Displays More Browser Info: This script does the same as the previous one, but it also displays browser type, browser version, and a few other items.

Get Name, Post Name: This script ask for the viewer's name and then posts it anywhere you want throughout the document.

Get Name, Post Name, 2: This is a different look from the previous one.

Date Stamp: This script posts the date on the page showing the last time the page was modified.

New Message at Bottom: This script displays a new message along the bottom of the browser.

Cleans Up URL: This script breaks the URL reading along the bottom of the page into Domain: and Page:.

Message Depending on the Date: You set the messages and, depending on the date, one pops up.

Animated Text on Status Bar: What more can I say?

Mouse Produces Words: You can set the words that appear when the mouse moves over a link on your page.

First/Last Name Post: This script asks for the viewer's first and last names and then posts them anywhere in the document.

Do You Have JavaScript Capabilities?: This script posts a message to the page whether or not the browser has JavaScript capabilities.

Random Sentence Generator: This is more like a random story generator. This script creates a new story every time someone logs in to the page.

New Greeting: Depending on the time of day, this script produces a new greeting.

Miscellaneous Scripts

These didn't really fit in any of the other categories.

Script Tester: Use this script to paste in and then test your scripts.

Something of the Day: This is a great joke-of-the-day script that you can change to be "anything" of the day.

No Right Click: This script disallows the right-click properties while the viewer looks at your page.

Holiday MIDI: This script lies in wait until a specific date arrives. Then, it pops to life, posts a message, and plays a MIDI. *Requires Microsoft Internet Explorer 4.0.*

Build Your Own Computer: This script was built for a site that builds computers. That site was nice enough to allow me to post it here. (Contents are in a Zip file.)

No Tripod Banner: The author claims this script will rid you of them.

Random MIDI Player: Try this one.

Guitar Notes: You enter the string and fret, and this script tells you the note.

A Constant MIDI: Want a MIDI to keep playing whether or not the user stays in the frames of your page? This script will do it.

Digital Clock Jumpers: This script sets up a table that shows you how to configure the jumpers in a PC case to adjust the LCD digits for the proper clock speeds.

Same Size Window: This script opens a window the exact same size as the viewer's screen.

Multi-Button/Multi-Platform Sound Player: The author claims it's the only one of its kind. See it work.

Hello and Goodbye: This script pops up a window that disappears on its own.

Quick Window: This script pops up a window using a MouseOver command.

Cross-Browser Sound Script: This script sees the browser and then chooses the EMBED or the BGSOUND option for the user—no more soundless pages.

Show Me the MIDI!: This is a random MIDI player that also posts the name of the MIDI being played.

Embed Sounds Through Java: This is an onLoad script that works across platforms to embed a sound.

Another Random MIDI Script: It does just what it says ....

Two Frames at Once with Radio Buttons: You are offered eight choices in two columns. Select one from each, click the button, and the two pages you chose load in two frames at once.

Download Script: Here's a button that starts an FTP download for you.

Adding Choices Script: This script enables your user to select from a list of items; it then adds them up.

Chi-square: For all the statistics people out there, use this script to figure a 2×2 Chi-square.

Date Verification: Enter a date, and this script tells you whether it exists.

Learning Tool: This script enables you to click boxes and then shows you the JavaScript to create what you did.

Random MIDI: This script plays a random MIDI file.

Chat Room Scripts: I have no idea how these work. There are seven of them, and they do things in chat rooms.

Guitar Chord Chart: This is another great guitar chord chart.

A Chord Finder: This script is great for guitarists trying to find that darn chord.

Sees Browser: This script tells you about your browser.

Age Verification: This script is not very functional. It simply asks your age and lets you in. It might scare off younger viewers, though.

Play a Music File: This script calls for, and plays, a .WAV file.

Auto Reload: This script reloads the page automatically.

Guitar Chord Chart: This is a script that shows the fingering of a chord you select. The root of the chord blinks.

Index

16.7 million colors script, 361–372

A

action property, 389

addition, 149, 386

after-effect event handlers, 41–44

alert boxes, 41, 44, 54–57

  escape characters and, 54–57

  forms and, 122–123

alert function, 117–118

alert method, 35, 51, 106, 390

alert scripts on HTML Goodies Web site, 430–432

alinkColor, 23, 25, 390–391

AM and PM for clocks, 183

anchors, 23

AND, 387

angle brackets, 77

animation, 93, 244–250

appCodeName, 24–25, 391

appName, 23, 25, 391

appVersion, 23, 25, 391

arguments, math operator, 159

arithmetic operators, 148–149

array method, 391–392

arrays, 59, 80–83, 209–241, 391–392

  combining user input using, 215–220

  commas in, 82

  creating, 82

  formats for, 210–215

  grading a test using, 239–240

  Guessing Game using, 223–227

  index number in, 212

  literals in, 82, 212

  multiple, 212–214

  ordering items in, 210–215

  parentheses in, 82

  Passwords using, 227–232

  plus signs, 82

  pulling information from, 219

  Quiz Form using, 232–241

  quotation marks, 82

  random banner ad script, 291–294

  random numbers and, 222

  random quotes as, 220–223

Web Developer Resources

www.internet.com/webdev

www.extremeflash.com

www.javascriptsource.com

www.webdevelopersjournal.com

www.flashkit.com

jobs.webdeveloper.com

WEB DEVELOPER'S™
‹VIRTUAL LIBRARY›

www.wdvl.com

www.flashplanet.com

www.justsmil.com

Webdeveloper.com.

www.webdeveloper.com

www.gif.com

www.scriptsearch.com

webhosts.thelist.com

www.javaboutique.com

www.streamingmediaworld.com

www.webreference.com

www.javascript.com

webdesign.thelist.com

www.xml101.com

internet.com's Web Developer Channel is the Web's leading gathering place for the developer community. Sites feature information resources that help developers do their jobs better, product reviews of key developer products, and collections of scripts and applets to add to sites to enhance their performance.

The Internet & IT Network